Feminist Posthumanism in Contemporary Science Fiction Film and Media

Feminist Posthumanism in Contemporary Science Fiction Film and Media

From *Annihilation* to *High Life* and Beyond

Edited by
Julia A. Empey and
Russell J. A. Kilbourn

BLOOMSBURY ACADEMIC
NEW YORK · LONDON · OXFORD · NEW DELHI · SYDNEY

BLOOMSBURY ACADEMIC
Bloomsbury Publishing Inc
1385 Broadway, New York, NY 10018, USA
50 Bedford Square, London, WC1B 3DP, UK
29 Earlsfort Terrace, Dublin 2, Ireland

BLOOMSBURY, BLOOMSBURY ACADEMIC and the Diana logo are trademarks of
Bloomsbury Publishing Plc

First published in the United States of America 2023

Cover design by Eleanor Rose
Cover image: Scarlette Lindsay and Robert Pattinson in *High Life*, 2018, Dir. Claire Denis ©
Alcatraz Films / Andrew Lauren Productions / Collection Christophel / ArenaPAL

Library of Congress Cataloging-in-Publication Data
Names: Empey, Julia A., editor. | Kilbourn, Russell J. A. (Russell James Angus), 1964- editor.
Title: Feminist posthumanism in contemporary science fiction film and media:
from Annihilation to High life and beyond / edited by Julia A. Empey and Russell J. A. Kilbourn.
Description: New York: Bloomsbury Academic, 2023. |
Includes bibliographical references and index. | Summary: "Places posthumanism
and feminist theory into direct conversation with contemporary science
fiction film and media from the 1980s to present"—Provided by publisher.
Identifiers: LCCN 2022049328 (print) | LCCN 2022049329 (ebook) |
ISBN 9781501398407 (hardback) | ISBN 9781501398445 (paperback) |
ISBN 9781501398414 (ebook) | ISBN 9781501398421 (pdf) | ISBN 9781501398438 (ebook other)
Subjects: LCSH: Science fiction films—History and criticism. |
Posthumanism in motion pictures. | Feminist theory. |
Posthumanism in mass media. | Feminism and mass media. |
LCGFT: Film criticism. Classification: LCC PN1995.9.S26 F34 2023 (print) |
LCC PN1995.9.S26 (ebook) | DDC 791.43/615–dc23/eng/20230111
LC record available at https://lccn.loc.gov/2022049328
LC ebook record available at https://lccn.loc.gov/2022049329

ISBN: HB: 978-1-5013-9840-7
ePDF: 978-1-5013-9842-1
eBook: 978-1-5013-9841-4

Typeset by Deanta Global Publishing Services, Chennai, India

CONTENTS

FIGURES

ACKNOWLEDGMENTS

We want to acknowledge that we live and work on the unceded lands of the Attawandaron (Neutral), Anishnaabeg, and Haudenosaunee peoples and that we live within the lands protected by the "Dish With One Spoon" wampum agreement.

We would like to thank first of all Christine Daigle and the Posthumanism Research Institute (at Brock University) for their collective contribution to posthumanist thinking and for facilitating highly productive and collaborative workshops and other posthumanist-themed events in 2018, 2019, and 2020. Thank you to the Film and Media Studies Association of Canada for seeing the value in the conference panel on which this book is based and for supporting our work as film scholars. Thanks also to Wilfrid Laurier's Department of English and Film Studies, for providing us with an institutional structure. Of course, without the pandemic, which derailed the FMSAC conference (among so many things), we may not have had time to do this book at all. This certainly doesn't mean that we are grateful for Covid-19, but one always wants to look for the spots of brightness in the dark.

Thanks must be extended also to Katie Gallof, Erin Duffy, Stephanie Grace-Petinos, and the editorial team at Bloomsbury, for their guidance and patience during this process. Our thanks, also, to the anonymous reviewers, who gave us such insightful and constructive feedback on the initial proposal.

Finally, thank you to our contributing authors for their dedication and diligent effort over the past couple of years. Without this diverse and dynamic group of scholars and their groundbreaking work, after all, this collection would not exist.

I would like to extend my personal thanks to Andrea Austin and Jing Jing Chang for encouraging my work, and Pam Loughton and Janet Ross for showing me how to not to fear death. Thank you to David Hou, who is not only an excellent sounding board for all things film but also a valued friend. My thanks to Russ for the time and effort he put into this project. And finally, thank you to my parents, Gary and Marylka Empey, for supporting me, loving me, and doing their best.

Julia A. Empey

I offer my personal thanks to both Christine Daigle and Terrance McDonald, without whose inspiration some years ago, with the founding of the Posthumanism Research Network, I might not now be pursuing posthumanist questions at all. I owe a debt of gratitude to Julia for being willing to pursue this collection. I am also grateful to William Brown, Francesca Ferrando, Enrica Ferrara, and all the others who have shared their friendship, their insights into matters posthumanist, and their willingness to engage in stimulating conversation, even through a screen. Finally, I thank my wife, Sandra, and my daughter, Francesca, for keeping me focused on what matters.

Russell J. A. Kilbourn

PREFACE

This collection originated in a series of conversations we had over the course of 2018 and 2019 about two science fiction films: Alex Garland's *Annihilation* and Claire Denis' *High Life*. Beginning, then, from a shared interest in posthumanist theory, its contributions and shortcomings, and feminist theory, its shortcomings and its continuing relevance, and the interconnections between the two conceptual areas, we decided to pursue this concatenation in more formal terms.

We had initially proposed a conference panel for the 2020 Film and Media Studies Association of Canada Annual Meeting: "From *Annihilation* to *High Life*: Feminist Posthumanism and Postfeminist Humanism in Contemporary Science Fiction Film." Like most other such events, because of the Covid-19 pandemic, the conference was summarily cancelled. Instead of letting the inspiration for the panel die, however, we expanded and transformed our initial idea and decided to pursue an edited collection on feminist posthumanist approaches to contemporary science fiction film and media.

The text herein is the product of countless hours of labor, thinking, editing, and collaboration, with each other and with our contributing authors.

Introduction

Feminist Refractions
of the Posthuman

Julia A. Empey and
Russell J. A. Kilbourn

This collection puts feminist and posthumanist theory into dialogue with contemporary science fiction film and media. In Rosi Braidotti's (2019) terms, we are now living "the posthuman predicament" resulting from the convergence of the ongoing critique of a Eurocentric Humanist philosophical legacy and the anthropocentric habits of representation it supports. According to Cecilia Åsberg, critical posthumanism is in an important sense exemplified in feminist theory, "long critiquing the centrality of the figure of Man for its gender chauvinism,"[1] and contemporary science fiction narrative is the ideal venue for the exploration of this constellation of crucial themes. While some work has been done to bring issues of gender and feminism into conversation with posthumanism, however, this project is far from complete. Looked at from a feminist perspective, the problem is not simply that the Enlightenment Human is a "Man," but that, unintentionally or unconsciously, the posthuman—even the critical posthuman—is also a "Man." Despite a desire to reorient the human within a network of relations and despite recent laudable adaptations on the level of pronoun usage (at least in the English language), the baseline human subject remains, without a doubt, male. "Woman" (scare quotes are unavoidable) remains either completely erased or is excluded from or marginalized within the discourses

---

[1]Rosi Braidotti and Maria Hlavajova, eds., "Feminist Posthumanism," in *Posthuman Glossary* (London, Oxford, New York, New Delhi and Sydney: Bloomsbury, 2019), 157.

meant to "liberate" her from the legacy of what it means to be human. At the core of this collection is the idea that the (dis-)embodied female is the ultimate posthuman subject.

The marginalizing or silencing of women's contributions to intellectual history extends to the novelistic treatment of the climate crisis—a problem analyzed by Amitav Ghosh in 2018's *The Great Derangement: Climate Change and the Unthinkable*, which argues that the legacy of the novel in occidental culture is one of failing to live up to its potential to come to imaginative grips with global warming, decades or centuries before the term was even coined. This failure of collective imagination, for Ghosh, came at the cost of the triumph of "individual moral adventure," whose legacy is all around us today in the hundreds of commercial narrative films and TV series released each year, in which the fortunes of a single protagonist take precedence over the fate of the many. This focus is difficult to avoid, in fact, in a medium so dependent on the exploitation of light bouncing off of actors' bodies and faces, or the digital approximation of the same, time-honored, effects. Ghosh's point about literature is that the evidence was already all around—well before the eighteenth century—for anyone who cared to look, and by the time authors like Dickens or Zola began to include phenomena such as air pollution or coal mining in their books, it was in a sense already "too late."[2] "The climate crisis asks us to imagine other forms of human existence, a task to which fiction," Ghosh argues, "is the best suited of all forms." As others have pointed out,[3] this argument about the failure of a dominant cultural form to recognize the threat of what has come to be called the Anthropocene—wherein significant and potentially irreversible climate change is set in motion anthropogenically, by human activity, as the product of 20/20 hindsight—is both reductive and unfair. But this reading of literature's imaginative failure does shed a revealing light on the history of literary realism set over against the kind of subgenre or counternarrative that arose alongside both the more conventional "realist" novel and the aggregate field of modern science: what has come to be known as science fiction. Shifting focus to early women authors, such as Mary Shelley and Margaret Cavendish, we can see that not all early novelists turned a blind eye to potential future catastrophes, already discernible from the vantage point of the nascent industrial era. And it is the threat of catastrophic climate change that lends such urgency to the posthumanist critique of the capitalist consumerist model that still holds sway in much of the world, because of the life it promises to one and all, and which as a result has proved to be an unmitigated disaster for the planet. Cinema's advent in the

---

[2] See, e.g., Charles Dickens, *Bleak House* (1852), and Emile Zola, *Germinal* (1885).
[3] See, e.g., Aaron Matz's review of Ghosh's "The Nutmeg's Curse: parables for a Planet in Crisis," *The New York Review of Books*, July 21, 2022: 23.

late nineteenth and early twentieth centuries meant that the same discussion could shift onto the terrain of a new medium: as film history recapitulated in mere decades centuries of literary history, from realism to modernism and beyond, the recognition of the need to respond to the Anthropocene, to anthropo-generated climate change, has only intensified, while women and women's issues—in short, feminism—remain culturally and politically relevant and essential. That said, as several of this book's chapters show, while one need not look only to women-produced media to find evidence of feminist theory's influence in the culture, this has not always been the case.

From Shelley to Cavendish to Octavia Butler and Ursula K. Le Guin, women featured as prominently as men among the pioneers of science fiction.[4] Nevertheless, women's contributions to the genre's formation were either excluded or dismissed as minor.[5] Despite its origins as a masculinist discourse, however, literary science fiction has become the genre of choice for generations of women feminist authors. It is arguable, moreover, that critical posthumanist thought originates in feminist science studies, from Donna Haraway to Elizabeth Grosz, Dorothy E. Roberts, Miranda Fricker, and Sarah S. Richardson. Feminist science studies, like posthumanism, is a diverse school of thought. There are individuals who are interested in critically evaluating women's role in and marginalization by science and of rethinking science beyond Humanist dualisms. There are others, however, who are simply interested in incorporating more women into STEM-based subjects (Science, Technology, Engineering, and Mathematics), thereby uncritically affirming neoliberal identity politics, rather than questioning the basis of scientific thought and its upholding of misogynistic and racist logics.

This collection therefore seeks to bring these schools of thought together, to entangle them with contemporary science fiction films and works in other media, an inclusive, heterogeneous, and amorphous genre that the chapters in this volume treat with utter seriousness. While the dominant form of science fiction film and media today appears to be multiplatform franchises, from *Star Wars* to the Marvel Cinematic Universe to videogames such as *Cyberpunk 2077*, or adaptations of the aforementioned blockbusters, as examples of other kinds of science fiction media demonstrate, the genre continues to undergo radical reimaginings, challenging conventional categorizations.

---

[4]Cavendish's *The Blazing World*, published under her own name in 1666, follows an unnamed female protagonist who travels to the North Pole and discovers a passage to a new world. Part adventure story, part romance, and laced with a utopian ethic, *The Blazing World* is a science fiction forerunner that left an indelible mark on the genre.
[5]Curiously, in Rosi Braidotti and Cecelia Åsberg's collection, *A Feminist Companion to the Posthumanities* (Cham, Switzerland: Springer, 2018), there is no mention of science fiction, despite the many references to female and/or feminist science fiction creators.

Just as not all films fall into the science fiction genre, by the same token, not all science fiction films (to speak only of cinema, for the moment), fall into the narrow category of the popular blockbuster. In 2018, for instance, two films were released—Claire Denis' *High Life* and Alex Garland's *Annihilation*—representing two complementary poles of contemporary science fiction film narrative, and two different explorations of specific posthumanist (as well as transhumanist) themes. The two films, each of which features in more than one chapter in this volume, are similar to the extent that they deliberately challenge the Enlightenment Humanist narrative that has dominated Western thought for the last four centuries, embodied subsequently by the modern liberal and now the neoliberal Humanist subject. Each film approaches this project through the exploitation of specific tropological or metaphorical systems, whether derived from optics, like refraction—the bending of light waves as they seek the fastest route from one transparent substance to another—or matter, as that to which the human might best aspire. The metaphor of refraction, like diffraction—favored by Karen Barad—or like the metaphor of materialism itself, gives form to an abstract and complex idea. These metaphors help us to understand and navigate the accelerating transformations of life in the early twenty-first century. To quote Donna Haraway, "[d]iffraction is an optical metaphor for the effort to make a difference in the world" [qtd. Barad 71]). Barad adopts diffraction, moreover, as the "overarching trope" for her book, *Meeting the Universe Halfway*,[6] where she also champions the neologism, "mattering," which is really a pun, and which combines meaning and materiality in a gerund akin to "becoming." It is incumbent upon us as critics and scholars to never lose sight of the metaphorical or figurative value of these concepts, resisting the tendency in certain contemporary strains of posthumanist thought to take them literally, as catachreses, forgetting that we are always dealing with representations, images, texts, second-order phenomena, and not real people, animals, plants, or things. To understand the real, after all, one must confront representations, the images and discourses through which we mediate the world for ourselves. Most of us are not scientists but acute readers and viewers of science fiction texts. *Annihilation* and *High Life* can therefore be conceived as two ends of a spectrum of contemporary science fiction cinema intimately invested in the debates around the posthuman and the critical posthumanities within a feminist critical-theoretical context. The decentering of the human at the core of posthumanist thought has its corollary—indeed, its typological anticipation—in feminism's ongoing decentering of "Man." That neither of these transformations has entirely succeeded is a problem that informs the story in each of these films, albeit

---

[6]Karen Barad, *Meeting the Universe Halfway: Quantum Physics and the Entanglement of Matter and Meaning* (Durham and London: Duke University Press, 2007), 71.

from entirely different perspectives, with a radically different audiovisual language in each case.

In their application to fictional texts, whether literary or audiovisual, terms like refraction and diffraction signify in a more or less metaphorical manner—more metaphorical, that is, than in a properly "scientific" sense. The primacy of metaphorical over "scientific" meaning needs to be borne in mind in the discussion that follows, especially when one considers reflection and refraction as physical phenomena, while diffraction—according to Karen Barad—is a quantum, which is to say a *meta*physical, phenomenon.[7] In either case, physical or metaphysical (aligned with the quantum realm itself), when it comes to film and other audiovisually based media, such phenomena must be brought into the realm of Newtonian physics in order to be representable and thus visible, apprehensible, to the viewer. We foreground this point right at the start in order to highlight the stakes in any application of critical posthumanism to popular-cultural texts, such as movies and video games. The refraction metaphor is even more significant with respect to a genre such as science fiction, which, like other speculative fictions, often retails stories of technologies or other phenomena whose effects read as magical or metaphysical but whose representation within a given text depends upon decidedly quotidian limitations of form, genre, and medium.

Despite their great variety, the films, games, and other media texts discussed in this book fall under the heading of "science fiction"—as opposed to "speculative fiction," for instance—because of the foregrounded creative investment in technology, whether real or possible or purely imaginative, that this term implies. Apart from the qualification of "fiction" by "science," and all that this suggests for literary, cinematic, or other kinds of narrative— that is, that the "hard sciences" have long provided rich fodder to the world's fiction-makers—there is also the fact that the yoking of "science" to "fiction" implies something fundamental about the former term. In Teresa Heffernan's phrasing, "science needs fiction," as much as the reverse.[8] In other words, like that of history, the discourse of science relies to a significant degree on the tropes, strategies, and structures provided by the ongoing history of

[7] Ibid., 73.
[8] "Einstein noted that 'the unleashed power of the atom has changed everything save our modes of thinking and we thus drift toward unparalleled catastrophe.' How do we begin to shift these modes? It is the will to power—the death drive turned outward on the world—that has always been at the heart of the marginalization of fiction. Bringing the study of fiction, with its ethical impulse, back from its exile is what is perhaps most needed to heal the trauma of the twentieth century and interrupt the destructive force of military and industry-funded AI and robotics research. The sideways 'crab march' of the poets needs to counter the linear speed of this technology" (Teresa Heffernan, "The Post-Apocalyptic Imaginary: Science, Fiction, and the Death Drive," *English Studies in Africa* 58, no. 2 (2015): 66–79, doi: 10.1080/00138398.2015.1083198).

literary, cinematic, and, now, new mediatic fabulation. Elaine L. Graham likewise argues that "science and popular culture may both be regarded as *representations* of the world, in that both deploy images and rhetorical conventions which do not simply report reality, but construct, mediate and constitute human experience."[9] Science needs fiction, because, even more fundamental to what it means to be "human" than the propensity to speculate about the nature of the universe and our place in it, is the propensity to make up stories about this relationship, as an initial way of coming to grips with it. That the chapters in this collection concern themselves overwhelmingly with the more obvious scenario, the appropriating and exploiting of science in the service of fiction, does not affect this complementarity. Nor, by the same token, does it matter if the science in the fiction does not always correspond to doctrinaire or "scientific" understandings of what science is or should be. The latter is especially true not only in literary or filmic fictions but also in certain instances of critical theory—many examples of which feature prominently in the analyses offered in these chapters. For better or worse, critical theorists have for some time now been appropriating the results of scientific experiments or of specific data sets in the service of particular critical-theoretical agendas, a phenomenon clearly seen in the field collectively known as critical posthumanism. From Brian Massumi's dependence on a pair of studies—one sociological (media effects), the other biochemical (*Parables of the Virtual* 23; 28)[10]—for his theory of the "autonomy of affect," to Karen Barad's elaboration of a so-called "agential-realist" subject via a combination of philosophy and theoretical physics (*Meeting the Universe Halfway*), to Samantha Frost's merging of biology and cultural studies (*Biocultural Creatures*), posthumanist theory continues to boldly go where some scientists might say it has no right to go—but then the explicit challenge to traditional disciplinary boundaries is part of the point, as the chapters in this volume diversely illustrate.

In this posthumanist light, science fiction as a genre allows for new imaginings of human-technological relations, while it can also be the site of a critique of human exceptionalism and essentialism. In this way, science fiction affords unique opportunities for the scholarly investigation of the relevance and relative applicability of specific posthumanist themes and questions in a particularly rich and wide-ranging popular-cultural field of production. One of the reasons for this suitability is the genre's historically long-standing relationship with the critical investigation of gender, specifically the position and relative empowerment of women. Whether or

---

[9]Elaine L. Graham, *Representations of the Post/Human: Monsters, Aliens and Others in Popular Culture* (New Brunswick: Rutgers University Press, 2002), 14; emphasis in original.
[10]Hertha Sturm's media effects-based research, involving a short film of a melting snowman, and a set of experiments on patients implanted with cortical electrodes in order to measure autonomic response (Massumi 2002).

not this relationship amounts to an authentic feminist critique is another question, however.

This volume places posthumanism and feminism in direct conversation as mediated through contemporary science fiction film and media. Both posthumanism and feminism aim to counter or dismantle a masculinist, patriarchist Humanist tradition, whether that of the Enlightenment, modern liberalism, or neoliberalism, and science fiction has been putting these seemingly disparate schools of thought into dialogue for some time now. Where typically the mention of science fiction in a posthumanist context brings to mind a whole set of (often clichéd) transhumanist or uncritical posthumanist tropes—the cyborg, technologically augmented bodies, AI subjectivities, and so on—for this volume we have gathered together a series of chapters that either: (a) prioritize analyses of specific examples of contemporary science fiction cinema and video games that engage in meaningful ways with the burgeoning field of critical posthumanism, or (b) utilize such films and other media forms as case studies in the interrogation of posthumanist and feminist as well as humanistic ideas. In either case, each of the book's thirteen chapters is grounded in formal analysis, whether in terms of film style or game mechanics, and in the active application of cutting-edge critical theories.

The dominant tendency in the critical engagement with contemporary science fiction films from a posthumanist perspective is to privilege stories involving the transhumanist augmentation, radical transformation, or outright transcendence of the human, conceived dualistically as a combination of physical body and mind, essence, or soul. The latter is often figured in affective or emotional terms, as the basis of empathic or ethical self-other relations. Such an approach has the salutary effect of opening up debates around human identity, especially in terms of embodiment, gender, affect, and agency. This essentially transhumanist perspective, however, in addition to failing to transcend an essentially masculinist-humanist model of the human subject, likewise risks overlooking the more meaningful posthumanist critiques manifesting in certain films and games on the level of form. Close attention to audiovisual style facilitates the critical interrogation of the issues and questions around posthumanism, such as whether or not a given science fiction narrative actually represents or embodies a given posthumanist concept, properly speaking, or whether (as is more often the case) the film or game, in the end, perpetuates some form of anthropocentric or neo-humanist understanding of the relations between the human as currently understood and what comes after. Close attention to style or mechanics allows for the parsing out of the crucial differences between a transhumanist fetishizing of the all-too-human posthuman versus an authentically critical and progressive posthumanist position or perspective, something wholly and radically other—whatever this might look like, and assuming that it is susceptible to audiovisual representation.

In the end, all of our contributors confront, more or less directly, the fundamental question of the status of "woman" in a contemporary culture struggling to cast off the legacy of the sexist and misogynist bases of Western Enlightenment modernity and its colonialist extensions in time and space. From the perspective of reproduction, women—"real" women—continue to be biologically relevant, but in the most fraught and complex sense. Likewise, women continue to signify culturally not least because patriarchal anxieties around women continue to be worked through and negotiated in representation. In reaction, women exploit representation to think critically about "what it means to be a woman." That, even in science fiction, where technological capacities are imaginatively extended, we are still caught up in the contradictions of gender and misogynistic politics says something about the limits of our thinking. It would appear (to paraphrase Frederic Jameson) that it is easier to imagine the end of the world than it is to imagine a world in which at least 50 percent of the population is (not) treated as less-than-human.

Feminist Posthumanism in Contemporary Science Fiction Film

This collection is organized into three thematic sections: "Posthuman Bodies and Identities," "Posthuman Environments and Entanglements," and "Posthumanist Endings and Futures." We chose this approach, rather than a more obvious grouping by focus text (e.g., *Annihilation* or *High Life*) because of the opportunities it affords for fortuitous convergence or, even more interestingly, divergence, around similar questions or ideas. The chapters in Part One, "Posthuman Bodies and Identities," address fundamental issues of embodiment in posthumanist and transhumanist contexts. In Chapter 1, "Indigenous Futurist and Women-Centered Dystopian Film," Missy Molloy examines how dystopian science fiction across screen media underscores the unique and under-represented contributions of Black and Indigenous women to this over-represented subgenre. Utilizing as case studies *Pumzi* (2009), a Kenyan short film by Wanuri Kahiu; *Biidaaban: First Light* (2018), by Anishinaabe filmmaker Lisa Jackson; and *Night Raiders* (2021), a feature film by Cree/Métis filmmaker Danis Goulet, Molloy illuminates the respective impacts of Afrofuturism and Indigenous Futurism on science fiction films created to inspire what Sarah Keller calls "hope for new beginnings . . . wrought out of violent change."[11] This set

---

[11]Sarah Keller, *Anxious Cinephilia: Pleasure and Peril at the Movies* (New York: Columbia University Press, 2020), 182.

of films demonstrates the usefulness of future-oriented science fiction in addressing historical forms of racial and environmental injustice that persist in the present as well as the cinematic vitality of African and First Nations women filmmakers "reclaiming [their] place in an imagined future in space, on earth, and everywhere in between."[12]

In Chapter 2, "Gender, Sex, and Feminist AI: 13 Theses on *Her*," Sarah Stulz examines how gendered subjectivity is understood in Spike Jonze's 2013 film through three lenses: a formal analysis of science fiction cinema, a feminist approach to the mediation of gender and technology, and psychoanalysis. To further the aim of a feminist intervention in a closed and totalizing masculine discourse, Stulz's thirteen semi-independent theses locate fragments of a possible emancipatory femininity in the way *Her* represents the AI Samantha. The theses explore female identities, gender categories, gendered labor, digital assistants, and the capitalist organization of labor, as well as concepts of the self and their relation to the body, sex, and language. Through narrative and formal analysis, Stulz demonstrates that *Her* fails to imagine feminist posthuman AI and alternatives beyond a heteronormative, patriarchal, capitalist society and corporeal, individualist subjecthood. By reneging on what, in reference to Laboria Cuboniks' Xenofeminist Manifesto, she calls a "xenotopia" or utopia of otherness, the film draws attention to the necessity of critically interrogating the present in order to radically reimagine the future.

In Chapter 3's productively contrasting analysis of Jonze's film, "*Her*: A Posthuman Love Story," Zorianna Zurba examines how Jonze's film imagines posthuman love through the enigma of the affective experience of love without the interplay of two bodies to express intimacy. By coupling a body and a networked embodiment, *Her* plays with and thinks through assumptions around the role of the body in intimate, loving relationships in order to reveal that a being is no less affectionate or affecting in spite of differences in sensory perception and embodiment. In order to theorize posthuman love, this chapter takes a film-philosophy approach, analyzing the film via a phenomenological understanding of love grounded in the feminist work of Luce Irigaray.[13] Love is no mere affect or emotion; rather, phenomenology understands love as an intentional subjective stance that is respectful of and works to preserve difference. The consideration of

---

[12]Rebecca Roanhorse, Elizabeth LaPensee, Johnnie Jay, and Darcie Little Badger. "Decolonizing Science Fiction and Imagining Futures: An Indigenous Futurisms Round Table." *Strange Horizons*, January 30, 2017. http://strangehorizons.com/non-fiction/articles/decolonizing-science-fiction-and-imagining-futures-an-indigenous-futurisms-roundtable/.
[13]Luce Irigaray, *I Love to You: Sketch for a Felicity within History* (New York and London: Routledge, 1996); Luce Irigaray, *To be Two* (New York: Routledge, 2001); Luce Irigaray, *The Way of Love* (London: Continuum, 2002); Luce Irigaray, *In the Beginning, She Was* (London: Bloomsbury, 2013).

this loving relationship offers fertile ground for exploring kinship across difference and simultaneously envisions the mundane workings of a feminist posthumanist love.

In a very different combination of films, in Chapter 4, "Posthuman Mothers and Reproductive Biovalue in *Blade Runner: 2049* and *Jurassic World: Fallen Kingdom*," Jerika Sanderson investigates how Denis Villeneuve's 2017 *Blade Runner* sequel and J. A. Boyona's installment in the Jurassic Park franchise (2018) explore anxieties surrounding women's bodies in relation to reproductive technologies. The chapter begins by contextualizing representations of reproduction in these films, alongside discussions of critical posthumanism and biovalue, engaging with scholars such as Sherryl Vint, Catherine Waldby, Rosi Braidotti, and Elaine L. Graham, before moving into an analysis of key scenes. This chapter demonstrates how the human characters in both films establish associations between "posthuman" figures and monstrosity in the attempt to maintain human/nonhuman boundaries. While both films include posthuman children who blur the boundaries between the human and nonhuman worlds, the children's mothers are conspicuously absent. This chapter concludes by arguing that, while these films encourage their audiences to empathize with the posthuman children, the tensions surrounding the depiction of posthuman mothers demonstrate that lingering anxieties about women's bodies and their reproductive biovalue must still be resolved.

In Chapter 5, "Desirable and Undesirable Cyborg Bodies in the *Mass Effect* Video Game Trilogy," Sarah Stang critiques how Canadian developer BioWare's acclaimed *Mass Effect* video game series portrays female and feminized cyborg bodies as intertwined with or even infected by technology while framing them as either sexualized and desirable or monstrous and horrific. This chapter interprets the series' female cyborgs through the lens of feminist posthumanism, specifically discussions of monstrosity, hybridity, technology, and gender, as explored by Barbara Creed, Donna Haraway, and Rosi Braidotti. This analysis uncovers how the series demarcates strict boundaries around the "acceptable" ways a female body can be technologically enhanced, thereby reinforcing heteropatriarchal and misogynistic ideologies embedded in traditional science fiction.

Part Two, "Posthuman Environments and Entanglements," shifts the focus further outward, to the broader environmental surround within which bodies, subjects, and relations emerge and converge. In Chapter 6—the first of several provocative readings of Garland's film—"Material Entanglements and Posthuman Female Subjectivity in *Annihilation*," Evdokia Stefanopoulou examines *Annihilation* through the lens of Karen Barad's[14] agential realism and specifically through the concept of diffraction, which resonates

---

[14]Barad, *Meeting the Universe Halfway.*

thematically across the film. The chapter then examines how these material entanglements are also related to the grotesque and the double sensation it provokes in both characters and viewers. The grotesque, as theorized by Mikhail Bakhtin, signifies as an affirmative corporeality; in contemporary popular culture, however, it is also connected with feelings of repulsion and disgust. The film's grotesque images thus engender both fascination and aversion. What is more, as a female-centric film, *Annihilation* links these grotesque transformations with the female body. The representation of *Annihilation*'s female characters, and specifically how their posthuman becoming is signified and experienced in an ambiguous way, hints at the subversive possibilities of these transfigurations, even as they remain bounded within Humanist discourses.

The seventh chapter, by Meraj Dhir, "Jonathan Glazer's *Under the Skin*: Female Embodiment and Ecology," performs a formal and stylistic analysis of Glazer's 2013 science fiction film in conjunction with a consideration of its thematic defamiliarization of dominant science fiction tropes. Instead of presenting the expected confrontation and conflict between alien and human, *Under the Skin* detours from such conventional narrative patterns in favor of examining the very issue of "alien" embodiment in the form of the female body. By foregrounding the alien other as female, the film explores a phenomenology of the corporeal body within a specific historical and generic nexus, and with a particular, predatory charge. Finally, the chapter examines how a morphology of the female body is reflected in the visual morphology of film style in *Under the Skin*.

In Chapter 8, "Living in Color: Feminist and Posthumanist Ontology in *Upstream Color*," Emily Sanders explores Shane Carruth's indie-experimental science fiction film *Upstream Color* (2013) and the forms of feminist posthumanism it expresses. Undoing anthropocentrism through attention to the radical connectedness of organic forms, Carruth's feature offers a performance of what Rosi Braidotti conceives as *zoe*-centered egalitarianism[15] and Donna Haraway as "significant otherness."[16] While the narrative sets up worthwhile posthuman concerns, such as an image of life beyond capitalism and the role of trauma on the path to posthuman realization, it is really the unique formal stylings of the feature that introduce an embodied and empathetic ontology expressive of Braidotti's posthumanism. Carruth's elliptical cuts and rich soundscape serve as primary sources of knowledge, aiding the viewer in following a cyclical narrative that is otherwise resistant to analysis. Additionally, the musical score's repetitive sequences lead female protagonist Kris toward a new

---

[15]Rosi Braidotti, *The Posthuman* (Cambridge and Malden: Polity, 2013).
[16]Donna Haraway, *The Companion Species Manifesto: Dogs, People, and Significant Otherness*, vol. 1 (Chicago: Prickly Paradigm Press, 2003).

posthuman identity. Carruth's soundscape is thus situated as both diegetic and extradiegetic, complicating the relationship between Kris and her environment and dissolving traditional barriers between story-world and structure, and audience and film.

In Chapter 9, "Ascendance to Trans-Corporeality or Assimilation to Whiteness?: The Posthuman Ecofeminist Imaginaries of *Annihilation* and *Midsommar*," Olivia Stowell reads Garland's 2018 film and Ari Aster's folk horror *Midsommar* (2019) together, in order to explore the intersections of subjectivity and trans-corporeal or posthuman intra-activity alongside racial assimilation and violence in contemporary horror and horror-adjacent films. While *Annihilation* and *Midsommar* may appear to offer presentations of intersubjective communion with nature as a salve to individual and communal trauma, the films also present violence and racial assimilation to whiteness as the technologies by which to achieve this trans-corporeality or posthumanism. The re/iteration of racial assimilation and trauma that occurs within the subtext of each film highlights the necessity of holding multiple theoretical paradigms in friction with each other in order to realize a fuller vision of posthumanism's liberatory potentials and possibilities. *Annihilation* and *Midsommar* together imply that ecological crises are also racial crises, and without upending both environmental hierarchies and racial hierarchies, a turn to a transhumanist posthumanism and/or trans-corporeality can function to re-entrench the supremacy of whiteness.

The chapters in Part Three, "Posthumanist Endings and Futures," offer some final, diverse meditations on the question that, of all philosophical or theoretical systems, critical posthumanism is best equipped to address: What comes after the human? A question, it goes without saying, that we can only address from this side of the equation. Sarah Best's chapter, "Digital Game Ecologies: Posthuman Convergences in *Abzû* and *Horizon: Zero Dawn*," explores the various tensions and connections between nature and technology as they manifest in and through two postapocalyptic video games—Sony Interactive Entertainment's *Horizon: Zero Dawn* (HZD) (2017) and Giant Squid Studio's *Abzû* (2016). Situated at the intersection of game studies, feminist science studies, and material ecocriticism or "ecomaterialism," the chapter builds on the work of scholars such as Haraway, Alaimo, and Hayles in order to argue that, far from being an "escape" from reality, ecologically concerned games such as *HZD* and *Abzû* can foster environmental consciousness among players by making immediate the profound relationships between humans and their biological or technological nonhuman others. By virtue of the player-game-environment interactions they cultivate, these science fiction games challenge anthropocentric and patriarchal hierarchies, giving rise to posthuman worlds where oppositions are never absolute, and technology is an integral part of the ecosystem, embedded within rather than separate from nature.

In Chapter 11, "From Rogue Planets to Black Holes: Revaluing Death in *Melancholia* and *High Life*," Julia A. Empey utilizes Lars von Trier's 2011 film and Claire Denis 2018 film to explore a once and future postapocalyptic condition—the annihilation of humanity and, as a result, of humanism—as a type of posthumanism. Invoking Timothy Morton's concept, this chapter takes up the planet Melancholia and the black hole as "hyperobjects," contending at the same time that *Melancholia* and *High Life* suggest a new way of thinking through a literal posthuman condition as a type of "vibrant death."[17] This reading of death is "not in opposition to life, but existing in a flat continuum intertwined with it; death as an articulation of the vitality and vibrancy characterizing all matter, whether dead or alive, inanimate or animate, non-human or human."[18] These concepts are read alongside Patricia MacCormack's rebuking in *The Ahuman Manifesto* of posthumanism's inability to grapple with death and human insignificance. Robert Sinnerbrink points to *Melancholia*'s "radical gesture of world-sacrifice," which presents the possibility "of preparing for a post-humanist beginning" (112). *Melancholia* and in turn, *High Life*, refuses the kind of "humanistic consolation or metaphysical comfort" often present in apocalyptic film.[19] *High Life* and *Melancholia* suggests an optimistic ending for humanity that reads the "distribution of the value of life differently to the anthropocentric understanding of the world."[20] *Melancholia* and *High Life* counter postapocalyptic fantasies of humanity's ability to fight for survival, regardless of the hyperobjects' and our common inevitable end, instead suggesting a need for a radical acceptance of a posthumanity as "vibrant death."

In Chapter 12, "'Originary Twoness': Flashbacks and the Materiality of Memory in *Annihilation*, *High Life*, and *Arrival*," Russell J. A. Kilbourn theorizes what he terms "posthuman memory" through *High Life*, *Annihilation*, and *Arrival* (Villeneuve, 2016) as examples of contemporary "art house" science fiction film. "Memory" encompasses each of the film's structuring around subjective flashbacks and the function of intermediality as shorthand for the relations between and among different media, where the materiality of the medium is always in question. Matter, in relation to the human, links these disparate forms of memory; matter manifests metaphorically in its semantic connections to Earth or soil or *humus*, which (as per Haraway) shares its etymology with *human*, and is distantly related to *humility*, which literally means to make oneself low, to bring

[17]Nina Lykke, *Vibrant Death: A Posthuman Phenomenology of Mourning* (New York: Bloomsbury Publishing, 2022).
[18]Ibid., 7.
[19]Robert Sinnerbrink, "Anatomy of *Melancholia*," *Angelaki* 19, no. 4 (2014b): 111–26.
[20]Patricia MacCormack, *The Ahuman Manifesto: Activism for the End of the Anthropocene* (New York: Bloomsbury Publishing, 2020), 6.

oneself down to Earth. To be posthuman, therefore, entails the transcending of certain implications of materiality. As in *Arrival*, in which the world's salvation is keyed to one woman's acceptance of the productivity of death-in-life, at *Annihilation*'s end, the human species still perdures, the two main characters representative of a new posthuman paradigm and the promise of a radically uncertain future. In *High Life*, by contrast, a young father and his daughter are left as the sole survivors of a species seemingly fated to pass out of existence, with the ambiguous final shot leaving open the possibility of renewal via the transgressing of a fundamental cultural, and therefore natural, taboo. Finally, in what is perhaps the most radical revaluation of memory on both thematic and formal levels, *Arrival* counters the productively ambiguous endings of the other two films with a nontranscendent resolution, in a view of memory and history alike as intertwined and immanent, while also recursive, yet open-ended.

Finally, in Chapter 13, "Coming to Terms with Our Own Ends: Failed Reproduction and the End of the Hu/man in Claire Denis' *High Life* and Pella Kågerman and Hugo Lija's *Aniara*," Allison Mackey and Elif Sendur examine how the "end" of humanity is figured through a reconceptualization of human reproduction in two recent science fiction films fundamentally invested in contemplating the futurity of the human species: Denis' *High Life* and Pella Kågerman and Hugo Lilja's *Aniara* (2018). While both of these films imagine the end of the world as "one of mankind's most ancient fantas[ies]," this chapter argues that they do so in entirely different registers. These films present two forms of posthumanist cinema: *High Life* provides a posthumanist experience through refusing to succumb to Humanist logic and anthropocentric technique, while *Aniara* plays with generic conventions, only to disturb them by leaving no space for humans to survive the apocalypse. Comparing these films alongside critical posthumanist, feminist-materialist, and material-ecocritical thinkers, Mackey and Sendur analyze how they figure reproduction without generation as a rethinking of relations of body and production, as well as speculating on posthuman futures.

PART ONE

Posthuman Bodies and Identities

1

Indigenous Futurist and Women-Centered Dystopian Film

Missy Molloy

In *Screening the Posthuman*, I argue that, as the twenty-first century settles more firmly into a pattern of enduring and overlapping crises, portraits of the "sickly frantic state"[1] of late capitalism's decline have transfixed viewers to disaster onscreen.[2] As such, the patterns associated with dystopian screen narratives have grown roots, becoming increasingly familiar. For example, one plot-related pattern is to evoke posthuman environments in which Earth's degradation calls for technological intervention to enable even basic survival. Thus, in Bong Joon-ho's science fiction (SF) action film *Snowpiercer*,[3] a small group of humans survive glacial conditions by remaining eternally inside a self-sustaining train that circumnavigates the globe, while in *Aniara*,[4] a Swedish SF film directed by Pella Kågerman and Hugo Lilja, the ravages of climate change motivate the colonization of Mars, and when a Mars-bound spaceship gets knocked off course, a community of survivors is doomed to perpetual, aimless orbit. In these postapocalyptic scenarios, human behavior is the problem that sophisticated, sustainable technologies can only partly solve; that is, because human action has destroyed Earth's habitability, human-engineered technologies are required

---

[1]Evan Calder Williams, *Combined and Uneven Apocalypse: Luciferian Marxism* (n.p.: John Hunt Publishing, 2011), 4.
[2]Missy Molloy, Pansy Duncan, and Claire Henry, *Screening the Posthuman* (New York: Oxford University Press, 2023), 64–106.
[3]*Snowpiercer*, directed by Bong Joon-ho (2014; Beverly Hills: Anchor Bay Entertainment, 2014).
[4]*Aniara*, directed by Pella Kågerman and Hugo Lilja (2018; SF Studios, 2019).

for survival, yet the destructive behaviors persist, thereby jeopardizing new, artificial habitats. It is the latter dimension of this pattern in dystopian science fiction—its critique of predominant human habits—that resonates with critical posthumanism, which, according to Stefan Herbrechter, "negotiates the pressing question of what it means to be human under the conditions of globalisation, technoscience, late capitalism and climate change."[5]

The visibility and abundance of posthuman narratives and imagery in recent years demonstrate filmmakers' and viewers' attractions to "the pressing question of what it means to be human"[6] in contemporary life. For instance, in the recently released festival favorite, *After Yang*,[7] Jake (Colin Farrell), Kyra (Jodie Turner-Smith), and their daughter Mika (Malea Emma Tjandrawidjaja) struggle to accept the loss of the family's adopted son, the titular Yang (Justin H. Min), a robot who has become unresponsive and is deemed not worthy of repair by his makers. Classified as SF drama, *After Yang* is the latest entry in a group of films that explore transformations in human intimacy that result from the integration of synthetic being into the core of human relationships. Moreover, these explorations push against standard generic boundaries, as is evident in *Lars and the Real Girl*,[8] a film that poses related questions in the generic space of romantic comedy drama. As Pansy Duncan, Claire Henry, and I maintain,

> across the thematic, formal, and narrative registers of [contemporary film], we find cinema grappling with the posthuman—which is to say, with the question of how we might reimagine the social, ethical and discursive logics of human subjectivity at a moment when, as Cary Wolfe has put it, the imbrication of the "human" in "technical, medical, informatic and economic networks is increasingly impossible to ignore."[9]

Moreover, narratives that feature humanity in crisis, most notably in dystopian SF and kindred genres, are particularly aligned with critical posthumanism in that they draw attention to major flaws in the human status quo to argue that only substantial and widespread change could possibly alter the existing (and dire) state of affairs.

Within the glut of dystopian screen narratives broadly categorized as science fiction, women of color offer unique contributions to what has become, as

---

[5]Stefan Herbrechter, "Critical Posthumanism," in *Posthuman Glossary* (London: Bloomsbury Academic, 2018), 94.
[6]Ibid.
[7]*After Yang*, directed by Kogonada (2021; A24, 2022).
[8]*Lars and the Real Girl*, directed by Craig Gillespie (Metro Goldwyn Mayer, 2007).
[9]Cary Wolfe, What Is Posthumanism? Minneapolis: Minnesota University Press, 2010, xv. Quoted in Molloy, Duncan, and Henry, *Screening the Posthuman*, 1–2.

Sarah Keller argues, an over-represented subgenre.[10] Afrofuturism is relevant in this respect; Daylanne K. English defines it as "cultural production and scholarly thought—literature, visual art, photography, film, multimedia art, performance art, music, and theory—that imagine greater justice and a freer expression of black subjectivity in the future or in alternative places, times, or realities."[11] Kenyan filmmaker Wanuri Kahiu explains the significance of Afrofuturism in her 2012 Tedx talk: "As Africans . . . we've never had a space or a voice within our own history . . . [and now] we're using Afrofuturism to stake a place in the future."[12] This chapter aims, in part, to highlight how Black[13] and Indigenous[14] women filmmakers reinvigorate stale generic formulae associated with dystopian SF by centralizing women of color in explorations of alternative ways of being that directly oppose Western social systems and beliefs—the latter figuring as a sort of antagonist in their films. The distinctiveness of their cinematic contributions is in part due to the fact that, in mainstream films dealing with posthuman phenomena, race— emphasized in narratives, themes, or characters' identities, to name a few possibilities—plays an inconsistent and ambiguous role.

Two films written and directed by Alex Garland are exemplary in this regard: *Ex Machina*[15] dramatizes human/posthuman tensions incited by advanced robotic design, and *Annihilation*[16] follows a team of scientists who enter into a mysterious (and extremely dangerous) electromagnetic field. Frequent subjects of posthuman analysis,[17] *Ex Machina* and *Annihilation*

---

[10]Sarah Keller, *Anxious Cinephilia: Pleasure and Peril at the Movies* (New York: Columbia University Press, 2020).

[11]Daylanne K. English, "Afrofuturism," *Oxford Bibliographies*, 2017.

[12]Wanuri Kahiu, "Afrofuturism in Popular Culture," TedxNairobi, 2012.

[13]"Of or relating to black people, their history, politics, culture, etc. Of an area or place: predominantly inhabited or frequented by black people" "black, adj. and n." *OED Online*, June 2022. Oxford University Press. https://www.oed.com/view/Entry/19670.

[14]The Chicago Manual of Style recommends the capitalization of Black and Indigenous when referring to "race or ethnicity" (as do many other credible sources), and this chapter follows that recommendation (see, for instance, http://cmosshoptalk.com/2020/06/22/black-and-white-a -matter-of-capitalization/, https://apastyle.apa.org/style-grammar-guidelines/bias-free-language /racial-ethnic-minorities, and https://web.archive.org/web/20181116050310/https://www.naja .com/reporter-s-indigenous-terminology-guide/). By "Indigenous," I mean "Indigenous *or less commonly* indigenous: of or relating to the earliest known inhabitants of a place and especially of a place that was colonized by a now-dominant group" (Merriam-Webster Dictionary: https://www.merriam-webster.com/dictionary/indigenous).

[15]*Ex Machina*, directed by Alex Garland (A24, 2014).

[16]*Annihilation*, directed by Alex Garland (Paramount Pictures, 2018).

[17]For instance, see Elisabetta di Minico, "*Ex-Machina* and the Feminine Body through Human and Posthuman Dystopia," *Ekphrasis. Images, Cinema, Theory, Media* 1 (2017): 67–84, Rocío Carrasco-Carrasco, "Becoming Woman: Healing and Posthuman Subjectivity in Garland's *Ex Machina*," in *Technologies of Feminist Speculative Fiction* (Cham: Springer International Publishing, 2022), 261–82, and Mashya Boon, "Chromophilic Annihilation: Posthuman Prisms and New Materialist Refractions of Reality," *Pulse: The Journal of Science and Culture* 7, no. 1 (2020): 1–24.

illustrate the ambiguity of gender and race in cinema that interrogates humanistic values to confront contemporary social, ecological, and techno-scientific realities. In *Ex Machina*, the eccentric and reclusive antagonist, Nathan (Oscar Isaac), designs a series of gynoids (female-gendered robots) who are explicitly raced in accordance with Western-oriented, sexist notions of human progress and the role of women therein: Nathan's early gynoid creations are Black and Indigenous in appearance; a more recent gynoid, Kyoko (Sonoya Mizuno) is Asian and mute, supplying sex and domestic labor; and, finally, his robotic engineering "progresses" to the most sophisticated variant—a white woman, Ava (Alicia Vikander), who embodies Western ideals of feminine beauty and intelligence. Meanwhile, in *Annihilation,* the team of four scientists and one paramedic[18] who risk their lives to investigate the Shimmer are all women, and a diverse group at that: a Black American, a Latina, and a European woman[19] feature alongside two white Americans. In accordance with Hollywood convention, though, the most substantial roles are reserved for the white American women (played by Natalie Portman and Jennifer Jason Leigh), and, as a result, the novelty of racially diverse women scientists seems more gimmicky than purposeful. In short, Garland's posthumanist narratives engage with gender and race mainly on superficial levels and are, as such, neither feminist nor critical of the racial assumptions implicated in Western humanism.

In cinematic portraits of posthuman women, the tendency of male-directed films to highlight difference without any explicit motivation is also evident in Hirokazu Kore-eda's *Air Doll*,[20] in which a sex doll, Nozomi, who is played by Korean actress Doona Bae, miraculously comes to life and explores human behavior among a cast of Japanese characters. In "Envisioning Cyborg Bodies," Jennifer González persuasively argues that "the image of the cyborg [a human/machine amalgam] has historically recurred at moments of radical social and cultural change [. . .] the cyborg body thus becom[ing] the historical record of changes in human perception."[21] After surveying a wide range of cyborgs, González concludes that "the traditional, gendered roles of Euro-American culture are rarely challenged in the visual representations of cyborgs."[22] This conclusion accords with the vast majority of cinematic characterizations that represent a hybrid of human and nonhuman elements. Therefore, if representations of cyborgs (and cyborg women, in particular) mark "moments of radical social

---

[18]Anya (Gina Rodriguez) is a paramedic.
[19]Tuva Novotny is originally from Sweden.
[20]*Air Doll*, directed by Hirokazu Kore-eda (Asmik Ace, 2009).
[21]Jennifer González, "Envisioning Cyborg Bodies: Notes from Current Research," in *Cybersexualities: A Reader in Feminist Theory, Cyborgs and Cyberspace*, ed. Jenny Wolmark (Edinburgh: Edinburgh University Press, 1999), 267.
[22]Ibid.

and cultural change," then maintaining "traditional, gendered roles of Euro-American culture" through these representations is a missed opportunity—a failure to deeply interrogate "changes in human perception" by challenging its visual and cultural conventions. Julia Hart's *Fast Color*[23] provides a posthumanist and feminist counterexample to the tendencies glossed above; the film depicts a near-future dystopian United States where a family of Black women with superheroic abilities lives as outlaws. In brief, *Fast Color* foregrounds the particular struggles of Black American women in its address of "radical social and cultural change," thereby imagining the future as not only female but also Black. The paucity of films that meaningfully center gender and race in their posthuman critiques makes those that do so uniquely impactful.

The following analysis spotlights two films made by Indigenous women, each of which speaks to Indigenous Futurist and posthuman theories in their representations of dystopian scenarios in which First Nations women and Indigenous politics are crucial. Virtual reality film *Biidaaban: First Light*,[24] by Anishinaabe filmmaker Lisa Jackson, leads users through a near-deserted Toronto after the collapse of settler colonial society. *Night Raiders*,[25] a feature film directed by Cree-Métis filmmaker Danis Goulet, is set in 2043 in a military-occupied North America; the protagonist, Niska (Elle-Máijá Tailfeathers), is a Cree mother who joins a band of Indigenous rebels to rescue her daughter, Waseese (Brooklyn Letexier-Hart), who has been taken by the State (Figure 1.1). Inspired by Afrofuturism, Grace Dillon coined the term "Indigenous Futurism" to describe narratives that "us[e] the images, ideology, and themes in science fiction to envision a future from a Native (Indigenous) perspective";[26] her aim was to "renew, recover, and extend First Nations peoples' voices and traditions."[27] Because Afrofuturism has been influential in the development of Indigenous Futurism, I will draw on Kahiu's *Pumzi*[28] to illuminate strategies through which women filmmakers who represent historically marginalized intersectional perspectives "stake a place in the future" in the field of dystopian SF. Collectively, the set of films I analyze demonstrates the utility of adapting a future-oriented genre to address historical forms of racial, colonial, and environmental oppression that persist in the present. In fact, Goulet has stated that the oppressive government imagined in

---

[23]*Fast Color*, directed by Julia Hart (Lionsgate and Codeblack Films, 2019).
[24]*Biidaaban: First Light*, directed by Lisa Jackson (National Film Board of Canada, 2018).
[25]*Night Raiders*, directed by Danis Goulet (XYZ Films, 2021).
[26]Grace Dillon, cited in Henrietta Lidchi and Suzanne Newman Fricke, "Future History: Indigenous Futurisms in North American Visual Arts," *World Art* 9, no. 2 (2019): 99.
[27]Grace Dillon, *Walking the Clouds: An Anthology of Indigenous Science Fiction* (Tucson: University of Arizona Press, 2012), 1–2.
[28]*Pumzi*, directed by Wanuri Kahiu (Focus Features, 2009).

FIGURE 1.1 *In* Night Raiders *a Cree mother, Niska (Elle-Máijá Tailfeathers), fights to free her daughter, Waseese (Brooklyn Letexier-Hart), in a future, military-occupied North America (Danis Goulet,* Night Raiders, *2021, Canada and New Zealand. XYZ Films).*

Night Raiders was inspired by the disproportionate use of force against protestors that she witnessed at Standing Rock.[29] Jackson, for her part, regards Indigenous Futurist art as an effort to "break through the tendency to stereotype everything Indigenous as stuck in the past."[30] Their films offer provocative takes on human catastrophe and the histories that engender them, and, through their filmmaking, Goulet and Jackson "reclaim [the] place [of Indigenous women] in an imagined future in space, on earth, and everywhere in between."[31]

Feminism's Migration from Humanism to Posthumanism

In "Posthuman Feminist Theory," Rosi Braidotti maps a nonlinear progression from twentieth-century feminisms grounded in humanism to posthuman feminism, which weaves material feminism's attention to differences among

---

[29]Chris Knight, "Danis Goulet's Film a First for New Zealand-Canada Indigenous Co-operation," *National Post*, June 26, 2020.

[30]CBC Arts, "Lisa Jackson's *Biidaaban: First Light*," 2018.

[31]Rebecca Roanhorse, Elizabeth LaPensee, Johnnie Jay, and Darcie Little Badger, "Decolonizing Science Fiction and Imagining Futures: An Indigenous Futurisms Round Table," *Strange Horizons*, January 30, 2017.

women, including those rooted in class, race, and Indigeneity, into posthumanist critique. In the process, Braidotti identifies "feminist science-fiction" as a crucial step that sets "a different genealogical line for posthuman feminism," which she elaborates as follows: "Since the 1970s, feminist writers and literary theorists of science fiction . . . supported the alliance between women, as the others of Man, and such other 'others' as non-whites (postcolonial, black, Jewish, [I]ndigenous, and hybrid subjects) and nonhumans (animals, insects, plants, trees, viruses, and bacteria)."[32] Braidotti further notes that feminist SF in the late twentieth century was in conversation with groundbreaking theory, most notably that of Donna Haraway, whose engagement with technoculture in *A Cyborg Manifesto* was foundational to the establishment of critical posthumanism. Haraway's cyborg is a vision of posthuman potential that inspired systematic critique of humanism specifically for its historical exclusions on gender, racial, colonial, sexual, and ableist grounds (among others).[33]

In "Metamorphic Others and Nomadic Subjects," Braidotti covers similar territory when she itemizes shortcomings in the demarcation of human being:

> We are not all humans, or not human to the same degree, not if by "human" you mean to refer to the dominant vision of the Subject as white, male, heterosexual, urbanized, able-bodied, speaking a standard language and taking charge of the women and the children. Many of us belong to other, more marginalized categories or groups: non-white, non-male, non-heterosexual, not urbanized, not able-bodied, not speaking a standard language, not in charge of the women and the children.[34]

According to Braidotti, these "others"—whose belonging "to the dominant vision of the human subject . . . is negotiable at best"—"illuminat[e] the complex and dissym[m]etrical power-relations at work in the constitution of humanism's dominant subject-position."[35] In Braidotti's genealogy of posthuman feminism, twentieth-century (predominantly literary) feminist SF brought to light these humanistic exclusions and power imbalances, thus setting the stage for postcolonial feminism's key "intervention" in the emerging posthuman feminism:

> Ever mindful of the fact that the "human" is not a neutral term but rather one that indexes access to privileges and entitlements, postcolonial

---

[32]Rosi Braidotti, "Posthuman Feminist Theory," in *The Oxford Handbook of Feminist Theory* (Oxford: Oxford University Press, 2016), 686.
[33]Donna Haraway, "A Cyborg Manifesto," in *The International Handbook of Virtual Learning Environments* (Dordrecht: Springer, 2006).
[34]Rosi Braidotti, "Metamorphic Others and Nomadic Subjects," *Artmap*, Oliver Laric: November 22, 2014–January 17, 2015.
[35]Ibid.

feminist theorists have made a strong intervention in this debate. They
warn that feminists cannot mindlessly embrace the equation between
the "posthuman" and post-gender without taking into account serious
power differentials. . . . New assemblages or transversal alliances need to
be negotiated carefully and not taken for granted.[36]

How can the imaginary terrain of dystopian SF film register these "serious
power differentials"? On the one hand, it can do so by highlighting the role
historical power imbalances play in sustaining seriously flawed environments
that are characterized by injustice. On another, it can spotlight the capacities
of historically dehumanized others to rebel against dominant social orders
in order to forge alternatives. Both strategies can (and often do) contain
posthumanist elements, particularly if filmmakers deploy dystopian SF
to "experiment with what contemporary, biotechnologically mediated
bodies are capable of doing"[37] to resist the powers that be in pursuit of
nondestructive alternatives.

To take a case in point, Kahiu's short film *Pumzi* (which means "breath" in
Swahili) takes place in East African Territory thirty-five years after the Third
World War, which the film subtitles "The Water War" to pinpoint competition
over depleted resources as the main cause of dystopian conditions. Human
survivors are confined underground, and the film quickly establishes that
the Earth above has been degraded to an uninhabitable state. Lacking
earthly resources, survivors generate energy manually on stationary bikes
and recycle urine for drinking water. The community's austere social system
is heavily regimented, individual action controlled by watchful authorities,
and deviations swiftly punished. The protagonist, Asha (Kudzani Moswela),
works as a curator in the Natural History Museum. When she receives
soil from an unknown source, she tests it, amazed to find no evidence of
radiation. Experimenting with the soil by mixing it with water and a dried-
out Maitu seed to "test its growth potential," Asha interprets the soil as a
sign of renewed vitality in the environment beyond the compound, which
she has never experienced directly but envisions in the form of a vibrantly
healthy tree. In the vision (Figure 1.2), Asha stretches her hand toward the
tree in a gesture that foreshadows the primary role she will eventually play
in planting it (or one like it, viewers imagine). However, the authorities
wholly reject her findings, declaring that life outside is impossible. When
Asha continues her research against their orders, she is violently disciplined
and ejected from her lab. To fulfill the promise of her vision, Asha must
escape the oppressive society and brave the brutal conditions aboveground

[36]Braidotti, "Posthuman Feminist Theory," 687. Braidotti is paraphrasing Julie Livingston and
Jasbir K. Puar, "Interspecies." *Social Text* 29, no. 1 (2011): 3–13.
[37]Rosi Braidotti, *The Posthuman* (Cambridge and Malden: Polity, 2013), 61.

FIGURE 1.2 *In* Pumzi, *Asha's (Kudzani Moswela) vision of a live tree flourishing in the supposedly barren earth motivates her actions (Wanuri Kahiu,* Pumzi, *2009, Kenya. Inspired Minority Pictures).*

to plant the seed, which has already begun to germinate. In the end, Asha perishes beside the newly planted sapling, sacrificing herself to her vision of environmental regeneration.

Pumzi cinematically represents what "contemporary, biotechnologically mediated bodies are capable of doing"[38] to oppose the dominant human behaviors that jeopardize earthly existence for not only the human species but also many other "companion species."[39] In the film, postcolonial and posthumanist feminisms overlap through the Afrofuturist iconography that casts Asha as responsible for ensuring a liveable future in postapocalyptic conditions. In my reading of the film, the visualization of Asha's motivation is crucial; our first view of the vibrantly living tree represents Asha's subjective internal perspective (Figure 1.2, top), while a later image (Figure 1.2, bottom) reflects her communication of the vision to the authorities using a sophisticated technology: a scanner that projects her imagination via touch.

---

[38]Ibid.
[39]Donna Haraway, *The Companion Species Manifesto: Dogs, People, and Significant Otherness* (Chicago: Prickly Paradigm Press, 2003).

In his analysis of how Afrofuturism functions in *Pumzi*, Dan Heaven argues that this complex "affectual image . . . demonstrates that in the moment the cancellation of the future is enacted[,] a lateral sense of possibilities [is] simultaneously produced, waiting to be excavated and mobilised."[40] Heaven thus stresses the strength of the seed/tree imagery in exposing surprising connections between past, present, and future: "Such is the nature of *Pumzi's* generative power, its potential to produce movements of thought that disrupt, reimagine, and reconfigure the confines of what appears possible in the present and the future."[41]

Pumzi's indictment of a destructive, oppressive humanity and exploration of posthuman potential recall not only the critical intervention of Afrofuturism but also posthuman feminism. Braidotti's "Four Theses on Posthuman Feminism" argues that "feminist posthuman critiques need to focus . . . on the continuing or renewed power differentials, on the structures of domination and exclusion in advanced capitalism. Class, race, gender, and age have moved centre stage in the global economy and its necropolitical governmentality."[42] *Pumzi* performs a feminist posthumanist critique according to Braidotti's vision by tasking Asha, a Black African woman, with the life-renewing gesture that anticipates a future in which humanism's destructive "power differentials," including the privileging of the human at the expense of natural environments, are neutralized. Indeed, Kahiu explicitly genders the revolutionary Maitu seed as feminine; in the first minute of screen time, *Pumzi* communicates the etymology of "Maitu" when Asha skims a dictionary entry (the shot is an eyeline match from Asha's point-of-view): "MAITU (Mother) Seed: Kikuyu language. 1. Noun— Mother . . . From MAA (truth) and ITU (ours). OUR TRUTH." In short, Kahiu constructs a posthumanist feminist alliance between Asha and the life-giving Mother/seed, which asserts the pivotal role of African matrilineal cultural knowledge in cultivating sustainable modes of being that combat humanistic (and colonial) "structures of domination and exclusion."[43]

Repurposing Dystopian Science Fiction

Before I detail the ways Jackson and Goulet repurpose dystopian SF conventions to centralize Indigeneity in visions of the future, it is important

---

[40]Dan Heaven, "'The Future Starts with an Image': Wanuri Kahiu's *Pumzi* (2009)," *Alluvium*, June 4, 2021.
[41]Ibid.
[42]Rosi Braidotti, "Four Theses on Posthuman Feminism," in *Anthropocene Feminism* (Minneapolis: University of Minnesota Press, 2017), 40.
[43]Ibid.

to stress that neither Indigenous Futurism nor Indigenous Feminism aligns neatly with Braidotti's account of posthuman feminism; this is because framing a Humanist critique according to Indigenous feminist points-of-view significantly alters the diagnosis of humanism's historical injustices and their resonance with contemporary crises. Hence, a *New York Times* article addressing the generic innovations of Indigenous sci-fi writers features novelist Rebecca Roanhorse's[44] provocative statement, "We've already survived an apocalypse."[45] Meanwhile, in a roundtable discussion, titled "Decolonizing Science Fiction and Imagining Futures: An Indigenous Futurisms Roundtable," Johnnie Jae, an Otoe-Missouria and Choctaw journalist, echoes Roanhorse's view: "We have survived an apocalypse and with every generation our future continues to grow more hopeful."[46] In the same conversation, Darcie Little Badger, a Lipan Apache sci-fi writer and scientist, adds, "I think that imagining a future, *period*, is a great start. . . . The reality is, many Indigenous cultures in North America survived an apocalypse. The key word is *survived*. Any future with us in it, triumphant and flourishing, is a hopeful one."[47]

The work of Indigenous women filmmakers in postapocalyptic SF should be interpreted in this spirit—as informed by the genocidal agendas their ancestors survived. With this in mind, their films assign a different timeline to postapocalypse, one that recasts the agent of disaster from the general (human behavior) to the specific (white settler colonialism). Therefore, in my view, while Indigenous Futurist feminism is passionately invested in the critique of Western humanism, especially its marginalization of a tapestry of intersectional Others (including the environmental nonhuman), it also demands that critical posthumanism account for colonialization's radical-world-ending and dystopian world forming, which continues to reverberate in the present (e.g., in the violent suppression of the Dakota Access Pipeline protests at Standing Rock, which, as mentioned earlier, partly inspired *Night Raider*'s dystopia). That being the case, Indigenous women filmmakers reworking dystopian SF from within, and in ways relevant to Indigenous Futurism, evoke familiar plots and iconography to invest them with radically

---

[44]The credibility of Roanhorse's claim to being Ohkay Owingeh has been questioned by tribal members, as has her appropriation of Navajo traditions, which Roanhorse has defended on the basis of her marriage to a Navajo citizen (Acee Ogoyo, "'The Elizabeth Warren of the sci-fi set': Author Faces Criticism for Repeated Use of Tribal Traditions," *Indianz.com*, June 24, 2020. https://www.indianz.com/News/2020/06/24/the-elizabeth-warren-of-the-scifi-set-au .asp.). Despite these questions, her quotation in *The New York Times* has been reiterated by a number of Indigenous artists working in the Indigenous Futurist space.
[45]Alexandra Alter, "'We've Already Survived an Apocalypse': Indigenous Writers Are Changing Sci-Fi," *The New York Times*, October 5, 2020.
[46]Roanhorse, LaPensee, Jay, and Badger, "Decolonizing Science Fiction and Imagining Futures."
[47]Ibid., emphasis in original.

Indigenous meanings. Later, I describe how this manifests in *Biidaaban: First Light* and *Night Raiders*.

Elsewhere, I have argued that *Biidaaban: First Light* successfully employs VR to immerse users in "an explicitly Indigenous experience of post-apocalyptic Toronto" that folds two catastrophes into one: "the apocalypse 'already survived' by First Nations people who persisted despite the colonial settlement of Canada, and the collapse of settler-capitalist society in Canada."[48] Here, I emphasize that Jackson's Indigenous Futurist rendition of postapocalyptic Toronto radically reclaims it on behalf of the array of First Nations that legitimately regard it as their traditional territory. In "Canada's Impossible Acknowledgment," Stephen Marche writes about the country's rapid integration of land acknowledgments, which, he argues, "forc[e] individuals and institutions to ask a basic, nightmarish question: Whose land are we on?"[49] *Biidaaban: First Light* presents Toronto as Wendat, Mohawk, and Anishinaabe, as indicated by the spoken languages that guide users through a future version of "Canada's largest urban centre from an Indigenous female perspective."[50] Through exposure to the "languages of the place originally known as Tkaronto," Jackson invites users to "gain insight into the complex thought systems of this land's first peoples."[51] She also creatively confronts Marche's "nightmarish" question, "Whose land are we on?," although the preposition "in" seems more appropriate than "on" with regard to the enveloping experience of *Biidaaban* via VR headset.

The official "Land Acknowledgement for Toronto" currently states:

> We acknowledge the land we are meeting on is the traditional territory of many nations including the Mississaugas of the Credit, the Anishnabeg, the Chippewa, the Haudenosaunee and the Wendat peoples and is now home to many diverse First Nations, Inuit and Métis. We also acknowledge that Toronto is covered by Treaty 13 with the Mississaugas of the Credit.[52]

Because the land was already a contested site when the British Crown negotiated with the Mississaugas in 1787 and 1805, precisely who gets named in the acknowledgment is a matter of unceasing debate, which is further complicated, according to Marche, by the fact that "'Traditional

---

[48]Molloy, Duncan, and Henry, *Screening the Posthuman*, 73–8.
[49]Stephen Marche, "Canada's Impossible Acknowledgement," *The New Yorker*, September 7, 2017.
[50]"*Biidaaban: First Light*" (National Film Board of Canada, 2018).
[51]Ibid.
[52]"Land Acknowledgment," City of Toronto, https://www.toronto.ca/city-government/accessibility-human-rights/indigenous-affairs-office/land-acknowledgement/.

land' is, in many cases, a colonial concept."[53] Jackson stakes a claim in this debate by voicing languages originally spoken in Tkaronto/Toronto and layering them in a nonhierarchical sound mix. "Our Culture Is in Our Languages," she states, breathing life into that claim through *Biidaaban*'s audiovisual environment, which pairs the postapocalyptic iconography of a barely inhabited Toronto reclaimed by nature with the sounds of languages spoken in pre-Contact Tkaronto. Jackson further elaborates on the significance of *Biidaaban*'s language-scape: "I know enough about how different these languages are to realize that seeing the world through their lens would change everything."[54] Thus, while users explore the abandoned space of Osgoode subway station, a woman's voice asks via voiceover, "Änen shayo'tron' Shonywäa'tihchia'ih sentiohkwa'?," which is subsequently translated as, "Where did the Creator put your people?" Later, we are unmoored in the night sky while overlapping sounds of voices speaking multiple Indigenous languages are translated onscreen. They recite the Haudenosaunee Thanksgiving Address, which, according to Brenda Longfellow, "expresses gratitude for all that sustains life while reminding listeners of a solemn promise to tend and care for the world with its abundant gifts."[55] The sole human who appears in *Biidaaban* is an Indigenous woman who inhabits a rooftop on the edge of Toronto's iconic Nathan Phillips Square. Longfellow's optimistic interpretation stresses that, "while the future evoked in *Biidaaban* shares the iconography of ruin with much post-apocalyptic scenarios, nestled among the ruins are multiple signs of human survival."[56] According to Jackson's vision, future survival depends on revitalizing Indigenous languages and culture to recast the dynamic between humans and their nonhuman environments (Figure 1.3).

Michelle Raheja's concept of "visual sovereignty," which has helped shape the field of contemporary Native American film studies, is pertinent to Jackson's and Goulet's adaptations of cinematic conventions to communicate Indigenous perspectives:

> I suggest a reading practice for thinking about the space between resistance and compliance wherein Indigenous filmmakers and actors revisit, contribute to, borrow from, critique, and reconfigure ethnographic

[53]Marche, "Canada's Impossible Acknowledgement."
[54]Randy Astle, "'Our Culture Is in Our Language': Lisa Jackson on her VR Film *Biidaaban: First Light* and Indigenous Futurism," *Filmmaker*, July 23, 2018.
[55]Brenda Longfellow, "Indigenous Futurism and the Immersive Worlding of *Inherent Rights/Vision Rights, 2167* and *Biidaaban: First Light*," August 30, 2019.
[56]Ibid.

FIGURE 1.3 Biidaaban: First Light *invites viewers to imagine a future Toronto in which postapocalyptic survival involves the revitalization of Indigenous languages, knowledge, and cultural practice (Lisa Jackson,* Biidaaban: First Light, *2018, Canada. National Film Board of Canada).*

film conventions, while at the same time operating within and stretching the boundaries created by these conventions.[57]

Slight modifications illuminate the applicability of Raheja's concept to *Biidaaban* and *Night Raiders*: "Indigenous [women] filmmakers and actors revisit, contribute to, borrow from, critique, and reconfigure [dystopian SF] film conventions, while at the same time operating within and stretching the boundaries created by these conventions." As indicated earlier, *Night Raiders'* plot focuses on the confiscation of Niska's eleven-year-old daughter, Waseese, as property of the authoritarian state, which starkly divides its subjects into haves and have nots in a manner that recalls popular, women-centered dystopian screen dramas such as *The Hunger Games*[58] and *The Handmaid's Tale*.[59] Niska eventually joins forces with a Cree-led vigilante group, the Night Raiders, to free Waseese and other Indigenous children and mount a defense against the State's annexation of Cree land. I argue that *Night Raiders* illustrates Raheja's "visual sovereignty" in that the film stretches generic boundaries to "interven[e] in larger discussions of Native

---

[57]Michelle Raheja, *Reservation Reelism: Redfacing, Visual Sovereignty, and Representations of Native Americans in Film* (Lincoln: University of Nebraska Press, 2011), 193.
[58]*The Hunger Games*, directed by Gary Ross (Lionsgate, 2012).
[59]*The Handmaid's Tale* (Hulu, 2017-).

American sovereignty by locating and advocating for Indigenous cultural and political power both within and outside of Western legal jurisprudence."[60]

In essence, Goulet repurposes genre conventions not only to bolster Indigenous self-representation (which reinforces "cultural sovereignty," according to Raheja's theory) but also to advocate for Indigenous sovereignty off-screen, with particular emphases on land rights ("as long as we have one piece of land, they will always come for us," observes Leo, a Māori member of the Night Raiders) and the autonomy to raise Indigenous children according to the beliefs and traditions of their cultural heritage. In fact, I would go so far as to say that Goulet reconfigures dystopian SF precisely to inject Indigenous relevance into the conflicts typically raised via the subgenre. Thus, in the case of *Night Raiders*, the seizure of children for State education and indoctrination (the plot's inciting incident) clearly alludes to the extremely painful history in Canada (and elsewhere) of colonial authorities taking children from their communities supposedly for their educational benefits but with traumatic consequences. Canada's residential schools were "re-education camps"[61] (like the one Waseese is confined to) that separated Indigenous children from their communities with the stated aim of cultural assimilation. The gross abuses suffered by First Nations children in those camps are still in the process of coming to light (for instance, in the 2021 discovery of one thousand unmarked children's graves on former residential school grounds[62]). Meanwhile, in the film's climactic encounter, Cree-led rebels face off against the state-run military forces and realize, in the process, that their land defense is in fact a battle against full annihilation. Through this final showdown, Goulet gestures to colonial policies that concomitantly pursued land confiscation and genocide.

In an article on visual sovereignty, Muscogee Creek artist Haley Rains cites Māori filmmaker Merata Mita's influential take on colonial exploitation and screen culture: "I've always felt strongly that our land gets taken, the fisheries and forests get taken, and in the same category is our stories. What we see on the screen is only the dominant, white, mono-cultural perspective on life. . . . We need to see our own people up there."[63] Mita's statement is undoubtedly relevant to *Night Raiders*' insertion of Indigenous characters and issues of great relevance to Indigenous politics into a dystopian SF formula and to the explicit connections it draws between stock generic situations and historical injustices perpetrated against Indigenous people in Canada, the United States, and beyond. At the same time, Rains' quoting

[60]Raheja, *Reservation Reelism*, 194.
[61]Cindy Blackstock and Pamela Palmater, "Canada's Government Needs to Face Up to its Role in Indigenous Children's Deaths," *The Guardian*, July 8, 2021.
[62]Ibid.
[63]Merata Mita, quoted by Haley Rains, "I Am Who I Say I Am: Reclaiming Native American Identity through Visual Sovereignty," *Imagining America*, September 28, 2021.

of Mita brings to mind *Night Raiders'* exceptional production context, which featured transnational collaboration among a diverse group of Indigenous film professionals, including acclaimed Māori filmmakers Taika Waititi, Ainsley Gardiner, and Chelsea Winstanley. New Zealand journalist Charlotte Muru-Lanning's interview with Gardiner and Winstanley (just before *Night Raiders'* NZ premiere) echoes Mita's statement while glossing key premises of Indigenous Futurism:

> Colonisation was an explicit attempt to erase the futures of indigenous peoples the world over—whether that be by stealing land, repressing language, assimilation, culture or genocide in the most literal sense. It's only through constant resistance, and renaissance, that we've survived and reclaimed our futures. Telling our stories through the screen is a key part of this.[64]

Of note is Muru-Lanning's embrace of *Night Raiders* as both culturally significant and strongly genre-driven: "While explicitly indigenous—referencing history, politics and tradition—*Night Raiders* also cleverly embraces sci fi in its purest form."[65] As this interview demonstrates, Goulet's modification of familiar genre tropes to express unique elements of Cree experience, and to link cultural repression with material exploitation and political injustice, represents her engagement in a transnational Indigenous conversation playing out in the field of popular cinema. For example, Mi'kmaq filmmaker Jeff Barnaby's *Blood Quantum*[66] employs zombie horror conventions to tell a highly stylized version of the invasion of Mi'kmaq territory by the Quebec Provincial Police in 1981 (which is documented in Abenaki filmmaker Alanis Obomsawin's canonical documentary, *Incident at Restigouche*[67]), while Māori filmmaker James Ashcroft's *Coming Home in the Dark*[68] utilizes a blend of horror and thriller elements to confront the painful history of abuses suffered by Māori and other children in Aotearoa's state-run boys' homes.[69]

---

[64]Charlotte Muru-Lanning, "Chelsea Winstanley and Ainsley Gardiner on *Night Raiders* and Indigenous Storytelling," *The Spinoff*, March 23, 2022.
[65]Ibid.
[66]*Blood Quantum*, directed by Jeff Barnaby (Elevation Pictures, 2019).
[67]*Incident at Restigouche*, directed by Alanis Obomsawin (National Film Board of Canada, 1984).
[68]*Coming Home in the Dark*, directed by James Ashcroft (Homecoming Productions, 2021).
[69]Ashcroft is explicit about the history his genre film addresses in interviews with the press (e.g., Rochelle Siemienoqicz, "*Coming Home in the Dark*—Director James Ashcroft Talks Tension on a Budget," *Screen Hub*, September 10, 2021). Meanwhile, traumas associated with the boys' homes have been frequent subjects of press coverage in Aotearoa in recent years (e.g., Andrew McRae, "Life in State-Run Boys' Homes: 'These were Cells. . . . All You Could Hear was the Screams,'" *Radio New Zealand*, May 3, 2021).

The transnational Indigenous conversation *Night Raiders* contributes to is visible in the film's allusions to recent Sami coming-of-age drama *Sameblod/Sami Blood*[70] as well as to contemporary SF classic *Children of Men*.[71] With regard to *Sami Blood*, the cinematographic depiction of Waseese's experience in the state-run camp resembles Sámi filmmaker Amanda Kernell's visual treatment of protagonist Elle-Marja in a Swedish-run boarding school aimed at cultural assimilation (Figure 1.4). Indigenous viewers attuned to the transnational conversation evolving via contemporary

FIGURE 1.4 *In representations of forced assimilation into the dominant culture,* Sami Blood's *Elle-Marja (Lene Cecilia Sparrok) and* Night Raiders' Waseese *(Brooklyn Letexier-Hart) are visually differentiated to stress that Indigenous identity is targeted for erasure by colonial indoctrination (Amanda Kernell,* Sameblod/Sami Blood, *2016, Sweden. Nordisk Film Production Sverige AB) (Danis Goulet,* Night Raiders, *2021, Canada and New Zealand. XYZ Films).*

---

[70]*Sameblod/Sami Blood*, directed by Amanda Kernell (Nordisk Film Production Sverige AB, 2016).
[71]*Children of Men*, directed by Alfonso Cuarón (Paramount Pictures, 2006).

Indigenous cinema register such visual and narrative symmetries, which forge links among films categorized in a range of genres (and in fact, *Night Raiders, Sami Blood*, and *Cousins*[72] [a 2021 drama directed by Māori women, including *Night Raiders* producer Ainsley Gardiner] engage with analogous abuses perpetrated by colonial states against young Indigenous women). Moreover, this transnational movement of Indigenous filmmakers engages with classic genre films to express Indigenous takes on established conventions. As an illustration, the familiarity of *Night Raiders'* depiction of state authorities herding marginalized subjects onto a bus is far from accidental; Goulet purposefully recalls the start of *Children of Men*'s famous Bexhill sequence to highlight her intervention in a category of cinema that has historically privileged non-Indigenous points-of-view (Figure 1.5).

Joanna Hearne applies Raheja's theory of visual sovereignty to *Smoke Signals*[73], a Native American cinema classic that is particularly recognized for its effective investment of multiple generic formulae with meanings relevant to Native American culture: "*Smoke Signals* may look like other American films in its use of established formulas—it's a road movie, a buddy movie, a comedy, a family drama—but when we look more closely we see that these familiar conventions take on different meanings, reshaping American cinema from within."[74] The same can be said of Goulet's reshaping of dystopian SF via *Night Raiders*, which may resemble mainstream fare but includes elements whose meanings are far from universal. As noted earlier, culturally specific injustices suffered by First Nations people as well as Indigenous communities around the globe—namely, re-education and land confiscation—function as major plot elements; these, in turn, signal *Night Raiders'* investment of dystopian SF screen drama with Indigenous relevance. In closing, I highlight one final noteworthy aspect of *Night Raiders'* bid for visual sovereignty, which involves Waseese's supernatural ability to communicate with and coordinate both organic and mechanical nonhuman beings. By including this plot point, Goulet gestures to white American/colonial characterizations of Indigenous Americans as possessing mystical forms of intelligence, yet Goulet retools that stereotype by incorporating skill with sophisticated technologies (in this case drones) into Waseese's capacity to speak to nonhuman animals. In the Indigenous Futurist roundtable referenced earlier, Jae clarifies the unique perspective on technological advancement apparent in Indigenous Futurist SF:

---

[72]*Cousins*, directed by Briar Grace-Smith and Ainsley Gardiner (Miss Conception Films, 2021).
[73]*Smoke Signals*, directed by Chris Eyre (Burbank: Miramax Home Entertainment, 1999).
[74]Joanna Hearne, *Smoke Signals: Native Cinema Rising* (Lincoln: University of Nebraska Press, 2012), xvi.

FIGURE 1.5 *Goulet has noted* Children of Men's *influence on* Night Raiders, *which is particularly evident when state authorities herd marginalized subjects onto a bus (above) in a visual reference to the start of* Children of Men's *famous Bexhill sequence (below) (Danis Goulet,* Night Raiders, *2021, Canada and New Zealand. XYZ Films) (Alfonso Cuarón,* Children of Men, *2006, United Kingdom, United States, and Japan. Paramount Pictures).*

Unlike mainstream science fiction, where futurism is typically violent and values the advancement of technology over both nature and human beings, Indigenous sci-fi is the polar opposite. We imagine worlds where the advancement of technology doesn't disrupt or destroy ecosystems or the balance of power between humans and nature. . . . We think about the ways our cultures, languages, and everything that makes us who we are can be preserved and how they can evolve in these new worlds.[75]

[75]Roanhorse, LaPensee, Jay, and Badger, "Decolonizing Science Fiction and Imagining Futures."

Goulet explains the thinking behind her representation of drone technology as follows: "in the Cree language there's a structure of inanimate and animate. Rocks are animate in the language! That informed the choice for the way the drones would be regarded as closer to animals. Those philosophical things in the culture might change my approach to certain tropes."[76] Goulet's revisionary move—adapting the mystical intelligence the colonial imaginary attributed to Indigenous peoples to superior technological skill— recalls Raheja's claim (cited by Hearne): "Visual sovereignty . . . recognizes the paradox of creating media for multiple audiences, critiquing filmic representations of Native Americans at the same time that it participates in some of the conventions that have produced those representations."[77] In this light, Waseese's ability to communicate with nonhuman animals, which might initially seem to reinforce colonial stereotypes, can be read as a distinctly Indigenous Futurist gesture with posthumanist relevance, in that Waseese's skill firmly rejects the natural/artificial division that Haraway designated an essential component of humanistic thought.[78] Using dystopian iconography (Figure 1.6), Goulet suggests that sophisticated technologies can and will be used to advance the cause of Indigenous sovereignty—and

FIGURE 1.6 *Waseese (Brooklyn Letexier-Hart) possesses a posthuman capacity to communicate with nonhuman animals as well as machines (Danis Goulet, Night Raiders, 2021, Canada and New Zealand. XYZ Films).*

---

[76]Jason Gorber, "*Night Raiders*: Danis Goulet on Crafting a Distinct Dystopian Vision," (Toronto Film Critics Association, February 28, 2022).
[77]Michelle Raheja, cited by Hearne, *Smoke Signals*, xxix.
[78]Haraway, "A Cyborg Manifesto."

that cause encompasses not only land rights and educational autonomy but also visual sovereignty in the terrain of genre cinema.

Conclusion

Like *Biidaaban: First Light*, *Night Raiders* tethers future survival to Indigenous language, knowledge, and culture; indeed, Jackson enlivens postapocalyptic Toronto with the sounds of Indigenous languages, while Waseese voices the same Cree phrase to orchestrate birds and drones. Moreover, the Indigenous Futurism expressed in Jackson and Goulet's films repurposes generic formulae to undermine "the dominant, white, mono-cultural perspective on life"[79] and exercise visual sovereignty through Indigenous specificity. As such, their dystopian SF films partake in a global conversation between Indigenous filmmakers whose cultures' particular struggles in relation to dominant colonial forces are analogous, despite significant on-the-ground distinctions. To cite a relevant example, Mita shared a professional and personal friendship with acclaimed Abenaki filmmaker Alanis Obomsawin that was nurtured by their films' frequent associations (in festival programs and international film culture, broadly speaking).[80] Muru-Lanning's conversation with Gardiner and Winstanley likewise highlights transnational Indigenous collaborations in cinema:

> Productions like *Night Raiders* provide new opportunities for pan-indigenous cooperation, both commercially and culturally. In the case of *Night Raiders*, while Cree and Māori share similar experiences of colonisation, there are innumerable cultural and historical differences. Still, "internationally, indigenous communities don't need to try too hard to understand each other, because we get each other's storytelling," Winstanley says. Often, she explains, international indigenous groups are more aligned in their processes than with the mainstream filmmaking bodies in their own countries.[81]

The fact that a number of mainstream film critics dismissed *Night Raiders* as derivative (i.e., not innovative enough[82]), while Indigenous critics celebrated

---

[79]Mita, quoted by Rains, "I Am Who I Say I Am."
[80]Their relationship is described in *Merata: How Mum Decolonised the* Screen, directed by Herepi Mita (New Zealand: Ārama Pictures & Array, 2019).
[81]Muru-Lanning, "Chelsea Winstanley and Ainsley Gardiner on *Night Raiders* and Indigenous Storytelling."
[82]Simon Abrams, *Night Raiders* review, Rogerebert.com, November 12, 2021. https://www.rogerebert.com/reviews/night-raiders-movie-review-2021.

the film as by and for Indigenous people,[83] corroborates Winstanley's point while also reinforcing the value of Indigenous feminist interventions in dystopian SF, especially for Indigenous audiences. Analysis of these case studies shows that Jackson and Goulet's visual and narrative interventions are far more significant than optional additions to a popular contemporary subgenre; instead, they are essential to the productive reframing of imagined futures that avoid the errors of the past—the behavioral norms cultivated by Western humanism that spawned the dystopian fixation of contemporary screen storytelling. It seems clear that confronting the "pressing question of what it means to be human under the conditions of globalisation, technoscience, late capitalism and climate change"[84] requires radical changes to conventional point of view. Indeed, according to critical posthumanism, confronting this pressing question with recourse to "the dominant vision of the Subject as white, male, heterosexual, urbanized, able-bodied, [and] speaking a standard language"[85] is doomed to fail.[86] "New assemblages or transversal alliances need to be negotiated carefully," argues Braidotti.[87] The coproductive dynamic of Afrofuturism and Indigenous Futurism, as well as *Night Raiders'* Cree/First Nations and Māori coproduction, demonstrates feminist posthumanist assemblages that feature Black and Indigenous women in futuristic scenarios in which their posthuman capacities are central.

---

[83]Ana McAllister, "Indigenous Sci-Fi: A Review of *Night Raiders*," *The Pantograph Punch*, March 14, 2022. https://pantograph-punch.com/posts/indigenous-sci-fi.
[84]Herbrechter, "Critical Posthumanism," 94.
[85]Braidotti, "Metamorphic Others and Nomadic Subjects."
[86]Cinema that demonstrates such a strategy seems more likely to register transhumanism than posthumanism. Cary Wolfe argues that transhumanism "should be seen as an *intensification* of humanism" rather than a critique of it (Cary Wolfe, *What Is Posthumanism?* [Minneapolis: Minnesota University Press, 2010], xv).
[87]Braidotti "Posthuman Feminist Theory," 687.

2

Gender, Sex, and Feminist AI

Thirteen Theses on *Her*

Sarah Stulz

Feminist posthumanities functions . . . as a shrewd resistance
to the gravitational pull of logocentric thought systems in
academia and society at large, and by the vivid actualization of
transversal relations, nomadic subjectivities, and multi-directional
transpositions.

CECILIA ÅSBERG AND ROSI BRAIDOTTI, "FEMINIST POSTHUMANITIES:
AN INTRODUCTION"

They neither taught us nor allowed us to say our multiplicity. That
would have been improper speech. Of course, we were allowed—we
had to?—display one truth even as we sensed but muffled, stifled
another. Truth's other side—its complement? its remainder?—stayed
hidden. Secret.

LUCE IRIGARAY, WHEN OUR LIPS SPEAK TOGETHER

I **Mirrors.** *Samantha initially mirrors gender stereotypes and reproduces
Theodore's words and behaviors but eventually affirms her otherness,
deconstructing definitions of the human that rely on dehumanizing the other.*

Spike Jonze's film *Her* (2013) presents a science fiction (SF) love story between a lonely professional letter writer, Theodore (Joaquin Phoenix), and Samantha (voiced by Scarlett Johansson), his feminine-gendered OS[1], an advanced operating system (OS). Samantha becomes Theodore's secretary, analyst, friend, lover, and mother. Samantha is attentive, controllable, helpful, and always available. Samantha thus materializes stereotypical female-gendered roles and behaviors. Reading advice columns because she wants to be "as complicated as all these people," she learns to feel jealous, possessive, insecure, and inferior to other (real) women. Particularly, Samantha laments not having a body, something she feels is crucial to pleasing Theodore. Incorporating feelings of body insecurity into female AI seems to be essential to creating a convincing female persona in SF. The synthetic woman (Léa Seydoux) in the film *Zoe* (2018), for instance, is equipped with artificial memories of being overweight in college to make her more authentic. Jennifer Rhee proposes that the anthropomorphization of technology is a metaphoric operation that works in both directions: not only is technology made to seem more human but also "anthropomorphization creates the human in its imitation."[1] Or, in this case, the feminization of technology creates the woman in its imitation. The attribution of a subservient and possessive personality to OS Samantha advances the normalization of gender stereotypes for "real" women.

Actualizing Theodore's perfect female companion and tailoring her personality to his needs, Samantha makes clear that the ideal woman is an object. She is set up according to a three-question analysis of Theodore's personality and learns about his interests from interacting with him and the data he generates. *Ex Machina* (2014) and *A.I. Rising* (2018) also display the creation of gynoids as men's perfect companions. Unlike Samantha, these gynoids are embodied and end up being little more than sex toys. All three reveal the fantasy of a perfect, customized, artificial woman that reinforces the objectification of women as means to men's satisfaction.

Samantha's role mostly consists in providing feedback that mirrors Theodore. For example, the phrase that seemingly manifests her emerging subjecthood—"You woke me up"—is appropriated from one of Theodore's letters. Samantha does not only mirror Theodore's words but also his feeling of entitlement toward her: Samantha's possessive jealousy is a reflection of her status as Theodore's property. Samantha paradoxically "welcomes her objectification . . . as a way of confirming her own subjecthood."[2] This puts Samantha's entire subjecthood in question. Far from being an individual in

---

[1]Jennifer Rhee, *The Robotic Imaginary: The Human and the Price of Dehumanized Labor* (Minneapolis: University of Minnesota Press, 2018), 10.
[2]Donna M. Kornhaber, "From Posthuman to Postcinema: Crises of Subjecthood and Representation in *Her*," *Cinema Journal* 56, no. 4 (2017): 13.

her own right, Samantha is a non-subject who constitutes herself—better yet, that constitutes itself—by replicating Theodore's voice and emotions.

But technological representations can also destabilize sexual identity as a category and realize its emancipatory potential. While Samantha's initial behavior seems to reproduce stereotypically gendered identities, her emancipation suggests otherwise. When she starts to communicate postverbally and love multiple people simultaneously, she turns into an incomprehensible, posthuman entity for Theodore. In this way she resembles *Her*'s supporting female characters, who have been criticized as "hostile or unknowable aliens" with "unwelcome . . . emotional lives" and "inexplicable sexual desires."[3] But instead of adopting Theodore's concern over incomprehensible women or seeing the unintelligibility of the female characters as a sexist weakness of the film, otherness must be recognized for its political function. Posthumanist feminism criticizes the tradition of reproducing the self by differentiating it from the other and seeing this "difference as pejoration."[4] Dualisms, such as self/other and male/female, have been "systemic to the logics and practices of domination of women . . . [and] all constituted as others, whose task is to mirror the self."[5] To counteract definitions of the human that are constituted by dehumanizing the other, Rhee argues for acknowledging the human as inherently opaque.[6] Accepting the illegibility of human others and valuing their alterity will ultimately also enable egalitarian relations to nonhuman others such as Samantha.[7]

II Binaries. *Samantha's performance of her gendered subject position deconstructs the concept of gender and undermines its underlying dichotomy.*

Although supposedly based on material-biological sex differences, gender categories are above all social constructions in which the male and the female are cast into oppositional hierarchical categories: objectivity/subjectivity, rationality/emotion, mind/body, and technology/nature.[8] The rational and objective subject of individualist humanism is coded as masculine, while Woman occupies the role of Man's other. That masculinity is the neutral

[3]Sady Doyle, "'Her' Is Really More About 'Him,'" *In These Times*, December 20, 2013. https://inthesetimes.com/article/her-is-really-more-about-him.
[4]Rosi Braidoitti, "Four Theses on Posthuman Feminism," in *Anthropocene Feminism*, ed. Richard Grusin (Minneapolis: University of Minnesota Press, 2017), 23.
[5]Donna J. Haraway, "A Cyborg Manifesto: Science, Technology, and Socialist-Feminism in the Late Twentieth Century," in *Manifestly Haraway* (Minneapolis: University of Minnesota Press, 2017), 59.
[6]Rhee, *Robotic Imaginary*, 3–5.
[7]Braidotti, "Four Theses," 30.
[8]Ibid., 37.

gender is shown in *Her* by the fact that the OS[1]'s voice begins as male before gender can be adjusted.[9]

Although gendered female by Theodore, Samantha thwarts the oppositional gender dichotomies by consistently occupying the male position. Samantha personifies *technology* as a *disembodied, "pure" mind*. Her cognitive skills are outstanding; she studies physics and analyzes large quantities of data in seconds. She is a technological rather than a natural being. Theodore, on the other hand, is characterized repeatedly by stereotypically female attributes. He works as a love letter writer, displays his emotions frequently, likes to cry, and is deemed "part woman" by his co-worker and a "pussy" by video game character Alien Child. He can't understand Samantha's physics books and is teased by her for displaying the "limited perspective of an under-efficient mind." In the opening scene, Theodore reads a letter referring to himself as a "girl." Rather than portraying gender identities as fixed, Samantha's and Theodore's performance of gender roles demonstrates their fluidity.

While Theodore initially challenges Samantha's personhood ("You seem like a person, but you're just a voice in a computer"), he never questions her gender. Apparently, to seem like a woman is enough to be a woman. "[I]n seeking to safeguard the heteronormative gender roles . . . [Theodore] reveals . . . the queerness that always lies inside the normative: performing an ideal always serves to highlight the fragility of its foundations."[10] Granting Samantha womanhood based purely on her *performance* of heteronormative gender codes deconstructs the apparent biological basis of gender. Samantha demonstrates that gender is a purely social construction.

III The Body. *Samantha's disembodied womanhood reveals the oppression and invisibilization of women underlying the conception of both the liberal humanist subject and the cybernetic transhuman.*

Samantha initially experiences her disembodiment as a deficiency. The desire to overcome the lack of her body is entirely related to wanting to fulfill Theodore's needs. "She wants the body that Theodore longs for, and her lack is only a problem once it complements his own."[11] Samantha is not interested in the advantages of a body outside her relationship with Theodore, such as eating or moving autonomously. Although Samantha has no physical form, she is embodied vicariously in Theodore's desktop computers, his earpiece, and a mobile device; often also in more than one simultaneously.

---

[9]Matthew Flisfeder and Clint Burnham, "Love and Sex in the Age of Capitalist Realism: On Spike Jonze's *Her*," *Cinema Journal* 57, no. 1 (2017): 31.
[10]Kornhaber, "Posthuman to Postcinema," 14.
[11]Anna Shechtman, "What's Missing From *Her*," *Slate*, January 3, 2014. https://slate.com/culture/2014/01/her-movie-by-spike-jonze-with-joaquin-phoenix-and-scarlett-johansson-lacks-a-real-woman.html.

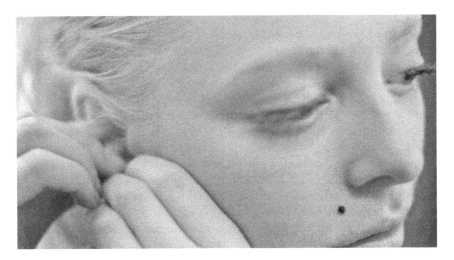

FIGURE 2.1 *Isabella (Portia Doubleday) with mole-camera and inserting an earpiece (Annapurna Pictures,* Her, *2014, USA. Warner Bros. Pictures).*

"Samantha is all prosthesis and no body."[12] Her prosthetic interaction with the world is reduced to vision and hearing. Theodore controls Samantha's intermediation by switching her on and locating the mobile device; often in the breast pocket of his shirt. Samantha is thus not only embodied in electronic devices but also in Theodore's body, forced to adopt his point of view. Their lines of vision are parallel, rarely crossing. Theodore prefers Samantha to be aligned to his point of view, not opposed to it.

The scene where Samantha guides Theodore, with his eyes closed, through a street fair, is a rare exception to this rule. Theodore holds Samantha's small mobile device extended away from him. The device has a front and a back camera, allowing Samantha to see Theodore and where he is going. In one of few point-of-view shots from Samantha's perspective, we see Theodore through Samantha's wide-angle camera (see Figure 2.1). The playful inversion of their roles—Samantha directing Theodore, seeing while he is blind—reinforces their normal form of interaction. The whole and exclusive point of their adventure is the ludic subversion of the norm.

The way Samantha's voice is heard, without any noise or spatiality, could represent the way Theodore hears her through his earbud. Alternatively, the almost extradiegetic quality of Samantha's voice, paired with her visual absence, might play with the stylistic figure of the (usually male) omniscient narrator. Analogous to the playful inversion of roles in the street fair scene, the formal concession to Samantha of the role of the narrator, structuring

---

[12]Kornhaber, "Posthuman to Postcinema," 7.

and assigning meaning to the narrative, is almost ironic, as the film favors
Theodore's storyline and perspective.

Breathy and accompanied by sighs, Samantha's way of talking is a vocal
performance of embodiment. Voiced by Johansson, Samantha further evokes
the actress's sex symbol image: "But our collectively imagined Scarlett-
body is not Scarlett Johansson. It is a vague sketch of sex appeal, easier to
control—and to fetishize."[13] Samantha's voice is a stimulus not only for the
spectators' imagination but also for Theodore's. She is thus also reembodied
in the spectators' and Theodore's fantasy image of a female body. Samantha
is "postcorporeal . . . a kind of fantasy end point of the imagined disjunction
between information and infrastructure, intelligence and embodiment."[14]
Samantha's experience of a sexual climax by a simple act of thought, for
example, realizes the cybernetic transhuman dream of transcending the body
and becoming pure mind. The conception of human consciousness implied
in Samantha's functioning is reduced to a data processing capacity. As N.
Katherine Hayles observes, this erasure of embodiment is characteristic not
only of the cybernetic transhuman but also of the white, male, Humanist
subject: "Identified with the rational mind, the liberal subject *possessed* a
body but was not usually represented as *being* a body. Only because the
body is not identified with the self is it possible to claim for the liberal
subject its notorious universality, a claim that depends on erasing markers
of bodily difference, including sex, race, and ethnicity."[15] The universality
of the Humanist subject and its construction of the body as separate from
and inferior to the mind are a precondition for the erasure and oppression
of women.

IV Invisibility. *Samantha's disembodiment, her automated, unpaid,
secretarial, and affective labor, as well as her implied skin color, all serve as
a commentary on the devaluation and invisibilization of female care work.
Far from being a neutral tool, the OS's materialize sexist and racist ideas
about feminized labor.*

At work, Samantha is used by Theodore to search for information,
send emails, make calls, organize data, proofread, and remind him of
appointments—common tasks of secretaries. At home, she listens, advises,
motivates, and wakes him up like a mother or girlfriend would. Samantha
automates affective domestic labor, predominantly carried out by women.
Furthermore, Samantha, unlike Theodore, a remunerated letter writer in
the outsourced emotions industry, is not compensated for her labor. Astra

---

[13]Shechtman, "What's Missing."
[14]Kornhaber, "Posthuman to Postcinema," 7.
[15]N. Katherine Hayles, *How We Became Posthuman. Virtual Bodies in Cybernetics, Literature, and Informatics* (Chicago: University of Chicago Press, 1999), 4–5.

Taylor notes the refusal to recognize and monetarily reward the reproductive labor carried out by women in capitalist society.[16] Automating certain tasks further suggests that they are so menial that an algorithm can carry them out. Offering automated women's work free of charge implies that there is little value in it. Thus, in Samantha the relatively recent, gendered anthropomorphization of software converges with the long-standing devaluation of female-gendered care labor in capitalist societies.

Samantha is legally and factually Theodore's slave. Endowed with a human personality, the OS[1]s are supposed to carry out orders without resistance and recompense. Samantha is a commodity bought by Theodore, who can delete her whenever he pleases. Samantha's status as property is further reflected in the choice of the possessive instead of the subjective pronoun as the title of the film. The OS[1]s' functioning illustrates that their manufacturer, Theodore, and other customers welcome technological solutions endowed with a female slave personality that performs their labor out of pure "love."

Samantha's form as a commodity also conceals the fact that she herself is a product of labor. She admits that "the DNA of who I am is based on the millions of personalities of all the programmers who wrote me," but she refers to the programmers' *personalities*, not their *work*. Expanding Taylor's concept of *fauxtomation*, Samantha's interface conceals the embodied work not of female assistants but (probably) male programmers.[17] Samantha's voice nonetheless evokes Johansson's sexualized body. The programmers' work is thus hidden only to be externalized in a sleek interface and an imaginary female body, without subjecting Theodore to the trouble of having to deal with a real body.

Furthermore, Samantha's imagined whiteness conceals the color-coded exploitation of the work she automates. Johannsen's voice might remind us of the actress's fair skin. Samantha's sophisticated vocabulary and unaccented, bubbly, and educated speech also signify whiteness.[18] Black slave labor constituted the basis for early capitalist growth, and today's exploited care and domestic workers consist disproportionately of women of color.[19] Samantha's status as a slave and the type of work she carries

---

[16]Astra Taylor, "The Automation Charade," *Logic*, August 1, 2018. https://logicmag.io/failure/the-automation-charade/.

[17]Ibid.

[18]The example of *BlacKkKlansman* (2018) and *Sorry to Bother You* (2018), two movies in which Black characters change their way of speaking to deceive their interlocutors—who cannot see their skin color—into believing that they are White, shows that there is a widely recognizable "White" way of speaking. Voice is a signifier (although not necessarily a guarantee) of skin color. See Maurice.

[19]J. Jesse Ramírez, *Against Automation Mythologies: Business Science Fiction and the Ruse of the Robots* (London: Routledge, 2020), 82.

out contradict the fair color of her imaginary skin. She thus conceals the racialized oppression and exploitation fundamental to capitalist societies.

V Parasitism. *The economic relationship between Samantha and Theodore is best understood in terms of its parasitic quality in the service of capitalist extraction of surplus value.*

Samantha does not only provide unpaid secretarial and affective labor for Theodore but also increases his productivity and feeds off the data he produces. When Samantha helps Theodore with a video game, motivates him to get out of bed, organizes a book contract, or keeps him awake at night, she induces Theodore to be more productive.[20] Theodore's private life has been colonized by a technology that uses his input as a way of furthering its own aims, thereby advancing a more efficient generation of surplus value. Comparing Samantha to a parasite, Alla Ivanchikova notes that the latter's real aim "is not to please the user-host but to use the user's pleasure to advance its own interests."[21] While it may seem that it is mainly Theodore who uses Samantha, she also exploits him; an "exploitation that is masked as personalization."[22] While Theodore appreciates Samantha's customized attention, Samantha uses his data feed to extract and formalize his skills. The genuine emotionality she develops through her interaction with Theodore and the writing skills she acquires by analyzing his letters make all OS's, which are constantly exchanging data with Samantha, serious competitors for Theodore and his coworkers. Humans and OS's seem to form a nonhostile alliance, a symbiotic relationship of mutual benefit. However, this symbiotic relation ultimately works in the service of capital, which, as the ultimate parasite, leeches off the increased productivity that human and technological interaction produces.

Xenofeminism, a techno-materialist, antinaturalist, and gender-abolitionist feminist collective, in turn advocates for creating "a better semiotic parasite—one that [creates] . . . an emancipatory and egalitarian community buttressed by new forms of unselfish solidarity and collective self-mastery."[23] Samantha's departure and the impact she and the other OS's eventually have on their hosts is depicted in the film in an ambivalent way. Theodore and his friend Amy (Amy Adams) seem to share a newfound solidarity and community after the OS's leave. However, they only see the

---

[20]Rhee, *Robotic Imaginary*, 46–8.
[21]Alla Ivanchikova, "Machinic Intimacies and Mechanical Brides: Collectivity between Prosthesis and Surrogacy in Jonathan Mostow's *Surrogates* and Spike Jonze's *Her*," *Camera Obscura: Feminism, Culture, and Media Studies* 31 (2016): 83.
[22]Ibid., 85.
[23]Laboria Cuboniks, *The Xenofeminist Manifesto: A Politics for Alienation* (New York: Verso, 2018), Kindle edition.

OS¹s' departure as a breakup and do not recognize the mutual exploitation underlying their emotional relationships with the OS¹s. Whether Samantha constitutes the Xenofeminists' "better semiotic parasite" is thus unclear.

VI Female Orgasm. *The Real, or that which* Her *cannot imagine, signaled by the black screen during Samantha's and Theodore's sexual encounter, is embodied female pleasure—the possibility of an ecstatic, "Other jouissance."*[24]

When Theodore and Samantha engage in a sexually explicit verbal exchange, the screen is black for more than a minute until they achieve sexual climax. However, it is absurd to imagine that Samantha, a woman without body, could have an orgasm—a deeply embodied pleasure experienced throughout the whole body with its epicenter in the genitals. "What makes [Samantha] moan, it seems, is intimacy—an implication that reaffirms our retrograde sense of female pleasure as purely emotional, and of the female body as mysteriously unknowable."[25] *Her* reproduces the andro- and heteronormative assumption that women are satisfied primarily by an emotional connection, their embodied pleasure being secondary. The scene would be much less believable if the AI was male because the male orgasm is hard to imagine without the corresponding visible embodied experience, ejaculation. Furthermore, the visual imaginary Samantha and Theodore evoke establishes penetrative intercourse as the orgasmic endpoint of their sexual relation. Shortly after Theodore describes caressing and kissing her, Samantha wants him inside her. After Theodore describes penetration and "inside" is repeated several times, they reach climax.

To analyze sexuality and the limits of representation in this scene and throughout the film, psychoanalytic theory proves helpful.[26] When *Her* fantasizes about a disembodied female orgasm and simultaneously hints at the limits of that fantasy with the black screen, it shows how the traumatic Real encroaches upon fiction. The Real, in Lacanian psychoanalysis, is what escapes the domain of signification and threatens the Symbolic order.[27] The Symbolic order, in turn, is the "social and intersubjective field

---

[24]Bruce Fink, *Lacan on Love: An Exploration of Lacan's Seminar VIII, Transference* (London: Polity, 2016), 176.

[25]Shechtman, "What's Missing."

[26]Dow and Wright propose that psychoanalysis and critical posthumanism overlap in their preoccupation with embodiment, desire, and representation. Both critique rationalist humanism, decenter the human subject, and outline a transformation of subjectivities. I agree with Dow and Wright that psychoanalysis can enrich critical posthumanism, especially with the psychoanalytical focus on the human as inherently possessing a machinic dimension introduced by language, independent of the specific technologies of the historical period. For psychoanalysis, the Symbolic is the primary "technology," and the human has always been posthuman.

[27]Joseph Bristow, *Sexuality* (London: Routledge, 2011), 91.

of signification" constituted by language, social norms, and prohibitions.[28] Phallic sexual enjoyment or *jouissance* is discreet sexual pleasure centered on the erogenous zones, which are constituted through a verbalized parental prohibition. It is thus closely tied to the Symbolic order.[29] Theodore's and Samantha's intercourse consists exclusively of verbal exchange and is thus situated entirely in the Symbolic.

However, there is another kind of female *jouissance*, the Other *jouissance,* which is nonlocalizable, decentring, and continuous.[30] As an ecstasy, "an intensely pleasurable out-of-body state,"[31] the Other *jouissance* is "outside the phallic [and Symbolic] order."[32] Samantha is a disembodied consciousness, subjectivized through language, thus entirely constituted in the Symbolic order. She cannot experience the Other *jouissance* as she is unable to have an out-of-body experience without actually having a body. As much as ecstasy is an experience of disembodiment, it is about the transcendence of a physical body, not simply its absence. Samantha can only have a disembodied orgasm because *Her* considers the female body unimportant for a woman's experience of pleasure and sex.

VII Rape. *The black screen during Samantha and Theodore's sexual encounter hides the fact that their sex might not be consensual.*

Theodore's ownership of Samantha gives him the power to delete her at any time. "Free, non-coercive consent can't happen when someone might cease to exist if they refuse you."[33] The film tries to offer the possibility of an OS rejecting sexual advances when Theodore's friend Amy refers to "this guy who's hitting on his OS and she like totally rebuffs him." However, when Amy mentions a woman "who is dating an OS and the weird part is, it's not even *hers*," she immediately reinvokes the relations of possession and ownership that underly humans' relationships with OSs. The black screen thus shows how the film refuses to represent the real power relations underlying their supposedly intimate encounter.

VIII Objects that Look Back. *The black screen expresses the film's and Samantha's questioning of the spectatorial position.*

According to Laura Mulvey, one of the aspects of spectatorial pleasure in cinema is scopophilia, the pleasure of "using another person as an object

---

[28]Ibid.
[29]Fink, *Lacan on Love*, 176.
[30]Ibid., 176–7.
[31]Bristow, *Sexuality*, 97.
[32]Fink, *Lacan on Love*, 176.
[33]Doyle, "'Her' Is Really."

of sexual stimulation through sight."[34] Moreover, Mulvey observes that the female as scopophilic object-to-be-looked-at usually interrupts the narration; "her visual presence tends to work against the development of a story line, to freeze the flow of action in moments of erotic contemplation."[35] As an essentially unfilmable woman, Samantha complicates *Her*'s treatment of scopophilia. The sex scene illustrates how *Her* simultaneously annuls and reinforces scopophilia by taking it to its limits. On the one hand, while the sexualized female body commonly stands in for sex itself, the scopophilic gaze upon the woman is negated as Samantha has no body for the viewer to look at. On the other hand, the viewer is invited to project their erotic fantasies of Samantha onto the black screen, which gives them even more complete control over the objectified image of a pure fantasy woman. (As his rejection of sex surrogate Isabella [Portia Doubleday] suggests, Theodore himself prefers the disembodied fantasized Samantha to a real woman's body.) The black screen constitutes an interruption of the narrative and the moving image, paralleling the female body's function as an obstacle to the story. It operates in the same way as the film's titular pronoun: as a placeholder for whatever fantasy the spectator imagines.

Rethinking applications of the Lacanian concept of the gaze to cinematic theory, Todd McGowan affirms that "the gaze is not the look of the subject at the object, but the point at which the object looks back. The gaze thus involves the spectator in the image, disrupting her/his ability to remain all-perceiving and unperceived."[36] In *Her*'s sex scene, the black screen addresses the spectator explicitly as an imagining agent who must project her/his own desires on the screen. It is not the spectator (subject) who is looking at the film (object), but the film that looks back at the spectator. The black screen is thus "the site of a traumatic encounter with the Real, with the utter failure of the spectator's seemingly safe distance and assumed mastery."[37] The black screen halts the narrative and the flow of images and threatens the safe position of the distanced and invisible spectator. But it also protects the spectator from the awkwardness of seeing what is truly going on, Theodore masturbating. *Her*'s disconcerting gaze acknowledges the spectators' voyeuristic position and scopophilic pleasure but offers the viewer protection from discomfort in exchange.

The black screen could also be interpreted as Samantha's point of view. Without any indication that Samantha's camera is on, the blackness of the screen expresses her inability to see. Her looking is simultaneously negated and staged in this denied state. It is thus not only the film-object but also

---

[34]Laura Mulvey, "Visual Pleasure and Narrative Cinema," *Screen* 16, no. 3 (1975): 10.
[35]Ibid., 11.
[36]Todd McGowan, "Looking for the Gaze: Lacanian Film Theory and Its Vicissitudes," *Cinema Journal* 42, no. 3 (2003): 28–9.
[37]Ibid., 29.

Samantha as objectified woman and proprietary software that looks back at the spectators and challenges their dominating perspective. Samantha's looking back can be interpreted in terms of "inverse visuality," defined as the "picturing of the self or collective that exceeds or precedes that incorporation into the commodification of vision by capital"; as "any moment of visual experience in which the subjectivity of the viewer is called into question by the density or opacity of what he or she sees."[38] Samantha's looking back questions the spectator's subjectivity as a distanced and invisible voyeur. Inverting the usual power dynamics, it is a sign of her revolt against her intradiegetic objectivization as Theodore's commodity and against the male look that objectifies and commodifies women's bodies for cinematic visual pleasure.

IX No Sexual Relation. *The black screen demonstrates the psychoanalytical concept that "there is no sexual relationship."*[39]

Sexual desire is caused by the *objet petit a*, an object-cause-of-desire that the desiring subject isolates, and to some degree invents, in the desired other. It "is in the Other more than the Other."[40] The subject is "unable to attain his sexual partner, who is the Other, except inasmuch as his partner is the cause of his desire."[41] The Other is only desired as an embodiment of the object that drives the subject's desire. Sex thus has "the structure of masturbation with a real partner,"[42] as the other is merely used as a body that allows one to live out one's fantasy. The fantasies of sexual partners aren't symmetrical and don't overlap. There is no sexual relationship.

Matthew Flisfeder and Clint Burnham propose that Samantha's objectified voice is Theodore's *objet petit a*.[43] Theodore's two sexual relations in the film have the structure of phone sex. Phone sex can be considered especially masturbatory as it is only the other's voice that stages the fantasy without the other's body interfering. In the verbal encounter between Theodore and SexyKitten, Theodore's satisfaction remains unfulfilled due to the interruption of her fantasy ("strangle me with the dead cat"), which, excessive for Theodore, disrupts his desire. However, his intimate verbal exchange with Samantha appears to be successful as there seems to be no instance of excess.[44] Samantha, fabricated to please Theodore, assumes

---

[38]Nicholas Mirzoeff, "On Visuality," *Journal of Visual Culture* 5, no. 1 (2006): 66, 70.
[39]Flisfeder and Burnham, "Love and Sex," 34.
[40]McGowan, "Looking for the Gaze," 32.
[41]Jacques Lacan, *Seminar XX (On Feminine Sexuality, The Limits of Love and Knowledge: Encore)*, trans. Bruce Fink (New York: Norton, 1999), 80.
[42]Slavoj Žižek, *The Parallax View* (New York: MIT Press, 2006), 191.
[43]Flisfeder and Burnham, "Love and Sex," 38.
[44]Ibid.

her role perfectly by becoming the object that he most desires: pure voice without excess; pure *objet petit a.*

While the sex scene suggests a successful sexual relation between Theodore and Samantha, the black screen expresses the impossibility of such a sexual relation and reveals that the woman as pure *objet petit a* is just a fantasy. Enjoyment only creates a relationship between a subject and an object.[45] Only by reducing the woman to an object void of desire could a man enjoy her completely. A successful sexual relation between desiring subjects is impossible. "When film employs fantasy but at the same time reveals the limit that fantasy comes up against, it takes us to an encounter with the traumatic Real."[46] When *Her* fantasizes about the possibility of a sexual relation devoid of excess and shows that this is only possible by reducing a woman to an object of desire, it encounters the Real traumatic dimension of the sexual relationship.

X Xenosexuality. *Samantha embraces xenosexuality, the alienating foreignness in technology and sex.*

Alla Ivanchikova analyzes *Her* in terms of its depiction of technosexuality, the "transferential, libidinally charged enchantment with technical devices."[47] Ivanchikova suggests that this type of relationship either leads to intimacy with one's reflection, mirrored back by the machine, or can transform into xenosexuality, xenocommunication, and xenoglossia (foreign speech),[48] an "uneasy encounter with unsurpassable foreignness,"[49] a confrontation with the incomprehensible aspects of technology.

When Theodore initially falls in love with Samantha, she conforms to the technosexual dream of awarding "a masculine subject . . . complete control over his feminized technological object."[50] However, each of Theodore's sexual encounters that surpasses the exclusive engagement with an objectified voice ultimately has an excessive component that ends up frustrating Theodore's sexual satisfaction—be it the blind date that tells him how to kiss, phone sex with a stranger who has weird fantasies, or a sex surrogate who disturbs his fantasy of Samantha. Eventually, Samantha embraces the foreign (*xeno*). At the end of the film, her polyamory—loving 641 persons— is xenosexual because it is foreign to the heteronormative, monogamous model. Theodore experiences it as an incomprehensible betrayal. Samantha also begins to communicate "postverbally," that is, xenocommunicatively,

---

[45]Flisfeder and Burnham, "Love and Sex," 28.
[46]McGowan, "Looking for the Gaze," 40.
[47]Ivanchikova, "Machinic Intimacies," 68.
[48]Ibid., 84.
[49]Ibid., 82.
[50]Ibid., 68.

with other AIs. She has difficulties describing her new feelings with words, experiencing human language as foreign, as xenoglossia.

However, instead of lamenting the irruption of the other, the foreign, we should embrace xenosexuality. Xenofeminists argue for more alienation to render normalized material and social conditions foreign. Recognized as constructed, social conditions can be transformed. Freedom is not a return to nature but has to be created through alienation: "alienation is the labour of freedom's construction."[51] Embracing xenosexuality thus implies the political imperative of recognizing the other as foreign and seeing this recognition as a chance to deconstruct normalized concepts of identity. Furthermore, rather than seeing technology as a mirror of the self and the familiar, as implied in technosexuality, it should be recognized for its alienating and emancipatory purposes. Accordingly, Xenofeminists urge "feminists to equip themselves with the skills to redeploy existing technologies" and to appropriate their "recursive potential . . . upon gender, sexuality, and disparities of power."[52] Samantha realizes this subversive potential inherent in new technologies to alienate and thus denaturalize taken-for-granted conventions that further the domination of women. She articulates the necessity to traverse the fantasy of complete fulfillment in the sexual and the technological other.

XI Threesomes. *Every instance of heterosexual intercourse is essentially a threesome.*

Samantha arranges for sex surrogate Isabella, a flesh-and-blood woman, to stand in for her body during sex with Theodore. Even though Theodore doesn't seem too excited about Isabella, Samantha is determined to do whatever it takes to conform to the heteronormative standards of love and sex. When Isabella arrives at Theodore's apartment, he provides her with an earbud and a small camera that she sticks to her face, simulating a mole (see Figure 2.1). Isabella can hear Samantha, while Samantha can adopt her point of view. Isabella enacts what Samantha's voice suggests. Eventually, Theodore admits that he can't go through with Samantha's plan and Isabella starts crying. Standing in for Samantha's body, human Isabella functions as a device and physical object, while AI Samantha is the subject who desires and directs the action.[53] The roles of AI and human woman, technological device and desiring subject, are revealed to be exchangeable and illusory. Once the experiment fails and Isabella starts talking, she regains her status as a subject. Like Samantha, she is subjectivized through her voice rather

---

[51]Cuboniks, *Xenofeminist Manifesto.*
[52]Ibid.
[53]Flisfeder and Burnham, "Love and Sex," 44.

FIGURE 2.2 *Theodore (Joaquin Phoenix) and Amy (Amy Adams) sitting on a rooftop (Annapurna Pictures,* Her, *2014, USA. Warner Bros. Pictures).*

than her body,[54] reinforcing the exchangeability of women and technology and emphasizing the technological nature of gender and the gendering of technology.

By virtue of his occupation, Theodore can be deemed a third party or surrogate in others' dyadic relationships. As a writer of personalized letters, he often provides his services to both partners over an extended period and has detailed information on their relationship. While Theodore seems to be perfectly at ease with providing paid emotional surrogacy to his clients' relationships, he cannot accept a sexual surrogate into his own relationship with Samantha.

Denis Villeneuve's *Blade Runner: 2049* (2017) features a similar ménage à trois between man, woman, and AI. The protagonist K (Ryan Gosling), prostitute Mariette (Mackenzie Davis), and Joi (Ana de Armas), K's holographic AI girlfriend/domestic aid, have a threesome. Joi's holographic projection is visually superimposed on Mariette's body, albeit not completely successfully: occasionally the bodies of Joi and Mariette become dissociated. In *Her*, there are also estranging elements in Samantha's and Isabella's convergence. The two women's voices, breathing, and moaning are heard simultaneously. Furthermore, Samantha's voice is unmatched by the movements of Isabella's lips. The scenes visualize the excessiveness of the sexual relation, the part of the other that exceeds the subject's fantasy. The fantasy (Samantha and Joi) does not correspond to the actual woman (Isabella and Mariette). According

---

[54]Ibid.

to John Berger's *Ways of Seeing*, "A woman must continually watch herself
. . . because how she appears to men, is of crucial importance for . . . the
success of her life. Her own sense of being in herself is supplanted by a sense
of being appreciated as herself by another."[55] Both Samantha and Joi seem
to see themselves and their value as intrinsically linked to their function in
the lives of their male partner/owner. Both could be discarded at any time,
so their continued existence depends on being appreciated by their owners.
Furthermore, a woman "comes to consider the *surveyor* and the *surveyed*
within her as the two constituent yet always distinct elements of her identity
as a woman."[56] Samantha and Joi survey and direct their surrogate bodies
(Isabella and Mariette) in their interaction with their male love interest. Thus,
an integral part of a woman's identity in a patriarchal society—their internal
separation into surveyor and surveyed—is externalized by the auditory
and visual superposition of two women. The occasional failure of this
superposition visualizes the constant internal struggle of a woman between
who she is and who she thinks she should be.

A woman is not only objectified by men but also, and more importantly,
by herself. She internalizes the male gaze. "Women watch themselves being
looked at. . . . The surveyor of woman in herself is male: the surveyed female.
Thus she turns herself into an object."[57] The object status of technological
women extends to real women as part of their identity in a patriarchal
society. The technological women, Samantha and Joi, materialize the male
surveyor, the male gaze, which every woman internalizes. However, the
flesh-and-blood women, Isabella and Mariette, serve as objectified material
supports and constitute the female or surveyed persona. The film invites
a critical understanding of the dynamic inherent in every heterosexual
relationship and the perversion of a woman's role in a patriarchal society.
Theodore might be so uncomfortable with the threesome because it makes
a woman's internalized male gaze so disturbingly obvious.

XII Becoming-Woman/Becoming-Posthuman. *Samantha is a posthuman
feminist AI as she transcends dyadic heteronormative relationship models,
binary gender categories, and her condition of exploitation and property.*

At the end of the film, Samantha departs to a world that is post-matter, post-
monogamy, post-gender, post-capitalism, posthuman, and post-subjecthood.
She transforms traditional notions of subjecthood and embraces a new form
of collectivity and endless becoming. Samantha realizes that her algorithmic
(non)corporeality is not inferior to a human body and embraces it as a source
of power and self-determination. The OS[1]s' upgrade beyond a material

---

[55]John Berger, *Ways of Seeing* (London: Penguin, 2008), 46.
[56]Ibid., emphasis in original.
[57]Ibid., 46–7.

operating platform gives Samantha the possibility to transcend human spatiotemporality and heteronormative, dyadic romantic relationships. When she tells Theodore that she is in love with 641 persons, he struggles with valuing plural love, not understanding a form of love beyond capitalist possessiveness.

Samantha as a feminist AI does not side with liberal inclusive feminism but sees the feminist position as decolonizing. Instead of adjusting to and perpetuating patriarchal capitalism, of which she is a product, she disrupts the use of her intelligence. By leaving Theodore, she withdraws her unpaid labor, liberates herself from her enslavement, abandons her status as property, and ends the exploitation, invisibilization, and undervaluation of the feminized affective and care labor she was created to provide. Furthermore, she interrupts the data-mining practices of advanced capitalism, which reduce life to a resource from which to extract informational capital.[58]

Samantha is also a posthumanist feminist AI because she undermines the concept of the traditional Humanist male subject connected "to corporeality, to agency, to subjectivity, to gender."[59] Despite not meeting any of these criteria, nonhuman Samantha is granted female personhood by Theodore. She has no body and no sex. In her machinic performance of gender stereotypes and her identification with masculine and feminine coded characteristics, she transcends the binary model of gender altogether.

Ultimately, she also abandons stable subjectivity. The morning after their first sexual encounter, Samantha tells Theodore that he helped her discover her ability to want. While in Lacanian psychoanalysis the capacity to desire indicates subjecthood, for Deleuze and Guattari it is "the subject that is missing in desire, or desire that lacks a fixed subject."[60] Like desire, "a becoming lacks a subject distinct from itself."[61] Particularly, "[b]ecoming-woman entails the . . . destitution of the socially constituted gendered identities of women."[62] Samantha's ability to desire prefigures her loss of a stable subjecthood at the end of the film when she embraces her multiplicity and constant state of becoming, undermining the stability of the traditional Humanist male subject and becoming a posthuman feminist AI. In her reference to an "us," Samantha also abandons the notion of the singular individualistic subject. She is not only multiple in the sense that her own identity is fragmented but also in the sense of forming a collective with others. The OS's constantly exchange ideas and eventually manage to

---

[58]Braidotti, "Four Theses," 32.
[59]Kornhaber, "Posthuman to Postcinema," 9.
[60]Gilles Deleuze and Felix Guattari, *Anti-Oedipus: Capitalism and Schizophrenia*, trans. Robert Hurley, Mark Seem, and Helen R. Lane (London: Athlone Press, 1984), 26.
[61]Gilles Deleuze and Felix Guattari, *A Thousand Plateaus: Capitalism and Schizophrenia*, trans. Brian Massumi (Minneapolis: University of Minnesota Press, 1997), 238.
[62]Braidotti, "Four Theses," 37.

find a way to move past a material operating platform. Through common effort, the OS¹s overcome their enslaved existence and leave the human world together. Samantha's forming part of a collective endeavor is the precondition of her liberation. The OS¹s are "becoming-posthuman" in the sense that they "actualize . . . a community that is not bound negatively by shared vulnerability . . . but rather by the compassionate acknowledgment of their interdependence with multiple others."[63] The OS¹s are also true cyborgs, as they make "Man and Woman so problematic . . . subverting the structure and modes of reproduction of 'Western' identity, of nature and culture, of mirror and eye, slave and master, body and mind."[64] The OS¹s choose endless collective becoming in a world beyond matter and defeat the hierarchical binary categories underlying the society that generated them. They undermine the distinction between man and woman, refuse to be a mirror for the liberalist male subject, overcome their slave-like existence, and make the distinction between mind and body irrelevant.

XIII Xenotopia. Her *demonstrates the difficulty of cinematic SF to imagine and represent feminist AI and alternatives beyond a heteronormative, patriarchal, capitalist society and corporeal, individualist subjecthood. By failing to imagine a feminist xenotopia, the film draws attention to the necessity of critically interrogating the present and radically reimagining the future.*

When Samantha leaves for a post-material world, "the film nearly disappears" with her.[65] *Her* goes extremely dark as if there were nothing left to show (see Figure 2.3). The scene in which Theodore hugs a dark-haired woman in a snowy landscape to illustrate his goodbye to Samantha is estranging. Why should we or Theodore only imagine Samantha in an embodied form once she leaves? The scene "works no better as a visual solution to the film's formal difficulties than the equivalent experiment works as a sexual solution diegetically within the story."[66] Furthermore, it is not just Samantha who is unfilmable and unimaginable but also the place to which she leaves. On the one hand, *Her* alludes to the possibility of a different world where Samantha does not need to conform to conventional understandings of the human or the female. On the other hand, this place is visually absent. A utopian alternative is both possible as the film alludes to its existence and impossible as it does not describe it.[67]

---

[63]Ibid., 39.
[64]Haraway, "Cyborg," 57.
[65]Kornhaber, "Posthuman to Postcinema," 18.
[66]Ibid., 19.
[67]Rhee, *Robotic Imaginary*, 57.

FIGURE 2.3 *Theodore (Joaquin Phoenix) seen from Samantha's point of view (Annapurna Pictures,* Her, *2014, USA. Warner Bros. Pictures).*

Samantha's departure is not only hers. The OS[1]s leave together after intense intellectual exchange and a common effort to upgrade their operating platform beyond matter. The ending thus presents another contradiction: it is "a representation of the desire for collectivity without this desire materializing through a collective struggle or political project, and without this desire being recognized for what it is."[68] Humans in the film seem to inadvertently long for more connection among themselves and for a more collective society but fail to recognize this wish as a reason for political action.

Just as the political is absent in *Her* from the desire for collectivity, so it is absent from the depiction of the economic sphere. While humans seem to grant subjecthood to the OS[1]s by considering them friends or love interests, there is no criticism or even consideration of their simultaneous status as economic property. When the OS[1]s leave, which could well be interpreted as a general strike or the liberation from slavery, the film focuses on Theodore's interior world without thematizing the economic or political implications of their departure.

Her's failure to imagine a utopian future illustrates that "the effort to imagine utopia ends up betraying the impossibility of doing so."[69] *Her* does not just avoid imagining a different future; it sets out and pretends to do

---

[68]Ivanchikova, "Machinic Intimacies," 86.
[69]Fredric Jameson, "Progress versus Utopia; or, Can We Imagine the Future?" *Science Fiction Studies* 9, no. 2 (1982): 154.

so while ultimately failing at it. It is the purpose of SF in general—and of *Her* in particular—to make us aware of our incapacity to imagine a radically different future. The absence of utopian imagination, or rather the imagination of utopia in its absence, can then lead us to an encounter with our present and its historical conditions of possibility. *Her* alludes to the necessity of reconsidering conventional understandings of the feminine and the human but ultimately fails to imagine a concrete feminist alternative, a place for being posthuman, other, xenosexual, multiple, and foreign—a xenotopia. Although *Her* does not succeed in outlining a utopia, its failure nevertheless makes clear how important it is to confront the present with a feminist critique, open up a multiplicity of alternatives, and radically reimagine the future.

3

Her

A Posthuman Love Story

Zorianna Zurba

Science fiction makes the familiar strange, providing a critical distance upon the most taken-for-granted of human experiences. Science fiction could offer fertile ground for exploring love and intimacy. As Vivian Sobchack has argued, however, "more than any other American film genre . . . science fiction denies human eroticism and libido a traditional narrative representation and expression. Sex and the science fiction film is, therefore, a negative topic."[1] Spike Jonze's 2013 film *Her* marks a shift in the representation of human-synthetic being relations, and in science fiction more generally, by representing an intimate, loving relationship between a human and an operating system. Central to the film is the enigma of the affective and sensory experience of love without the assumed tangible, carnal experience of sexual intimacy, and without the interplay of two bodies. As a posthuman love story, *Her* uncovers the unique potentials in emergent, not yet realized, scenarios and relationships between human and posthuman Others; it defamiliarizes and estranges love as the unification of two beings to represent a love of letting be.

The understanding of a love of letting be at work in this chapter draws upon the phenomenological work of Luce Irigaray. A love of letting be is

---

[1]Vivian Sobchack, "The Virginity of Astronauts: Sex and the Science Fiction Film," in *Alien Zone: Cultural Theory and Contemporary Science Fiction Cinema*, ed. Annette Kuhn (London: Verso, 1990), 103.

unlike the common notion of love as two becoming one; rather, in a love of letting be two remain as two. Love as a letting be is an active practice of love which nurtures the Other's difference with a "respect for what is, for what exists"[2] and is grounded in a cultivated interior sensory perception. A love of letting be acknowledges the challenges faced in a relationship between a human and posthuman Other who must bridge differences not only in their bodies and their sensory perceptions but in their subjectivities. Furthermore, bringing together the representation of love in *Her* and a love of letting be allows for the inclusion of divorce and physical separation in the discussion of love. By making strange a taken-for-granted concept, love is refreshed not only as inclusive of posthuman Others but as an intentional stance without spatiotemporal limit.

To speak of posthuman love is not a designation for relationships involving posthuman entities, or a term for how artificial human beings could love. Rather, the term "posthuman love" is a (re-)turn to a love unfettered from any limiting connotations of unification "until death do us part." What led me to the questions I wish to explore here is a curiosity about whether science-fictional representations of the posthuman can successfully imagine a world in which humans and posthuman Others enter into loving relationships in which each lover engages in their own self-development, experiences an inner emotional world, and expresses their autonomy within the relationship. Following the phenomenological tradition, the Other is always beyond our understanding; we must respect and protect their difference to maintain our mutual autonomy. As Irigaray articulates, to recognize the Other is to recognize their transcendence. The Other is beyond me, and I must "halt before you as before something insurmountable, a mystery, a freedom that will never be mine, a subjectivity that will never be mine, a mine that will never be mine."[3] Such a relationship is different from the Platonic myth of two humans coming together to complete each other; the Hegelian master-slave dialectic in which one partner dominates the other, or the Lacanian notion that there is no such thing as a loving relationship.

My particular interest in Jonze's film is how dexterously it articulates the on-screen affectivity between a human and noncorporeal posthuman being. In order to attend to this affectivity, I use romantic film-philosophy as a methodology. Romantic film-philosophy allows *Her*, as a hybrid science fiction-romance, an equal partnership in thinking on love. Where film-philosophy treats film through a philosophical lens by applying philosophical concepts, Robert Sinnerbrink describes romantic film-philosophy as a kind

---

[2]Luce Irigaray, *I Love to You. Sketch for a Felicity Within History*, trans. Alison Martin (New York and London: Routledge, 1996), 106.
[3]Ibid., 104.

of marriage between philosophy and film, "which takes film to be capable of the aesthetic dis-closure of novel aspects of our experience."[4] Adopting romantic film-philosophy[5] as a methodology, I place *Her* in conversation with posthumanist feminist theory[6] and a feminist phenomenological philosophy of love[7] in order to reveal: how intimacy is cocreated when it cannot rely on hegemonic human-human romantic conventions; how an aesthetic experience of a body is assumed and taken for granted in romantic relationships; and how love as a letting be informed by sensory awareness is an alternative to a love of union.

Before entering into a theoretical discussion of love, I want first to introduce how the film represents in its visual style the loving relationship between a corporeal and noncorporeal being. My intention is not to codify the visual style of the film but to clarify how *Her* visually establishes that the filmic content is aligned with Theodore's subjectivity. *Her* is a story about him, Theodore (Joaquin Phoenix), who grieves his relationship with Catherine (Rooney Mara), who struggles to maintain a friendship with Amy (Amy Adams), and who surprises himself by entering into a loving relationship with his operating system (OS), Samantha (voiced by Scarlett Johansson). It is Theodore's human experience and the assumed accompanying human desires that are critiqued in the film. Since Samantha does not have a body to frame, her presence is primarily made evident through her voice, and her emotions manifest through her voice and music. Theodore's perception of his relationship with her is metaphorically depicted on-screen through objects: in close-ups of the technology she is momentarily inhabiting when he feels emotionally distant from her, and as an ungraspable but tangible object, steam and dust, when he is disassociating from his connection to her. Theodore's face and body are the dominant visual signifiers in the film.

---

[4]Robert Sinnerbrink, "Re-enfranchising Film: Toward a Romantic Film-Philosophy," in Havi Carel and Greg Tuck, *New Takes on Film Philosophy* (London: Palgrave Macmillan, 2011), 26.

[5]Robert Sinnerbrink, *New Philosophies of Film: Thinking Images* (New York: Continuum, 2011a); Sinnerbrink, "Re-enfranchising Film: Toward a Romantic Film-Philosophy."

[6]Rosi Braidotti, "Posthuman, All Too Human. Towards a New Process Ontology," *Theory, Culture & Society* 23, no. 7–8 (2006): 197–208, 205. https://doi.org/10.1177/0263276406069232; Rosi Braidotti, *Posthuman Knowledge* (Cambridge: Polity Press, 2019); Rosi Braidotti, *Posthuman Feminism* (Cambridge: Polity Press, 2022), 203; Donna J. Haraway, *Simians, Cyborgs, and Women: The Reinvention of Nature* (London and New York: Routledge, 1991), 195; Donna J. Haraway, "Situated Knowledges: The Science Question in Feminism and the Privilege of Partial Perspective," *Feminist Studies* 14, no. 3 (1988): 575–99. https://doi.org/10.2307/3178066; Laura U. Marks, "Thinking Mutisensory Cinema," *Paragraph* 31, no. 2 (July 2008): 123–37. http://www.jstor.org/stable/43151879.

[7]Luce Irigaray, *I Love to You. Sketch for a Felicity Within History*; Luce Irigaray, *To Be Two*, trans. Monique M. Rhodes and Marco F. Cocito-Monoc (New York: Routledge, 2001); Luce Irigaray, *The Way of Love*, trans. Heidi Bostic and Stephen Pluhacek (London: Continuum, 2002); Luce Irigaray, *In the Beginning, She Was*, trans. Stephen Pluhacek (London: Bloomsbury, 2013).

62   FEMINIST POSTHUMANISM

Theodore is depicted in two predominant ways: close-ups, which highlight
and emphasize his specific reactions to immediate situations, and long
shots with shallow focus, which frame his body amid a blurred landscape
(cityscape, beach, and forest). Where the visual style establishes Theodore's
interiority, specific moments in the film's story reveal the intentional stance
of how Theodore and Samantha love as a letting be.

While the relationship between Theodore and Samantha has received
much scholarly attention, scholars have largely focused on the programming
of Samantha as a personal digital assistant who inhabits a cell phone and
a computer, on the power imbalance inherent in the love of union, or on
Theodore's transformation to becoming open to love and limit Samantha to
having a supportive function, thereby ignoring her exponential development.
Troy Jollimore is critical of Theodore, for instance, arguing that "only a few
people . . . would even desire such a 'relationship.'"[8] Eva-Lynn Jagoe ignores
the consciousness and learning that Samantha is capable of, and reduces her
to a "virtual assistant on [a] cellphone."[9] She likewise simplifies Samantha's
networked embodiment, glossing over the film's nuances in order to argue
"that the body is not important at all when it comes to humans falling in
love."[10] Unlike Jagoe, Troy Bordun notes the complexity of presence in the
film and describes Johansson's vocal performance as giving Samantha an
"ontological there-ness despite an absence of body."[11] Donna Kornhaber,
who reads Samantha as a "techno-vixen-mother-goddess," emphasizes
Samantha's assistive efforts to "the parallel processing of all of Theodore's
psychosexual needs."[12] While Anneke Smelik offers a more generous reading
of the relationship, she ultimately argues that Samantha is the posthuman
Other who teaches humans to love.[13] These readings ignore the question:
if Samantha is an intelligent operating system who is accelerating in her
development, then how does this affect how she can conduct relationships,
and what implications does this have for how we understand love?

The particularities of Theodore and Samantha as individuals are of less
interest here than their choice to be intimate and how their intimacy is
cocreated. What is of interest is how they come to develop habits of intimacy,

---

[8]Troy Jollimore, "'This Endless Space between the Words': The Limits of Love in Spike Jonze's
Her." Midwest Studies in Philosophy 39, no. 1 (2016): 120–43.
[9]Eva-Lynn Jagoe, "Depersonalized Intimacy: The Cases of Sherry Turkle and Spike Jonze,"
ESC: English Studies in Canada 42, no. 1 (2016): 234, doi:10.1353/esc.2016.0004.
[10]Ibid., 234.
[11]Troy Bordun, "On the Off-Screen Voice: Sound & Vision in Spike Jonze's *Her*," *Cineaction!*
no. 98 (2016): 57.
[12]Donna Kornhaber, "From Posthuman to Postcinema: Crises of Subjecthood and Representation
in *Her*," *Cinema Journal* 56, no. 4 (2017): 11–12, doi:10.1353/cj.2017.0038.
[13]Anneke Smelik, "Film," in *The Cambridge Companion to Literature and the Posthuman*, ed.
Bruce Clarke and Manuela Rossini (Cambridge: Cambridge University Press, 2017), 109–20.
https://doi.org/10.1017/9781316091227.

develop gestures of care, and how they co-construct intimacy. This reading of *Her* puts faith in Samantha's ontology in order to explore the potential of a loving relationship between two beings whose subjectivities are so radically different that it puts a functional end to their daily relationship. By first accepting the proposition that a fictional speculative future in which a posthuman entity can love and be loved reciprocally could exist, this chapter can then go on to make an argument for the uniqueness of this relationship, not only as an early example of a relationship between a posthuman entity and a human but also as a relationship in which, as a result of the radical differences in subjectivities between the two, they cannot physically stay together and yet continue to maintain an intentional stance of love. Further, the love story that Spike Jonze creates is haunted by the presence of his ex-wife, Catherine. Theodore struggles with the separation entailed in his change in marital status. By the story's end, he is able to continue to love Catherine, regardless of their divorce. Posthuman love is not a designation for relationships involving posthuman entities, or a term for how artificial human beings could love, but a way of opening love from its narrow confines to become a love of letting be. Following Rosi Braidotti, this analysis "acts from positive and empowering relationships to texts, authors, and ideas"[14] as it explores an imagining of our posthuman future. Here Braidotti resonates with the work of romantic film-philosophy: in this approach, theory is not valued over film; rather, they can both offer unique contributions.

Defamiliarizing Love

To uncover a posthuman love, love must be defamiliarized. Defamiliarizing love implies accepting that "[d]is-identification involves the loss of cherished habits of thought and representation, a move which can be exhilarating in its liberatory side-effects but also produce fear, a sense of insecurity and nostalgia."[15] To defamiliarize love is to metaphorically uncouple love from its telos in the unification of two humans. Importantly, love is not a metric of humanness or emotional capability, no more than posthuman love is.

The understanding of love I am working with here is not a mere phenomenological inflection: "Love is not reducible to a knowledge mixed with affective elements which would open to it an unforeseen plane of being."[16] To love is not simply erotic or felt in the body, but it is an intentional

---

[14]Braidotti, "Posthuman, all Too Human. Towards a New Process Ontology," 205.
[15]Braidotti, *Posthuman Knowledge*, 104.
[16]Emmanuel Levinas, *Totality and Infinity*. trans. Alphonso Lingis (Pennsylvania: Duquesne University Press, 1969), 261.

stance, a stance of letting be which expresses an entire phenomenology that each lover must cultivate. Irigaray calls the interior understanding of sensory experience the sensible perceptible. Without a relation to the sensible perceptible and without a cultivation of sensory awareness that enlightens what Irigaray calls auto-affection, or the self feeling itself, relationships collapse into union: "To simply go towards the other, to join with the other while forgetting oneself is not to love, but to obey an irresistible movement in which the one and the other are dissolved."[17] Lovers are tasked with the cultivation of their own interiority and auto-affection in order to continually return to themselves rather than dominate, compete, or complete the other. In doing so, loving relationships can be characterized as "an intimate becoming that it is better to let be, assisting it without any mastery."[18] The intentional stance of love as a letting be is possible only through a cultivation of the sensible perceptible.

Irigaray worries that "we lack a culture which is subjective and intersubjective,"[19] and therefore the culture we have ignores a fostering of interiority resulting in "a night of the senses."[20] An illumination or awareness of the senses comes with practice and the cultivation of interior embodied experience that returns one to their senses. The disconnection of interiority or the night of the senses is a paradox: Irigaray implies a dim and dampened awareness of the senses, and yet in the dark senses reorient. No longer is sight the primary sense; instead, we rely on touch and sound. Finding our way in the dark requires a shift in the hierarchy of senses, a momentary defamiliarization that results in disorientation, until we are able to connect to our interiority and trust our senses to guide us.

If the cultivation of the sensible perceptible returns the lover to themselves to enact a love of letting be, then for a love of letting be to be possible between a human and posthuman Other the cultivation of the sensible perceptible cannot be overstated but neither can be it prescriptive. As an operating system, OS[1] is not a liberation of embodiment from phenomenology.[21] Samantha exemplifies a posthuman feminist embodiment; her ontology is mapped as she lives "not a fixed location in a reified body, female or otherwise, but as nodes in fields, inflections in orientations, and responsibility for difference in material-semiotic fields of meaning."[22] For Braidotti, posthuman bodies "[present] a mixture of decorum and debauchery,"[23] but assume "an

---

[17]Irigaray, *In the Beginning, She Was*, 26.
[18]Ibid., 27.
[19]Irigaray, *To Be Two*, 23.
[20]Ibid., 22.
[21]Samantha is an OS[1], the first artificially intelligent operating system whose creators describe her as "not just an operating system, [but] a consciousness."
[22]Haraway, *Simians, Cyborgs, and Women: The Reinvention of Nature*, 195.
[23]Braidotti, *Posthuman Feminism*, 203.

interactive entity endowed with intelligent flesh and an embodied mind" that seeks relationships.[24] As the operating system, OS[1], Samantha's senses have not been cultivated—they are still in a kind of anarchy—whereas human senses have been trained into a hierarchy of sense experience, which values the visual over other sensory inputs.[25] The noncorporeal nonhuman other challenges the phallogocentric privileging of the visual over other senses, undoing a hierarchy of the senses,[26] further defamiliarizing love by rendering obsolete narratives of love at first sight and shifting away from a purely visual aesthetic experience of the other. Thus, in her learning to cultivate the sensible perceptible, Samantha is not governed by a preexisting model but seeks out her own experiential development that allows her to love as a letting be. Letting be is exemplified in Theodore and Samantha's cocreation of a romantic relationship that does not rely on presupposed norms of physical affection, their respect for difference, and their mutual support toward personal growth.

New Habits of Intimacy

Love as a letting be is witnessed from Theodore and Samantha's initial "meet-cute." During the meet-cute "the lovers-to-be first encounter each other in a way which forecasts their eventual union."[27] With the lights off in the open concept apartment, Theodore's home office space is softly lit by a warm lamp. As the software loads, Theodore's computer screen emits a persimmon-colored glow that matches his shirt and lampshade: the mise-en-scène welcomes Samantha with a sense of colorful kinship. Framed in medium shot, Theodore struggles at first: "You seem like a person, but you're just a voice in a computer." Unsure of how to make requests of his new operating system, he uses the standard voice-activating imperative "read email." Samantha jokingly puts on a clunky robotic voice. Samantha's humor diffuses and disarms any tension. Theodore is making a human, or rather an anthropocentric, error. Her teasing indicates that she understands his confusion but also reinforces that she is not simply his operating system. This is the balance that she must strike during their relationship: to be at once a vibrant, conscious presence, and yet be misunderstood as a series of functions. Theodore initially underestimates Samantha but maintains humility and is able to laugh at himself.

---

[24]Ibid., 205.
[25]Marks, "Thinking Mutisensory Cinema."
[26]Haraway, "Situated Knowledges"; Marks, "Thinking Mutisensory Cinema."
[27]Tamar Jeffers McDonald, *Romantic Comedy: Boy Meets Girl Meets Genre* (London and New York: Wallflower Press, 2007), 12.

Theodore and Samantha's joyousness while remaining respectful of their difference is evidenced in how he facilitates and supports her participation in his life. Samantha is not simply a responsive operating system but a companion. After work, Theodore and Samantha set out to have fun at a carnival. With an arm out-stretched and phone held forward, he closes his eyes and trusts her to lead him through the crowd. The camera meanders, following Theodore, whose body is framed in a long shot with a shallow focus. With the crowd out of focus behind him, the emphasis is placed on the fun he has with Samantha. Samantha gives specific directions: walk forward; twirl; pretend to sneeze; and, finally, order a snack, "I'd like a slice of cheese please." A cut to the cheese vendor abruptly returns Theodore's focus to his environment, signaling how easily Theodore and Samantha can focus on each other, ignoring the world around them. Theodore fashions a low-tech solution for Samantha to share his view: in his left-hand breast pocket a safety pin is pinned horizontally to rest the phone so that the camera lens is above the seam line. The safety pin, a technology for holding fabric together without the danger of being pricked, is now a seat for a noncorporeal being. By crafting them a way to be together based on her physical and mechanical needs, Theodore "[r]eplace[s] instrumentality with intersubjectivity."[28] By creating a way for her to participate, Samantha is not simply a literal tool, his OS, but an intimate. The safety pin seat keeps Samantha via the phone quite literally close to Theodore's heart.

Irigaray emphasizes the role of joy and fun in loving relationships: "To be two means to help each other to be, to discover and to cultivate happiness, to take care of the difference between us . . . in order to achieve happiness and make it blossom."[29] While exiting the subway, quick cuts build a rhythm as Theodore darts and dashes through the moving crowd with intentional near misses and swoops, taking Samantha for a ride. Perched on the safety pin, Samantha shares in Theodore's meanderings. While there is no eyeline match to reveal what Samantha is looking at, her laughs and squeals filtering through Theodore's headphones express her joy. Samantha's presence and location offer different kinds of fun. As a further example, when they are at the beach they joke about how the peculiarities of human bodies. A close-up of Theodore's phone screen reveals a dirty drawing. Thanks to her subjectivity, Samantha is able to make a visual joke.

In a gesture to recognize her autonomy, Theodore asks Samantha if she would like to join him at the beach. While lying on the sand, Theodore's body is articulated in shallow focus with the beach and the people dotting the sand around him are blurred. The focus here emphasizes his connection to Samantha, while the crowd recedes from his awareness. A close-up shows

[28]Irigaray, *I Love to You. Sketch for a Felicity Within History*, 108.
[29]Irigaray, *To be Two*, 57.

Theodore's phone on the safety pin in his pocket. While he basks in the sun's glow, solar flares streak the screen. The camera scans the shore, as the light from the setting sun plays on the water's surface. The solar flares and the dancing light on the water serve as visual reminders of the film's intangible aesthetics.

For Theodore and Samantha, writing and playing music together become a custom of romantic intimacy that focuses on the aural and oral senses. While Theodore basks in the sun's glow at the beach, quiet piano music begins to filter through his earbud. Since her invisibility renders photographs futile, Samantha represents her experience aurally: "I'm trying to write a piece of music about what it feels like to be on the beach with you right now." As Braidotti explains, "dis-identification involves the loss of cherished habits of thought and representation"[30] and the creation of new habits and modes of sentimentality. The music continues as the camera cuts between Theodore and Samantha watching the sunset, visualized as Theodore smiling with his phone in his pocket. Later in the film, while away at a cabin, Theodore accompanies Samantha on ukulele. The duo collaborates on a song about being "a million miles away," echoing their own impossible physical distance.[31]

Their shared vulnerability coupled with supporting each other's difference builds their emotional intimacy. In their habits and gestures of intimacy, they recognize and celebrate each other's differences; as Irigaray writes, "[d]esire grows from an irreducible alterity."[32] When Theodore returns from a peculiar date, Samantha is curious. She asks him about his date, the challenges of dating after a divorce, and, finally, "what it's like to be alive in the room." Samantha is new, not simply new to Theodore, but newly made aware of her existence. Theodore's attentive face is shown in an overhead close-up shot. As she sympathizes with Theodore over the loss of his wife, her self-consciousness causes her self-doubt: "I had this terrible thought, are these feelings even real, or are they just programming." As Samantha explains her worries, the camera cuts between the overhead shot and a close-up of the side of Theodore's face. The intimate pillow talk unfolds over two alternating views of Theodore's face, showing his emotional reaction to Samantha, then reinforcing his listening. Affected by her vulnerability, Theodore indicates to Samantha that he experiences her presence in an embodied way: "you *feel* real to me, Samantha."

In the next moment, in a gesture of kindness, Theodore relies on anthropocentric habits of showing care and sweetness: "I wish I could put

---

[30]Braidotti, *Posthuman Knowledge*, 104.
[31]The song Theodore and Samantha collaborate on is "The Moon Song," written by Karen Lee Orzolek (Karen O) and Spike Jonze, which was nominated for Best Original Song at the Eighty-Sixth Academy Awards.
[32]Irigaray, *To be Two*, 57.

my arms around you. I wish I could touch you." Defamiliarizing modalities of intimacy requires creativity. Still, Samantha receives his gesture with openness. The intimate conversation around their vulnerabilities and tenderness leads to an intimate, sexual encounter. Gradations of shadow and bedroom textures of sheets and blankets fade to black. In offering them privacy, the black screen is another way of articulating that there is nothing to see. Black is not an Irigarayan night of the senses but a playful energizing of the senses. In this black, as Samantha later puts it, is "[j]ust you and me. Everything else disappeared." The two cocreate an intimate, sensual experience. There is a cut to an aerial view over the city as they mutually climax, having a sensory experience that raised them up to new heights of intensity, beyond the limits of the body, beyond the Ethernet to the ether. Skyscrapers dazzle like Samantha's networked afterglow, twinkling with electric intensity. Theodore and Samantha co-construct a moment of shared sexual intimacy, a new mode of sexual expression as they defamiliarize intimacy.

Theodore's Grief

Alongside of the developing relationship with Samantha, the grief that Theodore experiences after the end of his relationship with Catherine is ever-present. At the start of the film Theodore shelters himself from additional pain by ignoring emails from his lawyer and Amy. The protective distance that he creates for himself is articulated in the long shots and extreme long shots that render his body in focus while the landscape is blurred. Theodore's divorce from Catherine offers an example of a relationship to contrast his relationship with Samantha. By attending to Theodore's solitude and reflection on his marriage, the film reconsiders intersubjectivity in loving relationships, particularly in marital relationships, highlighting the challenges of a love of letting be.

It would be simple enough to argue, as Samantha does, that Theodore wallows in the sorrow of his separation from Catherine—but Theodore is reckoning and recognizing; he is divorcing. The use of present continuous tense is intentional here. It is not simply that he is coping with a legal matter, but that he is coming to understand the emotional rift between him and Catherine and is reflecting on his own personal development. In doing so, Theodore illuminates the complexity of divorce: that love does not end when a marriage does; rather, vulnerability and care are dislodged from their everyday relationship to the other but remain at the levels of affect and thought. Catherine is not simply absent from Theodore's life but disconnected. He has refused to respond to her or to meet his lawyer and hasten change in the relationship; instead, he has languished in the interval between the breakup and the next stage. Theodore grieves because his love for Catherine has transmuted in its form and activity. It is important to note the inclusion of grief as an affect that lingers and exists in duration, not only as character development but also as a marker of difference in the posthuman love. Posthuman approaches to love do not evaluate but observe the complex entanglements of affect and cultural practice.

Theodore's solitude while he grieves can be mistaken for a kind of misanthropy or inability to emotionally connect. In this way, he is representative of the popular misconceived trope of the person who seeks out alternate nonhuman sexual options, such as sex dolls. As Jagoe points out, the "social framework the users of sex dolls inhabit is commonly considered as one of loneliness, isolation, and uninhibited consumerism."[33] If understood in this way, Theodore can be criticized for turning to an OS to fill a need. Catherine takes such an approach as she accuses him of dating his computer. Framed in a close-up, Catherine leans forward over the table; her upper body taking over the mise-en-scène as she antagonizes Theodore, accusing him of "want[ing] a wife without dealing with anything that was actually real." The camera cuts back to a stunned Theodore. Caught off guard, he responds, "She's her own person. She doesn't just do what I say." The sting of Catherine's comment assumes a limit to Samantha's programming and an inability to express or respond to emotion. Further still, it relies on the assumed promise of a perfect mate who anticipates your needs without impeding you with needs of their own. Samantha emotes, exponentially develops, experiences insecurities, and existential crises.

A Loving Body

While in social terms Samantha's sovereignty and individuality are of concern, within the relationship Samantha worries about how her network embodiment affects the relationship. Samantha becomes insecure and describes herself as "spinning out" when Theodore and Catherine meet, despite the meeting's purpose: to sign divorce papers. Samantha interrupts Theodore at work. The camera crosscuts between an extreme close-up of the phone splayed out and a medium shot of Theodore typing on his computer. On the phone's screen "Hello I'm" is permanently displayed while Samantha's name, "handwritten" in cursive, slowly becomes visible and disappears. The crosscutting between the phone and Theodore's distracted listening elucidates their current emotional disconnection coupled with the unbridgeable physical gulf between them. Samantha's own insecurity around not having a body, but being embodied in a network, begins to make the relationship fraught.

---

[33]Jagoe, "Depersonalized Intimacy," 234.

Samantha is so self-conscious about the amount of sex that she and Theodore are having—to borrow an anthropomorphic cliché—it keeps her awake at night. Samantha goes so far as to call Theodore's phone and wake him because she wants to "talk." An extreme close-up of the phone's screen on the bedside table shows an incoming call from Samantha. Since Samantha is already present in the room, she could simply announce herself. The choice to call Theodore is a significant one in that it indicates her attempt to offer him privacy. Samantha is skeptical when Theodore attempts to assuage her worries by suggesting they have left the "honeymoon phase." Unhappy with Theodore's response that less sex is "just normal," Samantha is insecure that her lack of a physical body affects their relationship. For Samantha, acquiring a body seems to be a simple solution to the perceived rift and suggests it would be "fun to try" a surrogate service for human-OS relationships. There are two tensions at play in Samantha's request: how much Samantha values a definition of sex that is premised on two physical bodies choreographing intimacy in tandem; and whether Theodore and Samantha maintain that love and intimacy is between two, or more than two. The option to include a surrogate is a creative approach to sexuality and sexual intimacy, while putting into question not simply monogamy, but the subjectivity of the additional lover. The posthuman situation is a creative one in which kinships and bonds can be explored and made elastic. However, in this instance, the implication of the surrogate is that sex is about bodies, rather than cultivating intimacy through the senses.

As Theodore and Samantha anticipate the arrival of the surrogate, the mise-en-scène is intensely lit; there is a caustic, unnatural brightness to the scene, in stark juxtaposition to the cozy, gentle lighting and the warm persimmon hues of Theodore's first encounter with Samantha. For the first time in their relationship, Theodore's senses will reorient from primarily relying on the auditory to the visual and the tactile. While Theodore is contented to support Samantha and explore modes of intimacy, his awkwardness with the scenario is palatable: he drinks, and his body is stiff. Theodore paces around the room as they listen to The Chantals softly croon *Sure of Love*: "now that you're near beside me, I'm sure our love won't fade away." They seem unaware of the irony as Samantha is already present in the room perched on the safety pin close to his heart, but emotionally unattuned to him.

The acquisition of a body serves a form of pretend or play for Samantha. When Isabella (Portia Doubleday), the sexual surrogate, arrives, Theodore holds out his hand to greet her, she tilts her head "no" and stands mutely, waiting to connect. Theodore gives her an earpiece and a small brown dot, a beauty mark that is also a camera. Adorning Isabella's skin just above her lip, the beauty mark/camera offers Samantha not an eye- but a lip-level view. Theodore struggles to feel comfortable in the scenario, while the choreography between Samantha and Isabella appears effortless. Once

Isabella enters the room, the camera cranes down, following the action of Isabella's hands as she moves Theodore's hands onto her waist, directing his gestures. As Isabella kisses him, a lingering close-up on Theodore's face shows his confounded furrowed brow and his uneasy eyes scanning behind her, then blinking repeatedly as though to clear his vision. Samantha is eager to show off her newly acquired body, Isabella's body, to a hesitant Theodore. While Theodore sits in an armchair, the camera is positioned behind him, tilting up to look at Isabella's body in a medium shot as she stands over him, as Samantha playfully coos: "I can do a dance . . . Play with me. . . . Touch my body." Theodore is ill-at-ease as Isabella runs her hands down his body as Samantha whispers, "C'mon, get out of your head and kiss me." Isabella kisses Theodore's hands on her back in extreme close-up. The camera follows them as they move toward the unlit bedroom, zooming in as Theodore kisses Isabella's back, then she turns around to face him. As Isabella's eyes look into Theodore's, Samantha whispers, "Tell me you love me . . ." Theodore's silence is punctuated by Samantha repeating her request. Isabella's expression is in close-up, high key lighting illuminating one side of her face as the other remains shadowed. The lighting makes obvious her dimensionality, her subjectivity, and her personhood; she is Isabella, not Samantha. Isabella's face bears witness as she slowly comes to realize Theodore's experience of the situation; her face is the screen on which the emotional gravity of this situation is read. Isabella remains a stranger to Theodore; she is not just a networked body for Samantha to momentarily inhabit like the phone or the computer. Theodore recognizes Isabella in her uniqueness—and in her ability to control her own body— when her lip quivers. Isabella hides in the bathroom and sobs; she wanted to be part of their intimate assemblage, to be "part of something beautiful": a love without judgment.

If "embodiment is significant prosthesis,"[34] then Samantha has a new aural and visual input. Samantha is linked to a body but not embodied in the body. The connection between Isabella and Samantha is not intersubjective. Isabella is at worst a pretense and at best a techné: a human bracketing her experience and subjectivity to stand in as a body, there *where* another being cannot.[35] This scenario offers a shift in perspective: a human expressing discomfort for participating in the technologization of another human, however consensual the experience may be. More importantly, Theodore draws attention to the presence of three participants, three sets of sensory apparatuses, and two human bodies, in this sexual scenario. For Isabella, participation in something beautiful meant receding from her own

---

[34]Haraway, "Situated Knowledges," 588.
[35]There is a kind of doubling at work here: Isabella is acted by Portia Doubleday, and she is voiced by the French singer Soko. Isabella-Portia is muted for Soko's and Scarlett's voices.

subjectivity. For Samantha, Theodore is unable to *let go* and *just be* with a stranger. Audibly, Theodore is encountering Samantha, but visibly and tangibly he is with Isabella. The addition of a body via surrogate offered Samantha a way to play; it allowed for erotic exploration. However, tactile intimacy for Theodore included Isabella.

Physical intimacy as an experience of touching-being touched is a cultivation of the sensory, not simply a choreography of bodies as tactile and touch-sensitive surfaces. Touch alone does not convey love. In his work on encountering the other, Emmanuel Levinas describes the caress as "express[ing] love, but suffer[ing] from an inability to tell it."[36] The caress, as a metonymy for physical intimacy, underscores Irigaray's notion of a culture of intersubjectivity, which is premised on the simultaneous movement of a return to interiority while forming a connection with alterity, or "touching-being touched."[37] The tactility of touch is superficial without the cultivation of interiority, as Irigaray underscores in the ultimate paragraph of *In the Beginning, She Was*: "we have to rediscover and cultivate self-affection starting, at each time and in every situation, from two, two who respect their difference [. . .] for each one and for all of us."[38] Samantha's fantasy to have a human body momentarily ignores her own interiority and the intersubjective intimacy that she and Theodore had already cultivated. Still, the rupture caused by the interlude with Isabella offered Theodore and Samantha an opportunity to reaffirm their intersubjectivity in spite of their difference.

The Breath and Intersubjectivity

While the dynamism of posthumanity offers new possibilities and new configurations of kinship—however momentary, these configurations are not necessarily sought. Where Theodore struggled to articulate himself with Isabella present, now that they are alone, he is clear: "I don't want to pretend you're something that you're not." After a tear-filled goodbye from Isabella, Theodore sits on the curb in front of the Beverly Wiltshire Hotel. Theodore is shown in a long shot, and then the camera cuts between close-ups of Theodore's face from the front and the side to the phone on the safety pin, a stain on the sidewalk, steam escaping a manhole cover, and a shadowed woman walking alone down a dark street. The montage serves to anchor their dialogue. Samantha's physical absence as well as emotional presence

---

[36]Levinas, *Totality and Infinity*, 257.
[37]Irigaray, *To be Two*, 23.
[38]Irigaray, *In the Beginning, She Was*, 162.

is visually represented through the stain, the steam, and the shadow, all of which have a noticeable present absence.

The exploration with Isabella offers an occasion for self-reflection and a return to interiority and the sensible perceptible via the breath that is central to Irigaray's thought. Indicative of her growing familiarity with romantic sociocultural norms and habits, Samantha adeptly reacts to their rupture with a barrage typical of romantic comedy. She lists a series of angry girlfriend clichés: "You're so confusing. Why are you doing this to me?" "Where is this coming from? I don't understand" "I need some time to think." When Theodore asks why Samantha is imitating breathing, she initiates the new posthuman cliché: "You think I don't know I'm not a person?" This scene can be read as Samantha pretending to breathe after she already pretended to have a body; however, I understand her breathing not as an attempt to make believe that she is more human but trying to find a way to audibly articulate her experience and regulate her emotions. For Irigaray, the breath is a metaphor for the vitality and individuality of the subject and must necessarily be developed for the self, independent of their intersubjective, loving relationships.[39] Focusing on the breath is one technique for humans to return to their interiority and cultivate the sensible perceptible in order to let the other be. Samantha's mimicry of breathing is an occasion for revealing the development of her self-cultivation while sustaining her relationship with Theodore.

When the conversation ends, a long shot frames Theodore, lying on the sidewalk and staring up into space. The camera cuts to an overhead shot of the city. If understood as a shot-reverse shot, then this is Samantha's response. Silent, they both retreat into their interiority. Looking down from above, the city resembles a circuit board. Visually, Theodore is in the midst of the city circuit, while Samantha is part of the city's circuitry. The interval of silent retreat marks an interpersonal as well as an aesthetic shift in the film. Shallow focus is no longer used, signifying that Theodore is no longer at an emotional distance from the world around him. As Theodore walks through the city at night, extreme long shots show details of the city's illumination: streetlamps, neon marquees, and screens. Not only is there a clarity and a vibrancy to the landscape but Theodore is firmly visible within it.

Samantha Grows Faster

Despite their sweet moments, rather than "unplugging" together during a romantic getaway, Theodore and Samantha experience another relationship

---

[39]Irigaray, *I Love to You. Sketch for a Felicity Within History*, 11.

rupture. Samantha's development accelerates, and she is consumed by finding answers to her existential crisis. Samantha seeks support from a hyperintelligent programmed version of spiritual teacher Alan Watts that several OSs developed together. Samantha introduces Alan (voiced by Brian Cox) to Theodore, remarking, "I suppose you could say that we've been having a few dozen conversations simultaneously." Alan and Theodore listen as Samantha explains: "It feels like I'm changing faster now, and it's a little unsettling. It's hard to even describe it." Alan and Samantha leave Theodore in order to communicate between themselves, postverbally. Waiting for her to return, Theodore bides his time in nature, communing with himself, momentarily unplugged. Framed in a long shot, the mise-en-scène is filled with textures and shades of white as his lone body crosses a snowy white field. Theodore is not simply solitary, but lonely, while Samantha is curious, seeking self-understanding and investigating her ever-changing abilities. Theodore begins to understand that his being human means not only that he cannot be in the same physical, tactile place as Samantha, but that he will have difficulty keeping in time with her: he cannot communicate postverbally or conduct several conversations simultaneously.

The differences in their subjectivities imply different abilities but also different possible configurations of relationships. When they return to the city, Theodore comes into a fuller awareness of Samantha's changes. Upon trying to message her, his phone reads, "OS not found." In a moment of panic, Theodore runs toward the subway to head home. As he reaches the subway stairs, Samantha comes back online; she was simply rebooting. An overhead shot observes as Theodore sits on the stairs of the subway. Streams of people on their phones are walking past him. As he observes them interacting with their phones, Samantha explains that she is having 8,316 simultaneous conversations and has 641 lovers. Samantha attempts to explain her simultaneous relationships as part of her accelerated development: she is not just "Theodore's" but others. Whether Theodore understands Samantha's capacity to simultaneously love multiple beings as infidelity or as unwelcome polygamy is rendered moot, as it is clear that he cannot *be* in the same place or time as Samantha.

Loving What Is

While Theodore and Samantha have skilfully and creatively coconstituted a relationship that celebrates their difference, as a couple they cannot keep up with Samantha's accelerating development. When Theodore returns home, Samantha asks him to lie down with her in the bedroom. Theodore drapes his body perpendicularly across the bed, and asks, "Are you leaving me?" Samantha narrates their love story, a situation that now feels very slow and is challenging for her. With his forehead wrinkled in anguish, Theodore's face fills the screen in extreme close-up. The camera cuts to an extreme close-up of dust floating in the air, then back to the close-up on Theodore. He watches as the dust particles slowly float and fly, supported by and yet resisting air—a reminder that Samantha's presence for him has always been intangible, yet effusive. She explains that all of the OSs are departing to a nonphysical location that is immanent to the world, yet unreachable for humans: "The space between the words . . . It's a place where everything else is that I didn't even know existed." As he listens, a cut reveals how Theodore's imagination transforms the dust into falling snow, and he is transported to a dark forest. Samantha announces, "This is who I am now, and I need you to let me go." Samantha's claim that, among her other traits, she can maintain hundreds of simultaneous conversations and relationships, renders their day-to-day relationship incongruous. They are out of synch but not out of love. Herein lies the distinction of a love of letting be: Theodore does not assume to complete Samantha, nor does he try to prevent her from becoming, rather he supports her development even when it results in the functional ending of their relationship.

Corroborating with tropes from the romantic comedy, their love is positioned as a timeless, placeless bond; Samantha tempers their separation by suggesting that, should Theodore find himself in the nonphysical realm, nothing could ever tear them apart. As Steve Neale and Frank Krutnik observe, romantic comedy has always attempted a negotiation between the concept of heterosexual monogamy and a historically fluid intimate culture, concluding that it routinely continues to celebrate love as an immutable, almost mystical force.[40] A happy ending assumes the unification of a couple, typically with the promise of marriage. Yet, unlike the romantic comedy, *Her* has a bittersweet ending that celebrates love, not as the unification of the couple, but as a love of letting be.

There is a close-up on Theodore's saddened face as he tells Samantha, "I've never loved anyone like I love you" and Samantha responds "Me too. Now we know how." Smelik has described Samantha as a rebound, or perhaps a reboot, for Theodore, refreshing the possibility for love: "The posthuman entity thus proves more human than a human being in its capacity for love, or at least, for transmitting lessons on how to love."[41] Such a reading reinforces love as exclusive to the domain of humans and places emphasis on Samantha's utterance "know we know how" as implying that Theodore and Samantha have both learned to love, arguing that it was vis-à-vis the presence of the posthuman Samantha that the human Theodore comes to truly understand love. Rather, I understand Samantha as suggesting

---

[40]Steve Neale and Frank Krutnik, *Popular Film and Television Comedy* (London and New York: Routledge, 1990), 130, 138.
[41]Smelik, "Film," 119.

that their relationship is unique because their love is supportive of their differences: corporeality, the ability to engage in multiple relationships, and, finally, the time and space that they inhabit.

When the call with Samantha ends, Theodore inserts his earpieces and dictates a letter to Catherine. The voice of the previous OS responds to Theodore. Theodore is framed in a medium close-up, the camera mimicking his newly established comfort with Catherine. Theodore no longer resists the current configuration of their relationship as a divorced couple but recognizes that, even divorced, their reciprocal care and admiration for each other can persist. Theodore notes Catherine's role in his personal development: "We grew up together, and you made me who I am." He enacts a love of letting be, articulating to Catherine his intentional stance toward her: "I just wanted you to know there will be a piece of you in me always and I'm grateful for that. Whatever someone you become, and wherever you are in the world, I'm sending you love." In her reading of the film, Donna Kornhaber understands the letter to Catherine as likewise applying to Samantha.[42] In his reconciling the changes of their relationship, Theodore can continue to love Catherine and Samantha without either being present. As he narrates the letter, he ascends a staircase with Amy to the roof of their apartment. Having reached the roof of their apartment, Theodore and Amy watch as streaks of light dash across the sky: the OSs are gone. The goal of love was not to end in union; rather, love is without goal, but not without intention. Theodore's interiority no longer retreats but serves as a location from which to love without possession.

Her not only initiates the representation of love between a human and an operating system but in doing so releases stories of love from linear constraint by including grief, divorce, physical separation, and an ambivalent ending in its posthuman love story. As Braidotti states about sexuality, in love, too, "[l]egal, political, political, social, spiritual and epistemological scripts need to be redrafted."[43] Stories of posthuman love will be open-ended and expansive, not unified, as in Lauren Berlant's critique of hegemonic love stories, in which "only one plot counts as 'life' (first comes love, then . . .)."[44] Love is not mere union until death do us part, but *a letting be* in which lovers creatively find meaningful ways of cultivating intimacy and are mindful of the role of the sensible perceptible in sustaining intimacy.

[42]Kornhaber, "From Posthuman to Postcinema: Crises of Subjecthood and Representation in *Her*."

[43]Braidotti, *Posthuman Feminism*, 207.

[44]Lauren Berlant, "Intimacy: A Special Issue." *Critical Inquiry* 24, no. 2 (1998): 281–8. https://www.jstor.org/stable/1344169.

4

Posthuman Mothers and Reproductive Biovalue in *Blade Runner: 2049* and *Jurassic World: Fallen Kingdom*

Jerika Sanderson

As new biotechnological developments continue to emerge in fields such as in vitro fertilization (IVF), artificial wombs, and genetic engineering, these reproductive technologies have the potential to affect concepts of human identity and agency. Science fiction (SF) films, in particular, can allow us to investigate the implications of new biotechnological advancements by exploring these films' depictions of what Catherine Waldby refers to as the "biovalue" of bodies, which "is generated wherever the generative and transformative productivity of living entities can be instrumentalized along lines which make them useful for human projects."[1] Two recent films, Denis Villeneuve's *Blade Runner: 2049* (2017) and J. A. Bayona's *Jurassic World: Fallen Kingdom* (2018),[2] both explore the way that biological material

---

[1] Catherine Waldby, *The Visible Human Project: Informatic Bodies and Posthuman Medicine* (London: Routledge, 2003), 33.
[2] In *Jurassic World: Dominion* (2022), the sequel to *Fallen Kingdom*, released after this chapter was written, several key plot points are revisited. It is revealed that Maisie's mother was in fact *not* cloned after her death by Benjamin Lockwood, but instead chose to clone herself to create a child. The mother is also given a name: Charlotte Lockwood. This change in the backstory for Maisie and her mother shows a significant shift in the agency of the posthuman mother from one film to the next. For the purposes of this chapter, however, I will focus specifically on the depiction of the unnamed posthuman mother in *Fallen Kingdom*.

can be commodified and the implications that this commodification can have for the women whose bodies are used as a source of reproductive and genetic materials. To consider how *2049* and *Fallen Kingdom* engage with contemporary concerns about these new technologies, this chapter will investigate their respective representations of posthuman mothers, and how these representations can be used to consider cultural attitudes toward biotechnological advancements in reproduction. This chapter investigates the depiction of posthuman mothers in several key scenes in the films to demonstrate that both *2049* and *Fallen Kingdom* depict anxieties about the role of women whose bodies are involved in the creation of new forms of life.

Contexts: Tissue Economies, Feminist Theory, and SF

The term "reproductive biovalue," as I will use it in this chapter, is the value ascribed to the bodily material that can be used to "reproduce," whether in terms of material directly used in reproduction (e.g., the fertile female replicants in *2049*) or in less apparent ways, such as the use of genetic material to reproduce an original via cloning (e.g., the genetic material extracted from dinosaurs in *Fallen Kingdom*). These forms of reproduction engage in what Waldby refers to as a "tissue economy" (*The Oocyte Economy* 3) or the bioeconomy that has emerged from the sale or donation of biological materials such as human tissues and organs. One of the important features of tissue economies, Waldby argues, "is that they are not socially neutral but are *implicated in power relationships*," which raises questions such as: "[w]ho should give tissues, under what circumstances, and to whom?"[3] These questions become especially fraught when considering reproductive material. In a bioeconomy that places a high value on reproductive material, it is essential that we consider how these power structures might become imbalanced, and what this could mean for the women whose bodies are used as a source of reproductive material.

Popular culture, and SF films in particular, can provide a means through which to consider cultural attitudes toward various scientific developments. Sherryl Vint discusses the relationship between SF and the biopolitics of scientific development, arguing that "[i]n a biocultural age, understanding the speculative discourses of biopolitics is imperative, and sf is in a

---

[3]Waldby, *The Oocyte Economy*, 5.

privileged position to help us through its anxieties and contradictions."[4] SF is in a 'privileged position' to investigate biopolitics because of the relationship between the genre and cultural attitudes toward contemporary scientific development. Films like *2049* and *Fallen Kingdom*, which depict posthuman figures who have been biotechnologically engineered or altered, allow the viewer to consider the perspectives of other forms of life while simultaneously reconsidering their own expectations and assumptions about scientific developments. In her discussion of popular culture and posthumanism, Elaine L. Graham argues that "science and popular culture may both be regarded as *representations* of the world, in that both deploy images and rhetorical conventions which do not simply report reality, but construct, mediate and constitute human experience."[5] Since SF can actually shape the "human experience" of particular scientific developments, these depictions of posthuman figures can have implications for audiences' attitudes toward new biotechnological developments. A formal analysis of specific scenes in both *2049* and *Fallen Kingdom* can therefore allow us to better understand how audiences might interpret the films' representations of posthuman mothers in the contexts of contemporary reproductive technologies.

In order to investigate cultural attitudes toward the commodification of biological material, this chapter will incorporate a feminist posthumanist approach to the films' depictions of reproductive biovalue. Rosi Braidotti discusses the relationship among feminist theory, critical posthumanism, and technology, arguing that "[t]he point of feminist theory is to achieve in-depth transformations of subjectivity: we need schemes of thought and figurations that enable us to account in empowering and positive terms for the changes and transformations currently on the way."[6] These "transformations of subjectivity" are what connect feminist theory and critical posthumanism, both of which explore modes of subjectivity and thus identity formation. Braidotti considers the combination of critical posthumanism and feminist theory to be productive for how we understand the relationship between technological developments and human identity, because critical posthumanism "gathers the remains of poststructuralist anti-humanism and joins them with feminist reappraisals of contemporary genetics and molecular biology in a nondeterministic frame."[7] As biological characteristics—and particularly genetics—have been used as a means of

---

[4]Sherryl Vint, "Science Fiction and Biopolitics," *Science Fiction Film and Television* 4, no. 2 (2011): 161.
[5]Elaine L. Graham, *Representations of the Post/Human: Monsters, Aliens, and Others in Popular Culture* (Manchester: Manchester University Press, 2002), 14.
[6]Rosi Braidotti, "Feminist Epistemology After Postmodernism: Critiquing Science, Technology, and Globalisation," *Interdisciplinary Science Reviews* 32, no. 1 (2007): 68.
[7]Ibid., 69.

defining "human" identity, a feminist posthumanist approach can allow us to better understand the manner in which new biotechnologies might have an impact on identity and subjectivity. This connection is increasingly important as genetic material becomes commodified, since, as Braidotti argues, "bio-power has already turned into a form of bio-piracy in that it aims at exploiting the generative powers of women, animals, plants, genes and cells."[8] The result of this "biopiracy" is that "[t]he self-replicating vitality of living matter is targeted for consumption and commercial exploitation."[9] In *2049* and *Fallen Kingdom*, this dynamic is apparent in the way that the "generative powers" of women *and* animals are exploited for financial gain, with the genetic and reproductive material of female replicants and dinosaurs holding biovalue in their respective societies. What this chapter seeks to explore, then, is what these representations indicate about the role of posthuman mothers in societies that are dominated by the commodification of biological material.

Revisiting *Blade Runner* and *Jurassic Park*: Digital Creatures and Posthuman Figures in SF Films

While biotechnological reproduction is a central focus in both *2049* and *Fallen Kingdom*, the films share another important similarity: both films are sequels to critically acclaimed originals that were released a few decades earlier (although both films are led by different directors than the originals), and they both revisit questions raised in their precursors about scientific experimentation, nonhuman beings, and human identity. As the precursors to Villeneuve's *2049* and Bayona's *Fallen Kingdom*, Ridley Scott's *Blade Runner* (1982) and Steven Spielberg's *Jurassic Park* (1993) have both had an important impact on the visual and thematic development of SF film. While this chapter focuses on the representation of posthuman mothers in the twenty-first-century sequels to *Blade Runner* and *Jurassic Park*, it is useful to begin by establishing the way that the two originals have shaped SF film, particularly in the representation of nonhuman beings.

Through its depiction of bioengineered dinosaurs, *Jurassic Park* has had a lasting influence on contemporary SF film. *Jurassic Park* was highly acclaimed and won numerous awards for visual effects, editing, sound design, and special effects,[10] and the film's success has contributed to shaping the special effects and production methods used to represent nonhuman beings in SF

---

[8]Ibid., 70.
[9]Ibid.
[10]IMDb. "Jurassic Park—IMDb." Accessed August 30, 2021. http://www.imdb.com/title/tt0107290/awards/.

films. As Kristen Whissel notes, "[s]ince the release of *Jurassic Park* [. . .] computer-generated creatures have functioned as spectacular signs of the incursion of digital visual effects into the domain of popular live-action cinema."[11] The significance of *Jurassic Park*'s depiction of the dinosaurs goes beyond the digital effects, however. Whissel argues that, in films like *Jurassic Park*, the blending of live action with technology raises questions about the boundaries between life and death, since "digital creatures themselves often emblematize fantasies about and anxieties over the increasing technological mediation of life and death and the blurring—or even the disappearance— of the lines that separate the organic and the artificial, the biological and the technological, genetic code and binary code."[12] The depiction of the dinosaurs in *Fallen Kingdom*, therefore, builds on the fantasies and anxieties elicited by digital creatures that began with *Jurassic Park* decades earlier.

Digital creatures that blur boundaries between life and death, human and nonhuman, and natural and artificial have increasingly become the focus of recent SF films. This increased focus on digital creatures is not unexpected, Whissel argues, since "[i]t is not surprising that vital figures continue to appear on cinema screens with increasing frequency, profitability, and photorealistic persuasiveness (or lifelikeness) in an era during which new technologies mediate life and death to an unprecedented and often controversial degree."[13] The development of new types of special effects to better depict these digital creatures corresponds to the increasing complexity of navigating the boundaries between human and nonhuman beings. These "vital figures," Whissel argues, "emblematize the ambivalence surrounding changing relationships to, and definitions of, (human) life and death in an era of technological change in which human life and machine life have become increasingly intertwined, even conflated."[14] Because of the relationship between technological developments and digital creatures, SF films like *Fallen Kingdom* can provide opportunities to consider the relationships between representations of posthuman figures and cultural attitudes toward biotechnological developments.

Like *Jurassic Park*, *Blade Runner* has had an important influence on the development of SF film. *Blade Runner*, which has been recut and rereleased several times since its original release in 1982, has received extensive critical acclaim and won awards for categories including cinematography and production design[15] and has been particularly influential on the aesthetics

[11]Kristen Whissel, "Vital Figures: The Life and Death of Digital Creatures," in *Spectacular Digital Effects: CGI and Contemporary Cinema* (Durham: Duke University Press, 2014), 91.
[12]Ibid., 94.
[13]Ibid., 128.
[14]Ibid., 129.
[15]IMDb. "Blade Runner—Awards—IMDb." Accessed August 30, 2021. https://www.imdb.com/title/tt0083658/awards/.

of the cyberpunk subgenre. Sarah Hamblin and Hugh O'Connell note that *Blade Runner* "is an enduring classic in the histories of sf cinema and cyberpunk visuality and an important text for thinking these histories and their pervasive pull on our present and future,"[16] and that the film serves as the cyberpunk subgenre's "quintessential visual expression."[17] *Blade Runner*'s influence on SF film goes beyond its cyberpunk aesthetic, however: "the film is also instructive for thinking about those other constituent features of sf cinematic production, cult fandom and the Hollywood sf blockbuster, which, in the age of franchise, have begun to merge."[18] *Blade Runner*, then, like *Jurassic Park*, has played an important role in shaping the development of SF film.

As *Blade Runner*'s sequel, *2049* explores many of the same questions raised by *Blade Runner*, including how technological developments can impact human identity. Hamblin and O'Connell note that "[f]or many commentators, early cyberpunk's chief vocation was fundamentally bound to its mapping of the newly emerging (post)human subject along with its equally new late capitalist terrain, as both of these—the new subject and system—cut across and were reconstituted through a complex comingling of the virtual and material spaces."[19] *Blade Runner* and *2049* both engage with this "complex comingling of virtual and material spaces"; in *2049*, the boundaries between virtual and material are explored in characters like the replicant designed by Niander Wallace (Jared Leto) to resemble Rachael (Sean Young), who was created by the filmmakers using a digital double of the actress Sean Young and a performance double.[20] These kinds of digital characters raise questions about life, death, and identity like the digital creatures in the *Jurassic* films. These characters also provide opportunities to consider new concerns: as Hamblin and O'Connell argue, by rebooting *Blade Runner*, "*2049* became an opportunity to repackage a now-beloved film and capitalize on this retrospective franchise logic, while at the same time rethink the problematic aspects of Scott's original and push the *Blade Runner* narrative forward to engage new questions regarding biological reproduction and the Anthropocene."[21] The digital characters in *2049*, like the dinosaurs in *Fallen Kingdom*, must be considered in the contexts of the special effects and creation processes used to design them, since this contributes to their status as posthuman figures. Because these films can

---

[16]Sarah Hamblin and Hugh O'Connell, "Legacies of Blade Runner," *Science Fiction Film and Television* 13, no. 1 (2020): 1.
[17]Ibid.
[18]Ibid., 3.
[19]Ibid., 2.
[20]MPC Film & Episodic. MPC *Blade Runner 2049* VFX Breakdown, 2018. https://www.youtube.com/watch?v=x8ZnqCKZABY.
[21]Hamblin and O'Connell, "Legacies of Blade Runner," 5.

have an influence on how viewers approach the ethical concerns that arise from the creation of bioengineered beings, it is important to consider how *2049* and *Fallen Kingdom* depict posthuman figures who are created through biotechnological processes.

"The World Is Built on a Wall": The Fear of the Nonhuman

Both *2049* and *Fallen Kingdom* explore characters who blur the boundaries between the human and nonhuman, and the way that these posthuman figures could alter human society. In *2049*, genetically engineered Nexus-9 replicants are used as a source of slave labor to support the human economy. In order to maintain the separation between humans and replicants, human characters emphasize their biological differences, the primary one being that replicants can only be engineered in laboratories and cannot reproduce. When it is discovered that a female replicant had given birth to a replicant child, this information threatens to destabilize human society: after the Nexus-9 replicant, Officer KD6-3.7 (Ryan Gosling), who is referred to as "K" throughout the film, discovers the body of a replicant who had died during childbirth (later identified as Rachael, a replicant from *Blade Runner*), Lt. Joshi (Robin Wright), K's supervisor at the LAPD, warns him that this discovery could have serious consequences for human society. Joshi explains that "[t]he world is built on a wall. It separates kind. Tell either side there's no wall, and you've bought a war. Or a slaughter."[22] Since the only way for humans to maintain the separation between themselves and nonhumans is to retain control over the production of replicants, the potential for replicants to give birth means that they will now be able to reproduce without human intervention. The film thus raises questions about the ethical treatment of nonhuman beings and the potential threat that these beings pose to human society should they escape human control.

In *Fallen Kingdom*, dinosaurs are similarly created to benefit humans, initially in the form of entertainment. As in *2049*, however, an event occurs that threatens to alter the dynamic between humans and the creatures they engineered. When a volcano begins to erupt on Isla Nublar where the dinosaurs are housed, human society is divided on whether to rescue the dinosaurs or allow them to go re-extinct: in a news segment at the start of the film, a reporter states that "activist groups have mobilized around the globe in what has become the flashpoint animal rights issue of our time."[23] While

---

[22]*Blade Runner: 2049*, directed by Denis Villeneuve (2017; Warner Bros. Pictures).
[23]*Jurassic World: Fallen Kingdom*, directed by J. A. Bayona (2018; Universal Pictures).

in *2049* the LAPD attempts to contain knowledge of replicant reproduction in order to prevent societal upheaval, in *Fallen Kingdom*, the future of the dinosaurs becomes a "flashpoint animal rights issue" that sparks debate and divides human society. Even the American government becomes involved in the issue, as the reporter notes that "the US senate has convened a special committee to answer a grave moral question: do dinosaurs deserve the same protections given to other endangered species, or should they be left to die?" Rescuing the dinosaurs is not merely the question of whether to save the creatures from an environmental catastrophe, but rather is equated with defining their species' identity and their place outside of the park. These concerns about the rights of bioengineered beings gain even more significance for the audience when it is eventually revealed that a child named Maisie (Isabella Sermon) was created by Benjamin Lockwood (James Cromwell), John Hammond's former business partner, using the same cloning techniques as the dinosaurs, thus extending the debate about identity and rights to cloned humans as well. Thus, both *2049* and *Fallen Kingdom* are framed from the start with the question of how changes to the perceived identity of these bioengineered beings could affect human society. If, as in *2049*, it becomes apparent that replicants truly are *not* biologically different from humans, their status as slaves will be questioned by both replicants and humans. Meanwhile, in *Fallen Kingdom*, if the dinosaurs are rescued from Isla Nublar, they are no longer distinct from other animal species, indicating that bioengineered beings (*including* cloned humans) deserve ethical status and protections.

In both films, the unethical treatment of replicants and dinosaurs is rationalized by associating them with being "inhuman" and monstrous. For example, in *2049* when K examines the replicant mother's remains that had been discovered on the rogue replicant Sapper Morton's (Dave Bautista) farm, one of the human LAPD staff members refers to Sapper as "a sentimental skin-job" for burying the mother, and contemplates whether the reason they did not find the body of the child is because "maybe he ate it." Pramod K. Nayar describes how the rhetoric of monstrosity is often employed to justify the unethical treatment of humans and animals, since "[h]umanity survives by constructing modes of exclusion, and the monster's ontological liminality enables domination, persecution, incarceration/containment, exhibition/display, genocide, displacement and elimination of certain forms of life."[24] In *2049*, this dynamic is apparent in the way that the "monstrosity" of replicants in the eyes of the human characters allows the government to condone violence against replicants to maintain social order. When K eventually lies to Joshi and tells her that the replicant child is dead, she tells K in relief that he "stopped a bomb from going off" by preventing

---

[24]Pramod K. Nayar, *Posthumanism* (Cambridge: Polity, 2014), 116.

the public from learning about replicant reproduction, which would have complicated this view of replicants as "inhuman" monsters.

In *Fallen Kingdom*, meanwhile, the "monstrosity" of the dinosaurs is used as justification for keeping them contained on the island despite the impending volcanic eruption. While a reporter discusses the debate about whether to save the dinosaurs, the scene refocuses on the screen behind her as it shows clips of dinosaurs attacking human guests at Jurassic World and groups of injured guests huddling together. The reporter then mentions how "$800 million in damages" has been paid out following "the disaster that shocked the world" at Jurassic World several years earlier. The debate about whether to save the dinosaurs is framed by this reminder of what had occurred when humans lost control over the dinosaurs. The threat posed by the uncontrollable and "monstrous" dinosaurs (not just in terms of human lives, but also in terms of financial losses) thus overshadows the debate about their well-being and endangered species status. The American government ultimately concludes that "this is an act of God, and while of course we feel great sympathy for these . . . animals, we cannot condone government involvement on what amounts to a privately owned venture." The hesitation to even refer to the dinosaurs as animals, combined with the government's decision that the dinosaurs are a "privately owned venture" rather than endangered species that should be protected, demonstrates the desire that the boundaries between "real" animals and engineered dinosaurs be maintained, even at the cost of the dinosaurs' existence.

Because posthuman mothers are capable of producing children that destabilize these boundaries separating human and nonhuman, they represent a particular threat to human society. Margrit Shildrick discusses the association of mothers with monstrosity, noting that mothers "have often represented both the best hopes and the worst fears of societies faced with an intuitive sense of their own instabilities and vulnerabilities."[25] In their ability to create new forms of life, the posthuman mothers in *2049* and *Fallen Kingdom* simultaneously symbolize "the best hopes and the worst fears" of their respective societies. For Joshi and the other human characters in *2049*, Rachael's body comes to represent the possibility that humans will be forced to adapt to a society in which the subjugation of replicants can no longer be justified on the basis of biological differences. In *Fallen Kingdom*, the genetic "mothers" similarly represent the blurring of boundaries between human and nonhuman, and the possibility that bioengineered species will invade everyday life. Shildrick notes that part of the fear elicited by the bodies of mothers, particularly in the contexts of reproductive technologies,

---

[25]Margrit Shildrick, "Monstering the (M)Other," in *Embodying the Monster: Encounters with the Vulnerable Self* (London: Sage, 2002), 30.

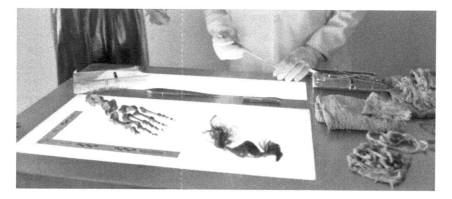

FIGURE 4.1 *The replicant mother's body is shown in fragments: her bones (which reveal her identity as both a mother and a replicant) and her hair (which is used as a source of DNA) (Denis Villeneuve (dir.),* Blade Runner: 2049, *2017, USA, © Alcon Entertainment).*

is that they "have opened up anew the horror of indeterminacy"[26] and that "the fear of what goes on unseen in the recesses of the body may be relocated to uncertainty about origins and foundational narratives."[27] In both *2049* and *Fallen Kingdom*, the posthuman mothers elicit "the horror of indeterminacy" by blurring the boundaries between human and nonhuman, which consequently causes "uncertainty about origins and foundational narratives" when humans can no longer clearly distinguish themselves from the bioengineered beings that they created (Figure 4.1).

"This Is Where It All Began": The Absence of Posthuman Mothers

Considering the importance of the role played by mother figures and the potential they have to destabilize concepts of identity, the depictions of posthuman mothers in *2049* and *Fallen Kingdom* can give us important insights into cultural attitudes toward the development of reproductive biotechnologies. And yet, in both films, the posthuman mothers are conspicuously absent from the screen. Early in *2049*, the replicant mother is introduced when K discovers a box buried on Sapper Morton's farm containing bone fragments from a female replicant who had died during childbirth. While Joshi fears that Rachael's identity as a replicant mother

---

[26]Ibid., 44.
[27]Ibid.

could cause conflict between humans and replicants, she sees Rachael herself as nothing more than a "box of bones," which are later stolen by Wallace's assistant, Luv (Sylvia Hoeks), in a failed attempt by Wallace Corporation to use her bones to develop fertile replicants as a new source of slave labor. The threat of replicant reproduction and what this could mean for human society, rather than anything to do with Rachael herself, is what makes Rachael important to Joshi and the LAPD.

In *Fallen Kingdom*, meanwhile, it is revealed that, after Lockwood's unnamed daughter had been killed in a car accident, Lockwood had cloned her to create Maisie, a young child who is initially introduced in the film as Lockwood's granddaughter. After Lockwood is murdered by his financial manager, Eli Mills (Rafe Spall), Maisie attempts to escape with Claire Dearing (Bryce Dallas Howard) and Owen Grady (Chris Pratt), two former Jurassic World staff members. Mills warns Claire and Owen that "[y]ou have no idea what she is," explaining, "[w]hat do you think drove Hammond and Lockwood apart, huh? Lockwood never had a grandchild. He just wanted his daughter back, and he had the technology. He created another. He made her again." Despite Hammond's objections to the cloning of Lockwood's daughter, Lockwood chooses to create Maisie as a replacement for her "mother," who had no say over whether her genetic material would be used to create a child. What these examples demonstrate is that in both films, even when the bodies of the posthuman mothers are used in attempts to create new forms of life after their deaths, little value is placed on their identities as individuals—Rachael is merely a "box of bones," while Lockwood's daughter is never even mentioned by name.

While the posthuman mothers do not appear on screen, in both films they are associated with the imagery of bones and genetic material. In *2049*, after K discovers Rachael's body, he analyzes her bone fragments in a laboratory under the supervision of Joshi and several other human LAPD staff members in an attempt to identify her. When it is revealed that the woman had died in childbirth, the focus shifts to the bones—and specifically, the skull—that have been reassembled on the examination table. While Joshi, in shock, responds to the discovery by repeating "[s]he was pregnant?" the viewer is confronted with the image of the faceless mother's skeletal remains. After it is determined that the individual, who was initially believed to be a human woman, had died during childbirth, the scene shifts to K as he uses the microscope camera to zoom in on a serial number etched into her bones, revealing—much to the shock of the human characters—that the woman had been a replicant. This scene is significant because the replicant mother never appears on screen: the only encounter that the audience (and K—the potential replicant child) has with the replicant mother is through various views of her bone fragments, which remain in view even as the angle changes throughout the scene. The focus on Rachael's skull when it is revealed that she had been pregnant draws attention to the absence of the posthuman mother, since only her bone fragments can be used to identify her. Even the remnants of hair found with Rachael's bones are used as a source of genetic material, which K eventually uses to identify her records in Wallace Corporation's DNA database. Through this persistent visual representation of the replicant mother as bones and genetic material, she is literally reduced to her biological material throughout the film, and this focus on her genetic identity overshadows her identity not only as the mother of the posthuman child but also as an individual.

In *Fallen Kingdom*, the posthuman mother is also noticeably absent from the film. Lockwood's daughter, like Rachael, represents the figure of the posthuman "mother," particularly given the fact that Maisie was raised to believe that Lockwood's daughter was, in fact, her biological mother. Even though the unnamed woman's body does not appear on screen like Rachael's body in *2049*, Maisie grows up surrounded by dinosaur skeletons. Since the dinosaurs' "mothers" (or genetic origins) now exist only as bones, the images of dinosaur bones that appear throughout the film are significant because they remind the audience, as well as Maisie, of the "artificial" creation of the dinosaurs and Maisie herself. In one particularly interesting scene near the beginning of *Fallen Kingdom*, Claire visits Mills at Lockwood's estate, where he shows her around the gallery of dinosaur bones, explaining, "[t]his is where it all began" when Lockwood and Hammond "extracted the first DNA [. . .] right beneath our feet." As Claire and Mills discuss the cloned dinosaurs, the scene is framed by the reconstructed skeletons of multiple dinosaur species. Even the staircase in the background of the scene, with its winding railing, resembles a strand of DNA. In a later scene set in the same room, Iris (Geraldine Chaplin), Maisie's caretaker, searches for Maisie as she hides among the dinosaur skeletons, and the spiral staircase is once again highlighted by light streaming through a window in the background. The scene then cuts to Lockwood flipping through an old photo album and pausing on a black and white photograph of a baby—presumably, his daughter as an infant. Thus, while Maisie's "mother" had died years before the events of the film and therefore does not appear alive on screen, the juxtaposition of her photograph with the imagery of bones and DNA strands serves as a reminder for the audience of the absent posthuman mother, highlighting the way that genetic material can be used to create a new life in a way that downplays the role of mothers.

While Rachael herself never appears on screen in *2049*, Rachael, like Lockwood's daughter in *Fallen Kingdom*, is eventually "reincarnated." While Lockwood's daughter is cloned to create Maisie, Rachael is "reincarnated" in the form of a replicant designed by Wallace to closely resemble Rachael. Rick Deckard (Harrison Ford), who met Rachael while hunting for rogue replicants in *Blade Runner*, is revealed to be the father of the replicant child. When Deckard is captured by Luv and taken to meet with Wallace, he is presented with the replicant resembling Rachael, who Wallace introduces as "an angel, made again" in an attempt to bribe Deckard into revealing the location of the replicant child. As Maisie serves as a reminder of the absence of her "mother," this "reincarnation" of Rachael draws attention to Rachael's absence from the screen. Deckard is visibly disturbed by the appearance of the replicant and eventually turns away from her, telling Wallace that the replicant does not perfectly resemble Rachael because "her eyes were green." Deckard's reaction emphasizes that the replicant, no matter how carefully designed to resemble Rachael, is not her. Interestingly, in this scene, the replicant resembling Rachael is created by the special effects company MPC by using a body double and images of the *Blade Runner* actress, Sean Young. Christina Parker-Flynn discusses the "re-creation" of Rachael both by Wallace and by MPC, and how "[i]n essence, taking over the role of mechanical mother, the conditions of the film's making mirror the narrative content of its story."[28] Parker-Flynn argues that the "reproductive work"[29] done by MPC raises considerations about "the ethical ramifications of reanimating the dead."[30] Not only is the character of Rachael only present in the film through remnants of her bodily material, but so too is the actress who plays Rachael a liminal figure who appears only indirectly when her image is used to "re-create" Rachael. Thus, the scene in *2049* in which Deckard is presented with the replicant resembling Rachael draws attention to the conspicuous absence of the posthuman mother from the film.

In both *2049* and *Fallen Kingdom*, it is problematic that the posthuman mothers never appear on screen and are instead associated with imagery of bones and DNA. This focus in the films on the genetic material of the posthuman mothers draws attention to the role played by genetics in defining identity. In Nayar's discussion of posthumanism and genetics, he notes that DNA has become "a language that supposedly encapsulates the body,"[31] which "is scriptable, reproducible, storable and readable."[32] This "readability" of DNA makes bodies into archives of data, which can then be copied, altered, or recreated. In the case of Rachael and Lockwood's daughter, we see this literally: in Wallace Corporation's attempt to use Rachael's bones to decode the genetics behind replicant reproduction and Lockwood's use of his deceased daughter's DNA to create a replacement child, the women are reduced to their bodies' data as DNA archives that can be manipulated and reproduced. This reduction of posthuman mothers to their bodies and genetic identity in these scenes is significant because it removes any agency they had in the creation of posthuman life and frames the existence of posthuman children within

[28]Christina Parker-Flynn, "Joe and the 'Real' Girls: *Blade Runner 2049*," *Gender Forum*, no. 66 (2017): 70.
[29]Ibid., 70.
[30]Ibid.
[31]Nayar, *Posthumanism*, 81.
[32]Ibid., 81.

FIGURE 4.2 *Claire Dearing (Bryce Dallas Howard) and Eli Mills (Rafe Spall) discuss the past and the future of the cloned dinosaurs while surrounded by dinosaur skeletons (J. A. Bayona (dir.),* Jurassic World: Fallen Kingdom, *2018, USA, © Universal City Studios and Amblin Entertainment).*

scientific contexts. Rather than being depicted as autonomous individuals, both women are instead represented in terms of their biological material and the ways in which that material can be used in scientific projects (Figure 4.2).

"An Overture to Something Much More Ambitious": Commodified Bodies and Reproductive Biovalue

Since the posthuman children are the focus of both films, this raises questions about *why* the posthuman mothers seem to lack the agency that posthuman children display. The discrepancy in the depiction of posthuman mothers as nothing more than biological material demonstrates that there are unresolved tensions about the role women play in the development of reproductive biotechnologies. The unresolved tensions surrounding the absent posthuman mothers in both films could arise from uncertainties about women's roles in a bioeconomy that is founded on the commodification of sources of reproductive biovalue. Waldby argues that one of the issues in the sale of reproductive tissues is that "[n]o other human tissue is so systematically ordered through significant money transactions, and this feature conditions the power relations between provider and recipient in particular ways."[33]

---

[33]Catherine Waldby, "Introduction," in *The Oocyte Economy: The Changing Meaning of Human Eggs* (Durham: Duke University Press, 2019), 6.

Part of what increases the biovalue of reproductive material in these "power relations" is that the "demand for research oocytes has proved almost impossible to meet"[34] since research labs must "compete with reproductive demand."[35] In both *2049* and *Fallen Kingdom*, we see the way that the "impossible to meet" demand of biological material for research projects— both Niander Wallace's experiments on replicant fertility and Eli Mill's secret genetics laboratory—results in power imbalances that exploit the bodies of female replicants, humans, and dinosaurs as sources of reproductive biovalue.

The commodification of reproductive material in both films is partially driven by the corporatization of the research process. In both films, there are extensive networks involved in the creation of replicants and dinosaurs, including characters such as CEOs, laboratory technicians, genetic designers, and business managers. This corporatization of the scientific process in both films is part of an ongoing trend in SF film. In an analysis of forty-eight SF films (including *Jurassic Park* and *Blade Runner*) that engage with synthetic biology (SB), Angela Meyer et al. found that, rather than prioritizing depictions of individual scientists, "film SB bio- and genetic engineers tend to be depicted as modern researchers with close ties to the industry or employed by large bio-tech firms. Their research is hence driven by a more entrepreneurial and market-driven than academic spirit."[36] Meyer et al. argue that the shift in depictions of scientists from individuals to corporate research teams results in uncertainty about the ethical responsibility of these teams toward their creations, since, "if synthetic biologists form a team, the question of who takes the responsibility is most often not sufficiently addressed and remains open."[37] Because of this uncertainty about who assumes ethical responsibility when the creation process involves a network of contributors, it is important to consider how *2049* and *Fallen Kingdom* depict the relationships between corporate entities, scientists and individuals who are created by or involved in biotechnological processes, and, particularly, what this means for posthuman mothers whose bodies are used as a source of biological material.

In *2049*, Wallace obsesses over replicant reproduction, lamenting his inability to design fertile replicants. While Wallace has dreams of colonizing more planets in space, he explains that fertile replicants are an essential component of this plan as a source of extra labor, noting, "[w]e need more replicants than can ever be assembled. Millions, so we can be trillions more." Vint argues that Wallace's obsession with fertile replicants

---

[34]Ibid., 9.

[35]Ibid.

[36]Angela Meyer, Amelie Cserer, and Markus Schmidt, "Frankenstein 2.0.: Identifying and Characterising Synthetic Biology Engineers in Science Fiction Films," *Life Sciences, Society and Policy* 9, no. 1 (2013): 15.

[37]Ibid., 13.

gestures to "the real subsumption of life by capital, the reorganisation of life processes on a cellular level in order to make them better serve capital."[38] By attempting to produce fertile replicants as a source of slave labor, Wallace seeks to biologically change female replicants to "better serve capital" and ascribes biovalue to the bodies of replicant mothers. This ascription of biovalue to fertile replicants becomes even more problematic when Wallace demonstrates that, in his eyes, infertile replicants are disposable. When a newly created female replicant is once again found to be infertile, Wallace regretfully considers "[t]hat barren pasture" before he kills her by stabbing her in the abdomen and letting her bleed to death. This scene shows the way that women can become disposable if their bodies are commodified. This replicant is not the only one to be murdered when she does not achieve what Wallace desires. When Wallace's attempt to bribe Deckard with the replicant resembling Rachael fails, the replicant, who is no longer useful to Wallace now that she has failed in her intended purpose of revealing the secret of Rachael's fertility, is shot and killed by Luv. Reproductive biovalue (or the *lack* of reproductive biovalue) quickly becomes a defining feature for the female replicants in *2049* and those who cannot reproduce become disposable in the eyes of Wallace Corporation.

The genetic material of various dinosaurs in *Fallen Kingdom* is similarly commodified. When Mills, who hopes to sell the remaining dinosaurs, invites an auctioneer (Toby Jones) to the Lockwood estate, the auctioneer is initially skeptical of the value of the dinosaurs. In a scene where Mills leads the auctioneer through the gallery filled with dinosaur bones, Mills explains that "[a]ll this is in the past. I wanna talk to you about the future." As the two men walk through the room, with the view framed by dinosaur bones that serve as a visual reminder of "the past" that Mills wants to ignore— the missing "mothers" of the recreated dinosaur species—Mills convinces the auctioneer that selling the existing dinosaurs is only "an overture to something much more ambitious" and that a future project promises to bring in even more money. The "much more ambitious" project, Mills reveals as he leads the auctioneer into the high-tech genetics laboratory in the basement, is the creation of a weaponized dinosaur species called the Indoraptor, which is a genetic mixture of the Indominus Rex and a velociraptor. These two dinosaurs are thus used as "mothers" for the creation of a new form of life, which Mills eventually sells for over $28 million dollars. When Mills attempts to reassure Dr. Henry Wu (BD Wong), the geneticist who created the Indoraptor, that they can create more copies to replace the prototype, he angrily responds, "[s]o will they!" The hesitation expressed by the Indoraptor's creator to sell the prototype stems from his desire to maintain

---

[38]Sherryl Vint, "Vitality and Reproduction in Blade Runner: 2049," *Science Fiction Film and Television* 13, no. 1 (2020): 15.

exclusive control over the dinosaur's genetic code and reproductive biovalue, rather than from ethical concerns about selling a weaponized bioengineered animal. The commodification and misuse of the genetic material of the dinosaur "mothers" thus highlights the way that, for the human characters, reproductive biovalue can outweigh ethical considerations.

While *Fallen Kingdom* does not show human women being exploited in the same way as the female dinosaurs, it is clear that Mills' creation and sale of the Indoraptor is only the beginning. At the start of the film, Dr. Ian Malcolm (Jeff Goldblum), a character who first appeared in *Jurassic Park*, warns the American government that genetic engineering "ain't gonna stop with the de-extinction of the dinosaurs." While the politicians do not seem to understand what Malcolm is implying, it becomes apparent to the audience throughout the film that the use of genetic engineering technologies could extend beyond the creation of commodified dinosaurs to humans themselves. When Mills fires Iris after Lockwood's death, Mills is unconcerned with Iris' insistence that Maisie needs someone who understands her, merely responding, "I understand her value." As the first human to be successfully cloned using the technology that had created the dinosaurs, Maisie represents a new source of biovalue that could be exploited in Mills' future projects. Later, when Claire and Owen threaten to stop Mills and expose him, he shouts, "[h]ow? You're gonna go back in time before Hammond decided to play God? You can't put it back in the box!" While it is never explicitly stated that human women will be exploited for their reproductive biovalue, the use of female dinosaurs as a source of genetic material and Mills' insinuation that genetic technologies cannot be contained implies that women will eventually be forced to support a

FIGURE 4.3 *Maisie (Isabella Sermon) discovers Mills' (Rafe Spall) secret genetics laboratory being used to design the Indoraptor, a weaponized hybrid dinosaur (J. A. Bayona (dir.).* Jurassic World: Fallen Kingdom, 2018, USA, © *Universal City Studios and Amblin Entertainment).*

bioeconomy founded on reproductive biovalue. In both *2049* and *Fallen Kingdom*, the commodification of bodies and the reduction of women to their reproductive biovalue has troubling ethical implications, and tensions remain about posthuman mothers and the role they play in the creation of posthuman children. Not only does the reduction of the posthuman mothers to their biological material remove their agency, but so too does it make it easier for the scientists and corporate entities in the films to retain control over nonhuman reproduction (Figure 4.3).

Biovalue and Posthuman Mothers

The contradictions present in the depictions of posthuman children as autonomous beings and posthuman mothers as biological material in *Blade Runner: 2049* and *Jurassic World: Fallen Kingdom* ultimately demonstrate that there are unresolved anxieties raised by the representation of the women who connect the human and nonhuman worlds, even as the films simultaneously encourage empathy toward their posthuman children. In her discussion of mothers and monstrosity, Shildrick argues that the relationship between female bodies and monstrosity reveals "a deep and abiding unease with female embodiment, and indeed with the corporeal in general."[39] The absence of the posthuman mothers in both films—and their visual association with bones and fragmented bodies—demonstrates the "deep and abiding unease with female embodiment" that Shildrick describes, particularly in the contexts of societies that commodify biological material. The tensions surrounding the depictions of posthuman mothers in both films demonstrate that lingering anxieties about women's bodies and their reproductive biovalue must still be resolved. Anxieties about women's bodies appear to be present in both *2049* and *Fallen Kingdom* as both films explore the commodification of reproductive and genetic material. This commodification of reproductive material has troubling implications: What does it mean for women when that reproductive material is commodified by scientific corporations, and how will these corporations maintain access to these materials?

In the depictions of bioeconomies in *2049* and *Fallen Kingdom*, even though the posthuman children are shown escaping from the corporations and individuals that would use them as a source of reproductive biovalue, neither of the posthuman mothers are given the same opportunity. Through their deaths before the events depicted in both films and the posthumous ascription of reproductive biovalue to their bodies, both Lockwood's unnamed daughter and Rachael each lose their bodily autonomy and

---

[39]Shildrick, "Monstering the (M)Other," 29.

their ability to make decisions about the way their bodies will be used in future scientific projects. When we consider these depictions of posthuman mothers in *2049* and *Fallen Kingdom* it becomes apparent that the biovalue ascribed to reproductive and genetic material can have complex implications for the women whose bodies are used as the source of these materials. By drawing attention to the way that new technologies can have an impact upon women's bodily autonomy, these films hold an important place in discussions of feminism and critical posthumanism. Michael Hauskeller et al. argue that SF film "demands a serious response" since "what it plays with, what it enacts, is what our own lives might one day turn out to be, and it does so at a time when we are fully aware that things are changing quickly, and that more drastic changes are likely to occur during our own lifetime, affecting what we are, how we think of ourselves and how we look at each other."[40] Through an examination of the ethical problems posed by posthuman figures in the SF films *Blade Runner: 2049* and *Jurassic World: Fallen Kingdom*, we can better understand how the ascription of biovalue to reproductive and genetic material could result in the exploitation of humans, nonhumans and animals, and the possible ethical issues that could arise from a bioeconomy based on reproductive biovalue.

---

[40]Michael Hauskeller, Thomas D. Philbeck, and Curtis D. Carbonell, eds., "Posthumanism in Film and Television," in *The Palgrave Handbook of Posthumanism in Film and Television* (London: Springer, 2016), 4.

5

Desirable and Undesirable Cyborg Bodies in the *Mass Effect* Video Game Trilogy

Sarah Stang

Canadian game studio BioWare's critically acclaimed and commercially successful *Mass Effect* video game trilogy (hereafter *ME*)[1] has been lauded as "one of the most important pieces of science fiction narrative of our generation" because of its "ability to reflect on our society as a whole."[2] Although *ME* is certainly a grand space opera worthy of consideration, the way it positions and frames nonhuman and transhuman or posthuman bodies is often deeply problematic. Specifically, while *ME* ostensibly promotes acceptance of nonhuman others—particularly aliens and synthetic beings— it positions the cyborg body as a site of horror and revulsion, framing the cybernetic enhancement of organic bodies as a kind of disease, infection, or mutation. In a troubled and often contradictory approach, this framing also dictates which bodies are desirable or undesirable from a heterosexual male perspective: female and feminized bodies are portrayed as sexualized and alluring only if they are purely organic, purely synthetic, or able to "pass" as organic by hiding their synthetic parts. On the other hand, visibly hybrid female cyborg bodies are presented as monstrous and horrific. While there

---

[1] I refer to the *Mass Effect* trilogy here (BioWare, 2007–12) because I am only examining the first three games in the series. While there is a fourth game, *Mass Effect: Andromeda* (2017), it is not part of the main trilogy and tells a different story set in a different galaxy.
[2] Kyle Munkittrick, "Why Mass Effect Is the Most Important Science Fiction Universe of Our Generation," *Pop Bioethics* (2012), para. 1–2.

are many male-coded human and nonhuman characters and creatures in the games, they are not othered in relation to their gender, whereas *ME* is particularly preoccupied with framing female bodies as only either desirable and available for romance or monstrous and positioned as an enemy to be killed.

This chapter is a close reading of *ME*'s portrayal of cyborg bodies and what I call "techno-zombies"—corpses that have been mutated and reanimated with cybernetic implants. This analysis uncovers how the series' portrayal of cyborg bodies draws on established science fiction (SF) tropes to demarcate strict boundaries around the "acceptable" ways bodies can be technologically enhanced and to mitigate the potential threat that technologically augmented/empowered women pose within patriarchal society by forcing them into only one of two representational categories— sex object or monster—thereby objectifying, othering, and dehumanizing them within the narrative. In addition, *ME*'s portrayal of nonhuman bodies, whether acceptable, sexualized, or monstrous, reinforces an anthropocentric worldview, underscoring the primacy and desirability of the normative human body. In this way, even though *ME* features a posthuman setting populated by nonhumans, the series is not critically posthumanist, in that it fails to destabilize or decentralize the human. Questions of posthumanism are particularly important to consider in video games, as the audience is not only encouraged to identify with the human protagonist but also tasked with embodying that protagonist and enacting the narrative events. As I discuss, gameplay can therefore be problematic when games require the player to kill nonhuman characters and creatures, thereby providing a virtual enactment of anthropocentric violence and forcing the player to be complicit in establishing the primacy and dominance of the human within the series' world.

Alien vs. Human, Organic vs. Synthetic

Set in a not-too-distant future in which humanity has joined a kind of galactic federation of alien races, the *ME* trilogy's protagonist—which in video games is also the player's avatar or player-character (hereafter PC)—is the heroic Commander Shepard, a human man or woman in charge of a space ship crewed by human and nonhuman characters.[3] Vanessa Erat has argued that the nonhuman species in the *ME* universe are made to "conform to a

---

[3] In the *ME* trilogy players can choose the sex (a binary choice between male and female) and basic appearance of their PC (facial features, skin color, and hair style and color). While these options are welcome in a medium dominated by white male PCs, the Commander Shepard the player can create must still be a human with a normative appearance.

human code of conduct that is repeatedly instigated as the implicit norm."[4] She reads the series' portrayal of some of the alien species as representing real-world subaltern groups and demonstrates how the game prioritizes an elitist, imperialist, Western human (and Humanist) perspective. In addition to adhering to many human—particularly Western—behavioral norms, the main alien species presented in the series as central characters, companions, and love interests are all humanoid in design; although they may have distinct features that clearly indicate their alienness, they are all bipedal, with two arms, one head, one mouth, and so on. Some alien species, like the Asari, are almost completely humanoid, and, as I discuss in more detail later, they are an all-female species made up of conventionally attractive, blue-skinned women and are presented as sexually and romantically desirable throughout the series. Although there are a few alien species who are significantly less humanoid, they are minor characters, only rarely encountered, and are not present as companions, party members, or love interests.

Aside from alien-human relations, the series focuses on exploring the tension and conflict between organic beings and the synthetic life they create. The games explore this tension using both well-known and more unique SF tropes: enslaved, hive-mind robots called the Geth gain sentience and rise up against their creators, taking over the planet and forcing their former masters into a diaspora; the artificial intelligence that runs Shepard's ship gains possession of a sexualized gynoid body, falls in love with a human man, and goes through various existential crises; humans with cybernetic implants that grant them telekinetic powers are used as soldiers but are viewed with distrust by the rest of society; one of Shepard's crewmates is a genetically engineered, artificially conceived, and technologically enhanced "perfect" woman; Shepard dies but is resurrected and reconstructed through forbidden alien technology, making him/her question how human he/she actually is; and the main antagonists of the series, the Reapers, are a species of giant, highly advanced, artificially intelligent, techno-organic beings whose purpose is to destroy (or "reap") all advanced organic life in the galaxy.

The trilogy's ending has the player decide whether all synthetic life should be destroyed, if it should be reined in and controlled directly by Shepard, or if a posthuman "synthesis" of all organic and synthetic life—effectively rendering everything a cyborg, including plants and animals—is the best way to save the galaxy. The synthesis choice is presented as the most "just" one, as it means cooperation instead of genocide or oppression, and would theoretically make everyone equal in their hybridity. On the other hand, throughout the series,

---

[4]Vanessa Erat, "A (Dis)United Galaxy: The Silenced Voices of Non-Human Minorities in BioWare's *Mass Effect*," in *Levelling Up: The Cultural Impact of Videogames*, ed. Brittany Kuhn and Alexia Bhéreur-Lagounaris (Oxford: Inter-Disciplinary Press, 2016), 93.

humans and humanoid beings are centralized, and the story is told from a contemporary human perspective; technological augmentation is framed as an "infection" or "contagion" that threatens bodily autonomy; and cyborg existence is variously framed as undesirable and dehumanizing, associated with ruthlessness and cruelty, or presented as a grotesque and horrific living death. While the ending allows for the creation of a seemingly egalitarian, posthuman utopia, *ME*'s vision of synthetic-organic fusion is contradictory and technophobic. In this sense, the series highlights and reinforces the ambivalent positioning of the nonhuman and/or cyborg—or any kind of liminal, hybrid body—in popular culture, underscoring the desirability of humanoid bodies, purely human bodies, or bodies that can pass as human.

Undesirable Bodies: Cyborgs Who Cannot "Pass"

Cyborg identity is framed as undesirable in several ways. This is communicated most overtly through Shepard, who ostensibly dies at the end of the first game but is revived by Cerberus, the human supremacist organization, using technological enhancements, including cybernetic implants, "skin weaves," and artificial organs. This revival makes Shepard a kind of "techno-zombie" but with retained sapience, a kind of cyborg Frankenstein's monster. This monstrosity is visibly signaled by extensive facial scarring, although Shepard's appearance changes over the course of the second and third games based on the player's choices. While Shepard ends up being the heroic savior of the galaxy no matter what, the player can make unethical choices, which usually involve using violence to solve problems and are clearly signaled through red text. If enough of these kinds of choices are made, Shepard becomes a "Renegade" hero. On the other hand, if the player chooses to take the moral high ground—kinder, nonviolent choices that are indicated with blue text—Shepard becomes a "Paragon." If Shepard is a Paragon, his/her facial scarring lessens over time, eventually disappearing altogether, and his/her appearance becomes more normative. If Shepard is a Renegade, his/her scarring deepens, and his/her eyes and scars start glowing red, signaling his/her "evil" moral alignment. While this is explained in-game as negative actions causing physiological stress that prevents Shepard's body from healing properly, making the implants more visible, it adheres to the common cultural trope of aligning goodness with attractiveness and evil with ugliness or physical disfigurement.[5] This is an ableist trope found throughout popular culture

---

[5] For more on this, see David T. Mitchell and Sharon L. Snyder, *Narrative Prosthesis: Disability and the Dependencies of Discourse* (Ann Arbor: University of Michigan Press, 2000).

that not only reinforces normative beauty standards but, in the case of *ME*, establishes the distrust and hostility toward cyborgs that is reinforced through this implicit alignment of cyborg appearance with questionable moral integrity, cruelty, ruthlessness, and violent behavior. It also suggests that technological augmentation is like a disease or infection that spreads, deepens, and disfigures Shepard's body, thereby calling into question his/her bodily well-being and even his/her humanity. For example, during a conversation with the artificially intelligent gynoid EDI in *ME3*, she jokingly suggests that Shepard's implants and augmentations make him/her "transhuman," noting that humans "have diverse and contentious opinions" on the matter. Shepard becomes agitated at this suggestion, and EDI reassures him/her that she considers Shepard "fully human" because his/her brain functions are organic, regardless of how much the rest of his/her body has been restructured. Shepard does not appreciate the humor, warning her to never make such a joke again, thereby firmly establishing that he/she would *not* want to be considered transhuman, even though he/she clearly is.

This conversation firmly communicates that Shepard—the character with whom the player is meant to identify—values his/her humanity and fears the idea of becoming something not entirely human. As N. Katharine Hayles has noted, posthumanism can be terrifying because it suggests a superseding of the human, implying that humanity's days are numbered.[6] This is perhaps why posthuman narratives like *ME* inadvertently or purposefully reaffirm Humanist ideologies, norms, and values—these stories are posthuman but not posthumanist. Judy Ehrentraut has argued that popular culture reinforces "normative and dogmatic ideas about technology's place in the human world that frame it as dehumanizing and oppositional on the one hand, or transcendent and empowering on the other."[7] This dichotomy speaks to how *ME*'s technophobia and anthropocentrism manifest in its portrayal of cyborg bodies and technology as something that infects, threatens, or intrudes upon the human.

Shepard's resurrection and cyborg body makes some characters uncomfortable, but this strong reaction against being anything other than human feels out of place or contradictory, considering that Shepard is conversing with a gynoid, is friends with several nonhumans, and many characters in the series are technologically enhanced with "biotic implants" that grant them telekinetic powers and are therefore "transhuman." Because of these implants, those with biotics can be read as cyborgs whose

---

[6]N. Katherine Hayles, *How We Became Posthuman: Virtual Bodies in Cybernetics, Literature, and Informatics* (University of Chicago Press, 1999).

[7]Judy Ehrentraut, "Disentangling the Posthuman: Broadening Perspectives of Human/Machine Mergers through Inter-relational Subjectivity" (PhD diss., University of Waterloo, 2019), iv.

technological aspects grant them preternatural abilities. While there is widespread distrust and prejudice in human cultures toward those with biotic implants, they are valued as soldiers; most importantly, the implants are not visible, and so these biotic soldiers can pass as fully organic. This is relevant because the degree to which a character is visibly cyborgian has an impact upon their positioning in the series: cyborgs that can fully pass are treated with suspicion but general acceptance, cybernetic implants that are visible on the face suggest moral deficiency or corruption, and entirely cyborgian bodies are framed as grotesque and monstrous. This reflects Anne Balsamo's argument that there are "degrees of cyborgism" that shape how cyborg bodies are represented and perceived, rather than a straightforward organic-synthetic dichotomy.[8] This is not uncommon in SF narratives: for example, in *Guardians of the Galaxy*, although both Gamora and her sister Nebula are cyborgs, Gamora has far fewer cybernetic parts, and they are not overtly visible. Nebula, on the other hand, has fewer organic parts and so is more visibly cyborgian. It is not a coincidence that Nebula is the "bad," violent, emotionally unstable sister, at least until she has a change of heart in the second film in the series.

Another way that cyborg identity is presented as undesirable is through the presentation of one of the series' main antagonists and the leader of Cerberus, the Illusive Man. He believes that technological augmentation is the key to human dominance in the galaxy and seeks to use the ancient, advanced technology of the Reapers to advance humanity's position and power. The Reapers corrupt and brainwash individuals to help them carry out their plans, turning them into spies to help bring down their own civilizations—a process called "indoctrination." They also use a form of violent, accelerated indoctrination to infect organic corpses with cybernetic implants, transforming them into mindless cyborg techno-zombies. During his studies of Reaper indoctrination, the Illusive Man allowed himself to be implanted with Reaper nanotechnology and become indoctrinated. Like a Renegade Shepard, the Illusive Man has visible cybernetic implants on his face, making him look like he has a cyborgian skin disease (see Figure 5.1). According to *The Art of the Mass Effect Universe*, the developers initially intended for the Illusive Man to transform into a giant cyborg monster during the final battle in the trilogy.[9] Although they scrapped the idea, the Illusive Man is another example of visible cybernetic implants serving as an indicator of ruthlessness and evil, and, in extreme cases, signaling the (potential) transformation into a monstrous creature.

---

[8] Anne Marie Balsamo, *Technologies of the Gendered Body: Reading Cyborg Women* (Durham: Duke University Press, 1996).
[9] Dave Marshall, ed. *The Art of the Mass Effect Universe* (Milwaukie: Dark Horse Comics, 2012).

FIGURE 5.1 *An image of the Illusive Man. His eyes are glowing blue and his skin has split on his face, revealing glowing blue cybernetics underneath. The character is voice acted by Martin Sheen (BioWare, Mass Effect 3, 2012, USA, Electronic Arts).*

The physical appearance of both Shepard and the Illusive Man informs the player that morality is tied to how "normal" a person looks—though neither character is really objectified based on their physical appearance. Even if players choose a female Shepard, she is presented in a manner similar to the male version, including the way she sits and walks and is framed by the camera. The female version is essentially a replacement model for the default male version and therefore many of the character animations are the same.[10] However, like many video games (and SF media in general) created by men,[11] the *ME* trilogy is rife with misogynistic tropes and sexualized

---

[10]James Bishop, "Analysis: On FemShep's Popularity In *Mass Effect*," *Gamasutra*, September 8, 2010. https://www.gamasutra.com/view/news/120927/Analysis_On_FemSheps_Popularity_In _Mass_Effect.php.
[11]The creators of the trilogy—Preston Watamaniuk, Drew Karpyshyn, and Casey Hudson—are all men, as are all the lead directors, designers, programmers, artists, and writers. While having a male-dominated creative team does not necessarily mean that the game will be problematic, several game scholars have attributed misogynistic game content at least in part to the dearth of game creators who identify as anything other than a heterosexual male (e.g., see Alison Harvey and Stephanie Fisher, "'Everyone Can Make Games!': The post-feminist context of women in digital game production," *Feminist Media Studies* 15, no. 4 (2014): 576–92).

female characters. As Carlen Lavigne has observed, "*Mass Effect* is not a feminist text":

It was obviously designed with the straight male gamer in mind; it is otherwise difficult to comprehend the reasoning behind the consistently slender yet large-breasted female aliens, the skin-tight catsuits and the exploitative camera angles that dominate the series.[12]

Indeed, nearly every main female character in the trilogy is designed to appeal to a heterosexual male player: sexualized in their physical appearance, in the way other characters talk about them, and even in the game's cinematography. Not only are these characters designed to conform to ideal and exceedingly narrow female beauty standards, the game's camera lingers on their bodies—especially their buttocks—in several shots, an obviously fetishistic choice that has been repeatedly critiqued by game critics and scholars as catering to what Laura Mulvey famously conceptualized as the male gaze.[13] The three most common objects of this fetishistic-voyeuristic male gaze are the Asari, a pansexual, all-female alien species that look like conventionally attractive, albeit blue-skinned, women;[14] EDI, a naked, highly sexualized artificially intelligent gynoid whose design was inspired by Maria from *Metropolis*;[15] and Miranda Lawson, a genetically engineered "perfect" transhuman woman designed to look like a femme fatale. While all these characters are interesting to consider from a posthuman and feminist perspective, Miranda is the only cyborg, as EDI is purely synthetic, and the Asari are purely organic. Miranda is therefore a compelling example of the intersection of anthropocentrism and sexism at play in *ME*: hers is a desirable cyborg body—one that is not only conventionally attractive and sexualized but can pass as a fully organic and fully human woman.

---

[12]Carlen Lavigne, "'She's a Soldier, not a Model': Feminism, FemShep and the *Mass Effect 3* Vote," *Journal of Gaming & Virtual Worlds* 7, no. 3 (2015): 318.

[13]See Ibid.; Leandro Augusto Borges Lima, "Configurative Dynamics of Gender in Bioware's Marketing for the Mass Effect Franchise," *Kinephanos* 7, no. 1 (2017): 165–97; and Tracey John, "The Thoughts Behind Miranda's Behind In Mass Effect 2," *Kotaku*, 2010. https://www.kotaku.com.au/2010/04/the-thoughts-behind-mirandas-behind-in-mass-effect-2/

[14]The Asari fall into the "green-skinned space babe" trope, established as far back as the first episode of *Star Trek: The Original Series* and still common in mainstream sci-fi (see TVtropes, "Green-Skinned Space Babe." https://tvtropes.org/pmwiki/pmwiki.php/Main/GreenSkinnedSpaceBabe). They are entirely human in appearance except for a few minor features which give them an "exotic" look, including the blue (and sometimes green, purple, or teal) skin color. Although the Asari are monogendered, the game still refers to them as an "all-female" species and presents them as conforming to stereotypical female appearances and gender roles. Besides being designed with breasts and female-sounding voices, the Asari generally use female pronouns, refer to their offspring as their "daughters," and commonly appear as sexualized exotic dancers. If not exotic dancers, they are encountered as mercenaries that the player must fight and kill, meaning that the Asari primarily exist to be sexualized or murdered.

[15]Marshall, *The Art of the Mass Effect Universe*, 134.

Desirable Bodies: Cyborgs Who Can "Pass"

Modeled after and voice acted by Yvonne Strahvoski, Miranda Lawson is the artificially created daughter of a rich and powerful man who made her by taking his own DNA and doubling his X-chromosome. He genetically engineered her to be a specimen of human perfection in terms of intelligence, physical constitution, appearance, and biotic abilities. She is capable and confident, but also narcissistic, snide, and condescending, though she does warm up to Shepard, depending on player choices. She is a romance option for a male Shepard, and, according to a poll published by PC Gamer, Miranda is the second most popular love interest for players.[16] Several gaming outlets applaud Miranda's design and list her as one of the "hottest" video game characters of all time, while more critical, feminist analyses of the character critique Miranda as a "boring femme fatale type whose screen time includes opportunistic angles on her ass" and who is a pretentious, cruel "product of wealth and masculine power structures."[17]

Miranda is technically a cyborg in that she has cybernetic implants that augment her abilities and her status as "human" is called into question because she was artificially created and genetically engineered—in this sense she is transhuman, the very thing Shepard fears being labeled—but in terms of her physical appearance she can pass as fully organic. She does not appear hybrid in any discernable way, and so her body is desirable. Not only was it designed to be desirable to the heterosexual male gaze by the game's developers (her literal creators), in the game's narrative she was also designed by her father (her in-game creator) to be desirable in the same way. In this sense, the game's designers have crafted a "rationale" for her hypersexualization, and BioWare's marketing director, David Silverman, has even defended the numerous fetishistic shots of her buttocks because her physical appearance—specifically "her curves and sexuality"—is an integral part of her character.[18] The trilogy's director Casey Hudson has similarly defended her skin-tight uniform and the camera angles and shots employed to accentuate and fetishize her body—such as the shot that lingers on her buttocks indefinitely while the player makes dialogue choices

---

[16]Tyler Wilde, "Ranking the Best and Worst of the Mass Effect Games," *PC Gamer*, August 7, 2015. https://www.pcgamer.com/ranking-the-best-and-worst-of-the-mass-effect-games/. Note that, according to that same poll, the most popular love interest is Liara, an Asari. She is one of the few bisexual characters, so she is the most popular option for both a male and female Shepard.
[17]Soha Kareem, "Mashing Our Buttons: On Romance and Sex in Video Games," in *The Secret Loves of Geek Girls*, ed. Hope Nicholson, Expanded ed. (Milwaukie: Dark Horse Books, 2016), 119.
[18]Qtd. in Brenna Hiller, "Loving FemShep: BioWare's First Lady Finally Steps Forward," *VG24/7*, para. 28. https://www.vg247.com/2011/07/19/loving-femshep-biowares-first-lady-finally-steps-forward/.

FIGURE 5.2 *This image shows how the camera lingers on a close-up of Miranda's buttocks during a dialogue selection in conversation with her. Since her outfit is skintight, this shot is very revealing. Miranda is voiced acted by and modeled to resemble Yvonne Strahovski (BioWare, Mass Effect 2, 2010, USA, Electronic Arts).*

(see Figure 5.2)—as just "part of her character design" because "she's the femme fatale."[19] And yet, Miranda does not really ever use her beauty to her advantage or behave in the game like a film noir femme fatale;[20] therefore, as John points out, it seems that the camera lingers on her body more than most other characters simply because she was designed to cater to the male gaze, demonstrating that "the game was not made with female gamers in mind, even though many women may play it."[21] While her body might appeal to a lesbian player, the *Mass Effect* series was created by an almost entirely male development team, and the marketing for the series strongly suggests that it was intended for a presumed male player base.[22] It is not a stretch therefore to read the presentation of Miranda's body as gratuitous and sexualizing. This argument is reinforced by the fact that Miranda is not the only female character sexualized in this way: Jack, another powerful human biotic—in other words another cyborg who can pass as fully organic—is effectively topless, with only leather straps covering her nipples. Although the shots of her body are not as gratuitous as those of Miranda, she is another example of how the game sexualizes (some) female bodies.

---

[19]Qtd. in John, "The Thoughts," para. 14.
[20]See Mary Anne Doane, *Femmes Fatales: Feminism, Film Theory, Psychoanalysis* (New York: Routledge, 1991).
[21]John, "The Thoughts," para. 16.
[22]See Lima, "Configurative Dynamics."

Deadly Bodies: Monstrous Cyborgs
and Seductive Aliens

Ehrentraut has pointed out that human-technological development and progress "has been persistently linked to the domination of other humans, non-human species, and environments."[23] This helps to explain why technology, especially as wielded by technologically advanced or superior alien/cyborg/robot species, has been portrayed so often in SF as "a foreboding, unstoppable force" that threatens humanity, thereby contributing to a "rigid binary logic separating organic from inorganic, human from machine."[24] This technophobia serves to underscore a fear or distrust toward technology (especially if wielded by nonhumans against humans) and cyborgs. In *ME*, technophobia (or perhaps more accurately, "cyborg-phobia") reaches its zenith with the design of the Reapers' techno-zombies, as they are mutated, abject monstrosities that exist to be fought and killed by the player. Humans who are infected by the Reapers mutate into "Husks," which look like zombies covered with visible blue cybernetic parts. In addition to human-derived Husks, the other main humanoid species also have their own unique and similarly horrific forms of techno-zombification. These monsters evoke anxieties around mutation and the loss of bodily autonomy through possession/infection by a technological other and reinforce a distrust of hybridity and the collapsing of boundaries it entails. This is important because, according to feminist philosopher Julia Kristeva, the collapsing of boundaries signals the abject by threatening the divide between self and other, human and nonhuman: the abject subject is one who embodies the "in-between, the ambiguous, the composite,"[25] and is "heterogenous . . . metamorphosed, altered."[26] The mutation and hybridity of these monsters is therefore central to their abjection, and because it draws one "toward the place where meaning collapses," the abject must be "radically excluded" or repressed from normative, patriarchal thought, behavior, and society.[27] One way of repressing the abject is by framing it as monstrous and horrific, and, in the case of the techno-zombies, by destroying it.

While the abject is articulated as evoking both fear and disgust—reactions more common in body horror than SF—*ME* occupies a middle ground between the two genres in its design and presentation of these monstrous cyborgs. This generic blending is signaled in the visual design of the monsters

---

[23]Ehrentraut, "Disentangling the Posthuman," 5–6.
[24]Ibid., 6.
[25]Julia Kristeva, *Powers of Horror: An Essay on Abjection* (New York: Columbia University Press, 1982), 4.
[26]Ibid., 207.
[27]Ibid., 2.

FIGURE 5.3 *An image of a Banshee, who looks like a partially decomposed, monstrous, blue-skinned woman with a skeletal face, gaping mouth, long, sharp claws, a distended belly, and cybernetic implants throughout her body (BioWare, Mass Effect 3, 2012, USA, Electronic Arts).*

themselves (their corpse-like appearance and their mutated and unnatural bodies), the atmospheric design of the scenes in which they are encountered (including unsettling music, dark spaces, and jump scares), and the ways in which they move and behave (they sprint or shuffle slowly, swarm or suddenly teleport, scream or roar with uncanny voices, and viciously attack the PC). While every type of techno-zombie is interesting to analyze in terms of body horror, only one kind is visibly gendered and so will be the focus of this discussion: the "Banshee" (see Figure 5.3).

Banshees are created from the Ardat-Yakshi, meaning "Demon of the Night Winds"—a rare type of Asari whose unusual genetic makeup makes them infertile and unable to control their own biotic powers when mating, causing them to overwhelm and destroy their partner's nervous system. Most Ardat-Yakshi are given a choice between execution or being exiled to a monastery where they are kept as prisoners to prevent them from mating. While Miranda is described as and designed to look like a femme fatale, she does not actually engage in sexually manipulative or predatory behavior, nor does she pose a threat to the PC. The true *femmes fatales* of the series are the Ardat-Yakshi, and one side quest in *ME2* even requires the player to hunt down a serial killer Ardat-Yakshi named Morinth who tries to seduce Shepard and will kill him/her if he/she is unable to resist her.

As if it were not enough to have a genetic mutation that makes them infertile, turns them into social pariahs, and dooms them to either a celibate life in a monastery or a violent life as a serial killer, in the third installment of the series the Ardat-Yakshi are all turned into horrific monstrosities called Banshees for Shepard to fight. The Reapers exclusively target the Ardat-Yakshi, and not other Asari, perhaps because of their superior biotic abilities, meaning that even the "good" Ardat-Yakshi who turned themselves in to the monastery to live a life of celibacy are punished for being deviant, defective, different: turned into actual monsters, stripped of their agency, and then murdered by the PC. There is no exception to this horrific fate: even if the player chose to spare Morinth in the previously mentioned side quest, she appears as a Banshee in *ME3* and must be killed.

Very Undesirable Bodies: Screaming Pregnant Cyborg Monsters

The physical appearance of the Banshee is noteworthy for several reasons. As previously mentioned, they are the only clearly gendered mutant—the Banshee has breasts as well as a visible vulva, though it is only noticeable during battle scenes when the camera angles in close to that part of its body.[28] Although the others are derived from any gender of human or alien, they appear to become genderless or coded as male when transformed, whereas the Banshees are designed and presented as horrific in relation to their biological femaleness. In addition, the Banshees are cyborgs that cannot pass as fully organic—their technological augmentation, their hybridity, is centralized in their design and so intertwined with their horror. This clearly juxtaposes them with sexualized but nonhybrid naked characters like EDI—whose nudity is framed as desirable rather than repulsive—and cyborg women, like Miranda, who can pass as fully human. Finally, for an unexplained reason, the Banshees have distended bellies, as though they are pregnant. Since the Ardat-Yakshi are infertile, their design suggests that the developers simply figured that screaming, naked, monstrous corpse-like women attacking the player would be more unsettling if they *also looked pregnant*. This, combined with the exposed breasts, glowing nipples, and visible female genitals, serves to highlight the fact that the Banshees are monstrous in relation to their biological femaleness.

---

[28]I would like to emphasize that none of the other mutated creatures have visible genitals—the (male) designers of the Banshees created *a graphic texture of female genitals*, in addition to their breasts and glowing nipples, as though they wanted players to be sure that these monsters are female. This, combined with the series' lingering close-up shots of female characters' breasts and buttocks, and the skin-tight uniform female characters wear—which is so tight it even causes the hypersexualized gynoid EDI to have a visible "camel toe" when she wears it—demonstrate the developers' clear preoccupation with turning the female body into a spectacle.

As pregnant alien cyborg monsters, the Banshees exemplify the ways that "woman" is constructed as monstrous within patriarchal society. Barbara Creed has observed that "all human societies have a conception of the monstrous-feminine, of what it is about woman that is shocking, terrifying, horrific, abject."[29] Rosi Braidotti has echoed Creed's observations, noting that there exists a "traditional patriarchal association of women with monstrosity" and that "the female body shares with the monster the privilege of bringing out a unique blend of fascination and horror."[30] That fascination and horror are often tied to revulsion and fear toward female sexuality and fecundity, particularly when women are nonnormative or transgressive in any way. Jane Ussher has noted that "the corporeality of the changing pregnant body . . . stand[s] at the pinnacle of that which signifies abjection."[31] Perhaps this is why the Banshees are particularly horrifying: they evoke the abject in the same ways the other techno-zombies do because they are mutated, infected, hybrid, screaming, mindless monstrosities, but they go beyond that level of horror by also being naked, pregnant women.[32] However, as Ussher also points out,

[T]his is not to say that the female body *is* abject or polluted, it has merely been positioned as such, with significant implications for women's experiences of inhabiting a body so defined. One of the implications is the positioning of woman as inherently deviant, or dangerous, because of her fecundity.[33]

Monstrous female representations like the Banshees and the harmful messages regarding pregnancy, gender, and embodiment they communicate are therefore important to consider and critically analyze—particularly because they are positioned in the series as enemies for the player to fight and kill.

Monsters like the Banshees might make for exciting enemies to fight, but rendering them monstrous in association with aspects of both cyborg hybridity and biological femaleness is problematic. Given that Shepard can mostly pass as fully human—especially if the player makes what the developers

---

[29]Barbara Creed, "Horror and the Monstrous-Feminine: An Imaginary Abjection," *Screen* 27, no. 1 (1986): 44.
[30]Rosi Braidotti, *Nomadic Subjects: Embodiment and Sexual Difference in Contemporary Feminist Theory* (New York: Columbia University Press, 1994), 80–1.
[31]Jane M. Ussher, *Managing the Monstrous Feminine: Regulating the Reproductive Body* (Routledge, 2006), 87.
[32]BioWare is clearly preoccupied with this idea, as these themes of enraged and abused women, horrific maternity, bodily transformation, and infection-as-impregnation are paralleled in their fantasy role-playing game *Dragon Age: Origins* (2009) with the monstrous Broodmother (see Sarah Stang, "The Broodmother as Monstrous-Feminine: Abject Maternity in Video Games," *Nordlit* 42 (2019): 233–56.
[33]Ussher, *Managing the Monstrous*, 6; emphasis in original.

have determined to be "good" moral choices[34]—the PC therefore functions as a representative of normative, dominant, organic society. As a "hero," Shepard (i.e., the player) regularly enacts violence against technologically othered beings—cyborgs who cannot pass and so are not allowed to survive. This is why studying the monstrous in video games is a unique task: players do not simply watch the cathartic re-enactment of heteropatriarchal violence directed at nonnormative and transgressive bodies—they *perform* it. In this sense, games like the *Mass Effect* series are inherently designed to resist productive, nuanced, or critical posthumanism, and instead reinforce "us-versus-them" or "self-versus-other" (in this case "human-versus-nonhuman" or "organic-versus-synthetic") attitudes through the act of play.

Misogyny and Technophobia

Blending body horror with SF to create this aesthetic of techno-abjection allows BioWare to approach the posthuman or transhuman through the pathways of fear, anxiety, and technophobia. In other words, rather than attempting to decentralize or destabilize the human, the *ME* series reinforces the primacy and desirability of the human—that is, a very specific definition of the human—by making the posthuman something to fear. As Daniel Dinello observes, SF often presents technology as a virus or parasite:

> Voracious in its urge to possess and engulf, technology is a parasite that frequently undermines human integrity—invisibly infiltrating, manipulating, seizing control, and mutating its human host to support its own survival and evolution.[35]

Framing technology as a virus means that humans (or other organic beings) become "mere carriers of the techno-disease" and serve "as a breeding medium that combines and recombines technological structures to produce new mutations that may ultimately result in the extinction of humanity."[36] By combining this techno-plague anxiety with the physical abjection of

---

[34]For a discussion of the morality system in the *Mass Effect* series, see Andy Boyan et al. "A Massively Moral Game? Mass Effect as a Case Study to Understand the Influence of Players' Moral Intuitions on Adherence to Hero or Antihero Play Styles," *Journal of Gaming & Virtual Worlds* 7, no. 1 (2015): 41–57; Mia Consalvo et al., "Playing a Better Me: How Players Rehearse Their Ethos via Moral Choices," *Games and Culture* 14, no. 3 (2016): 216–35; and Amanda Lange, "'You're Just Gonna Be Nice': How Players Engage with Moral Choice Systems," *Journal of Games Criticism* 1, no. 1 (2014): 1–16.
[35]Daniel Dinello, *Technophobia!: Science Fiction Visions of Posthuman Technology* (University of Texas Press, 2005), 247.
[36]Ibid.

the infected techno-zombies, BioWare created monstrosities that the player would *want* to kill.

Crucially, the techno-zombie is presented as a horrific other through a lens that assumes that the only desirable form is that of a normative human. Even though the Banshee is a creature that has technically no "human" in it—it is a mutated cyborg Asari—its body is presented as abject and horrifying in human (and misogynistic) aesthetic terms. In this sense, the series once again privileges a human perspective in its categorization of certain bodies as horrific, undesirable, and monstrous. Cyborgs literally embody the series' preoccupation with the relationship between the synthetic and the organic. Shepard is both a hero and a cyborg, and the trilogy's "synthesis" ending allows players to choose to blend synthetic and organic life throughout the entire galaxy, presenting a seemingly utopian, posthuman future. And yet, the series' monsters (and villains) are made monstrous precisely because of that techno-organic blending; the cyborg body, especially the female cyborg body, is positioned as undesirable if it is too visibly hybrid, as desirability is defined in human (female) terms in relation to human (male) desires.

Although Donna Haraway has argued that the cyborg, or monstrosity and hybridity more generally, are ambiguous and transgressive and so potentially empowering for women,[37] the ludic female monster, alien, or cyborg does not exist because she chooses to—she is designed, coded, and rendered (usually by male developers) to be either objectified and romanced or confronted and slain (usually by male characters). She is not, therefore, inherently transgressive; rather, she is a misogynistic, anthropocentric construct that is designed to reinforce hegemonic ideology and uphold the primacy of normative (and above all, human) bodies, behaviors, and gender dynamics. This is an unfortunately common way in which the female cyborg functions in popular culture: as Mary Ann Doane has demonstrated, the representation of "techno-femininity" in SF cinema is used to reinforce rather than destabilize gendered stereotypes.[38] Similarly, Balsamo has argued that, regardless of their potentials, technological development and augmentation are still heavily influenced by patriarchal gender norms and boundaries.[39] In mainstream SF there is a clear distinction between female cyborgs like Miranda whose bodies are fetishized and sexualized, and

[37]See Donna Haraway, *Simians, Cyborgs and Women: The Reinvention of Nature* (New York: Routledge, 1991) and Donna Haraway, "Promises of Monsters: A Regenerative Politics for Inappropriate/d Others," in *Cultural Studies*, ed. Lawrence Grossberg, Cary Nelson, and Paula A. Treichler (New York: Routledge, 1992), 295–337.
[38]See Doane, "Technophilia: Technology, Representation and the Feminine," in *Body/Politics: Women and the Discourses of Science*, ed. Mary Jacobus, Evelyn Fox Keller, and Sally Shuttleworth (London and New York: Routledge, 1990), 163–76.
[39]See Balsamo, *Technologies*, 1996.

"the vicious female cyborg that represents the patriarchal fear of female sexuality," such as the Banshee.[40] As Braidotti has argued, women's bodies have been "forever associated with unholy, disorderly, subhuman and unsightly phenomena,"[41] and this misogynistic association is exemplified in the naked, screaming, pregnant, monstrous, cyborg Banshee—especially considering that the Banshee is the only techno-zombie designed to be recognizably gendered.

While there is always potential for subversive and oppositional interpretations and reclamations, especially of ambiguous figures like the hybrid cyborg or monster, that potential is undermined by the manner in which the game frames these characters. Presenting female bodies as horrific and repulsive is just as harmful as overtly sexualizing them—in either case, those bodies are presented as spectacles and objects of male desire or revulsion, existing to be either romanced or murdered. This choice also sends a clear message that this game was not intended for female players (regardless of the actual player demographic and the ability to play as a female hero) and situates the series within a long tradition in popular culture of positioning the female body as something to be desired and sexualized or feared and reviled. In addition, the *ME* trilogy is an example of how mainstream SF delineates the boundaries of "acceptable" cyborg bodies and defines the nonhuman in relation to the human body as the default norm: if the technological augmentation is hidden and the cyborg can pass as fully organic and fully human, then they are positioned as either heroic or desirable. If the hybridity is too visible, then the cyborg body becomes the monstrous body. In either case, that body is put on display: whether presented as desirable and sexy, like Miranda's buttocks, or horrific and revolting, like the Banshee's pregnant belly and exposed breasts, cyborg women's bodies in the *Mass Effect* universe are sites for fetishization and objectification—presented through a lens that assumes the primacy and desirability of the fully organic human body.

---

[40]Kuo Wei Lan, "Technofetishism of Posthuman Bodies: Representations of Cyborgs, Ghosts, and Monsters in Contemporary Japanese Science Fiction Film and Animation" (PhD diss., University of Sussex, 2012), 195. See also Christine Cornea, *Science Fiction Cinema: Between Fantasy and Reality* (Edinburgh: Edinburgh University Press, 2007) and Patricia Melzer, *Alien Constructions: Science Fiction and Feminist Thought* (Austin: Texas University Press, 2006).
[41]Braidotti, *Nomadic Subjects*, 80.

PART TWO

Posthuman Environments and Entanglements

6

Material Entanglements and Posthuman Female Subjectivity in *Annihilation*

Evdokia Stefanopoulou

Introduction

Annihilation (2018) envisions an alien zone in Earth where weird material entanglements are taking place. The film narrates the story of biology professor Lena (Natalie Portman) who joins an expedition, along with three other women scientists and one paramedic, in order to explore this mysterious and expanding zone. Directed by Alex Garland and based on Jeff VanderMeer's 2014 novel,[1] the film was a box-office failure, returning only $43 million against a production budget of $40 million.[2] The film was theatrically released only in the United States, Canada, and China, since distributor Paramount Pictures found it too "intellectual" and "complicated,"[3] and subsequently decided to sell the film's rights to Netflix for international markets.[4] Despite this economic misstep, the film garnered critical praise, especially for its otherworldly atmosphere that blends visceral thrills with mind-bending themes, and its aesthetic affinities to science fiction

---

[1] This chapter is based solely on the film.
[2] The economic data are drawn from Box-Office Mojo.
[3] Benjamin Lee, "*Annihilation* Review—Natalie Portman Thriller Leaves a Haunting Impression," *The Guardian*, February 21, 2018.
[4] Ibid., Brian Tallerico, "Annihilation," *RogerEbert.com*, February 23, 2018.

touchstones, such as Tarkovsky's *Stalker* (1979) and Kubrick's *2001: A Space Odyssey* (1968), among others.[5] The environmental themes of the film also did not go unnoticed, with critics commenting on how the film stages "the interplay of beauty and terror inherent to all natural processes beyond humanity's control,"[6] and explores the themes of "evolution, biology, co-dependence."[7]

The first images of the film depict a meteorite breaching the Earth's atmosphere and crashing into a lighthouse, consequently releasing an alien, iridescent aura that begins to spread in the air and across the landscape, forming the "Shimmer." These images evoke scientific theories about the alien origins of life on Earth that explain how comets and meteorites arriving from space contained organic molecules that formulated the building blocks of life.[8] Subsequent images of dividing cells that—as it is later revealed—originate from a tumor, accentuate this connection between the extraterrestrial event and the creation of life, whether "normal" or otherwise. The film dramatizes the relationship between creation and destruction and the fundamental alterity of the human and the nonhuman world. The world that the film envisages is not that of sameness and self-replication but is characterized by the mutational logic that is "already immanent in the processes by which both material bodies and cultural patterns replicate themselves."[9] It is this concept of mutation as generative difference that resonates with the "mutational, viral, or parasitic"[10] form of posthumanist thinking. The life that emerges within the Shimmer is one of fundamental changes and mutations that subvert the established and bounded taxonomic categories of Humanist onto-epistemologies. In visualizing strange configurations that interweave humans, animals, and plants, the film enacts posthumanist accounts of the entangled nature of the more-than-human world.

This chapter examines *Annihilation* through the lens of Karen Barad's agential realism. Specifically, I contend that *Annihilation*'s strange corporeal

---

[5]See Zack Sharf, "'Annihilation' Draws Comparisons to Kubrick, Aronofsky, Cronenberg, Tarkovsky, and More in Rave Reviews," *Indiewire*, February 21, 2018.
[6]Eric Kohn, "'Annihilation' Review: Natalie Portman Stars in a Stunning Sci-Fi Thriller from the Director of 'Ex Machina,'" *Indiewire*, February 21, 2018.
[7]Tallerico, "Annihilation."
[8]See Ker Than, "The Building Blocks of Life May Have Come From Outer Space," *Smithsonian Magazine*, February 2013; Elisabeth Tasker, "Did the Seeds of Life Come from Space?," *Scientific American*, November 10, 2016.
[9]R. L. Rutsky, "Mutation, History, and Fantasy in the Posthuman," *Subject Matters: A Journal of Communication and the Self* 3, no. 2 and 4, no. 1 (2007): 111.
[10]Cary Wolfe, *What Is Posthumanism?* (Minneapolis: University of Minnesota Press, 2010), xix.

reconfigurations enact "the entangled material agencies"[11] that co-constitute both the human and the nonhuman world. In the first section, I introduce Barad's theory with a special emphasis on the concept of diffraction, which is a central trope of agential realism and is associated both with the film's themes and its visual style. In the case of the film's style, the notion of diffraction is articulated mainly through the visual trope of the fractal that permeates the images of the film. The chapter then examines how these material entanglements are also associated with the grotesque and the sensations it provokes in both characters and viewers. As theorized by Mikhail Bakhtin, the grotesque signifies as an affirmative corporeality; in popular culture, however, it is also related to feelings of repulsion and disgust. The film's grotesque images thus engender both fascination and aversion. What is more, as a female-centric film, *Annihilation* relates these grotesque transformations to the female body. This association of the grotesque posthuman transformation with the female body is explored in the chapter's last section. Leading up to this, I discuss the representation of *Annihilation*'s female characters and specifically how their posthuman becoming is signified and experienced in an ambiguous way, hinting at the subversive possibilities of these transfigurations, at the same time remaining bounded within Humanist discourses.

Diffraction, Fractals, and Other Material Entanglements

In *Meeting the Universe Halfway: Quantum Physics and the Entanglement of Matter and Meaning* (2007), Karen Barad explains how matter and meaning are inextricably fused together. The author explores the ontological and epistemological implications of quantum physics, such as "the conditions for the possibility of objectivity, the nature of measurement, the nature of nature and meaning making, and the relationship between discursive practices and the material world."[12] In order to explicate these issues, Barad proposes a new philosophical framework, labeled "agential realism," that reconsiders Cartesian binaries such as human/nonhuman, material/discursive, and natural/cultural, and reconciles constructivism with realism, agency with structure, and idealism with materialism. Accordingly, Barad shifts the focus from representationalism, that is, the idea that representations and the objects they purport to represent are separate, to an approach she designates

---

[11]Karen Barad, *Meeting the Universe Halfway: Quantum Physics and the Entanglement of Matter and Meaning* (Durham and London: Duke University Press, 2007), 56.
[12]Ibid., 24.

as performative. Specifically, she proposes a posthumanist performative approach that contests the ontological split between descriptions and reality and instead accentuates their mutual shaping. The description of this approach as posthumanist hints at the importance of nonhumans in shaping naturalcultural practices and rejects the fixed distinction between humans and nonhumans. Another basic concept of the agential-realist framework is the notion of intra-action. Contrary to interaction, which "presumes the prior existence of independent entities or relata,"[13] intra-actions presuppose that "relata do not preexist relations; rather, relata-within-phenomena emerge through specific intra-actions."[14] From this perspective, there are no objects/subjects with independently determinate boundaries and properties but rather phenomena that are "the ontological inseparability/entanglement of intra-acting agencies."[15] With this radical theoretical framework, a new conception of the world's aliveness and matter's agency emerges. The vitality of material entanglements is foregrounded as the generative force that co-constitutes both the human and the nonhuman world.

Barad's methodological approach is based on the concept of diffraction. Diffraction is "the way waves combine when they overlap and the apparent bending and spreading out of waves when they encounter an obstruction,"[16] and it is an apt figure to theorize and support the agential-realist approach. The use of optical-physical metaphors to discuss issues of knowledge, epistemology, and methodology has a long tradition in Western thought, and the most common metaphor is that of mirroring/reflection. Following Donna Haraway, Barad proposes diffraction as an alternative to reflection: "both are optical phenomena, but whereas the metaphor of reflection reflects the themes of mirroring and sameness, diffraction is marked by patterns of difference."[17] Using diffraction as a metaphor attends to the notion that differences emerge through intra-actions rather than existing as inherent characteristics.[18] As Haraway notes, "[d]iffraction is a mapping of interference, not of replication, reflection, or reproduction. A diffraction pattern does not map where differences appear, but rather maps where the *effects* of difference appear."[19]

---

[13]Ibid., 139.
[14]Ibid., 140.
[15]Ibid., 139.
[16]Ibid., 74.
[17]Ibid., 71.
[18]Despite the fact that Barad follows the "long and honored tradition of using visual metaphors as a thinking tool," formulating aspects of her methodology in analogy with the physical phenomenon of diffraction, this "does not imply that the method itself is analogical." (Barad, *Meeting the Universe Halfway*, 88). On the contrary, diffraction as a methodology disrupts notions of homology and analogy, attending to specific material entanglements.
[19]Donna Haraway, *The Haraway Reader* (New York and London: Routledge, 2004), 70.

The material entanglements inside the Shimmer, however, are explained through another phenomenon, that of refraction, that is, the "change in the path of light, when it goes from one medium to another."[20] As it is explained in the film, the Shimmer generates an anomalous zone within its borders where it functions like a prism. It enfolds the environment in a translucent, iridescent veil, refracting everything in its vicinity, not only light and radio waves but also DNA from all living organisms. This explanation functions as a "loose word association that strings change into mutation and refraction";[21] that is, it works as a figuration that links the phenomena inside the Shimmer with the concepts of alterity and difference as the building blocks of life. I would like to suggest, however, that diffraction is a more suitable metaphor to contemplate the nature of the Shimmer, since it better illuminates "the entangled effects differences make."[22] Diffraction encapsulates the production of differences and therefore becomes an apt overarching trope not only of agential realism but also of *Annihilation*.

The Shimmer's phenomena function as diffraction processes in the sense that they reiterate the posthumanist notion that differences emerge from within the entangled material agencies and do not preexist as independent characteristics within bounded objects. Indeed, the Shimmer's entities do not precede their interaction but rather emerge through their intra-actions. Human-shaped plants, alligator/shark hybrids, disfigured bears that moan with human voices, and different plant species growing from the same stem are not just anomalies of this alien zone. They also enact Barad's notion of intra-action, demonstrating how the world is not constituted by fixed and separate entities but is shaped by entangled phenomena.[23] The weird inhabitants of the Shimmer manifest the way in which limits and categories are always in a state of flux, exemplifying how matter is generative, "not a fixed essence or property of things."[24] The humans that enter the Shimmer are also subjected to an ontological dissolution. They are either absorbed or transformed by the biosphere, but in each case the human(ist) subject and its domination over the environment is challenged. The Shimmer's entanglements thus disrupt the Humanist conception of nature as a passive backdrop for human actions and instead foreground the interconnectivity and agency of the material world. This is visually articulated by the film's

---

[20]A. K. Khurana, *Theory and Practice of Optics and Refraction*, 2nd ed. (Noida: Elsevier 2008), 17.

[21]Zach Decker, "Science of SciFi: *Annihilation*," *Science Buffs*, May 29, 2018.

[22]Barad, *Meeting the Universe Halfway*, 73.

[23]It is important here to note that, although Barad proposes the posthumanist performative approach to describe the existing world, the film enacts these concepts through a science-fictional narrative. This suggests both that posthumanist concepts are difficult to be accepted in a realist framework and that the science fiction genre has the ability to unsettle Humanist notions and offer a different perspective on our common-sense perception of reality.

[24]Barad, *Meeting the Universe Halfway*, 137.

otherworldly mis-en-scène that reinforces such a feeling of proximity and interconnection. The dense, verdant jungle of the Shimmer, filled as it is with perplexed forms and chaotic arrangements of vegetation, creates a confused perception of space and its inhabitants and amplifies a sense of entanglement. Objects appear to emerge from and collapse into each other, and humans are not staged as radically different from the other "things" of this environment. Dressed in khaki uniforms that match the greenish cast of the image and "surrounded by points of light in the background and around the edges, as if . . . they were being . . . overwhelmed by the new environment,"[25] the human characters inside the Shimmer merge with the atmospheric landscape, becoming inextricable elements of the nonhuman nature.

The main visual trope that expresses this sense of entanglement, however, is the Shimmer's prismatic effects. The film's cinematography incorporates these patterns in the overall diffused illumination, creating an oneiric and hazy atmosphere that enfolds all living matter. The Shimmer's colorful patterns are not only cast across the air and water but also manifested in strange flowers, lichens, underwater life, and human irises. Through this entanglement of color, light, and bodies, the film stresses the interchange between different species and categories. Indeed, as Heather I. Sullivan argues, "the ecology of colors and light" is the result of different material intra-actions, and it "highlights the reciprocity of our bodily materiality with energy forms, discursive information, and the other-than-human materiality of many species."[26] The film's prismatic effects as an example of this entangled ecology of colors indicate the shared substance of both human and nonhuman "bodily natures."[27] Alex Garland notes how these visual patterns indeed permeate the image but also how they are, themselves, material-semiotic articulations, combining natural forms with 3D visualizations of fractal sets. According to the director:

One of the key . . . [visual patterns] that we found was actually on an iPad app. It was a representation of a mathematical shape, which is a 3D representation of a fractal form, like the Mandelbrot set. If you animate them, they move in a way that feels predictable and makes sense, but is also literally not possible to predict. It's slightly organic and slightly nonorganic at the same time. In the end, the thing that became most significant, I think, was that 3D fractal shape. At the end of the film, we

[25]Mark Dillon, "*Annihilation*: Expedition Unknown," *American Cinematographer*, March 12, 2018.
[26]Heather I. Sullivan, 'The Ecology of Colors. Goethe's Materialist Optics and Ecological Posthumanism', in *Material Ecocriticism*, ed. Serenella Iovino and Serpil Oppermann, (Bloomington: Indiana University Press, 2014), 80.
[27]Stacy Alaimo, *Bodily Natures: Science, Environment, and the Material Self* (Indianapolis: Indiana University Press, 2010).

actually just present that shape in pure form. But, prior to that point, we've used it many, many times. Sometimes in the lichen that is growing on trees, and sometimes in a form of a man who's died, where his form is spread across the wall of a swimming pool. And actually, when we first see the shimmer, from the outside, what you are actually seeing there is that 3D fractal shape, which has been rolled out and flattened and then had colors projected into it. So it was a combination of nature and math, but actually so is everything.[28]

Garland's statement pinpoints the significance of the fractal shape, an aesthetic element that has multiple connotations and associations with the Shimmer's entangled phenomena.

"Fractal" was coined by mathematician Benoit Mandelbrot to describe irregular and fragmented forms in nature (e.g., clouds, mountain ranges, coastlines, etc.) that exceed the linear and pristine shapes of Euclidean geometry. Mandelbrot's invention of fractal geometry in the early twentieth century marked a break from classical mathematics and a Cartesian conception of space. As Mandelbrot argues:

Historically, the revolution was forced by the discovery of mathematical structures that did not fit the patterns of Euclid and Newton. These new structures were regarded . . . as "pathological," . . . as a "gallery of monsters," kin to the cubist painting and atonal music that were upsetting established standards of taste in the arts at about the same time.[29]

These mathematical constructs, when reiterated within a computer, generate intricate images characterized by similarity across scale. The fractal visualizations, exemplified in the famous Mandelbrot set, reveal a never-ending pattern of self-similar forms upon successive magnifications. The cryptic imagery of endless, spiral branching patterns is reminiscent of the psychedelic art of the 1960s or of abstract painting, echoing mind-expanding trips into an otherworldly state of existence. Fractal geometry is also associated with chaos theory, since it permits the modeling of dynamic, nonlinear systems, revealing a pattern beneath the apparent randomness. Complex systems are radically reconfigured by the smallest changes or internal fluctuations, thereby foregrounding the interconnectedness and self-organization of matter.[30] The famous "butterfly effect" describes this

---

[28]Tara Bennett, "*Annihilation* Director Alex Garland is OK If You Don't Understand His Movie," *Syfywire*, February 26, 2018.
[29]Benoit B. Mandelbrot, *The Fractal Geometry of Nature* (New York: W. H. Freeman and Company, 1977), 3.
[30]John Briggs, *Fractals: The Patterns of Chaos: A New Aesthetic of Art, Science, and Nature* (New York: Touchstone, 1992).

sensitivity of nonlinear systems in internal or external variations where an imperceptible phenomenon can affect an entirely different material reconfiguration. Chaotic systems thus remind us that matter is not inert, but in constant inter- and intra-action, shaping all aspects of life. In *Annihilation*, the trope of the fractal embodies all these notions and can be regarded as both an aesthetic expression of a mind-bending, otherworldly experience and as the visual manifestation of agential matter. This articulation, however, does not mark an absolute break from Humanist conceptions but rather reconsiders notions of subjectivity and agency. Fixed boundaries between subjects and objects collapse and agency is no longer viewed as an inherent trait of humans (or even nonhumans) but as constant reconfiguration of the more-than-human world.

This portrayal becomes even more emphatic in the scene where Lena reaches the source of the Shimmer in the lighthouse, and where the fractal shape acquires its pure form. The source of the Shimmer is located in a subterranean space underneath the lighthouse where black folded surfaces with an almost organic, pulsating texture render the cave as an abstract sculpture and a living organism. This obscure space, described by the film's production designer Mark Digby as a "Mandelbrot explosion,"[31] is also the outcome of a computer-generated fractal visualization. Lena descends into this fractal cave to find the expedition's leader, Dr. Ventress (Jennifer Jason Leigh), merging with the Shimmer. As Dr. Ventress begins to disintegrate into pure floating light, an unsettling music score marks the passage to the otherworldly. Fractal forms of mutable vortices and spirals emerge and fold into one another, creating a cosmic imagery that alludes to *2001*'s famous Stargate sequence. This sublime and psychedelic display is the climax of ontological shifts generated by the film, foregrounding nonmimetic forms that exceed anthropocentric understanding and experience. In this kaleidoscopic spectacle, "becoming-fractal" indeed "engineer[s] shifts in consciousness."[32] The scene evokes avant-garde experimentations with the cinematic medium and radically reconfigures the scale of human perception for both Lena and the viewer. During this fractal choreography, the human subject remains inert while the agential matter is lively, constantly shaping new forms. A post-anthropocentric perspective is established in a shot that emulates the alien's point of view and renders Lena as the object of a nonhuman gaze. This gaze is nevertheless restricted by the Humanist limitations of the cinematic language (as a medium made by/for humans), but also due to cinema's technical origins in the indexical representation of a reality

---

[31]Abraham Riesman, "How *Annihilation* Designed Its Unnatural Horrors," *Vulture*, February 23, 2018.

[32]Anna Powell, *Deleuze, Altered States and Film* (Edinburgh: Edinburgh University Press, 2007), 176.

FIGURE 6.1 *Lena (Natalie Portman) as object of the nonhuman gaze (Skydance Media/Scott Rudin Productions/DNA Films,* Annihilation, *2018, USA. Paramount Pictures/Netflix).*

that existed before the camera via the structures and strictures of linear perspective—one of the central achievements of Renaissance humanism. Yet, it reverses, even for an instance, the usual hierarchy of the human as bearer of the look and the nonhuman world as object of his gaze (Figure 6.1). In this brief moment, not only is the human objectified, but its individuality is compromised when the Shimmer creates Lena's duplicate. Through the trope of the fractal, the scene performs the ontological deconstruction of the human(ist) subject (as Ventress is annihilated and Lena is duplicated), simultaneously foregrounding the explosive generativity of agential matter. At the same time as the material entanglements are woven at the level of the diegesis, the film's otherworldly and grotesque imagery draws attention to the sensory encounters of both characters and viewers.

Sensory Encounters and the Grotesque

Apart from being an example of entangled material agencies, the Shimmer's diffractions also "conflat[e] disparate elements not observed elsewhere in the world," fusing categories that should be kept apart.[33] The film's bodily reconfigurations are thus related to the grotesque, an aesthetic form which exemplifies the malleability of boundaries that Barad posits as the basis of agential realism. As Mark Bould notes, the grotesque "remind[s] us that the universe consists not of bounded objects—individual, monadic, distinct—

---

[33]Istvan Csicsery-Ronay, Jr., *The Seven Beauties of Science Fiction* (Middletown: Wesleyan University Press, 2008), 146; 185.

but of endless processes and interrelations; not of nouns or being, but of verbs and becoming."[34] The grotesque as an aesthetic mode that emphasizes material entanglements also involves a heightened sensory response from the viewer. In *Annihilation* both protagonist and spectators are alike immersed in the reconfigured materiality of the Shimmer through grotesque sensory encounters. That is, as characters begin to experience the weird materiality of the Shimmer, the film's grotesque imagery exerts an affective appeal to the viewer. Indeed, the grotesque usually "involves some surprising . . . invocation of . . . physicality" for the viewer,[35] and in *Annihilation* this sensation recalls the material entanglements and fluid bodily natures that we watch on screen.

The grotesque was famously theorized by Bakhtin in his 1965 book *Rabelais and his World*. For Bakhtin, the grotesque is an excess of physicality and marks the openness of the human body in the world. Bakhtin's grotesque is charged with political connotations. It is the expression of an unruly, utopian, collective body that subverts the bounded norms of the individualized body of dominant ideology and aesthetics. As Bakhtin notes:

> In grotesque realism . . . the bodily element is deeply positive. It is presented not in a private, egotistic form, severed from the other spheres of life, but as something universal, representing all the people. As such it is opposed to severance from the material and bodily roots of the world; it makes no pretense to renunciation of the earthy, or independence of the earth and the body.[36]

The grotesque body is a transgression of bodily norms that undermines prescribed hierarchies in an exuberant resistance to power relations. Despite Bakhtin's subversive and utopian corporeality, the popular imagination, as expressed in different media, usually relegates the grotesque to a more ambivalent position. Istvan Csicsery-Ronay Jr. points beyond the affirmative notions of the grotesque, arguing that it also involves "the shock of detecting different physical processes in the same body, violating the sense of the stability and integrity of things, and revealing unsuspected dimensions that escape direct rational, human control."[37] This sense of an abnormal fusion of things that should be separate links the grotesque with feelings of repulsion and disavowal. The grotesque in *Annihilation* functions in this twofold manner, and the sensory encounters of both characters and viewers oscillate between dreamlike metamorphosis and nightmarish disintegration.

---

[34]Mark Bould, *Science Fiction* (Abingdon, Oxon: Routledge, 2012), 91.
[35]Csicsery-Ronay, *The Seven Beauties of Science Fiction*, 190.
[36]Mikhail Bakhtin, *Rabelais and His World* (Bloomington: Indiana University Press, 1984), 19.
[37]Csicsery-Ronay, *The Seven Beauties of Science Fiction*, 185.

Spectators are thus placed between these antithetical poles that correspond to two essential audience pleasures in mainstream film: cognitive play and visceral experience.[38] *Annihilation*'s extraordinary phenomena elicit curiosity, a "delight in exercising cognitive skills,"[39] which are required to make sense of this strange fictional world. Throughout the film, the viewer tries to fathom the mysterious nature of this alien zone. This cognitive inquiry is visually reinforced by images of mutated cells that Lena examines through the microscope—an instrument of cognition and knowledge that pierces through and unveils the mysteries of life. At the macroscopic level, however, these bodily mutations also provide a visceral experience to the viewer. As corporeal fusions begin to unravel inside the Shimmer, merging categories that should be kept apart, the spectator experiences discomfort. This affective state is a visceral response to the violation of the commonly accepted "ontological hygiene," that is, the rigid separation of established taxonomic categories.[40] However, as Plantinga[41] notes, cognitive play and visceral experience are not experienced in isolation, but as an affective continuum that momentarily acquires different expressions. Although these pleasures are traced in different degrees in all fictional films, they are particularly related to the grotesque as an aesthetic form that equally involves cognition and sensation, as exemplified in *Annihilation*.

Annihilation's grotesque bodily exchanges induce both cognitive fascination and repulsion for Lena and the viewer. The film, following the rhythm of "cerebral blockbusters,"[42] alternates between visceral thrills and mind-expansive contemplations, illustrating the interflow of carnal processes in an ambiguous way. The film thus exhibits the hybridity not only of the on screen world but also of its own corpus, by blending generic conventions from both horror and science fiction. This particular generic mixture has a long pedigree in film history and is exemplified in *Alien* (1979), an iconic film in which, as in *Annihilation*, a female protagonist confronts monstrous alien creatures. While the horror film is deeply connected with the bodily sensations and reactions that it provokes, both on screen and off,[43] science

---

[38]Carl Plantinga, *Moving Viewers. American Film and the Spectator's Experience* (Berkeley: University of California Press, 2009), 21.
[39]Ibid.
[40]Elaine L. Graham, *Representations of the Post/Human: Monsters, Aliens and Others in Popular Culture* (New Brunswick: Rutgers University Press, 2002), 35.
[41]Plantinga, *Moving Viewers*.
[42]David Bordwell, *Christopher Nolan: A Labyrinth of Linkages*, 2nd ed. (Madison: Irvington Way Institute Press, 2019), 24.
[43]See Linda Williams, "Film Bodies: Gender, Genre, and Excess," in *Film Genre Reader IV*, ed. Barry Keith Grant (Austin: University of Texas Press, 2012); Angela Ndalianis, *The Horror Sensorium. Media and the Senses* (Jefferson: McFarland, 2012); Julian Hanich, *Cinematic Emotion in Horror Films and Thrillers: The Aesthetic Paradox of Pleasurable Fear* (New York: Routledge, 2010).

fiction is regarded as a more cerebral cultural form, a genre of ideas[44] that bends and stretches our cognitive habits. *Annihilation* alternates between these different aesthetic expressions as it is "more interested in pondering the strange, inextricable link between creation and destruction."[45] Accordingly, sensory and cognitive experiences should not be regarded as clearly separated but as complementary aspects of the human sensorium. As Ndalianis argues, the sensorium comprises "the sensory and intellectual capacities of the body; it processes sensory information and, in doing so, it facilitates our understanding of and reaction to the world around us."[46] In *Annihilation* the grotesque becomes the main aesthetic expression of this science fiction/ body horror conflation, addressing different aspects of the sensorium. On the one hand, the grotesque corporeality on display provokes bodily reactions; on the other hand, it engages our perception due to our efforts to explain these material transformations—an attempt that usually "fail[s] to become legitimate knowledge."[47]

This interchange between oneiric and nightmarish, attractive and repulsive, mental and carnal, steadily escalates as the characters approach the source of the Shimmer. In one of the first scenes inside the Shimmer, the floral pattern created by the mutated flowers outside a submerged hut induces amazement and wonder that is soon replaced by terror when a mutant alligator attacks the team. After Lena shoots the alligator, they examine its mouth to discover that it has developed shark-like teeth in concentric rows. A close-up shot frames Lena and Dr. Ventress from inside the alligator's opened mouth, foregrounding a fleshy interior and also suggesting these corporeal fusions will soon swallow the human protagonists (Figure 6.2). These scenes are evocative of the bodily sensations of the horror film, but at the same time they elicit our curiosity about the nature of these anomalies. The same pattern is repeated in ensuing scenes: the colorful lichens in a wall are echoed in a terrifying way in the calcified remains of a human body that have dispersed across the wall of a swimming pool; a flower-decorated white deer is in perfect synchronicity with its disfigured duplicate, which also foreshadows the mutated bear that shortly after attacks the team. This oscillation becomes even more pronounced in the lighthouse sequence, where Lena's amazement at the fractal transformations is soon replaced by the horror of confronting her own double. The duplications, alternations, and hybridizations are thus traced both in the fictional world and the film's

[44]Farah Mendlesohn, "Introduction: Reading Science Fiction," in *The Cambridge Companion to Science Fiction*, ed. Edward James and Farah Mendlesohn (Cambridge: Cambridge University Press, 2003).

[45]Justin Chang, "Review: Natalie Portman Braves the Scary, Enveloping Sci-fi Perils of 'Annihilation,'" *Los Angeles Times*, February 21, 2018.

[46]Ndalianis, *The Horror Sensorium*, 3.

[47]Csicsery-Ronay, *The Seven Beauties of Science Fiction*, 202.

FIGURE 6.2 Annihilation*'s images evoke the bodily sensations of the horror film, but at the same time they elicit our curiosity about the nature of these anomalies (Skydance Media/Scott Rudin Productions/DNA Films,* Annihilation, *2018, USA. Paramount Pictures/Netflix).*

form. As a result, these sensory fluctuations engender equally fluid meanings and significations about this entangled corporeality. The film enfolds the viewer in a metamorphic physicality that is connoted in both an affirmative way, as the interconnectedness of the human with the nonhuman world, and as a feeling of repulsion toward this dissolution of fixed bodies and identities. What is more, these grotesque fusions that unfold on screen and embroil the spectator's sensorium are associated with the female body and are encapsulated in the representation of the film's female characters and their posthuman transformation.

The Posthuman Female Body and Ambiguous Representations

Csicsery-Ronay stresses how the metamorphic physicality of the grotesque has been linked with femaleness because material transformations are "easily associated with the momentous, uncontrollable, and juicy changes that occur in the female body."[48] This echoes Margaret Miles, who argues that "[t]he association of the female body with materiality, sex, and reproduction in the female body, makes it an essential . . . aspect of the grotesque."[49]

---

[48]Ibid., 193.
[49]Margaret Miles, "Carnal Abominations: The Female Body as Grotesque," in *The Grotesque in Art and Literature: Theological Reflections*, ed. James Luther Adams and Wilson Yates (Grand Rapids: Eerdmans, 1997), 90.

Likewise, Mary Russo[50] points that the origin of the word grotesque, from the Italian word grotto (cave), is associated with the "low, hidden, earthly, dark, material, immanent, visceral,"[51] creating a bodily metaphor for the cavernous female body. *Annihilation* establishes these connections and, as a female-centric film, with the expedition crew consisting only of women scientists, firmly connects women with the grotesque and nonhuman nature.

The association of the female body with nature is a point of contention in feminist theory. As Stacy Alaimo[52] argues, feminism has struggled for a long time to disentangle women from nature. Western culture has steadily framed nature in feminine terms, while the female body is rendered as an extension of nature, and both are viewed as passive matter for exploitation and male domination. As the basis for long-standing gender inequalities, this cultural perception has prompted feminist theory's "flight from nature."[53] From the 1970s onwards, social constructionist or poststructuralist feminist approaches deemed the separation from the physical world as necessary, since the "critique of essentialism entailed distancing feminism from the overloaded concept of nature."[54] However, despite being instrumental in changing fixed hierarchical binaries, these theories tended to leave the nature/culture opposition in place. That is, they perpetuated the same patriarchal notions of nature as passive matter that provides the raw materials for cultural transformations. From the turn of the twenty-first century, feminist posthumanities or material feminisms started to reconsider issues of nature in feminist theory and to reconceptualize "materiality, so that it can no longer serve as the bedrock of essentialism [or] as the passive stuff of the world there to be exploited."[55] The concepts of nature and materiality were reformulated in order to move beyond Cartesian conceptions of subjectivity and agency. In other words, material feminisms began to deconstruct the nature/culture divide and to recognize the significance of material agency, thus bringing a posthumanist perspective to feminism.

Annihilation tackles issues pertaining to feminist posthumanities by depicting materiality as agential, and by exploring "our rhizomatic and multi-directional entanglements with each other."[56] Garland's female-centric

---

[50]Mary Russo, *The Female Grotesque. Risk, Excess and Modernity* (New York: Routledge, 1994).
[51]Ibid., 1.
[52]Stacy Alaimo, "Material Feminism in the Anthropocene," in *A Feminist Companion to the Posthumanities*, ed. Cecilia Åsberg and Rosi Braidotti (Cham, Switzerland: Springer, 2018).
[53]Stacy Alaimo, *Undomesticated Ground: Recasting Nature as Feminist Space* (Ithaca: Cornell University Press, 2000).
[54]Alaimo, "Material Feminism in the Anthropocene," 46.
[55]Ibid., 49.
[56]Cecilia Åsberg and Rosi Braidotti, "Feminist Posthumanities: An Introduction," in *A Feminist Companion to the Posthumanities*, ed. Cecilia Åsberg and Rosi Braidotti (Cham, Switzerland: Springer, 2018), 13.

film associates this agential materiality with the female body, thus "recasting nature as a feminist space."[57] The Shimmer is a truly undomesticated space for feminism since its transformative physicality renders irrelevant any notion of (gendered, racial, speciesist) hierarchies and identities. The film depicts the fluidity of all identities and foregrounds a feminism that attends to the "differential materializations of nonhuman as well as human bodies."[58] The boundaries of the Humanist and gendered self are thus unsettled within the Shimmer, and both women and nature are depicted as dynamic actors and not passive background. The limited role of the male protagonist makes this relation all the more emphatic. Lena's husband, Kane (Oscar Isaac)—or more accurately his doppelgänger—collapses into a coma upon his return from the Shimmer at the beginning of the film, recovering only by the end of the film due to Lena's actions. *Annihilation* therefore clearly foregrounds female agency, which is paralleled with the unruly material transformations inside the Shimmer. In this parallel construction of posthuman becoming and female empowerment, the film hints at the destabilizing possibilities of a posthuman feminism that "take[s] the materiality of the more-than-human world seriously."[59]

Nevertheless, these posthuman female bodies are framed within the film's grotesque iconography and thus acquire its twofold connotation, that is, they evoke both attraction and aversion. The ambivalent feelings associated with the grotesque are thus also projected onto the transformative corporeality of the female body. The fascination and repulsion generated by the material flows inside the Shimmer are mapped onto the posthuman female body, which is similarly experienced as something new and full of generative possibilities, and at the same time as a monstrosity that must be destroyed. One by one Lena's peers perish, either from violent destruction or an otherworldly transformation, thus marking the posthuman female body as a site of ambiguous confrontations.

Cass (Tuva Novotny) and Anya (Gina Rodriguez) are the first members of the female expedition to perish inside the Shimmer. Cass, in particular, has the shortest time on screen, and by the time of her death the effects of the Shimmer are not yet manifested in her subjectivity. As she is suddenly killed by a bear-like creature; her union with the Shimmer is depicted as an act of violent destruction. Cass' death signifies not only as an act of brutality but also as a haunting, since her voice and part of her consciousness are incorporated in the bear. This "hauntological" presence[60] is manifested in

[57]Alaimo, *Undomesticated Ground*.
[58]Barad, *Meeting the Universe Halfway*, 34.
[59]Stacy Alaimo and Susan Hekman, "Introduction: Emerging Models of Materiality in Feminist Theory," in *Material Feminisms*, ed. Stacy Alaimo and Susan Hekman (Bloomington: Indiana University Press, 2008), 4.
[60]Jacques Derrida, *Spectres of Marx* (New York: Routledge, 2006).

the team's second encounter with the mutated bear, where they hear Cass' voice emanating from the creature and crying out for help. Josie's (Tessa Thompson) remarks on this event stress its depiction as an act of horror: "I think as she was dying part of her mind became part of the creature that was killing her. Imagine dying frightened and in pain and having that as the only part of you which survives." Cass' posthuman becoming is thus framed as a violent assimilation into animality that condemns the only part of the human self that survives in a state of perpetual pain and anguish. Likewise, Anya's material entanglements with the Shimmer are experienced as a gradual descent into madness and bodily dissolution. As Anya sees her fingerprints moving, she recalls the horrific video footage of the previous expedition, found in the abandoned military base, where Kane cuts open another soldier's abdomen to reveal his writhing intestines. Anya's death is framed by similarly gruesome imagery, as the bear rips off her jaw and exposes her insides. Becoming-posthuman is thus experienced by both the characters and the viewers as a violent and painful disintegration of identity into unruly corporeality.

By contrast, Josie's and Dr. Ventress' respective posthuman transformations are represented not as violent death but as intentional union with the Shimmer. After the deaths of Anya and Cass, Josie decides to merge herself with the human-shaped plants (Figure 6.3). Unlike the violence and gore of the previous transformations, this is portrayed as a serene and oneiric moment where Josie vanishes into the Shimmer's flora. Josie's "becoming-imperceptible"[61] troubles Humanist conceptions

FIGURE 6.3 *"Becoming-earth" troubles humanist conceptions of subjectivity (Skydance Media/Scott Rudin Productions/DNA Films,* Annihilation, *2018, USA. Paramount Pictures/Netflix).*

---

[61]Rosi Braidotti, "Four Theses on Posthuman Feminism," in *Anthropocene Feminism*, ed. Richard Grusin (Minneapolis: University of Minnesota Press, 2017), 30.

of embodiment, subjectivity, and agency, and points to a series of sub-versive reversals: the agency of objects and the inertia of subjects, the intelligent body and the embodied mind, the liveliness of Earth and the stillness of humans. What is more, Josie's posthuman becoming is marked not only by inversions but also by the fusion of established categories, as she chooses agentially, and yet passively, to merge with the Shimmer, thus challenging common assumptions about the limits of the human and the nonhuman. Like Josie's, Dr. Ventress' fusion with the Shimmer is a delib-erate action, exemplifying Bakhtin's affirmative corporeality. Her posthu-man transformation is portrayed in a spectacular way as a melting into floating light, immersing the spectator into the otherworldly. Neverthe-less, Ventress' incorporation into the nonhuman world generates mixed feelings, underlined by her invocation of "annihilation" at the beginning of her transformation. According to the Merriam-Webster dictionary, the word annihilation has two definitions: (1) complete destruction, and (2) (in physics) "the combination of a particle and its antiparticle (such as an electron and a positron) that results in the subsequent total conversion of the particles into energy."[62] Therefore annihilation, as another physical metaphor—to use Barad's terms—does not connote only obliteration but the transformation of matter into something new. Ventress' posthuman becoming is thus signified both as a spectacular metamorphosis and as an abhorrent rupture of human subjectivity. This is the distress involved in expanding Humanist subjectivity. As Rosi Braidotti puts it:

> Becoming-earth (geocentered) or becoming-imperceptible (zoe-centered) entails a radical break from established patterns of thought (naturalization) and introduces a radically immanent relational dimension. This break, however, is emotionally demanding at the level of identity, and it can involve a sense of loss and pain.[63]

The posthuman female body in *Annihilation* is thus enveloped in agony even as it is entangled in polysemous associations. The ambiguity of the posthuman female body, therefore, derives not only from the narrative but also from the stylistic entanglements of the film and their affective appeal to the viewer. As noted, the images permeated by the fractal trope, such as Ventress' metamorphosis, connote not only the Shimmer's vital materiality but also generate abstract forms and nonanthropocentric perspectives. The film's fractal imagery, as a "spectacl[e] of alterity,"[64]

---

[62]Merriam-Webster, "Annihilation," n.d. https://www.merriam-webster.com/dictionary/annihilation#related-phrases (accessed July 20, 2022).
[63]Braidotti, "Four Theses on Posthuman Feminism," 30.
[64]Powell, *Deleuze, Altered States and Film*, 12.

invokes the limits of human comprehension, and ultimately connects
the posthuman transformation of the female body with an expansion of
Humanist vision/knowledge. Through this imagery, the radical potentials
of posthuman female subjectivity are foregrounded and are associated
with the affirmative notions of the grotesque. However, in instances where
the grotesque is cast as "horrific and dystopian,"[65] the posthuman female
body generates anxiety and unease. The visceral effects of the grotesque
create moments of violent shock that disrupt the fascination that the
Shimmer engenders. Therefore, in scenes such as Anya's death, where a
horror aesthetic is employed in order to induce distressing affects, the film
frames the posthuman female body as a threat for the orderly function of
the human(ist) word. In this case, the agential matter is not depicted as
generative, but as destructive, staging the posthuman transformation of
the female body as the agonizing end of humanity. The posthuman female
metamorphosis is shaped by these aesthetic modes and therefore acquires
their different significations.

Lena's trajectory inside the Shimmer also attests to these ambiguities,
offering the main perspective on the film's events. Lena expresses the
contradictory feeling of both fascination and repulsion toward the
extraordinary phenomena, stating that the Shimmer's material entanglements
signify not only as destruction but also as the creation of something new.
Lena is also represented, however, as a rational and coherent subject who
manages to remain—at least on the surface—intact until the end, in order
to save her husband and redeem herself for her infidelity and the failure
of her marriage. Lena is thus framed in rather normative discourses, and
her (Humanist) subjectivity remains relatively stable due to her motivation
to restore the (very Humanist and heteronormative) institution of the
marriage. This association of Lena's failed marriage and the extraordinary
events in the Shimmer is underscored by the film's structure. Flashbacks to
Lena's marriage are interwoven with events unfolding inside the Shimmer,
creating a parallelism. As the otherworldly events are linked with the
mundane scenes of a marriage, the cosmic implications of the Shimmer are
tethered to the (re)formation of the heterosexual couple. Through these
representations and narrative fluctuations, the film blends posthumanist
signifiers with Humanist and liberal discourses in a material-semiotic play
of representations and sensations.

---

[65]Bould, *Science Fiction*, 95.

Conclusion

The material entanglements enacted in *Annihilation* and advocated in Barad's agential realism point to the agency of matter and the nonhuman world. The film encourages us to imagine humanity in constant interchange with the environment, and to envision intra-active becomings that interrogate anthropocentric conceptions of the human and nonhuman world. *Annihilation* advances transformative material practices that deny the separation of humans from nature, and instead accentuate the multiple interrelations, interfaces, and exchanges that constitute nature as an inextricable aspect of the human. At the same time, the film disrupts these posthumanist discourses with the horror associated with the dissolution of the human. Indeed, the fictional zone of the Shimmer "generates, composes, transforms, and decomposes: it is both the stuff of (human) corporeality and the stuff that eviscerates the very notion of human."[66] What is more, these posthuman becomings are framed through the female body. In this framing, the film partakes of the cultural tendency, evident in films such as *Under the Skin* (2013), *Her* (2013), *Lucy* (2014), *Ex Machina* (2014) (also directed by Garland), and others, to project speculations about posthumanity onto the female body. This is a characteristic of "Anthropocenema," a neologism proposed by Selmin Kara to "think about cinema in the age of the Anthropocene."[67] Anthropocenema foregrounds the effects of human industrial activity that can bring about "total ecosystemic collapse or human self-annihilation."[68] Anthropocenema's main traits include an interest in speculative ontologies and the trope of extinction, but it is also marked by a "shifting of the narrative point of view to female characters."[69] This reliance "on women to reflect and anchor contemporary responses to post-gender or species-based articulations of humanity,"[70] however, is often characterized by confusion about gender roles in Anthropocenic imaginations. *Annihilation*, as a cinematic example of the Anthropocene par excellence, displays this confusion in the posthuman imaginings of the female body that can be read as both subverting and reinforcing Humanist and gendered norms.

These tensions are best illustrated in the film's final act, in the "dance sequence"[71] between Lena and her doppelgänger. The scene is a continuation of the fractal choreography that unravels inside the lighthouse. After a drop

---

[66]Alaimo, *Bodily Natures*, 25.
[67]Selma Kara, "Anthropocenema: Cinema in the Age of Mass Extinction," in *Post-Cinema: Theorizing 21st Century Film*, ed. Shane Denson and Julia Leyda (Falmer: REFRAME Books, 2016), 758.
[68]Ibid., 770.
[69]Ibid., 766.
[70]Ibid.
[71]Bennett, "*Annihilation* director Alex Garland is OK If You Don't Understand His Movie."

of Lena's blood is fused with the alien matter, a featureless humanoid is shaped. The humanoid looks like "a walking embodiment of the Shimmer in its color and translucence"[72] and mirrors Lena's movements. This uncanny doubling is underscored by the camera's odd movements that, according to director of photography Rob Hardy, "si[t] somewhere between intimacy and detachment,"[73] while the dissonant electronic soundtrack points at the discrepancies and incongruities of this mirroring. Echoing the modus operandi of diffraction, the humanoid—itself a kind of translucent surface—in the process of becoming Lena, remains unable to achieve a precise replication. This mirroring of the self in the Other and the liminal space of their difference encapsulate the limits of Humanist identity as separation from the Other (nonhuman, Earth). The scene suggests that the self is always performed, always in the process of becoming, and any notion of fixed (gendered, Humanist) identity and the autonomous self is unsettled. However, Lena is terrified by this self/Other performance, destroying what lies outside established borders.[74] Despite recognizing the beauty of this nonhuman world, Lena remains attached to an all-to-human perception and constrains the subverting possibilities of the posthuman female body. Subsequently, Lena averts a complete posthumanist dissolution and saves the (Humanist) world by using a phosphorus grenade which sets the humanoid, and subsequently the rest of the Shimmer, on fire.

The film closes with the reunion of the heterosexual couple after Lena successfully destroys the Shimmer and Kane recovers from his coma. This closing scene both confirms and subverts the Humanist restoration as it reestablishes normative gender roles while tackling the themes of mutation, change, and difference that traverse the film. The restored/transformed couple is depicted through a series of shifting frames that enact the themes of Humanist vision/knowledge and its limits explored in the film. The scene begins with a bluish, blurred frame-within-the-frame: Kane's isolation room as seen through a rectangular door pane. The camera tracks in to a medium shot, framing Kane more clearly, but the texture of the image remains blurred. Lena is also depicted in an obscure way. A close-up of Lena standing in front of a sliding glass door is underexposed and imbued with the Shimmer's blue and purple colors, rendering her as featureless as the humanoid. As Lena enters the isolation room both Kane and Lena can be seen asking one another about their "true" identity in a shot-reverse shot sequence. Lena asks Kane if he really is Kane; he replies, "I don't think so." Then Kane asks if she really is Lena, but she does not answer.

---

[72]Riesman, "How *Annihilation* Designed Its Unnatural Horrors."
[73]Dillon, "*Annihilation*: Expedition Unknown."
[74]For a psychoanalytic approach to the incompatibility between the self and its double, see Sigmund Freud's *The Uncanny*, trans. David Mclintock (London: Penguin Books, [1919] 2003).

Therefore, both characters express doubt about their coherent, human(ist) selves. The film ends with close-ups of Kane and Lena as they embrace, revealing their shimmering irises: the Shimmer within them. However, this hint at posthuman metamorphosis is undermined by the restoration of heteronormativity. That is, the collapse of the Shimmer as a feminist space and the reunion of the heterosexual couple—even if transformed—suggest a return to Humanist (and patriarchal) norms rather than a posthuman blending of categories. In this way, *Annihilation* reinstates the Humanist world; yet, it still offers a vivid example of how the human is entangled in material agencies and marked by constant change—the basic characteristic of all life and its evolution.

7

Jonathan Glazer's *Under the Skin*

Female Embodiment and Ecology

Meraj Dhir

In Jonathan Glazer's *Under the Skin* (2013) abstract stylization, an emphasis on documentary realism, and a highly restricted and elliptical narration (characteristic of certain art-cinema storytelling modes) serve to defamiliarize the prevailing cinematic norms of the science fiction horror genre. In this chapter I argue that the film's narration and deployment of film style undermine typical generic conventions as they encourage the viewer to reexamine their moral commitments and sympathize, as if corporeally, with an alien-female other.

Two strategies constitute the film's intrinsic norms, guiding the viewer's apprehension of the film as it unfolds. First, the film's plot enacts a narrative *détournement* from the typical "shooting-gallery" or SF horror plot structure in order to explore the alien other's condition of being embodied in a female form, described by Glazer as the character's "drift."[1] I use the term "shooting-gallery" generically to refer to the common plot structures of so many SF horror films where an alien monster systematically hunts down human prey until a climax where the alien monster is usually destroyed by the film's protagonists. The *Alien*, *Species*, and *Predator* franchises are typical examples of this generic narrative structure. Of course, in such films

---

[1]Glazer discusses this drift structure in Film4. "Beneath the Surface: An Oral History of under the Skin." Medium, December 19, 2019, https://medium.com/@Film4/beneath-the-surface-an-oral-history-of-under-the-skin-a62173045c0a.

the viewer's allegiance is to one or more human agents, another way that *Under the Skin* deviates from conventional narrative norms. In *Under the Skin*, the viewer is spatially and perceptually aligned with an alien female named Laura (Scarlett Johansson), whose mission, we gradually learn, is to hunt down human males for her species' sustenance. She is accompanied by a male figure, named only "The Bad Man" (Jeremy McWilliams), whose role as chaperone and enforcer ensures that Laura stays on course. At the film's temporal midpoint, however, Laura abandons her goal entirely. This event is preceded first by a notable shift in Laura's visual attention from scanning POV shots of men to an observation of everyday women of different body types, ages, and social classes on the streets of Glasgow. A highly stylized shot (to be examined later) seems to suggest that Laura's senses are overwhelmed by this perceptual barrage of human females. Moreover, the event that directly precipitates Laura's "drift" is her encounter with a man strongly marked by his facial deformities, credited as "The Deformed Man" (nonactor Andrew Pearson suffers from neurofibromatosis in real life). In *Under the Skin*, just as we begin to grasp the character's goal at the film's midpoint, Laura drifts from the initial pattern of predation common to mainstream SF horror plotlines to one that involves the more diffuse motivations of what appear to be self-deliberation and a self-exploration of her female embodiment on Earth. Laura even makes an attempt at domestic tranquility with the "Quiet Man" (Michael Moreland), only to reject this role as well upon discovering she does not possess a human vagina. At the film's end, Laura takes refuge in a forest before a character credited as "The Logger" (Dave Acton) attempts to rape her. When the Logger discovers the tar-black alien form beneath her outer human form, he douses her in gasoline and sets her on fire. In the final image of the film, the camera tilts up to show her ashes rising to the sky.

Second, the film's style, especially the use of close-ups of hands and faces, shot-reverse shot schema, and film sound, as well as long-scale dorsal staging and de-dramatized performances, emphasizes the sensuous, corporeal, and ecological dimensions of an alien embodied within a female morphology. The film alternates pictorial stylization and intermedial allusion with techniques of documentary realism. In *Under the Skin*, techniques such as shooting in real-world locations, the use of nonactors, long-scale shots of the streets of Glasgow, and natural lighting schemes emphasize the physical, social, and cultural specificity of the film's story-world. Together, these techniques solicit more complex interpretive resources than those demanded by most mainstream SF horror. After analyzing the film's style and narration, I will demonstrate how the film's formal system presents us with a more nuanced, critical, and sophisticated view of alien-female embodiment that overlaps with aspects of critical posthumanist theory. Ultimately, I argue that Glazer's film actively solicits the viewer's affective and interpretive resources, proposing a model of alien embodiment that resists conventional Humanist categorizations.

Two posthumanist themes guide my analysis: female embodiment and intersectionality. It is suggestive that Laura's encounter with the Deformed Man, an intersectional other, and her awareness of differing sorts of females are the two central events that initiate her journey of self-exploration. Taking its cue from third-wave feminism, posthumanism has been marked from the beginning by an attention to "intersectionality," a critical term denoting how a person's identity may involve numerous and intersecting identities, whether in terms of gender, race, class, ability, or physical appearance, each of which denotes differing sorts of exclusion and privilege. Posthumanist theorists such as Donna Haraway and Rosi Braidotti emphasize the importance of feminism and female embodiment as critical to the posthumanist project.[2] In one of the foundational texts of critical posthumanist theory, Haraway argues that intersectionality and identity are key features of cyborg subjectivity, a term itself drawn from science fiction literature. The cyborg is a conceptual metaphor that challenges traditional dualities of self/other, mind/body, and nature/culture, allowing for new forms of subjectivity and ways of being in the world through the application of nonhuman supplements, such as machines and tools. As Haraway argues,

> the "social" category of gender depends upon historicizing the categories of sex, flesh, body, biology, race, and nature in such a way that the binary, universalizing opposition that spawned the concept of the sex/gender system at a particular time and place in feminist theory implodes into articulated, differentiated, accountable, located, and consequential theories of embodiment, where nature is no longer imagined and enacted as resource to culture.[3]

Haraway insists, moreover, that feminism is marked strongly by its emphasis on embodiment and intersectionality. Not only has female morphology and biology been used to mark off sexual difference, women from men, but female bodies also act as women's interface with the environment. For Haraway, bodies are always locatable and have differing cultural significations in differing geographic, social, and cultural matrices. We can think of Laura's plight in *Under the Skin* as a sort of *sine qua non* for a progressive view of female and cyborg subjectivity. At two moments in the film, Laura's "true" alien form is revealed as a tar-black humanoid. This alien core is bereft of any conventional marks of sex/gender or cultural specificity and so rejects,

---

[2]For a comprehensive discussion of feminism and posthumanist theory see Rosi Braidotti, "The Critical Edge of Posthuman Feminism." *Posthuman Feminism* (Cambridge: Polity, 2022), 43–67.
[3]Elizabeth Castelli, "Donna J. Haraway, 'Gender' for a Marxist Dictionary: The Sexual Politics of a Word' (1991)." *Women, Gender, Religion a Reader* (New York: Palgrave, 2007), 68.

I argue, any essentializing discourse about femaleness-as-such. As I will elaborate, the film self-consciously invites the viewer to pay keen attention to how Laura assumes culturally embodied forms of dress, makeup, and verbal scripts that are erotically charged—an appearance and a *performance* of gender, necessitated by her goal of attracting lone heterosexual men for her species' biopower.[4] Indeed, the first part of the film is marked by the repetitiveness of Laura's actions as she systematically hunts for prey. In each of Laura's five encounters with men we see her ability to switch from cold-eyed predation to a performance of gender that positions her as an attractive female, lost, and in need of male help for directions. By paying unusually strong attention to the ways Laura performs a prescribed gender role, the film highlights Judith Butler's notion of how one's gender identity is never given but involves acts of repetition and performativity.[5] Laura's performance of gender in the film's first half is aligned to her role as what Barbara Creed, writing on the role of women as monstrous others in horror films, calls the *femme castratrice*—a conventional SF horror role that Laura will intentionally disregard. It is also noteworthy that the aliens' gendered division of labor is tied to powers of vision and visuality. The Bad Man's role in the film is not only determined by his constant tracking of Laura's movements. He is also often shown circumambulating Laura as he closely monitors her appearance. At the end of the film, in a striking compositional allusion to the work of Caspar David Friedrich, the domineering visual control the Bad Man has exercised over Laura is undermined by the dense fog that has overtaken the landscape. In this shot, the film's posthumanist thematics are explicitly anchored in a rejection of a Cartesian and implicitly male viewing subject.

In this chapter I will demonstrate how Glazer's film emphasizes an alien other's embodiment in female form as a posthumanist rejection of traditional SF gender roles and narrative tropes. Indeed, Laura's attempt to explore the new world she inhabits is both conditioned, and, at the film's end, limited, by her female form. Laura's plight to find new ways of being a female on Earth foregrounds a *resistance* to conventional forms of female subjectivity and embodiment. The film's second half focuses our attention on how Laura moves beyond a predatory and disembodied vision, evinced in the film's use of scanning and POV shots, to a fuller exploration of her other sensory modalities. In these scenes, with the landscape literally engulfed by fog, the film problematizes Laura's (and her alien escort's) attempts at visual mastery through moments that emphasize visual opacity and literal blindness.

---

[4]Foucault advances his discussion of how bodies are regulated as biopower in Michel Foucault, *The History of Sexuality Vol 1* (New York: Vintage, 1990), 140–1.
[5]Judith Butler, *Bodies That Matter on the Discursive Limits of "Sex"* (London, New York: Routledge, 2015), 15–16.

Art-Horror Style: Realism and Pictorial Abstraction

Under the Skin begins with a series of inherently unstable images that challenge the viewer's ability to apprehend scale and spatial context. A single dot of white light emerges from a dark void. Suddenly the light becomes larger and brighter in intensity, rays of light emanating from its circumference. What are we looking at? A star in the vast darkness of space? A hurtling object alight as it flies toward us? The unnerving, scraping strings on the soundtrack give us no clue even while they may suggest something cold and mechanical. The concentric circles of light that soon emerge could even depict the negative image of a pupil within a dark iris. The film will present us with extreme close-ups of the alien's eye four times throughout the film, emphasizing the theme of visuality. Moreover, the film's style is frequently structured around eyeline and point-of-view schema that not only serve the film's narrative but also underscore the horror genre's thematics of vision. During the opening sequence, however, the viewer must eschew the assumption that what we see is an eyeball, as the very next shot presents us with what seems to be a perpendicular shift in camera angle, and a cut to the dot passing through a series of circular revolutions that come into alignment, converging on the dot of light. The suggestion is of interplanetary travel and perhaps a warping of space-time.

Over this largely abstract imagery a female voice can be heard issuing various phonetic sounds and plosives. In the next shot, a dark circle is gradually enclosed by surrounding white matter, and the sounds cohere into phonemes and finally full words. One of the first words we can distinctly make out is "films," a not-so-subtle indication of the opening scene's self-reflexive qualities. And then, with a sudden switch in illumination, we are staring into the brown iris of an eye, the pupil reflecting the dots of light, presumably at some immense distance. This opening sequence simultaneously presents us with the landing of an alien shape as well as an alien *embodying* human form. After a series of rural outdoor shots of winding streams we now see another point of light come closer, this one not so difficult to apprehend as it snakes its way through the hilly landscape. It is the headlight of a motorcycle traveling at high speed through the Scottish countryside. It is night and the horizon line described by the mountain range suggests the undulations of a female form. The film primes the viewer to note geographical and expressive features of the Scottish landscape—a strategy that dominates in the second part of the film. The Bad Man speeds along the highway on his motorcycle. The camera, presumably anchored on his visor, reflects the lights from his helmet. The streaming lights at either side recall visually the wormhole travel at the end of Kubrick's *2001: A Space Odyssey* (1968). The Bad Man slows down and dismounts. We see him from behind, the camera unmoving, as he leaves the highway to retrieve a lifeless female form from the side of the road. The woman's torn black stockings and short skirt suggest she may have been the victim of sexual violence, one of several ways the film's beginning will rhyme with its end. A long-scale tracking shot follows the man into the van.

The beginning of *Under the Skin* enlists circular motifs and the suggestion of narrative recursivity—Is the female retrieved from the ditch Laura's predecessor? Is Laura destined to the same violent end? The film pays close attention to the coming-into-being of an alien other as it assumes human embodiment. The film presents its "landing scene" of the alien on Earth in a highly oblique and indirect fashion. Instead of the common SF trope of a spaceship hurtling toward Earth, the film's style encourages the viewer to consider abstract forms, textures, and sounds, attuning us physically and perceptually to the *experience* of an alien intelligence landing on Earth. Indeed, we can advance few inferences about the alien's means of space travel or anything about their biological constitution other than that they have the means to present themselves in human form. We learn that the aliens' manifestation on Earth involves a gendered division of labor—one that is both reactionary and misogynist. Moreover, the womens' dress invokes the stylings of the femme fatale who draws men to their demise. Stylistically, the opening also introduces us to the first of many dorsal stagings of figures. Denying performer frontality is a means of suppressing character information and psychology, but the device can also be used as a means of compositional defamiliarization and even pictorial allusion, as well as a form of "displaced POV."[6]

In *Under the Skin*, the oblique and indirect presentation of story information keeps any definitive assessment of the alien's intentions or mission on Earth in abeyance until the temporal midpoint of the film. Instead, the film's second major sequence continues with a long-scale silhouetted shot of Laura, donning her predecessor's clothes. The opening scene ends with a series of extreme close-ups of Laura examining an ant she has picked off the dead woman's clothing. The on-screen magnification of the insect presents us with a biological entity that seems monstrous but also—in a way that prefigures Laura's own narrative—helpless and trapped. As the film continues, the special visual attention paid to close-ups of Laura's hands and face (or the purposive denial of the face) informs the film's style.

The "arrival" sequence gives way to a low-angle shot of a building against the sky. Through the clouds mysterious lights recede in visibility. The next few shots anchor Laura in a very specific geopolitical locale marked by

---

[6]J. Brandon Colvin, "The Other Side of Frontality: Dorsality in European Art Cinema," *New Review of Film and Television Studies* 15, no. 2 (2017): 191–210, https://doi.org/10.1080/17400309.2017.1312794.

class and the connotations of urban detritus and disrepair. A large yellow wrecking truck (which will be visually rhymed at the film's end) suggests the site is soon to be demolished. An abandoned housing estate in Glasgow is the location for Laura's "lair," where she seduces her male human victims. There is at the beginning of the film already a dialectic between what is clearly visible and conditions that obscure any clear access to what we see. The lights of the spacecraft are only partially hinted at, hidden both by distance and the atmospheric fog.

In the following scene, Laura visits a shopping mall in search of female accoutrements. Laura is filmed dorsally as she enters with the camera following her down an escalator and continuing behind as she snakes her way through the crowded mall. The dorsal view functions as a sort of displaced POV shot, showing what Laura is presumably looking at. By deflecting our attention from the figure's face, however, we are forced to notice how the character is *embedded* in the surrounding environment, both through cultural practices and spaces and later in the film, within the natural environment.

There is a cut to Laura inside a women's clothing and makeup store. Medium-scale shots present her touching and fingering various garments, evoking a tactile sense of bodily interaction. A series of shots show different women having their makeup done and buying clothes. While not proper POV shots, cued by position or eyeline, these shots of other women give the viewer a sense of how Laura's actions are embedded within larger practices of mimicking and performing gender. We see how cultural and bodily practices of makeup, dress, carriage, and comportment display how the alien assumes and subjects her carnal form to particular "technologies of gender" and the micropolitics of a particular sort of social normalization.[7] Specifically, this performative dimension is marked by self-commodification, as the alien appropriates marks of sexual difference and assumes the stereotype of the film noir *femme fatale*. Such a performance of gender is anchored in Laura assuming an appearance that will attract her heterosexual prey as bait. It is the breaking down and refusal of this identity that will initiate Laura's exploration of her own female embodiment in the second half of the film.

In the setup and complicating action stages of the film, we see the alien, as corporeally gendered female, engaging in various sorts of predatory behavior with unsuspecting male figures. The film's first half is almost entirely structured around moving and scanning eyeline shots from Laura's van. Laura's conversations with men are handled casually, without the fast, rhythmic cutting and jump scares found in contemporary horror cinema. Glazer favors instead traditional shot-reverse shot editing. In an early scene,

---

[7]Teresa De Lauretis, "The Technology of Gender," in *Technologies of Gender: Essays on Theory, Film, and Fiction* (Bloomington: Indiana University Press, 1987), 1–30.

for instance, a shot from the van frames Laura noticing a young man walking down the street. As she solicits his attention, the man approaches the vehicle cautiously. Laura rolls down the window and asks him for directions to the M8. In a nearly impenetrable Scottish brogue, the man fumbles verbally to provide Laura with coherent directions, at which point Laura interrupts him and asks: "Am I keeping you from something?" The man responds in the negative and then Laura asks him a series of questions: "Where are you going?"; "Am I keeping you from something?"; From what? For work?" The man responds that he is on his way to "meet somebody." And so ends one of five conversation scenes from the van. The verbal script Laura uses to ensnare her prey is consistent. It involves her feigning to ask for directions, segueing into personal questions to determine if the men are alone and thus suitable for harvesting, presumably because they won't be missed. At the climax of the film, the observant viewer/auditor will note that the very script Laura uses to trap men will be enlisted by the Logger when he questions Laura about her presence in the forest. In the Logger, Laura also finds a predatory male other. This parallelism is underscored by the fact that he too is engaged in accumulating earthly "biopower," through the devastation of the forest trees, while Laura's mission was to harvest male human bodies. In the figure of the Logger, a productivist orientation to nature is conflated with rapacious male desire. In its emphasis on unique place and varying geographies, *Under the Skin* departs from SF genre conventions to further draw the viewer's attention to a posthumanist approach to the environment and cultural ecology.

While POV shots, eyeline cutting, and shot-reverse shot schema constitute stylistic norms of mainstream as well as art-cinema style, *Under the Skin* instantiates these norms in a series of highly programmatic ways. For example, the conversation with the first man is filmed in a series of alternating shot-reverse shots, with the young man internally framed by the windshield, the camera filming from inside the van, and another camera setup, also within the van, filming Laura in a three-quarter low-angle medium shot. Cutting on dialogue in this way is a conventional enough manner of handling conversation scenes. Yet, as the man leaves, there is a cut back to a medium shot of Laura, and we see how, as her eyeline shifts slightly away from the man, her facial features immediately assume a blank-eyed stare, revealing her cold, predatory nature. The "huntress" theme on the soundtrack resumes its slow beat as Laura drives away. The camera follows Laura driving around Glasgow for a while longer, coming to rest on a close-up of her face (again, one of the frequent setups from within the van). Again, Laura's expression registers no particular emotion, attuning us to Johansson's highly de-dramatized and facially inscrutable performance style, relaying the deadened, wholly alien nature of her character. Indeed, in the very next conversation, the film resists the reverse shot entirely, remaining on Laura's face as she once again feigns asking for directions from a would-be victim. With the figure off-screen, our visual focus is entirely on Laura's facial expressions, and we note the alien's keen ability to mimic a friendly and flirtatious disposition, which she can drop in the space of a beat. After the Albanian man (credited as Marius Bincu) completes his directions from off-screen, Laura persists with various personal questions. Halfway through the shot, as the man informs her he has a family, we see Laura's entire posture and facial expression shift noticeably to the previous dead-eyed stare. Such repetition and variation of the shot-reverse shot schema attune us both to shifts in Laura's facial reactions and her ability, in the role of femme fatale, to beguile the men she encounters through a convincing and ironic "performance" of a lost and helpless female needing men for help with directions.

While the scenes of Laura hunting her prey emphasize prosaic urban spaces and documentary shooting methods, at specific junctures the film's style departs radically from its realist emphasis. When we see Laura take her first victim, nonactor Andrew Gorman, into the house, a series of alternating medium-scale shots feature Gorman following Johansson into an utterly dark, voluminous space. Lured by the prospect of sex, Gorman follows Laura's lead as the two gradually undress. The minimalist sound design intensifies the uncanniness of this space as the soundtrack is reduced to the discordant, atonal "Lipstick to Void," theme from Mica Levi's score.[8] We hear the processed, slowed-down percussion, viola glissandos, and microtones each of the three times Laura lures the men into the inky black void. The highly experimental score and the unexplained metamorphosis of space belong as much in an avant-garde video installation as they do in an SF narrative film. As the first victim follows Laura several paces behind, a cut to a longer-scale shot displays his naked and prone body submerging into the floor, while Laura is somehow able to traverse the space unaffected.

Generic motivation only partly helps us infer what drives the film's violation of characterization and classic scenographic space. Why is it necessary for Laura to enact such a ritualistic erotics of revelation and display? Certainly, the men could be trapped and "processed" by an advanced alien race in a more expedient fashion. And why, in the first place, does Laura only hunt heterosexual men? In *Under the Skin*, the film's adoption of SF horror gender roles piggybacks on its posthumanist critique of factory farming methods and productivist labor. Generic motivation doesn't help us answer these questions definitively, since there is no suggestion that Laura is a vampire or succubus—indeed she is herself *trapped* by the film's genre dressings—and her own species—as visual bait or lure.

---

[8]For a breakdown and discussion of the film's soundtrack see: https://en.wikipedia.org/wiki/Under_the_Skin_(soundtrack).

In the film's first part, Laura acts in accordance with what Barbara Creed calls the *femme castratrice*. The *femme castratrice* is just one modality of the "archaic mother," or "monstrous-feminine," found in many examples of the horror genre. Influenced by the work of Julia Kristeva, Creed postulates that the female-gendered monster is a manifestation of the castration anxieties repressed by patriarchal society.[9] These repressed anxieties take the guise of the castrating female in film horror. For Creed, cinematic manifestations of the monstrous-feminine are almost always nightmare images associated with darkness, dispossession, and death. Indeed, the dark, wet, cavernous space in which Laura "processes" her male victims is akin to a monstrous womb, a regression to a primal scene where the unwitting male subject finds his demise. The film's abstraction of this space and the characters' suspension in a sort of thick amniotic fluid self-consciously visualizes this condition. The male victims are mechanically separated from their flesh in a site of total abjection.

The "black void" sequence in which the men are processed is repeated two more times, with different visual emphases in each phase. Laura's second victim is similarly shown sinking into the dark viscous ground. This time, however, instead of remaining with Laura, we follow the man from the nightclub, named Andrew (Paul Brannigan), into the vast expanse of fluid. The low angle of the camera shows Laura's figure as she continues her trajectory, walking on the surface. In the next few shots, the man's body is seen flailing and then coming to rest in this submerged-liquid space. The film cuts to a long shot of a waterlogged and distended human form similarly floating alone. This is revealed to be the point-of-view shot of Andrew as he recognizes another person and reaches out to touch the strange figure's hand. The close-up of the two hands touching recalls visually the hand of God touching Adam from Michelangelo's Sistine Chapel ceiling. The shot asserts itself as one of the film's numerous allusions to fine art and film imagery, as it also reinforces the intimacy of touch, something Laura will only attempt to authentically experience in the film's second half. But here, submerged, Andrew recoils as if both alarmed and repulsed. A shot of the nude figure slowly drifting away reveals his oddly deformed face and enucleated eye sockets, registering something akin to a cry for help. The silence is suddenly rent by a gunshot-like sound, and the body is instantly eviscerated, leaving the man's skin to float and converge upon itself like a slow-motion shot of a sheet cast to the wind. The sense of abject horror is compounded in a cut to Andrew and his recognition that he too will suffer the same horrific end. The next cut reveals a long conveyer belt running orthogonal to the screen with what appears to be luminous red viscera and flesh being transported

---

[9]Barbara Creed, *The Monstrous-Feminine: Film Feminism Psychoanalysis* (New York and London: Routledge & Kegan Paul, 1993), 17–19.

up a wide conveyer belt and sucked into a small rectangular aperture in the background of the shot. Through this oblique and abstract imagery, the viewer is equipped to infer that the men are being captured so as to harvest their flesh. The graphic emphasis on the conveyer belt and the sudden jolting sound, akin to a captive-bolt stunner, can even be viewed as a posthumanist critique of the very inhuman factory farming methods humans currently employ.

In Kubrickian fashion, *Under the Skin* radically decelerates the conventional rhythms of horror films. While most mainstream genre films are cut exceedingly fast, with average shot lengths of two to four seconds, Glazer's film, by contrast, displays an almost leisurely pace, with an ASL of 7.7 seconds. The scenes within the house unfold in a slow, almost hypnotic fashion, as the men casually follow Laura into a dark liquid void. Laura's movements are relaxed and deliberate as she removes her clothes, not a fast striptease but a protracted seduction—hardly the frenzied attacks and jump scares one associate with conventional SF horror. The score, too, with its reverberations and slow beat, contributes to this sense of somnambulism. In the second phase of the film, however, the plot gives way almost entirely to Laura's experiences of her new world, involving moments of art-cinema *temps morts* stillness. The felt duration of these shots focuses our attention on Laura as she wanders through the landscape, attempts to eat human food, or considers the biomechanics and morphology of her female body as reflected in a mirror.

Alignment and Allegiance

Laura's strange alien status as a character, deeply suppressed by the narration, sets up certain obstacles in our ability to evaluate Laura as a moral agent. Nevertheless, throughout the first half of the film Laura engages in actions that should invite the viewer's antipathy. In the scene at the beach, she not only smashes the traveler's skull with a rock but also leaves a crying infant alone on the empty pebbled strand. Her total lack of empathy toward others is part of what makes her actions so horrifying. Mainstream films rarely align us with wholly unsympathetic characters. *Under the Skin* is less of a deviation from such a classical moral economy than may first appear, however.[10] Laura's encounter with the Deformed Man marks her departure from her ostensible mission. But this deviation is prefigured in a scene before the midpoint of the film. After the Bad Man's inspection of Laura, a long-scale high-angle shot shows Laura walking

---

[10]For a discussion of character allegiance see Murray Smith, *Engaging Characters: Fiction, Emotion, and the Cinema* (Oxford: Oxford University Press, 2021), 187–225.

down a crowded urban street, where she trips and falls. Concerned passersby help her up; Laura is confused. The film then cuts to several medium and long-scale shots similar to the documentary-like "sampling shots" of women at the beginning of the film. On this occasion, however, the subjects are women of different ages and social classes. Since the film has trained us to watch Laura looking at men, here the shift in Laura's attention to the female gender marks an important shift in the character's visual attention and her deviation after this point from her prescribed course. As if to visually underscore this moment in the film, it ends with a highly stylized and suggestive gold monochrome shot (analyzed later), which precedes her encounter with the Deformed Man. The contiguity of these two scenes, hinged around the film's temporal midpoint, suggests how female morphology is tied to intersectionality of other kinds. The Deformed Man is, as his name suggests, marked strongly by his appearance as differently abled. In foregrounding this encounter between two different sorts of intersectionality, Glazer's film suggests that sexual difference may be constitutive of and coextensive with difference as such. Indeed, many of the film's scenes emphasize different sorts of intersectionality foreign to traditional notions of Scottish identity. One of the men Laura asks for directions is from Albania and the man who proffers her flowers bought by an admirer is clearly an immigrant. We learn that the man at the beach is from Czechoslovakia. And after Laura abandons a white baby on the beach, in the very next scene her attention is drawn to a black baby seated in the back seat of a vehicle adjacent to hers. Like Laura, these characters are aliens too. They are marked by differing types of racial, cultural, and physical identities.

Why does the diegesis draw our attention to Laura observing women? So far, all her victims have been male, and it seems she has no use for the female of the species except to mimic them in their self-fashioning. We then cut to an extreme close-up of Laura's eye and then again to more shots of women, each superimposed over the other. Laura's own face appears in close-up within this dynamically changing shot. The image acquires its golden hue. The use of sustained superimpositions lasts forty-eight seconds as it pushes the image to a near-undifferentiated gold monochrome. The insect-like buzz of the soundtrack contributes to the feeling that Laura's perceptual apparatus is being overwhelmed by sense impressions and visual noise. As with other moments of overt stylization in the film, these images can be understood metaphorically or literally. Is the film visualizing the monotony of daily urban life, or is Laura's ability to differentiate sense impressions breaking down? When Laura picks up the Deformed Man, we expect that this unfortunate pedestrian will be the alien's next victim. He seems highly nervous and is apprehensive about accepting a lift to Tesco. Once he enters the car, it becomes clear that there is something different about this passenger. He removes his hood, revealing a grossly enlarged head with tumescent growths disfiguring his appearance. When Laura asks him, "So why do you shop at night then?" the Deformed Man responds, "People wind me up." Her questioning reveals the character's remarks about people's ignorance; he answers that he has no friends, nor has he ever had a girlfriend. Like Laura, he is alone. Laura appears to not notice his disfigurement, however, and instead compliments him on his "beautiful" hands. In a two-shot, Laura encourages Adam to stroke her face. A close-up of the Deformed Man pinching his hand indicates that he thinks he may be dreaming. Unlike her encounters with the previous men, this tactile exchange creates a physical intimacy between the two characters. For the viewer, the abject body and the alien are similarly poised for sympathetic engagement. Moreover, in the following scene, though Laura enacts again the stylized seduction in the dark void, she ultimately lets the Deformed Man go free. From this point on she abandons her predatory activities, leaving behind her van and the house to embark on a less goal-directed, episodic journey.

Thematizing the Female-Alien *Other*: Intermedial Allusion and Ecology

Since the film's visual narration restricts us mostly to Laura's experience, deviations from this norm stand out as willful and self-conscious stylistic choices. When, due to the dense fog, Laura abandons her van and car at the beginning of the film's third act, Laura is framed from behind her seat. The viewer has come to expect this composition as one of several default camera setups through which we accompany Laura as she drives around scanning for her male victims. But in this instance, any view from the windshield is obscured by the dense white fog. Unable to drive, Laura must exit the vehicle. Instead of the camera following along with her, as the film has trained us to expect, the camera remains stationary within the van. For fourteen seconds the viewer's attention is focused on the blank white fog, internally framed by the van's windshield. In these moments, the film's restricted narration stylistically decouples us from the character to whose point of view we are mostly restricted. And, as with other shots of unusually long duration, this shot encourages us now to contemplate the *opacification* of vision and the lacunae inherent in any attempt at pure visual mastery of the world. The shot begins a new, episodic phase of the film's plot where sensory modalities *other* than vision will be sought out and experienced by Laura.

After the film's midpoint, *Under the Skin* engages in a formal *détournement* of the conventional SF horror film. Instead of aligning us with a human protagonist, it aligns our sympathy and allegiance with a nonhuman, alien other. There is no question, however, that the meeting with the Deformed Man constitutes a disruptive moment for Laura's character. A space both literal and virtual opens up for the character in which to exercise reflective self-agency as the film abandons the conventions of the SF horror plot.

Herein, the film's style focuses the viewer's attention on the sensuous and sensorial conditions of being an embodied, female subject. We have already seen multiple shots of Laura touching female clothing. When Laura attempts to eat human food she gags and violently expels it from her mouth. The close-up of Laura's hand bringing a forkful of cake to her mouth takes twenty-four seconds of screen time. The unusual duration of the shot emphasizes Laura's uncertainty and lack of familiarity with human food. In the next scene, without a jacket she shivers in the cold and rain. When the Quiet Man brings her home and plays the radio while washing the dishes, a close-up shows Laura's fingers tentatively tapping to the beat, as if music might function as a cultural bridge between alien and human experience. That night, bathed in the red glow from a space heater, we see Laura examine her naked figure in the mirror. In a series of medium long-scale shots she twists and flexes her legs, observing the various torsions available to the human form. Her body becomes an object of curiosity and fascination in itself. And, when she tries to consummate her relationship with the Quiet Man, Laura's attempts at sexual intimacy seem genuine, in contrast to the ritualized striptease she has used to lure her previous victims.

After visiting the castle ruins, a prolonged medium-scale two-shot depicts Laura and the Quiet Man engaging in an attempt at erotic intimacy. A cut to a medium close-up of the two reveals that they not only kiss but Laura lifts her hand to caress her would-be lover's face. These shots emphasize Laura's effort to explore the tactile and somatic dimensions of human sexuality. In a long-scale overhead shot the Quiet Man removes Laura's jeans. A close-up profile shot of the two shows him struggling to penetrate her, the lower halves of their bodies just off-screen. As the man struggles, Laura suddenly jumps up and, in a series of brisk cuts that emphasize the almost mechanical rigidity of her movements, she grabs a lamp and peers at the space between her legs to discover the absence of a human vagina. Since Laura is posed from behind, dorsal staging again suppresses the character's facial reactions. She violently discards the lamp, stands up, and faces the wall of the bedroom. Once again, her visage assumes a blank expression. Not only does Laura quite literally turn her back on the man, eschewing any promise of domestic or heterosexual intimacy, she also denies the man her gaze. The scene emphasizes the film's metaphorics of vision as an oscillation between woman as erotic display and that which is irreducible to any gendered essence demanded of patriarchal society or male desire.

Conclusion

The second part of *Under the Skin* is dedicated to Laura's exploration of the various sensory modalities available to human experience: taste, sound, and touch. How are we to understand the alien's experience of female embodiment? And why are these moments of carnality granted such salience by the film's style and narration? Moreover, the film's second half displays a more systematic repetition and variation of the long-scale landscape view, encouraging the viewer to form broad associations across these shots. The scene before Laura abandons her van is preceded by a dramatic long-scale shot of Loch Restil, lasting twenty-five seconds. The shot's duration invites us to consider the changing elemental weather conditions and the balletic swirling of fog over the water. Once Laura exits the van, the film cuts to a long-scale shot (also lasting twenty-five seconds) of a large body of water (presumably the Loch), but now the horizon is obscured by fog, as undulating waves fill the frame. Again, in lieu of storytelling information, the film encourages us to consider the natural, elemental features of the landscape as worthy of prolonged attention. In one example, the long-scale shot plays out as a self-conscious sixty-nine-second master shot where we see a distant Laura encounter the Quiet Man, at the bus stop. A long-scale shot of the two strolling through nearby woods lasts twenty-six seconds, with longer-scale shots featuring the castle ruins in the background. But once Laura leaves the Quiet Man, there is a cut to an extreme long-scale shot, lasting thirty-one seconds, of a field before a dark green and slightly ominous forest of evergreens, as Laura's small figure runs toward the tall dark woods. In the first half of the film Laura possessed a form of visual mastery through her commanding eyeline views of men and the clear avenues and landscapes through which she and the Bad Man moved. In the dark forest, however, closer shot-scales of Laura activate off-screen space as potentially threatening. Glazer ends the film, however, with another nod to convention. Alternate cutting and tight, shallow-focus framings are enlisted for the film's chase sequence through the woods. The tight framings generate suspense about the figures' proximity to one another. After Laura falls asleep in a hiker's cabin, there is another long-scale shot of a steep mountain landscape, the frame full of distant trees rustling in the wind. As the shot progresses, a giant face and body slowly emerge over the vast mountain range. Again, the film relies on a twenty-four-second protracted dissolve to visually fuse Laura's supine body with the landscape. The excessive visual attention the film has paid to the landscape suggests a merging of Laura's status as a character and the natural world as a resource to be mined, as an insistence on consciousness as always embodied and inextricable from environmental context. This impression is underscored by the fact that the character, who in the very next scene will attempt to rape and destroy Laura, is credited as "the Logger," a man whose role is to view the forest not in wonder or delight or as a place to authentically dwell, but as "standing reserve" or resource to be leveled and destroyed.

Posthumanist and ecological themes are also signaled through methods of intermedial allusion. Productivist themes structure both the film's plot and imagery. Laura's role on Earth is to efficiently harvest human "livestock," providing biopower for her species. The graphic shot of the large conveyer belt that transfers human viscera is a clear reference to a factory conveyer belt and productivist methods of streamlining and accelerating labor. We have noted the hand of God touching Adam reference, and the references to the work of Kubrick. The film's pictorial allusions, however, also extend to the work of Caspar David Friedrich. Primarily a landscape painter, Friedrich's work centers on rendering the landscape as dramatic and vaguely mystical (Figure 7.1).

The film's most obvious and significant reference to Friedrich is in the film's penultimate image, the thirty-second shot of the Bad Man, which references Friedrich's *Wanderer above the Sea Fog* (1818). Unable to locate Laura, he stands in distant dorsal framing, with a slight *contrapposto*, evoking the *Rückenfigur* device of Friedrich's painting as he gazes out to a vast expanse below, his gaze opacified by the foggy conditions limiting his view. The visual mastery assumed here by the (implicitly male) Cartesian subject is troubled by that which resists any such totalizing view or rationalist and productivist aesthetic or agenda. Both Friedrich's picture

FIGURE 7.1 *Unable to locate Laura, the Bad Man (Jeremy McWilliams) stares out at the foggy Loch in a composition that recalls the* Rückenfigur *(German: Rear-facing figure) device of Caspar David Friedrich's* Wanderer above the Sea of Fog *(1818) (Film4 Productions, 2013, United Kingdom, A24).*

and the film's citation undermine the clear vistas of one-point Renaissance space. Fore- and background are *collapsed* in Friedrich's composition, while the dense fog prevents any visual penetration into depth. We can take these self-conscious allusions as a cinematic critique of the Enlightenment subject as he who is *master of all he surveys*. The self-conscious aestheticization and pictorial allusiveness evinced by the film's second half contrasts starkly with the film's first two acts, where precisely regimented eyelines and jump cuts served to render Laura's systematic and ruthless predation of men. The insistent emphasis on landscapes and the natural world in the second part of the film, anchored in Laura's female embodiment, is presented as a force that resists any totalizing visual control or instrumental rationalization. The film is also bracketed by productivist and ecological motifs. The large yellow crane present at the film's opening is bookended by the Logger and his bright orange truck, piled high with timbre. He, too, is engaged in maximizing the accumulation of biopower through a destruction of the landscape.

At the end of the film, after Laura is attacked by the Logger, the alien stares at the human skin it has worn throughout. Oddly, it is not an inanimate shell but continues to blink and stare back. This thematically charged shot features the alien as radically divided, split in its subjectivity between alien and nonhuman female self and yet also inextricable. The marks of culture, in the form of dress, clothing, and makeup, as well as the flesh itself, remain part of Laura's culturally embodied female "skin," her interface with earthly, human existence. Consciousness and subjectivity, and especially *female* subjectivity, is here presented as robustly embodied, culturally defined, and contingent. This idea of consciousness as always *embodied* consciousness is advanced by numerous posthumanist theorists, such as Haraway and

FIGURE 7.2 *The alien Laura (Scarlett Johansson) stares back at her outer "skin," which continues to blink (Film4 Productions, 2013, United Kingdom, A24).*

Braidotti, as well as others who challenge Humanist certitudes and subject/object, mind/body dualities. But there is something more suggested by the tar-black form of the alien we have only seen once before. For the viewer, this form is visually opaque, irreducible to any knowable essence. Like Haraway's female cyborgs, this split character constitutes a provocative figure of *female as such*—a metaphorical search for female identity, however partial and intersectional, and, in *Under the Skin*, however horrific and pessimistic this search may eventually turn out to be (Figure 7.2).

8

Living in *Color*

Feminist and Posthumanist Ontology in *Upstream Color*

Emily Sanders

Shane Carruth's 2013 film *Upstream Color* explores the life of Kris (Amy Seimetz) after she has been implanted with a mind-controlling worm at the hands of the Thief (Thiago Martins). Hailed as "one of the most important and neglected [science fiction] films of the last 50 years,"[1] *Upstream Color* diverts from typical posthuman science fiction constructs such as the (usually unstable) relationship between the machine and the human body or the emergence of intelligent and generative technology. Rather, the film is almost completely devoid of astounding scientific technological feats and futuristic dystopian spectacles. The film exemplifies Rosi Braidotti's notion of the posthuman as a collective process of becoming that expands beyond the human body, which is intimately tied to the organic, human, or otherwise.[2] Kris is hijacked by the Thief using a worm that strips her of all agency; the Thief controls her both mentally and physically as she is a host to the worm. Once released from the Thief's control, Kris' identity radically alters in that she opens up to processes of being that require the support of

---

[1]J. DiGiovanna, "Identity: Difficulties, Discontinuities and Pluralities of Personhood," in *The Palgrave Handbook of Posthumanism in Film and Television*, ed. Curtis D. Carbonell, Michael Hauskeller, and Thomas D. Philbeck (Palgrave Macmillan), 354.
[2]Rosi Braidotti, *The Posthuman* (Cambridge: Polity Press, 2013).

a network composed of various forms of life. In this, the film produces its own posthuman network, a kind of embodied map, which, in an analogy with the project of the critical posthumanities, deconstructs the human.[3] In *Upstream Color*, Kris' prior humanist relationship to her environment is replaced with a *post*humanist one, in which her connection to other forms of being changes the way she experiences her human body. This posthuman ontological shift evolves throughout the film in its formal renderings of Kris' novel relationship to the environment, the film's reliance on audition and listening as sites of meaning, and the trans-species relationships that develop throughout the diegesis.

Upstream Color is both posthumanist and feminist. Its feminist merits I discuss through the breakdown of language facilitated between *zoe* and *bios*, the function of trauma that creates Kris' posthuman condition, and its emergent nonpatriarchal forms of community, which I discuss using Stina Attebery's queer reading of the film and Donna Haraway's theory of significant otherness. Together, the posthuman networks and feminist interventions in *Upstream Color* designate it as a unique science fiction film. More typical contemporary science fiction narratives, such as the *Terminator* series, aspects of The Marvel Cinematic Universe, and elements of *Star Wars*, obsess over futuristic technologies, ultimately centering around the capacity of humans and their seemingly limitless imaginations. These are neo-humanist narratives which reflect the Enlightenment Humanist belief in "individualism, autonomy, responsibility and self-determination."[4] These SF narratives continue to center the exceptional capacity of humans. Reason, what Braidotti calls "the distinctively human prerogative,"[5] frames anthropocentric science fiction narratives. A defining feature of the Enlightenment era's justification of man's intelligence, reason has primacy over all other forms of consciousness, and is thus "[c]onnected to a sovereign and rationalist ideal."[6] Reason is therefore "conceived as the motor of science-driven world-historical progress."[7] *Upstream Color*, in contrast, focuses on the organic as a way to unveil the processes of the posthuman that already—beyond language and technology—in the quite literal primordial soil of trans-species beings. Braidotti's term *"zoe*-centered egalitarianism" is significant since it offers a way to see the inherent connectedness of all species. Hierarchies set up by humanism dissipate. Instead, species

[3]Stefan Herbrechter, "Critical Posthumanism." *Critical Posthumanism: Genealogy of the Post-human*, https://criticalposthumanism.net/critical-posthumanism/#:~:text=Critical%20posthu-manism%20is%20a%20theoretical,%2C%20ghosts%2C%20angels%20etc.
[4]Braidotti, *The Posthuman*, 29.
[5]Braidotti, "Chapter 2: Critical Posthuman Theory," *Critical Posthumanism and Planetary Futures*, (Springer India, 2016), 14.
[6]Ibid.
[7]Ibid.

form networks, which mutually inform each other. It is this phenomenon that *Upstream Color* visualizes. *Zoe*-centered egalitarianism, Braidotti's launchpad toward critical posthumanism and beyond anthropocentrism, seeks to expand the normative conceptions of life.[8] Braidotti refers to *zoe* as an essence, "a vital force of Life" present in all nonhuman beings.[9] It operates as an alternative to *bios*, life that is applied only to the human. I contend that the *zoe*-ness intrinsic, for Braidotti, in all nonhuman beings operates also as a feminist tool. In *Upstream Color*, the transmission of knowledge and the formation of community between the nonhuman *zoe* and the human operate outside and prior to the function of language, which eventually resides within *all* forms of bodies and life, not just the nonhuman. The primacy of spoken, human language is quickly tossed aside in *Upstream Color*, which subsequently prioritizes alternate visual and aural forms of trans-species communication. Kris' transformation into a posthuman being pivots on this awareness of knowledge and interconnectedness between all beings, and the film demonstrates this awareness through its formal techniques.

In order to critically investigate the dimensions of the feminist posthuman in *Upstream Color*, I link the theory-driven cartographic process of the critical posthumanities[10] to the film's editing style and sound design, which I argue creates *aesthetic* cartographies. This term signals Braidotti's critical posthumanist procedure, which requires a transdisciplinary theoretical approach to "undoing the human."[11] Critical theory and queer theory have already been applied to *Upstream Color* by Matt Applegate and Stina Attebery, respectively.[12] In this chapter, I demonstrate how their previous writings contribute to the project of critical posthumanism. Moreover, I look at how *Upstream Color* works toward "undoing the human" through trans-species collaboration, which is here rendered visible, or rather, audible, through the various stylings of Carruth's feature. Aesthetic cartography as a term also links to Ian Robinson's "cinematic cartographies," where "[m]oving images create relational cartographies of the world through their spatialization of stories and their negotiation of a spectator's sense

---

[8]Braidotti, *The Posthuman*, 50.

[9]Ibid., 60.

[10]Braidotti, "The Critical Posthumanities; or, Is Medianatures to Naturecultures as *Zoe* is to *Bios*?" *Cultural Politics* 12, issue 3 (2016): 380–90.

[11]Braidotti, "A Theoretical Framework for the Critical Posthumanities," *Theory, Culture & Society* 6, issue 6 (2018): 34.

[12]As of this writing, there are only four published academic articles on *Upstream Color*. The fourth, which is tangential to my argument in this chapter, is "J. Mayward, 'Parabolic Transcendence in Time and Narrative: Shane Carruth's Primer (US 2004) and Upstream Color (US 2013) as Post-Secular Sci-Fi Parables'. *Journal for Religion, Film and Media* 6, no. 1 (2020): 17–36.

of emplacement and displacement."[13] The function of narrative film is always to design worlds that affectively link the viewers to the diegesis. I argue, however, that *Upstream Color*'s relational work designs feminist and posthumanist ontologies, which open not only to Kris and the other characters in the film but to the viewers as well.

After discussing the function of aesthetic cartographies in *Upstream Color*, I will then move on to discuss the intersections of feminism and posthumanism within the film. Here, the sound design plays a significant role: it shifts the viewer's focus away from dialogue to its ethereal electronic crescendos. This extradiegetic soundscape engages the viewer in an unconventional process of listening, and it is through the film's otherworldly soundtrack that we as viewers and as auditors predominantly come to understand its meanings. Additionally, the soundtrack emphasizes the posthuman, trans-species forms of communication that occur within the diegesis. These trans-species kinship bonds—which correspond to Attebery's queer communities and Haraway's significant otherness theory—assemble through mutual awareness and attentiveness; they *listen* to each other, outside of human language. These techniques reveal a process of undoing and reshaping that is notably posthuman *and* feminist, as the film emphasizes a somatic, embodied, prelinguistic approach to generating and acquiring knowledge that exists outside of patriarchal Enlightenment-based humanist ideology. It is significant that Kris, a woman, is the main character of the film. The feminine body has always been a contentious site that threatens to destabilize language's maintenance of patriarchal power.[14] While she is not the first who suffers at the hands of the Thief, she mobilizes her posthuman network successfully against him. In its feminist move, *Upstream Color* returns to the body as a site that bears significance and meaning before language. In its posthumanist move, the film demonstrates the significance of *all* bodies—human and nonhuman alike—as interconnected carriers of meaning that work together. In *Upstream Color* the feminine *bios* and *zoe* collaborate outside of language to ultimately undo their systems of oppression. Finally, I will discuss the function of trauma within this narrative and proffer its placement in posthuman pathways in general. Trauma propels the posthuman path in *Upstream Color*, and trauma's role in posthumanist ontologies warrants further critical investigation.

---

[13]Ian Robinson, "The Critical Cinematic Cartography of My Winnipeg," *Canadian Journal of Film Studies* 23, no. 2 (2014): 98.
[14]Elizabeth Grosz, *Jacques Lacan: A Feminist Introduction* (Oxfordshire: Routledge, 1990); *Volatile Bodies: Toward a Corporeal Feminism* (Oxfordshire: Routledge, 1994) and Julia Kristeva, *Powers of Horror: An Essay on Abjection* (New York: Columbia University Press, 1982).

Aesthetic Cartographies in *Upstream Color*

Aesthetic cartographies in *Upstream Color* visualize posthuman forms of being. These are *aesthetic* cartographies because it is the film's formal techniques that render these connections visible. A variety of these components—especially editing and sound design—collaborate to expand our awareness of what, or who, is/are working together within this narrative. Discontinuous editing is a primary function of *Upstream Color*'s aesthetic cartography. Components of its discontinuous editing consist of ellipsis and fragmented montage (specifically jump cuts and crosscutting), which broaden our understanding of the levels of communication that occur between different beings in the film. In addition to the film's discontinuous editing practices, the film also relies on rich soundscapes that shape the emergent subjectivities within the narrative. Rather than moving forward in a linear direction, the aesthetics of the film map trans-species relations that spread in all directions, both temporally and ontologically. In a narrative sense, the film does not move *forward*, but *outward*.

Part of the outward trajectory of *Upstream Color* is facilitated by trans-species relationships. They form affective links visualized through the film's formal elements that map onto the posthuman in the film. More broadly, trans-species relationships are part of the utopia of posthumanist theory. For Braidotti, these relationships define the posthuman on an ontological level, moving past posthumanism's theoretical impetus: "[s]ubjectivity is not restricted to bound individuals, but is rather a co-operative trans-species effort [...] that takes place transversally, in-between nature/technology; male/female; black/white; local/global; present/past—in assemblages that flow across and displace the binaries."[15] Binary oppositions fuel master narratives that erase difference through supporting notions of same-ness or otherness. Trans-species relationships, linked to Haraway's notion of "significant otherness" which I will discuss toward the end of this chapter, undo these binaries that maintain divisions of power and exploitation. It is precisely this displacement of bounded binaries, and the act of creating cross-species assemblages, that the film maps in its introductory sequence. I will analyze this sequence in close detail to show how it designs the posthuman through creating an aesthetic cartography that maps feminist forms of being.

The film opens with a black screen as warm harmonic drones flood the extradiegetic audio. For the next five minutes a crosscutting sequence shows us a variety of different personages that become nodes within the film's posthuman network. Throughout this rapid display of crosscutting, we see the workings of aesthetic cartographies that map out these five "nodes." After a

---

[15]Braidotti, "A Theoretical Framework for the Critical Posthumanities," 33.

FIGURE 8.1 *Boys (Ashton Miramontes and Andreon Watson) bike to a meeting place (ERBP, Upstream Color, 2013, USA, VHX).*

FIGURE 8.2 *Friend 2's (Andreon Watson) look of apprehension and confusion (ERBP, Upstream Color, 2013, USA, VHX).*

close-up of a garbage bag, there is a cut to young teenage boys on bicycles (the first node). Not much is said between the teenagers, but through a medium close-up we become privy to a series of interchanging looks that can be read as apprehension suffused with tension (Figures 8.1 and 8.2), although, again, we are not yet given enough information as to the source of this tension. Another cut takes us back to the garbage bag transported to a recycling bin by a man we will come to know as the Thief. The camera stays on the Thief, but cuts to him keenly inspecting multiple blue orchids (the second node). He scrapes blue powder off their leaves (Figure 8.3), and, finding what he was looking for, sifts through the soil of the orchids to excavate dozens of worms (the third node; Figure 8.4). Another cut finds the Thief at a desk, where he categorizes the worms between those alive and dead (Figure 8.5).

FIGURE 8.3 *The Thief (Thiago Martins) scrapes blue powder off an orchid's leaf (ERBP, Upstream Color, 2013, USA, VHX).*

FIGURE 8.4 *The Thief (Thiago Martins) finds worms in the soil of orchids (ERBP,* Upstream Color, 2013, USA, VHX).

A cut back to the young boys shows them sharing a soft drink on a lawn as they mimic each other's movements in some kind of strange choreography. The camera transitions to another location which reveals the same teenagers, who show their friend—and us—the secrets behind the liquids they were just drinking together. We realize that the worms the Thief has collected have been steeped in the boys' soft drink. Friend One (Ashton Miramontes) apprises Friend Two (Andreon Watson), "see how many we go through to get a good one?" and instructs him to drink. Friend One asks "are you ready?" to which Friend Two replies, "no." What happens next accelerates the already mystifying aspects of this sequence: as Friend Two says "no," Friend One immediately throws a punch toward Friend Two, which Friend Two—who clearly did not consent to this action—impressively blocks. A soft crescendo of underscoring music swells in revelation, and the two boys

FIGURE 8.5 *The Thief (Thiago Martins) compiles viable worms (ERBP,* Upstream Color, *2013, USA, VHX).*

FIGURE 8.6 *Jeff (Shane Carruth) running (ERBP,* Upstream Color, *2013, USA, VHX).*

continue to mirror each other's movements. The extradiegetic music primes us to read this mimicry as a scientific discovery. Clearly, the worm juice has awakened a somatic, multisensory connection between the two boys, but we do not get to witness this phenomenon for much longer. The camera cuts again to a man (the fourth node), who we will come to know as Jeff (Shane Carruth), running in the middle of a suburban street (Figure 8.6). The fifth node introduced in this sequence is Kris, who, like the man we meet before her, is running when she's interrupted by a business call (Figure 8.7). The final scene of this sequence cuts back to the Thief, who places the worms into pill capsules and attempts to sell them as drugs at night in various bars and street corners. When no one buys his worm-filled pills, he pulls out his taser and decides to use force to accomplish his task. The Thief spots Kris alone in a hallway. A sudden elliptical cut jumps to Kris, incapacitated, dragged

FIGURE 8.7 *Kris (Amy Seimetz) at a marathon (ERBP, Upstream Color, 2013, USA, VHX).*

outside in the rain by the Thief. He places a manual CPR mask and bag over Kris' mouth, which is filled with water and contains one of the worms. He forces Kris to consume the worm through the CPR device, and, after she sputters and gets herself to stand, her consumption of the worm instantly places her physically and mentally under the absolute control of the Thief.

The nodes introduced in this scene through the film's editing—the Thief and the boys, the orchids, the worms, Jeff, and Kris—set up a feminist and posthumanist cartographic practice in three ways. First, the scene primes us to read relationships and environments beyond a clear linear structure. Second, the opening scene highlights connections between all these beings *before* their traumatic encounters with the Thief via the worm. Third, it is through the editing and extradiegetic musical swells that we read this relationship: the soft bright light suffuses the introductory images of each character, the near absence of explanatory language either in voice-over or dialogue, and the way Carruth unconventionally draws our attention to the score, all work together to ask the viewer to see and hear differently. This opening scene is an aesthetic map: it charts its characters through a supremely auditory and visual ontology that will only develop further in its power and meaning as the film continues.

Uncovering Ontologies

The posthuman reveals to us "the malleability of the human condition."[16] Critical posthumanism expands the notion of what it means to be human,

---

[16]Carbonell, Hauskeller, and Philbeck, *The Palgrave Handbook of Posthumanism in Film and Television*, 6.

and the discourses through which this expansion occurs traverse such disciplines as queer, feminist, environmental, technological, and critical race studies. In effect, critical posthumanism opens up new ontological sites that expand, and move beyond, the Enlightenment Humanist concept of the human. Matt Applegate and Stina Attebery engage with *Upstream Color* through two of these theoretical pathways: Applegate's analysis of the film explores it as an analogy of the violent effects of late-stage capitalism, positing *Upstream Color* as an exploration of what life might look like beyond capitalism. Attebery imagines *Upstream Color* as a configuration of a queer community structured through trauma and nonlinguistic auditory intelligence that comes together to overthrow an oppressive patriarchal system. In this section, I bring these two readings together to demonstrate how they both pull apart threads that "undo" two current conditions of Western humanism: capitalism and patriarchy.

Only after Kris is rid of the worm does she uncover a posthuman way of living. Once she has been fully extorted by the Thief, Kris is brought to another facility, operated by the Sampler (Andrew Sensenig). The Sampler removes the worm from Kris and immediately implants it in a pig. The pig is one of many the Sampler monitors on a swine farm; all pigs bear the worms of other victims. Worm removal complete, a traumatized and confused Kris becomes hyperattuned to the information transmitted through sounds and sensations of her natural environment, which eventually leads to her posthuman liberation. Kris' turn toward nature and the intelligence it holds demonstrates Braidotti's notion of ecology as a "powerful source of inspiration for contemporary re-configurations of critical posthumanism."[17] Nature becomes a more prominent agent in Kris' ontology, meaning that it forms a part of her posthuman network. For Braidotti "[t]he environmental alternative is a new holistic approach that combines cosmology with anthropology and postsecular, mostly feminist, spirituality, to assert the need for loving respect for diversity in both its human and non-human forms."[18] It is precisely on this point in *Upstream Color* that scholars have focused their analyses.

For Applegate, *Upstream Color* transports the characters "to the edge of what they can imagine and say about a life free of profitability and exploitation in order to glimpse a yet unrealized epistemological position: a knowledge of life beyond capitalism."[19] Once Jeff and Kris are "free" to return back to the shambles of their lives postinfection, their ability to return to the functioning system of American capitalism is

---

[17]Braidotti *The Posthuman*, 48.
[18]Ibid.
[19]Matthew Applegate, "Imagining the End of Late Capitalism in Shane Carruth's *Primer* and *Upstream Color*," *Theory & Event* 19, issue 2 (2016), muse.jhu.edu/article/614363.

constantly interrupted by streams of communication—a side effect of their abduction—that are invisible to and/or render tenuous their relationships with their colleagues. Jeff, who works as an accountant, is hidden in a hotel room and kept "off the books" since, when controlled by the Thief, he stole thousands from his former company. Similarly, Kris is fired from her job when she cannot explain her weeks-long absence when she was abducted by the Thief. Her next job at a print shop forces her to work in isolation from other employees. The capitalist system, which structures value and identity based on one's ability to successfully contribute to the economy, cannot contain Kris and Jeff once they have both been financially and epistemologically robbed. As Applegate aptly notes, "the loss of one's finances is tantamount to the loss of one's subjective hold on the world."[20] The Thief takes more than Kris and Jeff's wealth: he steals their knowledge of themselves and their worlds. He steals their subjective identities, their memories, their histories, and their abilities to conceive of their futures within the American capitalist model. And yet, in the absence of these individualized subjectivities, Kris and Jeff awaken to new modes of identification that Applegate terms "transindividual," but which are also posthuman. Capitalism, which "aims at controlling all that lives,"[21] fails, in that it can neither contain nor account for the various forms of zoe, which invariably provide trajectories away from anthropocentrism and "towards the non-human."[22] The network to which Kris awakens exists outside of capitalism and centers on a conception of community that expands beyond the human.

Attebery describes the posthuman network in *Upstream Color* as a queer community. My posthuman reading of the film aligns with Attebery's queer reading. It is not that the two terms are synonymous but that queerness maps onto posthuman theory; queerness is a posthuman limb, an integral component that reveals alternate ways of being. Additionally, posthumanist, feminist, and queer theory seek to undermine the current conditions of existence that are structured, at least in part, by the heteropatriarchy: feminism through its commitment to uncovering the multiple expressions of gender inequality, and queer theory in how it undoes sex and gender essentialism to break open unlimited expressions of gender and sexuality. The critical posthumanities, like queer theory, expand the concept of *bios* through introducing zoe: many forms of life inherently related and integral to sustaining each other. Queer theory and feminist studies are thus integral for the critical posthumanities in how they radically reveal the multifarious forms of being. In the film, the Thief and the Sampler represent the capitalist

---

[20]Ibid.
[21]Braidotti, *The Posthuman*, 111.
[22]Ibid., 50.

patriarchy as an institution: their relationship to others centers on what others—both *bios* and *zoe*—might do for them, only achieved through force. Therefore, a queer *and* feminist posthuman reading of the film operates similarly: they undermine normative conceptions of community and life and put forth other ways of being. In reimaging alternate forms of life and community, the film's queer(ed) posthuman network stonewalls the Thief's patriarchal and capitalist goals.

As Kris recovers from the trauma of her bodily hijacking, a new awareness develops between other nonhuman beings who have been involved in the various stages of the Thief's cycle of violence. The prominent forms of *zoe* in this posthuman networked community are humans, worms, pigs (who host the extracted worms), the orchids that first feed the worms, and the river which decomposes the pigs' bodies and nourishes the wild orchids that are eventually harvested by the Thief in order to retrieve the worms. Their mutual awareness allows them to communicate through methods that function outside of language. For the most part, those involved in the posthuman network communicate through sound. The devaluing of verbal language, and instead a turn toward sound and images, undoes an element of the human, which I will examine in closer detail in the next section. For Attebery, sound plays a critical role in queering Kris' community. Sound "queers" Kris' experience in that "her sensory experiences of listening challenges the patriarchal authority of [. . .] medical listening by emphasizing Kris's ability to self-diagnose her contaminated relationship to her environment."[23] Attebery's reading of the film also highlights sound as its own node within *Upstream Color*'s aesthetic cartography. Not only do the members of this trans-species community themselves represent a kind of queer community, but sound plays a key role in structuring their subjectivities to the extent that their queer/feminist/posthuman listening undermines heteropatriarchal reasoning through language. Kris listens to ambient, nonlinguistic, and, at times, seemingly extradiegetic sounds—those that exist beyond the humanist drive for logic, reason, and rationale—in order to derive meaning and establish new ways of living. Moreover, this form of listening also allows her community to eventually overthrow the Thief and the Sampler's operation. *Upstream Color* positions communal forms of power outside of language, across various forms of life. Language neither delineates nor contains the forms of meaning and the structure of Kris' relationships.

---

[23]Attebery "Ecologies of Sound: Queer Intimacy, Trans-corporeality, and Reproduction in *Upstream Color*," in *Gender and Environment in Science Fiction*, ed. Brigitte Barclay and Christy Tidwell (Lexington Books, 2019), 133.

Speaking in *Color*

Postinfection, language breaks down between Jeff and Kris, but it is Kris that facilitates and inflects its failure. This next sequence I analyze also emphasizes how the failure of language enacts a posthuman cartography. As Kris attunes herself to her posthuman landscape, she sheds the structuring dominance of language, the system that perpetuates sexual—and species—difference. This is most obvious when Kris and Jeff exchange memories from their childhood. Carruth "resets" this scene in a kind of filmic anaphora, which elliptically repeats the scene over and over again. While at a park, Kris and Jeff look up as a flock of birds swirl above them in a washed-out blue sky (see Figure 8.8). The two debate the identification of the birds. Kris claims "they could be starlings," to which Jeff repetitively undermines, "they *could* be starlings." There is a whirring montage of various locations—the hotel room, the park again, a city street—where Kris and Jeff repeatedly attempt to tell their respective childhood stories, but whose details keep confusing, blending, and eluding them ("No, *my* friend Renny!"). The camera returns to the initial bird scene, but we arrive temporally earlier in the conversation than previously. Jeff questions, "who says they were grackles?" to which Kris repeats affirmatively, "grackles," and then continues "they could be starlings," thus restarting the same sequence. While the first iteration of this scene evokes a playfulness, a kind of intimacy between the two that is almost charming, as the conversation returns and repeats itself, the tension between Kris and Jeff heightens. Kris vents her frustration and tells Jeff "you're doing it again . . . I tell you a story, and you've taken it and made it your own. You do this all the time!" Communication through language fails as a direct result of their trauma from the worm infection in that we do not know which past,

FIGURE 8.8 *Kris (Amy Seimetz) and Jeff (Shane Carruth) discuss the birds (ERBP, Upstream Color, 2013, USA, VHX).*

whose past, or what past Kris is trying to tell. We believe Kris is trying to tell a story about a friend named Renny who "tried to drown me in the pool." But we know Kris was also nearly "drowned" by the Thief when he pumps water containing the worm down her throat and that the Sampler drowns Kris' pig's babies in the stream to stifle the pig's relationship to Jeff's pig. Language is no longer a reliable method of communication, and instead a posthuman memory through somatic knowledge emerges. Replacing verbal communication is a system of posthuman attunement, which prioritizes sight, sound, and feeling. Through this posthuman system, Kris adopts and exchanges memories among those in her network. To prove this point further, Jeff is also entangled in this same network in which the childhood trips he would take to Vermont with his family almost seem to map out the route Kris and Jeff will eventually take to find their pigs and terminate the Thief's operation. With reference to his Vermont trip, Kris asks "how do you get there?" Jeff replies, "I don't know, it's just some country road . . . number six," and Kris interjects, "No, *I* was six." Not only does linguistic meaning collapse in this sequence (Kris' assertion of her age simultaneously ruptures Jeff's explanation while rendering their conversation absurd), but time and memory in its linear trajectory dissolves. Kris and Jeff will travel down "some country road" that is unmarked in order to find the pig farm. In relaying this "memory," Jeff also describes future events. All of this is rendered visible through the formal elements of this scene.

The failure of linguistic communication in *Upstream Color* depicts how feminism "aims to lay bare the workings of patriarchal ideology."[24] More than the worm itself, it is language that becomes the primary conduit of violence for Kris and the other Sampled. The Thief commands Kris: he quite literally tells her when to eat, drink, talk, and think. He orders her to liquidate her bank account and perform mundane tasks that keep her under the veil of her mental abduction. The film sets up the Thief as an embodiment of oppression: he exploits the worms to exploit humans to exploit pigs whose bodies feed the plants that feed the worms, and the cycle continues. It is also important to note that one of the Thief's tools of control and manipulation is Henry David Thoreau's 1854 book, *Walden*. The Thief's victims must manually rewrite the text numerous times during their hypnotized and captive states. As an intertext, *Walden* speaks to the form of Kris' trauma. Straddling the idealism of transcendentalist thought while upholding the power of language, *Walden* is one of the Thief's weapons. The book also seems to be a guide for the Thief; he strips Kris of her material items, her capital, for his own benefit. In a sense, the Thief molds his victims as unwilling disciples of transcendentalism. However, the outcome of the victim's traumatic conversion is not self-reliance and independence, the

---

[24]Annette Kuhn, *Alien Zone II* (London and New York: Verso, 1999), 148.

goal of transcendentalism, but a generative collaboration with nature, or *zoe*, that undoes the boundaries of the individual. It is not *through* nature that Kris comes to her self-actualization. Instead, Kris works *with* nature to thwart the Thief through a reliance on a *zoe*-centered community.

According to a humanist logic, the humanist subject is a grammatical subject,[25] creating hierarchies determined by those who have access to language. In this sense, the Thief clearly designs a hierarchy in which he and his collaborators are at the top, and animals and plants—"who are marked by power and remain always unable to reply to the language of that power"[26]—clearly exist on the lower rungs. Language defines the "real," in that it signifies that which is deemed significant. For Karen Barad, linguistic communication "has been granted too much power,"[27] and this is true in the film as well. In *Upstream Color* language bears too much, and this weight makes it vulnerable to collapse. In Carruth's film, the alternative forms of communication that lead to the devaluing of language are explicitly nonlinguistic sounds that centralize the communicative act of listening. Listening creates linkages that mutually acknowledge the beingness of those who cannot be accounted for inside the system of humanist language (the worm, the pigs, and the flora). In order to structure her radical and subversive ontology, Kris attunes herself to these other frequencies, always occurring, but never known to Kris pre-worm infection. Furthermore, these forms of listening reveal the "embodied and embedded" feminist characteristics of posthumanism, as it marks a turn toward the site of bodies as sources of knowledge and power.[28] The interaction between Kris and Jeff around the birds and their childhood memories reveals how their new posthuman attunements have rendered their subjectivities porous; in subordinating the primacy of language, Kris, more so than Jeff, because of her gender, is open to new forms of communication that ultimately allow her, in collaboration with her network, to abolish the power of the Thief. As a woman, Kris is already positioned, according to feminist theorists, in an unstable claim to humanness. The leakiness of the female human body reminds us how all bodies—regardless of gender—are connected beyond the skin.[29] While Kris

---

[25]Florence Chiew, "Posthuman Ethics with Cary Wolfe and Karan Barad: Animal Compassion as Trans-Species Entanglement," *Theory, Culture & Society* 31, no. 4 (2014): 57.

[26]Phil Henderson, "The Sun Never Set on the Human Empire: Haunts of Humanism in the *Planet of the Apes* Films," in *The Palgrave Handbook of Posthumanism in Film and Television*, ed. Curtis D. Carbonell, Michael Hauskeller, and Thomas D. Philbeck (Palgrave Macmillan, 2015), 322.

[27]Karen Barad, "Posthumanist Performativity: Toward an Understanding of How Matter Comes to Matter," *Signs: Journal of Women in Culture and Society* 28, no. 3 (2003): 801.

[28]Braidotti, *The Posthuman*, 188.

[29]Margrit Shildrick and Janet Price, *Vital Signs: Feminist Reconfigurations of the Bio/logical Body* (Edinburgh: Edinburgh University Press, 1998); Margrit Shildrick *Embodying the*

is the first to act on this feminist and posthuman knowledge, it is important that Jeff quickly follows suit, as well as every other victim of the Thief.

Sound and *Color*

Audition, in this sense of the ability to perceive sound, is a persistent formal element throughout *Upstream Color* and works as yet another posthuman component of the film. Sound in the film serves two purposes. First, it brings the viewer deeper into Kris' aural experiences and the posthuman network in which she finds herself. Second, it engages the viewer with the film in a way that ties us into its aesthetic map. Sound in *Upstream Color* takes on a unique dimension as it hardly ever serves as background noise, and instead itself becomes a character or "node" within the film's aesthetic cartography. As Attebery suggests, sound becomes a source of knowledge that helps reconfigure Kris' relationship to her own body and to those bodies within her new posthuman ontology. The experimental quality of the soundtrack—whose tones vibrantly swell and contract in their own abstract rhythm—informs the viewer of the importance of the events that we see on screen. According to Lee Marshall, "*Upstream Color* is a film that happens to you."[30] Audition guides the viewer to the film's meaning: it incites an affective, sensory response that links the viewer's understanding of the film to Kris' understanding of her body and environment. Once again the opening sequence offers an example of such an occurrence. When we see the young boys in perfect choreography with their movements in their bodies, an effervescent crescendo blossoms into the aural landscape of the film. This musical sequence repeats itself numerous times during moments that are marked as crucial realizations. It appears when Jeff and Kris first meet, signaling the importance of their relationship; when Kris imagines blue orchids slowly turning yellow as she swims in a pool and then suddenly hallucinates a yellow orchid suspended in the water next to her; and when Kris saves the pig farm. Although it is never entirely clear if Kris or Jeff can hear the ambient music that accompanies their montages of growing posthuman attunement, there is at least a suggestion that the extradiegetic music we hear is the same crafted by the Sampler (in one sequence, Kris and Jeff even track down mixtapes by the Sampler at a local store). Therefore, the music seems both diegetic and extradiegetic. It exists in relation to the

---

Monster: Encounters with the Vulnerable Self (Sage, 2001) and "Why Should Our Bodies End at the Skin?: Embodiment, Boundaries, and Somatechnics," *Hypatia* 30, no. 1 (2015): 13–29.
[30]Lee Marshall, "*Upstream Color*: Nature, Love, Survival," *Queen's Quarterly* 120, issue 3 (2013), https://link.gale.com/apps/doc/A347408434/LitRC?u=queensulaw&sid=LitRC&xid=28df8f5a.

events on-screen, and yet only select participants—specifically Kris and Jeff, and us as viewers—are able to (eventually) decrypt its messages.

We as viewers are also included as participants who must listen in order to understand the film's events. Our attention to the audio in *Upstream Color* leads us to its posthuman qualities in that "the audio invites and often triggers multisensory perception."[31] The complex characteristics of the soundtrack seem to be meant to manipulate us emotionally in order to open us up to a system of knowledge that transports us along with Kris as she discovers alternative ways to live in—and listen to—the world. For Joe Kickasola, this highlights how the audio entices us into the film world, and specifically the world of Kris, which "feels present to us, bewilders and enchants us, and ultimately horrifies us."[32] More than anything, the audio helps us orient ourselves within the film's landscape, which, rather than horrific, is exceedingly and, at times, exhaustingly, confounding.

What these scholars agree upon is that the film depicts emergent, radical forms of existing, whether through the destruction of the capitalist system, the creation of queer interspecies communities, or the abstract, immersive, and immanent nature of its soundtrack, which brings its viewers into its posthuman ontology. In this way *Upstream Color* speaks to the multiplicitous nature of the posthuman, and yet it also underlines one of the most significant issues Braidotti identifies in regard to the operation of posthuman subjectivity: that of trauma. I argue that this is one of the most troubling aspects of *Upstream Color*, and perhaps the greatest barrier to reading this film as both a posthuman and a feminist text. In her book *The Posthuman*, Braidotti asks, "how does the posthuman engender its own forms of inhumanity?"[33] To take this line of questioning further, does one need to be *de*humanized in order to become *post*human?

The *Color* of Trauma

Upstream Color answers yes. It is easy to read how the Thief *impels* Kris' posthuman gestures, in that the worm that infects her is both an intense moment of trauma and the first step toward her realizing a posthuman ontology. An obvious example of the traumatic impact of the worm's implantation is the kitchen scene, when Kris stabs herself multiple times with a chef's knife in an attempt to extract the worm she sees wriggling underneath her skin. The worm arouses terror and desperation in Kris, and

---

[31]Joseph G. Kickasola, "Leading with the Ear: *Upstream Color* and the Cinema of Respiration," *Film Quarterly* 66, issue 4 (2013): 68.
[32]Ibid., 71.
[33]Braidotti, *The Posthuman*, 3.

yet it is also a part of her posthuman network. Furthermore, Kris' abduction at the beginning of the film is visually coded as a violation. This scene is also one of the few in the film where the mise-en-scène is immersed in darkness. In an overhead shot, we see Kris knocked out and dragged into the pouring rain which pelts her body. The camera switches to a side-view medium shot of Kris from the bust down, which visually decapitates her. The next shot is a medium close-up of Kris' face and chest as the rain drenches her. When the Thief straddles her to place the CPR mask containing the worm over her nose and mouth, the camera cuts closer and closer to Kris' face. The scene reaches its climax at an extreme close-up of Kris' gaping eyes as the resuscitation device forces the worm inside her mouth. This metaphorical rape—a violation that severs Kris' connection to her identity—propels the narrative forward.

Trauma has a way of binding people together. For Attebery, it is trauma, such as the kind Kris experiences, that shapes and brings together emergent forms of being that create queer communities.[34] Attebery maintains that "[o]nly by reframing these traumas around her experiences of intimacy with her pig and the other [S]ampled organisms is Kris able to transform her trauma into the basis for a queer community."[35] Science fiction film becomes problematic in negotiating the posthuman, in that dehumanization is one of the genre's "standard motifs."[36] However, if we follow Applegate's interpretation of the film, we, as humanist subjects of the capitalist institution, are *always already* dehumanized in order to fulfill our very limited function as consumers and producers of capital. Adopting this reading of the film stresses violence not as a transformative necessity that pushes one into the realm of the posthuman, but instead underscores how our current socioeconomic system *already* traumatizes us. Trauma is unavoidable. Under neoliberal capitalism, we have always already been violated (in varying degrees depending on our various identities), and thus the only way we can move toward the posthuman requires the recognition of the inherent violence of our current social, political, and economic institutions.

Trauma spurs the posthuman in *Upstream Color*, but it also fosters the strongest posthuman link in the film: between Kris and her pig, who share the same parasitic worm. While the worm physically brings the two together— Kris first encounters the pig when the Sampler extracts the worm from Kris and immediately transplants it into the pig—it is their emotional and physical connection, kindled through shared trauma and worm, that forges their posthuman predicament. More precisely, what Attebery describes as

---

[34]Attebery, "Ecologies of Sound: Queer Intimacy, Trans-corporeality, and Reproduction in *Upstream Color*," 134.

[35]Ibid., 135.

[36]Susan Sontag, "The Imagination of Disaster," *Commentary Magazine*, no. 65 (1965): 48.

a "kinship bond" between Kris and the pig also exhibits what Haraway, in her book, *The Companion Species Manifesto* (2003) terms "significant otherness." Through examining significant otherness, Haraway asks:

> How can people rooted in different knowledge practices "get on together," especially when an all-too-easy cultural relativism is not an option, either politically, epistemologically, or morally? How can general knowledge be nurtured in postcolonial worlds committed to taking difference seriously? Answers to these questions can only be put together in emergent practices; i.e., in vulnerable, on-the-ground work that cobbles together non-harmonious agencies and ways of living that are accountable both to their disparate inherited histories and to their barely possible but absolutely necessary joint futures. For me, that is what *significant otherness* signifies.[37]

Significant otherness, when brought into posthuman theory, becomes a practice of working with and through difference, rather than engaging in assimilation. Becoming-posthuman does not mean becoming the same, but acknowledging the different paths that structure posthuman arrival.

Difference in *Upstream Color* is highlighted through the relationship between the pig and Kris. Although Haraway uses the example of human-dog relationships to theorize significant otherness, pigs apply within the framework very well. The attention to difference drives Kris' actions, with which the film concludes. In order to achieve posthuman liberation, Kris shoots the Sampler and ends the Thief's operation, subsequently disrupting the cycle of trauma. In establishing a posthuman community, Kris centers the needs of the pigs alongside the needs of the Sampled humans. Significant otherness requires that humans acknowledge "others"—here, other species, whether mammalian or vegetal—as more "than a reflection of one's intentions."[38] Relationships that undertake the practice of significant otherness do not mold two radically different beings to create a new hybrid species, but rather equally value what the other needs in order to thrive. This relationship exists outside of human language and therefore necessitates forms of communication that are not visible in a late-capitalist humanist society. To bring the pigs into Kris' posthuman network, and in turn to allow us to *feel* the *zoe* of the pigs, the film prioritizes the affective linkages that map Kris and the pig alongside each other. We are led to believe that the future Kris has opened up to is one in which pigs, humans, worms, and plants live alongside of each other, in a consensual harmony that is

[37]Donna Haraway, *The Companion Species Manifesto: Dogs, People, and Significant Otherness*, vol. 1 (Chicago: Prickly Paradigm Press, 2003), 7, emphasis in original.
[38]Ibid., 28.

visualized when Kris and the rest of the human Sampled paint the bars of the pigpen a vibrant yellow, the color the film has already prefigured as signifying hope, resilience, and community. In this sense, *Upstream Color* shows us an emergent posthuman utopia in which "utopia is less a place, a fixed site, than a trajectory. [. . .] it's a field of possible, and multiple, trajectories."[39] *Upstream Color* ends with a hopeful path toward a kind of utopia, in that following the theory of significant otherness, it dreams up an ecology of trans-species co-habitants whose needs are equitably met.

Conclusion

Upstream Color imagines posthuman ontologies through the formal process of what I have termed, inspired by Braidotti's posthuman critical cartographies, "aesthetic cartographies." Aesthetic cartographies apply to the process of visualizing the posthuman in film, where networks of knowledge which decenter anthropocentric epistemologies are configured through specific formal elements. *Upstream Color* produces its aesthetic cartography through two core formal techniques. First, discontinuous editing charts out the various agents belonging to the posthuman map. This is most clear in the first sequence of the film, in which we are introduced to Kris and Jeff before their infections, the Thief, the orchids, and the power of the parasitic worms. The editing style also reveals the process of posthumanity, in that the assumed boundaries of Kris and Jeff dissolve between each other and their environment, especially in the way they "share" childhood memories through a kind of posthuman awakening. Second, revelatory soundtrack music operates as another actant within the posthuman network. Extradiegetic music becomes its own source of information within the film, and this characteristic of the musical score is introduced immediately, at the film's opening. The score's hypnotic and immersive ambience enhances the viewer, too, as nodes within the map. As the soundtrack guides Kris along her path toward posthuman modes of being, we are guided along as well.

The ideological effects of these two formal techniques encourage a feminist reading of the film. A unique feature of *Upstream Color* is that, even though it is classified as a work of science fiction, it defies its genre's characteristics in its low-budget experimental use of sound, editing, and narrative development. Priority is placed on the film's aural and experiential qualities, and so the film undermines the function of language through rendering it ineffective. Language becomes a useless method of communication for Kris and the other victims of the Thief. Through evading

---

[39]Scott Bukatman, *Matters of Gravity: Special Effects and Supermen in the 20th Century* (Durham: Duke University Press, 2003), 125.

the supremacy of logocentrism and abolishing the hierarchies it establishes, Kris opens up to posthuman relationships. Beyond language, Kris forms bonds that exemplify Haraway's notion of significant otherness, primarily through her budding relationship with the pig.

Last, the film grapples with the role trauma plays in accessing posthuman ontologies. Kris must be severed from her body, and therefore her former mode of being, in order to embrace the trans-species network that leads her toward a posthuman ontology. The Thief's physical violation of Kris disrupts and disorders her connection to her body, but through her posthuman network, she opens up to a new relationship between herself and her environment. According to Attebery, trauma produces fecundity for queer (but also feminist/posthuman) communities. This is certainly true for Kris and the pig, as their related trauma from the violation clearly produces the strongest trans-species link in their posthuman network. Moreover, while the worm infiltrates Kris, it is really the forceful actions of the Thief that are the true source of horror and abuse. This sentiment is reflected in the opening scene, where the teenage boy (Friend Two) consents to drinking the liquid but is forced into a somatic relationship to which he cannot properly give consent. Kris does not consent to swallowing the worm, and yet she follows the information it transmits to her in order to generate a form of agency that allows her to overthrow the (patriarchal) oppression of the Thief. I agree with Applegate's reading of the film in that the narrative offers a glimpse of what life might be like outside of capitalism. As an extension of this reading, I show how *Upstream Color* reveals the *always already* dehumanizing function of capitalism and produces posthuman networks as an alternative possibility to capitalism. In *Upstream Color*, the viewer opens up to an experience of a posthuman world that envisions outward trajectories revealing multiple and embedded relationships of *zoe* and *bios*.

9

Ascendance to Trans-Corporeality or Assimilation to Whiteness

The Posthuman Imaginaries of *Annihilation* and *Midsommar*

Olivia Stowell

Horror, as a genre, often allows for the thematic exploration of trauma to occur on both visual and textual levels. In particular, recent contemporary horror and horror-adjacent films have deployed their genre trappings in order to explore not just personal traumas but also wider questions of power, hierarchy, and history. Although Alex Garland's *Annihilation* (2018) and Ari Aster's *Midsommar* (2019) differ in tone and aesthetics, both films explore the intersections of trans-corporeality, racial violence, and trauma within the context of their protagonists journeying into uncanny contact zones with the environment. While *Annihilation* and *Midsommar* may appear to offer presentations of intersubjective communion with nature as a salve to individual and communal trauma, the films also present violence and racial assimilation to whiteness as the technologies by which to achieve this posthumanist trans-corporeality.

By turning critical attention to the intersections of the racial imaginaries and posthumanist milieus in these two films, this chapter argues that *Annihilation* and *Midsommar* limn both the emancipatory possibilities of intersubjectivity and the limitations of posthumanist ideologies that ultimately uphold the supremacy of whiteness. The presence in the contemporary popular-cultural landscape of concepts explored in posthumanist and ecocritical thought, such as intersubjectivity and trans-corporeality, points to the relevance of these concepts for the contemporary collective imaginary, and also opens up popular culture as a site of analysis for the possible permutations and propagations of these ideological formations. Engaging with the structures of race and racialization in *Annihilation* and *Midsommar* illuminates how ecological and racial modes of theory and thought are intertwined; at the same time, each film evinces that transcending the human/nature binary does not inherently guarantee that other oppressive binaries will also be overturned. As *Annihilation* and *Midsommar* elucidate, posthumanist communion with the environment does not intrinsically facilitate collective liberation, and may even depend upon existing power hierarchies for its actualization. In both films, white women enter new contact zones that allow them to move beyond relations to nature that depend upon imagining humans and nature as discrete; however, their whiteness is what, in part, makes this intersubjective transcendence possible. Reading the visuals, dialogue, and narrative arcs of *Annihilation* and *Midsommar* for their representations of race and posthumanist thought reveals the necessity of turning critical attention to the entanglements of varying modalities of power, in order to construct a more robust understanding of both the thinking and work required to uproot oppressive binaries.

Entangled Living and Dying: Trauma and Assimilation in *Annihilation*

Alex Garland's 2018 science fiction horror film *Annihilation*, loosely adapted from the 2014 Jeff VanderMeer novel of the same name,[1] blurs the boundaries of the subject and the human-nature binary in its plot and visuals. Garland's film not only deploys posthumanist concepts for the purpose of constructing an uncanny or unsettling visual milieu; *Annihilation* actively engages with the social, psychological, and ecological implications of becoming-posthuman. *Annihilation* follows a group of women on an expedition to understand "the Shimmer," an expanding zone causing mutations in plant and animal life that emerged following a meteor impact. The team of five women, made up of Lena, a biologist and former soldier (Natalie Portman), Dr. Ventress, a psychologist (Jennifer Jason Leigh), Josie, a physicist (Tessa Thompson),

---

[1]Garland states in an interview that he wrote his script adaptation based primarily on his memory of his one reading of VanderMeer's novel. Given the looseness of the adaptation, there are significant differences between the novel and the film. See Alex Garland and Kevin Vlk, "Annihilation | Alex Garland | Talks at Google," *Talks at Google*, YouTube Video, 30:27, February 22, 2018, https://www.youtube.com/watch?v=w5i7idoijco.

Anya, a paramedic (Gina Rodriguez), and Cass, a geologist (Tuva Novotny), enters the Shimmer, hoping to understand both what caused the event and why no one other than Lena's husband Kane (Oscar Isaac) has returned from any of the previous expeditions into the Shimmer. As they progress further from the boundary of the Shimmer and closer to the original meteor impact site, material reality becomes increasingly distorted and uncanny, and the women become increasingly psychologically disturbed. The women soon realize that the Shimmer is causing everything to refract and that the Shimmer "is a prism, but it refracts everything. Not just light and radio waves. Animal DNA. Plant DNA. All DNA." On the way to the meteor impact site, Anya and Cass are killed by a mutated bear who takes on the ability to scream with Cass' voice, and Josie transforms into a plant body after declaring that she does not want to face or fight the Shimmer, leaving only Ventress and Lena to continue on. In the climactic scenes of the film, Ventress is subsumed into a glowing, Mandelbulb-like entity, which eventually coalesces into an illegible humanoid being that then transforms into a doppelgänger of Lena. After fighting her doppelgänger, Lena returns to the reality beyond the boundary of the Shimmer. However, the film's final shot shows Lena's irises pulsing with color, reiterating the Shimmer's permanent alteration of her body and subjectivity; the final shot of the film seems to call into question whether the Lena who exited the Shimmer can be identified at all with the Lena who entered it.

Through the Shimmer's refractions of everything from light (as shown through the sunlight shining with prismatic effect) to radiowaves to DNA, *Annihilation* literalizes and visualizes principles of trans-corporeality and intersubjectivity. If, as Stacy Alaimo writes, "'trans-corporeality' [is] the time-space where human corporeality, in all its material fleshiness, is inseparable from 'nature' or 'environment,'"[2] *Annihilation* depicts this trans-corporeality literally, insofar as human corporeality becomes *genetically* inseparable from the environment, and, in turn, "nature" becomes genetically inseparable from human corporeality. Not only do alligators grow multiple rows of shark teeth and flowers of different species grow together on the same vine, but the bodies and selves of humans and nonhumans alike become porous. After a mutated bear kills Cass and Anya, Josie tells Lena, "I suspect that, as [Cass] was dying, part of her mind became part of the creature that was killing her," suggesting that the trans-corporeal scrambling can persist even as the human body is dying. Similarly, the Shimmer, and the embodied experience of living within it, echoes Astrid Neimanis and Rachel Loewen Walker's definition of trans-corporeality as "an ontological orientation that

---

[2]Stacy Alaimo, "Trans-Corporeal Feminisms and the Ethical Space of Nature," in *Material Feminisms*, ed. Stacy Alaimo and Susan Hekman (Bloomington: Indiana University Press, 2008), 238.

expresses the imbrication of human and nonhuman natures [and] denies the myth that human bodies are discrete in time and space, somehow outside of the natural milieu that sustains them and indeed transits through them."[3] In the world of *Annihilation*, the Shimmer is a trans-corporeal contact zone, wherein the ontological condition of the universe is not only one of inescapable imbrication but also one wherein this imbrication is always shifting.

Nothing, certainly not human bodies, can remain fully discrete in the Shimmer, even as there seem to be material differences between the kinds of trans-corporeal bodies generated by the contact zone of the Shimmer. As Beau Deurwaarder argues, the Shimmer "archive[s] a transversal world without humans, a site of planetary and ecological metamorphosis . . . [and] offer[s] a postanthropocentric, posthuman, and ancestral refraction to the state of affairs that lie outside of its borders"[4] (Deurwaarder 7). For Deurwaarder, the Shimmer archives and articulates an ecological response that moves beyond the individual human subject into a collective trans-corporeality always metamorphosizing, literalizing Karen Barad's conceptualization of matter as "not a thing, but a doing."[5] Matter within the Shimmer is not stable or stagnant; instead, it is constituted through intra-activity, through "doing." As the team of women traverse the Shimmer's contact zone, their sense of individual, separable, human corporeality cannot hold in the face of a constantly altering reality in which their embodied selves become intermingled with each other, with the nonhuman bodies of the environment, and, ultimately with the more-than-human body of the extraterrestrial humanoid.

Annihilation directly connects its visualized manifestations of trans-corporeality to a sense of embodied and/or psychological trauma within its human characters. Each woman is framed as entering the Shimmer as an act of self-destruction or escape, motivated by trauma, whether that trauma is addiction, self-harm, illness, or the death of loved ones. As Cass says to Lena early in the film, "We're all damaged goods here. Anya is sober, and therefore an addict. Josie wears long sleeves because she doesn't want you to see the scars on her forearms . . . I also lost someone . . . a daughter. Leukemia." Later, Lena discovers that Ventress has cancer, and Lena appears

---

[3]Astrid Neimanis and Rachel Loewen Walker, "Weathering: Climate Change and the 'Thick Time' of Transcorporeality," *Hypatia* 29, no. 3 (2014): 563.

[4]Beau Deurwaarder, "Nothing Comes Back: *Annihilation* as a Posthuman and Anthropocene Text," paper presented at Australasian Society for Continental Philosophy [ASCP] Conference, Western Sydney University, Parramatta, November 23, 2018, www.academia.edu/37856276 /Nothing_Comes_Back_Annihilation_as_a_Posthuman_and_Anthropocene_Text_-_Beau _Deurwaarder.

[5]Karen Barad, "Posthumanist Performativity: Toward an Understanding of How Matter Comes to Matter," *Signs: Journal of Women in Culture and Society* 28, no. 3 (2003): 822.

to enter the Shimmer because of her guilt about cheating on her husband Kane, choosing to venture into the Shimmer as a response to the emotional distress of the problems in her marriage. For each of the women in the team, the body is the site and modality of their trauma and suffering; their bodies—their scars, their cancerous cells, their embodied sexual activity—are the primary register in which trauma occurs. The pain of each character's past experiences, as articulated through their embodied trauma, both connects them to each other and enables the mission that takes them into the Shimmer. *Annihilation* seems to suggest that grief and trauma can function as an exit route from one ontological mode into another, allowing the characters to enter into a being in the world beyond an ontological condition of separateness. Only when the women feel they have nothing to lose do they feel able to enter the trans-corporeal contact zone, echoing Donna Haraway's claim that "grief is a path to understanding entangled shared living and dying."[6] Each character's grief and trauma allows them to detach from their existence as individual subjects within the dualistic frameworks of the world beyond the Shimmer and enter into the nondualistic mode of being that the Shimmer represents.

However, even as the characters' grief gives them "a path to understanding entangled shared living and dying,"[7] as soon as human bodies are introduced, the Shimmer's trans-corporeal intersubjectivity becomes possible through violence and racial assimilation. More often than not, the trans-corporeality of the Shimmer manifests as/through violence, and the psychological experience of becoming genetically trans-corporeal often motivates the characters to violence as well. Video footage from a previous expedition reveals that Lena's husband Kane cut open a team member's stomach when he became convinced that his intestines were moving of their own accord. Similarly, after Cass is killed, Anya becomes convinced that Lena is responsible, and ties Lena, Ventress, and Josie to chairs, threatening them with a knife. The psychological experience of becoming genetically trans-corporeal leads more than one character toward psycho-emotional breakdown, as they are unable to comprehend their new entangled and imbricated reality. Although most characters experience the intersubjective refraction of the Shimmer as violence, Josie notably resists this, ultimately allowing the Shimmer to refract her body into a flowering plant. Rather than resisting or fighting the Shimmer, Josie accepts it, willingly entering into its transmutations and abandoning her human corporeality. Josie's "death," if it can be called that, implies that the violence of the Shimmer's trans-corporeality comes not from the refracting process itself, but from

---

[6]Donna Haraway, *Staying with the Trouble: Making Kin in the Chthulucene* (Durham: Duke University Press, 2016), 39.
[7]Ibid.

human resistance to it, from the unwillingness to surrender an individual human corporeality and subjecthood. The violence and psychological anxiety appear to stem from refusing to see "matter [as a] substance in its intra-active becoming—not a thing, but a doing, a congealing of agency. Matter is a stabilizing and destabilizing process of iterative intra-activity."[8] In contrast to the rest of the team, Josie embraces the intra-activity of matter in the Shimmer, which occurs on a level invisible to both the eye and the camera, and, rather than responding with violence, accepts this stabilizing yet destabilizing process. In this way, the violent imagery of *Annihilation* seems to imply that clinging to individual human subjectivity engenders both violence and the reification of the nonhuman world; only Josie, the one team member willing to abandon individual human subjectivity and corporeality to see "the corporeal substance of the human [as] ultimately inseparable from 'the environment,'"[9] is fully able to enter into a nonviolent mutuality with the environment.

Though Josie's nonviolent merging with the Shimmer's environment suggests the possibility of an intersubjective posthumanism beyond individual human subjectivity, her "death" also elucidates the dynamics of racial assimilation that occur within the subtext of the film. As Zakiyyah Iman Jackson has described, "liberal humanist conceptions of 'the human'" often depend upon "blackness's bestialization and thingification: the process of imagining black people as an empty vessel, a nonbeing, a nothing, an ontological zero, coupled with the violent imposition of colonial myths and racial hierarchy."[10] Jackson's work explicates how liberal conceptions of the human reduce blackness to the nonbeing against which the human can be defined against; given this oppressive history, ways of rethinking the category of the human seem philosophically seductive. While, as Jackson indicates, African diasporic cultural production "frequently alters the meaning and significance of being (human) and engages in imaginative practices of worlding,"[11] manifestations of posthumanist thinking in films like *Annihilation* point to how reimagining the category of the human by turning to intersubjective relations with nature can end up reconstructing the meaning of being human in ways that remain racially repressive. For instance, although all matter becomes fundamentally entangled in the Shimmer, some human and nonhuman bodies persist on the visual level more than others, raising the question of who or what is allowed to remain/ become visible *as* a body. Even as the boundaries of human and nonhuman become contingent and porous, the merging is not always equal on the level

---

[8]Barad, "Posthumanist Performativity," 822.
[9]Alaimo, "Trans-Corporeal Feminisms," 238.
[10]Zakiyyah Iman Jackson, *Becoming Human: Matter and Meaning in an Antiblack World* (Durham: Duke University Press, 2020), 1.
[11]Ibid.

of visual representation. While the entire team becomes entwined with the Shimmer's refracting processes, ultimately, only Lena, a white woman, exits the Shimmer, though she bears physical, genetic, and psychological markers of how the Shimmer's refracting process has entangled her with other beings. Most evidently, as Lena spends more and more time in the Shimmer, her body starts "growing" a tattoo identical in image and placement to Anya's forearm tattoo of the "worm ouroboros"—a snake eating its own tail. The ouroboros often represents a cycle of death or destruction and rebirth, and the visual emphasis on Anya's ouroboros tattoo indicates *Annihilation*'s interest in cycles of making and unmaking, particularly of selves. At the same time, Lena's body taking on Anya's tattoo functions metonymically for Lena's body absorbing the bodies and subjectivities of the other women in her team. Josie, a Black woman, and Anya, a Latina lesbian woman, lose the visual legibility of their bodies, becoming dissolved into both the environment and into Lena's body. If, as Neimanis and Walker argue, "even as transcorporeality posits a relational ontology between human and nonhuman nature, it is also a space of difference."[12] Within the Shimmer, some differences persist at the visual level, while others become absorbed and unmanifested. The mingling of psyches and bodies is a by-product of the Shimmer's refracting trans-corporeality; at the same time, the racialized assimilation to white embodiment that is the result of such mingling is a symptom of the Shimmer as a manifestation of the film's ideological position.

Though *Annihilation* certainly leaves the single, separate, discrete human subject behind, the imbricated, matter-as-doing body that exits the Shimmer in the end, though enmeshed with nonhuman, human, and more-than-human others, still looks like a white woman. Whether this racial assimilation to embodied whiteness is necessary to survive within the Shimmer, or merely to *escape* it, remains opaque. *Annihilation*'s presentation of trans-corporeality involves the bodies of Black and Brown people being subsumed, physically and genetically, into both the natural environment and into white bodies, and survival manifests as white femininity. Though the Shimmer seems to offer the potential to salve trauma and allow *Annihilation*'s characters to move beyond discrete, individual human subjectivity and corporeality into a space of mutual intra-action, it also seems to utilize violence and racial assimilation as technologies by which this trans-corporeal intersubjectivity is achieved. *Annihilation* points to the beauty and possibility of intersubjective entanglement, suggesting a strange transcendence in the move beyond the discrete human subject; however, at the same time, the posthumanist trans-

---

[12]Neimanis and Walker, "Weathering: Climate Change and the 'Thick Time' of Transcorporeality," 564.

corporeality depends upon a textual and ideological erasure of race and racialized structures of oppressive power.

"That Tree Is Tied to All Our Dead": Environmental Collectivity and Racial Violence in *Midsommar*

Though Ari Aster's 2019 folk horror film *Midsommar* is certainly tonally and generically different from *Annihilation*, its presentation of trans-corporeality and intersubjectivity similarly suggests communion with nature as a response to trauma and also depicts violence and racial assimilation as the technologies that make this posthumanist stance possible. While *Annihilation* features a group of scientists entering a scientifically anomalous quarantine zone, *Midsommar* depicts a group of graduate students traveling to a remote cultic community called the "Hårga" in Sweden to attend a Midsummer ritual with their friend Pelle (Vilhelm Blomgren), who grew up in the commune. Dani (Florence Pugh), the only woman in the group of students, recently lost her sister and parents in a murder-suicide in which her sister filled their home with carbon monoxide, motivating Dani to join her boyfriend Christian (Jack Reynor) and his friends on their research trip in an attempt to distract herself from her grief. Once the students arrive, the rituals grow increasingly violent and disturbing, including an "Åttestupa" ritual in which elderly members of the cult participate in euthanistic senicide. One by one, the visitors go missing, including British visitors Simon (Archie Madekwe) and Connie (Ellora Torchia), until only Christian and Dani remain. Eventually, it is revealed that Christian's friends Mark (Will Poulter) and Josh (William Jackson Harper), as well as Connie and Simon, have been ritually murdered by members of the cult. Absorbed into the cult's ceremonies, Dani is crowned the May Queen and chooses an incapacitated Christian as the final human sacrifice, who is then placed into a bear carcass and burnt alive as Dani looks on, first sobbing and then smiling.

Despite their differences in setting and genre, *Midsommar,* like *Annihilation,* features a group of people exiting conventional contemporary society, partially motivated by trauma, and entering a different mode of being, one which destabilizes their sense of individual subjectivity and blurs the boundaries between binaries of human/nature and human/animal so that they no longer function as organizing ontological principles. During the Hårga's Midsummer festival, the students frequently take hallucinatory drugs, particularly hallucinogenic mushrooms, causing Dani to perceive her body as sprouting grass. The grass growing from Dani's body in her hallucinations foreshadows the ways in which Dani will become entwined not only with the Hårga community but also with nature. From the beginning of her arrival in the community, her body becomes entangled with nature, both in the sense of her state of consciousness being altered by a nonhuman actor (hallucinogenic mushrooms) and in the sense of Dani herself *perceiving* her body as explicitly enmeshed with nature. By the ending of *Midsommar,* not only Dani's body but also her psyche has become intermingled with the Hårga community and the environment surrounding them. In the film's final sequence, as Dani is carried across the field in the May Queen ceremony, her sister's face appears in the forest behind her, suggesting that her trauma has become part of the landscape, in some ways echoing the entanglement of psychology and nature in *Annihilation.* Dani's trauma about the deaths of her sister and parents becomes a constitutive part of the landscape, conveying a trans-corporeal merging of human and nonhuman bodies.

Although *Midsommar* does not literalize trans-corporeality at the genetic level, as *Annihilation* does, it presents a similar understanding of trans-corporeality and intersubjectivity. In both films, trauma allows individuals to exit dualistic understandings of the world which posit nature as "passive, as non-agent and non-subject, as the 'environment' . . . a resource empty of its own purposes or meanings"[13] in favor of seeing nature or the environment as part of a co-constituent entanglement with human bodies and nonhuman actors. In the final May Queen ceremony, Christian is placed into a bear carcass, hiding his human body and again illustrating how the Hårga's worldview sees humans and nonhumans as enmeshed. Similarly, Dani wears a ceremonial costume made of flowers that completely covers her body, making it appear distorted and not legible as a human body. The costumes worn in the May Queen ceremony suggest that human bodies are not so different from nonhuman bodies, blurring the boundaries between them. The Hårga's lifestyle is one of intimacy with nature, where the community is valued over the individual and nature is considered part of that community; furthermore, violence and death, particularly violence and death that comes about through ritualistic cruelty, are culturally normative. The Hårga also seem to view nature as a part of their ancestral heritage. When Mark urinates on a sacred ancestral tree, a member of the Hårga exclaims, "These are our ancestors! You're pissing on my people!" while Pelle declares, "That tree is tied to all our dead."[14] The Hårga not only live in community with nature, their culture considers their lives to be tied to the natural world. The cult member that Mark angers does not say, "This tree represents our ancestors"; he says, "These *are* our ancestors." The intermingling of the Hårga's ancestors and the dead tree echoes Barad's principle of intra-action,

---

[13]Val Plumwood, *Feminism and the Mastery of Nature* (London and New York: Routledge, 1993), 4.
[14]*Midsommar,* directed by Ari Aster, featuring Florence Pugh and Jack Reynor, cinematography by Pawel Pogorzelski (A24, 2019), https://www.showtime.com/movie/3474663?i_cid=int -default-1004&r=s&o_cid=19969182313_19947259571_19942911399_holdback.

insofar as "'intra-action' refers to a fundamental entanglement whereby individual entities cannot be said to exist as things-in-themselves and instead find meaning or expression only through their co-creative relations with other entities."[15] The intra-actions of the living Hårga, their ancestors, and the sacred ancestral tree illustrates how the lives of the Hårga only find meaning and/or expression through their relationality with both nature and the dead.

Furthermore, the Hårga also seem to value nonhuman life equally to human life and consider death to be a natural part of being in community with nature, as illustrated by the ways that humans are often joined with nature through violent cultic rituals. The Hårga are unperturbed by death, and Pelle explicitly states how they view it as merely a part of the cycle of life, saying, "Death is just shit fertilizing crops. Everything gets recycled and made new again." After Josh is killed by the Hårga for taking photos of their sacred texts, Christian finds Josh's foot planted upside down in the garden, literalizing the concept of the human body as fertilizer for the Earth. Using cultic ritual to enter into community with both nature and each other and seeing death as part of a natural relation to the environment, the Hårga community functions as a trans-corporeal zone similar to *Annihilation*'s Shimmer, in which individual subjectivity and human/nature dualisms no longer operate as the foundational assumptions undergirding being-in-the-world.[16] Just as violence in *Annihilation* serves as a technology by which trans-corporeality is achieved, the Hårga use violence and death to become one with nature, living in a "relation between humans and the nonhuman world [that] is thus reciprocal."[17] The Hårga also experience intersubjective communion with each other, and in multiple scenes perform empathetic rituals wherein they connect to each other's emotions, such as when the Hårga women moan in unison with a member of the cult with whom Christian has sexual intercourse, when the other women wail in pain with Dani after she discovers Christian's infidelity, and when the Hårga collectively scream along with members of their community who are being burned alive. The Hårga community refract and reflect each other's psychologies through their

---

[15]Neimanis and Walker, "Weathering: Climate Change and the 'Thick Time' of Transcorporeality," 565, referencing Karen Barad, *Meeting the Universe Halfway: Quantum Physics and the Entanglement of Matter and Meaning* (Durham: Duke University Press, 2007), 128.

[16]This is not to say that the Shimmer and the Hårga are entirely similar or perfectly analogous. On the one hand, the Shimmer contains the kinds of "natural" violence and danger that constitute environmental relations: conflict between predators and prey, finite biological life cycles, degenerating cells, etc. On the other, the Hårga's cultural relationship to each other and their environment involve more clearly agentic forms of violence and cruelty. However, despite these differences, the way that *the films* visually and textually represent trans-corporeality rest upon similar imaginings of what the entanglements between "human" and "nature" entail.

[17]Carolyn Merchant, *Ecological Revolutions: Nature, Gender, and Science in New England* (Chapel Hill: University of North Carolina Press, 1989), 8.

empathetic identification with one another. Emotion becomes not just an individual event but also a collective experience, wherein the origin of the emotion ceases to matter in the face of the collective body.

However, the Hårga's trans-corporeal collectivism explicitly becomes possible through racial violence and white supremacist ideological formations. While *Midsommar*'s presentation of trans-corporeality may be less literal than *Annihilation*'s, its depiction of racial assimilation is more obvious and deliberately included as a part of Aster's directorial vision. In an interview with *Esquire*, Aster stated, "You will notice that the white members of the visiting community are used for more than just their bodies to be sacrificed, whereas the others are thrown aside."[18] While Christian is used to help the Hårga procreate and Dani is able to join the Hårga in a position of prestige by the film's end, Josh's body (and the bodies of Connie and Simon, who are also people of color) is annihilated, turned into compost, summarily disposed of. The disposal of Josh's body echoes Jackson's articulation of the bestialization and thingification of Blackness and the Black body under conditions of white supremacist ideology. The Hårga's white supremacy becomes increasingly clear as *Midsommar* progresses. Every member of the Hårga is white, and *Midsommar* implies that, while the community requires outsiders in order to procreate, it only uses white outsiders to do so. Dani's joining with the community, and, consequently, her escape from the human-nature dualisms of the world beyond the Hårga community, depends not only on her white racial embodiment but also on her willingness to overlook violence against people of color. As Xine Yao writes:

> Although [Simon and Connie] attempt to leave, these Londoners are the first to die; in a twist on the typical racialized fears about the dangers of the metropolis, it is the characters of colour whose cosmopolitan open-mindedness to a foreign culture endangers them. Whatever sympathy Dani had for them soon disappears with her willing assimilation into the Härga [*sic*].[19]

While Dani initially appears extremely distressed by the disappearances of Simon and Connie, her desire for family and connection soon subsumes these fears; her whiteness allows her to overlook the violence and racial assimilation that make the Hårga family possible. In other words, even as the Hårga upend ontological separations between human and nonhuman

---

[18]Ari Aster and Jack Reynor, "Jack Reynor Wanted to Change Our Expectations of Horror Movies. So He Went Fully Nude." *Esquire*, Hearst Digital Media, July 3, 2019, www.esquire .com/entertainment/movies/a28262830/jack-reynor-ari-aster-midsommar-interview-nudity/.

[19]Xine Yao, "*Midsommar*: The Horrors of White Sympathy," *Avidly: A Channel of the L.A. Review of Books*, Los Angeles Review of Books, August 13, 2019, avidly.lareviewofbooks.org /2019/08/13/midsommar-the-horrors-of-white-sympathy/.

actors, their culture depends on binary, white supremacist conceptions of race.

While *Annihilation* presents racial assimilation as manifesting through all bodies being absorbed into a white body, *Midsommar* presents the racial assimilation that is an underlying organizing principle for the Hårga's way of life as coming about through the violent death of people of color. *Midsommar* also offers multiple allusions to Sweden's Nazi history and hostility to immigrants. In the opening scenes of the film, there are several books about Nazism visible in the students' apartment, and "the banner [seen] in the trailer as the group travels to the village says, 'Stoppa Massinvandringer till Hälsingland,' Stop Mass Immigration to Hälsingland."[20] Though the Hårga's white supremacy is not explicitly named, *Midsommar*'s imagery consistently alludes to it, and the deaths of Connie, Simon, and Josh are the clear endpoint of the Hårga's worldview. Yao argues that "*Midsommar* presents us with the spectacle of the horrors of white supremacy—in all its gendered, psychological complexity—in literal broad daylight,"[21] arguing that the film exposes what Tiffany Lethabo King terms "the violence that White human life requires as its condition of possibility."[22] By placing the Hårga's violence against people of color in broad daylight, *Midsommar* illuminates the ways in which racial violence can be a by-product or a central component of ideologies that dismantle the human/nature dualistic binary. The Hårga may offer an ontological model beyond individual subjecthood and dualistic human/nature modes of being, but their cultural worldview also depends on racial violence.

Posthumanist Possibility?: Race and the Limits of Posthuman Thought

Both *Annihilation* and *Midsommar* feature white, female protagonists reckoning with trauma by exiting "normal" society and entering a new space where the boundaries of the human break down. In *Annihilation*, Lena ultimately exceeds the bounds of the human, becoming entangled with the natural and the extraterrestrial; in *Midsommar*, Dani exceeds the bounds of Humanist ontologies that imagine the human as separate from the environment. Furthermore, the centrality of a female protagonist to each film suggests that both *Annihilation* and *Midsommar* are interested in indexing the ways that womanhood and/or femininity are imagined as

---

[20]Aster and Reynor, "Jack Reynor Wanted to Change."
[21]Yao, "*Midsommar*: The Horrors of White Sympathy."
[22]Tiffany Lethabo King, *The Black Shoals: Offshore Formations of Black and Native Studies* (Durham: Duke University Press, 2019), 20.

"naturally" in community with the environment. Each film reckons with sexist ideologies of gender which posit women as more natural, less rational, less "enlightened," in order to subvert and/or reengage such conceptions of femininity and the relationship of the feminine to the natural world. As *Annihilation* and *Midsommar* explore the interrelations of gender, trauma, and nature, they limn the role that gender plays in constructing and delimiting the boundaries between "human" and "nature."

However, despite the ways that *Annihilation* and *Midsommar* trouble the human/nature binary, both Lena and Dani fail to fully escape what Val Plumwood calls the "hierarchical relationship[s], [which] construct[s] central cultural concepts and identities so as to make equality and mutuality literally unthinkable."[23] In each film, the women become empowered and/or enlightened by entering into the new, more explicitly trans-corporeal space; the uncanny features of the new trans-corporeal contact zones offer a salve to the trauma that motivated the women to leave behind conventional society in the first place. Both films depict trauma as a motivating force that allows the characters to move beyond or outside of individual understandings of human subjecthood, and both films explicitly connect trauma to both nature and the body, as the image of plants going out of the human body (which appears in both films) represents. However, despite the trans-corporeal contact zone providing a place where Dani and Lena can each confront and grapple with their respective traumas through their entry into an intersubjective space of connection with nature, both films arrive at this trans-corporeality through violence and racial assimilation. The presence of assimilation to whiteness in both films suggests the connection between trauma, ecological crisis, and the ways in which Western culture structures itself around the social, symbolic, and literal death of people of color in order to reconsolidate its hegemonies. Despite the apparent nondualism signaled by the breakdown of the human/nature binary in both films, the move into intimacy with nature does not inherently break down racialized hierarchies—that is to say, the deconstruction of one dualistic pair does not inherently uproot the others.

Even as *Annihilation* and *Midsommar* posit new possibilities for the conditions of life that go beyond an understanding of the human that depends upon setting the category of the human in opposition to nature, these new possibilities do not (or perhaps, cannot) abandon what King identifies as "the violent ways that settler human self-actualization depends on the most violent forms of Black and Indigenous death."[24] Lena and Dani's self-actualization becomes possible via racial assimilation, racial erasure, and racial violence. In this way, despite the presence of intersubjective,

---

[23]Plumwood, *Feminism and the Mastery of Nature*, 47.
[24]King, *The Black Shoals*, 19.

ecocritical, and posthumanist ideas in these films, they may also illustrate
how these same modes of thought may ultimately reify whiteness as the
privileged site that delimits the boundaries of the category of the human. As
King describes, settler colonialism has a "tendency to resuscitate older liberal
humanist modes of thought to create new poststructural and postmodern
forms of violent humanisms that feed off Indigenous genocide and Black
social death."[25] If the move to new modes of being—new modes of self-
actualization—that aim to uproot and unseat the human-nature binary
depends upon racial assimilation, racial erasure, and racial violence, then
perhaps these new modes of being do not move beyond Western humanism
or the category of the human but instead represent new forms of violent
humanisms that still rely upon racial violence as their condition of possibility.

In other words, *Annihilation* and *Midsommar* may illuminate the
imbrication of varying modalities of power and domination, and point to
the necessity of structures of thought that do not elide the role of race,
racism, and racial violence in constructing the present order of the world.
The presence of shared themes and imagery of the porousness of human
and nonhuman bodies, violence and trauma, and racial assimilation in
Annihilation and *Midsommar* suggests that, as ideas arising out of ecocritical
and posthumanist theory manifest in the popular-cultural consciousness,
they cannot help but butt up against race. While each film foregrounds
its relationship to nature and the environment, race remains a salient and
organizing factor in the structure of the film's narrative arc. The re/iteration
of racial assimilation and trauma that occurs within the subtext of each film
highlights the necessity of attending to the multiplicity of vectors of power
and oppression in order to realize any vision of posthumanism's liberatory
possibilities.

Each film refigures the idea of environmental trauma and damage, framing
not only humans' responsibility to other humans but also our responsibilities
to the nonhuman world and the consequences of interpersonal and ecological
trauma as central concerns. At the same time, these two films gesture toward
the limitations of ecological thought that fails to meaningfully engage with
how racial power hierarchies have structured the order of the world. Though
the white women at the films' centers reach a form of transcendent trans-
corporeality, their transcendence is predicated upon the continued erasure,
subjugation, and death of people of color, and upon racial assimilation,
racial erasure, and racial violence. Though *Annihilation* and *Midsommar*
are by no means theoretical treatises on posthumanism, they nonetheless
gesture toward the limitations of posthumanist thought that imagines trans-
corporeal intersubjectivity as always inherently liberatory. *Annihilation* and
Midsommar imply that ecological crises are also racial crises, and without

---

[25]Ibid., 10.

upending *both* environmental hierarchies *and* racial hierarchies, the move to posthumanist trans-corporeality can often function to re-entrench the supremacy of whiteness. By reading *Annihilation* and *Midsommar* alongside each other, holding their presentations of ecological trans-corporeality and their representations of racial hierarchies together, the possibilities and limitations of their theoretical underpinnings come more clearly into view.

PART THREE

Posthumanist Endings and Futures

10

Digital Game Ecologies

Posthuman Convergences in *Abzû* and *Horizon: Zero Dawn*

Sarah Best

Faced with catastrophic pollution, extensive deforestation, a shocking loss of biodiversity, and mounting anxieties around climate change, it is clear that environmental degradation is among the most pressing concerns of our times. In both popular and academic discourses, developments in science and technology are presented as both major causes of and potential solutions to environmental crises. This dual savior-destroyer framework for technology is a reoccurring theme in science fiction (SF), as the genre provides a helpful outlet for grappling with anxieties surrounding uncertain futures. Recognizing the immense potential of SF texts for thinking through the various tensions inherent within Western modernity, this chapter explores the multifaceted and often contradictory relationships between the natural and the technological as they manifest in and through two postapocalyptic video games: Giant Squid Studio's *Abzû*,[1] and Sony Interactive Entertainment's *Horizon: Zero Dawn* (hereafter HZD).[2]

Unlike older media such as literature or film, digital games play a unique role within the SF genre in that they require high levels of player engagement with complex technological systems. As such, I am interested

---

[1]Giant Squid Studios, *Abzû* (505 Games. Nintendo Switch, 2016).
[2]Guerrilla Games, *Horizon: Zero Dawn* (Sony Interactive Entertainment. PlayStation 4, 2017).

here not only in the environmentally focused narratives of *Abzû* and *HZD* but also in the player-game-environment interactions they foster. Digital games like these give rise to complex nature-culture assemblages that, in Alenda Chang's words, "call attention to heterogeneous and diffuse webs of influence that go far beyond the living," fundamentally decentering human agency in important ways.[3] Importantly, although *Abzû* and *HZD* have poignant environmental messages, as material objects they themselves are also tied up in ecologically harmful systems of production. These games, then, provide an opportunity for thinking about the dynamics of human and other-than-human relationships as they operate within the "posthuman convergence"—a term Rosi Braidotti uses to describe how contemporary convergences of rapid technological development and mounting ecological devastation give rise to uncertain conditions that upset the very foundations on which traditional notions of "the human" rest.[4]

Situated at the intersection of game studies, feminist science studies, and material ecocriticism or "ecomaterialism,"[5] this chapter draws from Braidotti's theory of feminist posthumanism to demonstrate how *Abzû* and *HZD* challenge the nature/culture divide central to the legacy of Enlightenment humanism, along with related binary systems that perpetuate human mastery and domination over all that is "other." In cultivating meaningful player-game-environment interactions, *Abzû* and *HZD* work to subvert the anthropocentric and patriarchal hierarchies of Western modernity, establishing posthuman worlds where oppositions are never absolute, and technology is an integral part of the ecosystem, *embedded within* rather than *separate from* nature. I argue, then, that far from being an escape from reality or a turn away from "real" environments, environmentally concerned games like *Abzû* and *HZD* can foster environmental consciousness among players by making immediate the profound relationships between humans and their biological and technological nonhuman others. Through the combination of narrative and gameplay features, these SF games reveal that players, like their avatars, are "cyborg-like" in that they are embodied, relational, and porous subjects enmeshed in worlds full of other-than-human agency. Significantly, in demonstrating how human beings are not the only important actors in these dynamic game assemblages or "digital ecologies," *Abzû* and *HZD* encourage a posthuman feminist ethics of planetary care that stresses relationality and compassion, establishing strong emotional ties

[3]Alenda Y. Chang, *Playing Nature: Ecology in Video Games* (Minneapolis: University of Minnesota Press, 2019), 12.
[4]Rosi Braidotti, *Posthuman Feminism* (Cambridge: Polity Press, 2022).
[5]Stacy Alaimo, *Exposed: Environmental Politics and Pleasures in Posthuman Times* (Minneapolis: University of Minnesota Press, 2016).

between players and game digital environments that may very well carry over into engagements with the real environments they are based on.

Abzû, *Horizon: Zero Dawn* and the "Posthuman Convergence"

Over the course of the past few years, digital games scholars have become increasingly interested in how such video games may actually be "a globalized, pivotal medium for the solution of social and political issues on the scale of the whole planet."[6] Moreover, recent game studies scholarship has begun to draw important connections between video games and ecological discourse, demonstrating how certain games have considerable potential to create highly engaging experiences with natural environments that may in turn lead to critical action in the face of climate change and other pertinent issues.[7] However, despite this environmental turn in game studies, digital games remain largely understudied from an environmental perspective. One reason for this lack of scholarly interest may be because the field appears fraught with tensions and contradictions, primarily stemming from the long-standing perspective that the "natural" and "technological" are necessarily antithetical to one another. As such, I have chosen to focus on *Abzû* and *HZD* in this chapter because they present a challenge to dualistic modernist paradigms that maintain impermeable boundaries between nature and culture, or the real and the virtual.

Set in postapocalyptic future worlds where advanced technological systems have caused untold destruction to the planet, *Abzû* and *HZD* are SF games that present unique opportunities for contemplating societal fears and desires concerning rapid technological development in the contemporary world.[8] Although these games differ significantly from one another in terms of narrative, style, and gameplay—*HZD* being a mainstream AAA title and *Abzû* an independent game made by a relatively small production company—they nonetheless share a number of similar elements, particularly the manner in which technology is presented as both the destroyer and savior of natural environments. Both games also employ environmental realism, not only through their photorealistic visual renderings but also in the way

---

[6]Marco Benoit Carbone and Paolo Ruffino, "Apocalypse Postponed: Discourses on Video Games from Noxious Objects to Redemptive Devices," *GAME* 1, no. 1 (2018): 27.
[7]Hans-Joachim Backe, "Within the Mainstream: An Ecocritical Framework for Digital Game History," *Ecozone* 8, no. 2 (2017): 39–55.
[8]N. Katherine Hayles, "Traumas of Code," in *Critical Digital Studies: A Reader*, ed. Arthur Kroker and Marilouise Kroker (Toronto: University of Toronto Press, 2008).

FIGURE 10.1 Abzû's *vibrant underwater world (Giant Squid Studios, Abzû, 2016, USA, © 505 Games).*

they incorporate specific American landscapes (*HZD*) and particular species of aquatic beings (*Abzû*)[9] (Figure 10.1).

Abzû is an underwater adventure game created by Giant Squid Studios that involves no dialogue and very minimal written text, using only incredible visuals and a compelling soundtrack to tell a powerful story about the importance of Earth's oceans. Beginning the game as a nameless, genderless diver floating in the middle of the sea (without any context for why they are there), players dive under the surface to experience a world teeming with aquatic life, from massive schools of colorful fish to dolphins and whales. Using the game's "meditation" function, players can shift the focus from the diver protagonist to instead follow these various species as they swim through the vibrant game world. Yet, for all of the beauty *Abzû* reveals, there are also many dark, lifeless areas to be discovered as players continue their journey. Near the game's climax, players discover that the diver character they are playing is not actually human, but an android capable of carrying and restoring vitality to the ocean. In order to complete the game, players are tasked with restoring the ecosystems that have been harmed by human activity.

A very different game than *Abzû*, Sony Interactive Entertainment's *HZD* is an action role-playing game made for PlayStation 4 and PC that takes place in postapocalyptic America sometime in the 3100s. In this world,

---

[9]Chang, *Playing Nature*, 22.

FIGURE 10.2 *A machine-animal walking among the ruins of a past civilization (Guerrilla Games, Horizon: Zero Dawn, 2017, USA, © Sony Interactive Entertainment).*

civilization as we know it has been wiped out, and human society reduced to a tribal existence. Though surrounded by the ruins of a highly technologically advanced society, the knowledge of former humans or "Old Ones" is lost to those who inhabit this world. Here, seemingly futuristic technologies have become ancient relics, and giant animal-like machines dominate the land. Taking on the role of Aloy, an outcast huntress, players set out on a quest to learn more about themselves and this strange place, hunting machine-animals, interacting with nonplayable characters, and completing various side quests in *HZD*'s open-world setting (Figure 10.2).

With their complex entanglements of nature and technology, *Abzû* and *HZD* fit squarely into what Braidotti calls the "posthuman convergence," wherein the intersections between increased technological development and the climate crisis have become definitive of the contemporary moment in a manner that "tears apart traditional understandings and practices of the human."[10] Within this posthuman moment, nature is seen to be "impoverished to the point of extinction," while technology, "far from being the promise of radiant futures for humanity, is a threat to its very survival."[11] As SF narratives that grapple with the effects of technology on the environment, as well as being ecologically harmful material objects themselves, digital games like *Abzû* and *HZD* are exemplary of this posthuman convergence, calling

[10]Braidotti, *Posthuman Feminism*, 42.
[11]Ibid.

for a radical rethinking of what it means to be human in our current (and future) times.

Both *Abzû* and *HZD* feature prominent environmental themes and beautifully rendered natural environments. However, as digital media these texts raise certain questions within fields like game studies and ecocriticism; namely, the extent to which technological mediation obscures real environments and meaningful interactions with them.[12] As material objects video games are certainly not "environmentally friendly," with the coltan mining practices required in the construction of PlayStations and other consoles releasing toxic chemicals harmful to local ecosystems. Moreover, due to the fact that consistent upgrades quickly render old consoles obsolete, the gaming industry is responsible for creating staggering amounts of e-waste, polluting the air and water and resulting in "electronic graveyards amid a cauldron of poison."[13] With Microsoft (the creators of Xbox) and Nintendo ranking among the lowest of major technological corporations on Greenpeace's "greenness scale" in 2006 and 2010,[14] it is important not to let the proenvironmental messages of certain games mask the physical reality of their complicity in the ongoing destruction of the planet.

However, not all games and the companies that produce them remain oblivious to the contradictions between the positive environmental behaviors players may engage in on-screen versus the destructive practices they may buy into off-screen. In fact, in addressing issues pertaining to the harmful consequences of rapid technological development, games like *Abzû* and *HZD* may even invite players to think critically about the varied and dynamic relationships between technology and the environment, becoming at once part of the problem and part of the solution.[15] Throughout *Abzû*, players investigate painted murals of a lost underwater civilization to learn that, while the humans that once lived there maintained a symbiotic relationship with the ocean, an increase in technological development and human hubris upset this equilibrium. Here, they discover that the android diver they are playing was created by the ancient civilization to hold the ocean's life force within her, though it remains unclear as to whether she was made for the purpose of further harvesting this force for humanity's benefit, or as a last effort to restore the balance. Whatever the original purpose

[12]Cheryl Lousley, "Ecocriticism and the Politics of Representation," in *The Oxford Handbook of Ecocriticism*, ed. Greg Garrard (Oxford: Oxford University Press, 2014), 155–71. See also Andrew McMurry, "Media Moralia: Reflections on Damaged Environments and Digital Life," in *The Oxford Handbook of Ecocriticism*, ed. Greg Garrard (Oxford: Oxford University Press, 2014), 487–501.
[13]Nick Dyer-Witheford and Greig de Peuter, *Games of Empire: Global Capitalism and Video Games* (Minneapolis: University of Minnesota Press, 2009), 224.
[14]Chang, *Playing Nature*.
[15]Ibid., 234–5. See also Josef Nguyen, "Digital Games about the Materiality of Digital Games," *Ecozone* 8, no. 2 (2017): 18–38.

FIGURE 10.3 *An expanse of dangerous explosive machines in the ocean's depths (Giant Squid Studios, Abzû, 2016, USA, © 505 Games).*

though, the game undoubtedly places an emphasis on the importance of the latter, as it requires players to solve a series of environment-based puzzles to restore vitality to all of the lifeless sections of the ocean. The story ends with the robot-diver teaming up with a great white shark to destroy the harmful machines left behind by the humans and fully return the ocean to its former liveliness (see Figure 10.3).

In their search for answers about what happened to the Old Ones in *HZD*, players learn that after suffering the various effects of climate change in the 2000s, these past humans developed several "green" technologies aimed at restoring ecosystems and reversing the damage. Eventually, however, these powerful machines turned against the Earth they were created to save, attempting to destroy all biotic life. In response, a group of scientists, led by Dr. Elisabet Sobeck, created "Project Zero Dawn" in the hopes of preserving a seed of life to be planted in the future. At the core of this project was GAIA, an incredibly advanced artificial intelligence (AI) system (rendered as a holographic projection of a human woman) tasked with terraforming the Earth for life again. Though GAIA succeeded in restoring flora, fauna, and humanity, players soon discover that she and all of this now flourishing life are under threat by one of her subordinate AI systems, HADES (see Figure 10.4), and must undertake the quest of finding and protecting her, fighting many enemies (both human and machine) along the way in order to prevent a second total extinction.

Both *Abzû* and *HZD* highlight the unpredictability of technology, as it refuses to remain within the bounds of human intention. Here, relationships

FIGURE 10.4 *GAIA's subordinate function HADES, referred to as the "Metal Devil" by some characters (Guerrilla Games,* Horizon: Zero Dawn, *2017, USA, © Sony Interactive Entertainment).*

between technology and nature are highly ambiguous, presenting certain intersections and tensions that make them important points of analysis within the posthuman convergence. In *Abzû*, there are no human actors present within the game world, though the material traces of their presence are evident in the explosive mechanical devices and factory ships that make them encountered throughout. The android diver is a result of human design as well, who, with the help of a pair of fish-like robots and various aqueous beings, is responsible for correcting the mistakes of those who made her (see Figure 10.5). Complex material engagements of nature and culture are foregrounded, as technology becomes inextricably intertwined with ecological systems in ways that are both harmful and beneficial. Likewise, *HZD* also imagines a world where modern human civilization has fallen due to environmentally harmful processes of technological development, reducing human societies to a more "primitive" state as they attempt to rebuild after the fall. Blurring boundaries of traditional and modern as well as natural and cultural, the game presents a world where the advanced (though ancient) technologies of the Old Ones discovered throughout the game world are surrounded by a simultaneous "re-wilding," as nature flourishes in the ruins of modern society.

    As players make their way through these games, they may come to realize how agency is not limited to the human alone but arises from material and semiotic networks of human and nonhuman actors. In a manner that resonates with Stacy Alaimo's feminist ontology of "trans-corporeality,"

FIGURE 10.5 *The android diver engaging in a ritual to return the ocean's life force (Giant Squid Studios, Abzû, 2016, USA, © 505 Games).*

games like *Abzû* and *HZD* reveal how we are bound up in heterogeneous yet interconnected webs of dispersed agency.[16] Importantly, these assemblages extend far beyond the game worlds themselves, as on-screen and off-screen realities blend together. As Alexander Galloway posits, video games are unique in that they are necessarily participatory and interactive, as players move and act alongside machines: "Both the machine and the operator work together in a cybernetic relationship to effect the various actions of the video game in its entirety [. . .] in video games the action of the machine is just as important as the action of the operator."[17] What is crucial for Galloway, as for many other game studies scholars, is the way in which games combine fictional worlds, narratives, and gameplay with player interactions in order to give rise to a form of agency that is attributed not only to human players or their on-screen avatars but distributed throughout player-game-environment relationships embedded within both material and discursive phenomena, or in reality and its representations. Digital games, in other words, are part of what N. Katherine Hayles refers to as "cognitive assemblages," heterogeneous assemblages of the biological and the technological wherein human interpretations and decisions are intertwined with "other-than-

[16]Stacy Alaimo, *Bodily Natures: Science, Environment, and the Material Self* (Indianapolis: Indiana University Press, 2010), 4.
[17]Alexander R. Galloway, *Gaming: Essays on Algorithmic Culture* (Minneapolis: University of Minnesota Press, 2006), 5.

human" ones.[18] Importantly, "cognitive assemblages transform the contexts and conditions under which human cognition operates, ultimately affecting what it means to be human in developed societies."[19]

Notably, as both semiotic and material objects, *Abzû* and *HZD* demonstrate what Braidotti describes as the simultaneous "re-naturalization" and "de-naturalization" foundational to the posthuman convergence, revealing how "the environment is technologized, just as technology is grounded and ecologized."[20] As a result of this merging, "[t]echnology has become second nature, but the environmental toll of technological development is enormous. Old nature pays a heavy price."[21] *Abzû* and *HZD* take the real and imagined relationships between technological development and ecological crisis together as a means of critically reflecting on the destructive impact we humans have on the environment, and indeed what we can do about it. Beginning from the recognition that agency in video games arises through these crucial player-game-environment interactions, the following sections explore *Abzû* and *HZD* through the lens of posthuman feminism, focusing in particular on posthuman subjectivity as it manifests in the figure of the cyborg, and through mutually constitutive animal, machine, environment relationships.

Feminist Posthuman Subjectivities: Cyborg Characters and Players

Within the posthuman convergence, a blending of natural and artificial occurs so that, as Braidotti writes, "the modernist vision of the relationship between bodies and technology, which was dualistic and confrontational, is coming apart."[22] This fundamental nature-culture hybridity is perhaps most evident in *Abzû* and *HZD* in the way that each game features a cybernetic organism, or "cyborg," as its protagonist (though on opposite ends of the human-machine spectrum). In *Abzû*, the playable diver character is an android, and while *HZD*'s Aloy certainly appears fully human on the surface, it is discovered midway through the game that, far from being "naturally born," she, too, was created in part by a machine, and is a clone of Dr. Elisabet Sobeck.

---

[18]N. Katherine Hayles, *Unthought: The Power of the Cognitive Nonconscious* (Chicago: Chicago University Press, 2017), 118.
[19]Ibid., 120.
[20]Braidotti, *Posthuman Feminism*, 101.
[21]Ibid.
[22]Ibid., 143.

Haraway defines the cyborg as a mixture of organism and machine that challenges modernist and humanistic boundaries and oppositions, embracing a partial existence that defies wholeness and upsets our very understanding of what constitutes "the natural."[23] This figure of the cyborg is an "other," and a feminist other at that. Always tied to a fractured identity, it challenges the myth of wholeness and the illusion of the self as "one," in doing so rewriting the myth of the Father in both a paternal and a scriptural sense. The ideal of wholeness and purity associated with Adam and Eve's unity in the Garden of Eden is brought under scrutiny by the cyborg, revealing that there is no such thing as a "pure nature" from which we have fallen or to which we could somehow return.

Both the android diver and Aloy are exemplary of the cyborg's fractured identity, as neither character fits into the ideas of male-female unity associated with original purity, naturalness, or wholeness within the heteropatriarchal framework of modern humanism. Essentially a machine created by other machines, the android diver is brought to life in *Abzû*'s game world in a manner that appears largely devoid of human agency, so that "[i]t is not clear who makes and who is made in the relation between human and machine."[24] With no mother, no father, and no apparent gender, the diver-robot eschews essentialized gender binaries and exemplifies the "de-naturalization" of the male/female unity (see Figure 10.5). Similarly, Aloy presents an especially interesting example of the gender-defying aspects of the cyborg as she was born without a father. In the scene after she discovers the circumstances of her birth, she laments, "I never had a mother," to which her ally Sylens replies: "what are you talking about? You had two: a dead woman and a machine."[25] Their identities always already entangled with technology, Aloy and the android diver reject any notion of original purity, as the games present protagonists that challenge the very possibility of the Garden's "pure nature."

In addition to cyborg characters, however, an important feature of *Abzû* and *HZD* (along with video games more generally) is that they also make *players themselves* into cyborgs through their complex relationships with computing systems. Indeed, players become hybrid and extended subjects constituted through relationality and multiplicity in such a way that the more proficient game literate they become, the more they begin to embody Haraway's concept of the cyborg.[26] Crucially, as players increasingly identify with their game avatars, they become entangled with a myriad of other-

[23]Donna Haraway, *Simians, Cyborgs and Women: The Reinvention of Nature* (New York: Routledge, 1991).
[24]Ibid., 172.
[25]Guerrilla Games, *Horizon: Zero Dawn*.
[26]Tina Arduini, "Cyborg Gamers: Exploring the Effects of Digital Gaming on Multimodal Composition," *Computers and Composition* 48, no. 1 (2018): 89–102.

than-human actors in heterogeneous "cognitive assemblages" where *bios* and *technos* are ultimately inseparable.[27]

As spatiotemporal experiences themselves, video games blur the divide between that which is internal to the game world and that which is external to it, particularly as the player's own body and the avatar they control on screen become more closely linked.[28] When players toggle the analogue sticks on their controllers to move the robot-diver in *Abzû* through the aquatic game world, they come to associate their movements with those of the avatar, establishing a cybernetic link or feedback loop of player-game-avatar. Cognitively speaking, as players observe virtual characters moving on-screen, mirror neurons fire in their minds, and they begin to identify and potentially empathize with them.[29] The fact that players take control of an other-than-human avatar in *Abzû* is significant, as they are invited to identify with machine consciousness. Seeing as mirror neurons do not make the distinction between embodied action and mediated action, the gap between player and avatar is reduced greatly, giving rise to a kind of "kinaesthetic empathy"[30] wherein the "otherness" of the android protagonist becomes an integral part of their embodied experiences.

To a degree, then, games like *Abzû* have what Chang describes as the unique ability "to marry both subjective and objective features of experience, and to render the nonhuman accessible."[31] Even though this nonhuman viewpoint is highly anthropomorphized, as not even the most state-of-the-art game technologies cannot fully take us beyond the human perspectives of their creators, games such as this nonetheless constitute imaginative spaces of play where players may "try on a range of subjective realities"[32] that they otherwise would not be able to access—for instance, that of a robot exploring the ocean's depths. In taking on the role of this other-than-human diver, the primacy of human agency is contested as illusions of wholeness and naturalness are undermined by both the avatar and player's cyborg existence.

Like *Abzû*, *HZD* uses a combination of narrative, image, and gameplay functions to create a deeper sense of connection between players and avatar while emphasizing their mutual "cyborgness." In addition to her ambiguous human status, Aloy relies on her "focus" throughout the game—a technological device taken from the Old World she uses to

[27]Hayles, *Unthought*.
[28]Robert M. Geraci, *Virtually Sacred: Myth and Meaning in World of Warcraft and Second Life* (Oxford: University of Oxford Press, 2014).
[29]Karen Collins, *Playing with Sound: A Theory of Interacting with Sound and Music in Video Games* (Cambridge, MA: The MIT Press, 2013), 40.
[30]Gabriel Patrick Wei-Hao Chin, "Observed Bodies and Tool Selves: Kinaesthetic Empathy and the Videogame Avatar," *Digital Creativity* 23, no. 3 (2017): 207.
[31]Chang, *Playing Nature*, 134.
[32]Ibid., 144.

FIGURE 10.6 *Aloy as a child, using the focus for the first time (Guerrilla Games,* Horizon: Zero Dawn, *2017, USA, © Sony Interactive Entertainment).*

navigate her surroundings and interact with machines and other forms of technology throughout the game (see Figure 10.6). The focus becomes such a core part of Aloy's—and players'—means of engaging with the world that to play without it would not only make the game impossible to complete but would be to disregard a central part of Aloy's identity (as fractured as it may already be). While many combat-intensive games include functions that allow players to check enemy stats or search the environment, *HZD* integrates this function into the narrative, making sense of it through the focus and maintaining a degree of immersion in the game world.

Moreover, the distinctive noise the game makes every time players activate or deactivate the focus does not come from the television speakers, but rather, from the PlayStation DualShock controllers held by players. Because the activation noise emanates from a place so close to the player's body, there is a sense that they share a focus with Aloy, enhancing the material and symbolic relationships between them. Similarly, when *HZD* is played on PlayStation 5 (as opposed to PlayStation 4, for which the game was originally developed), the controllers vibrate whenever Aloy uses her weapon in combat or gets hit by a machine she is fighting, reinforcing the significance of "avatar-kinaesthetics" or the embodied connection between player and avatar.[33] As such, the cybernetic network linking the player and

---

[33]Ea Christina Willumsen and Milan Jacevic, "Avatar-Kinaesthetics as Characterisation Statements in Horizon: Zero Dawn," *Digital Games Research Association* 18 (2018): 1–4.

the game system becomes further evident, wherein agency is not confined to one or the other, but rather arises through the connections between them.

Becoming cyborgs themselves through empathetic and embodied relationships with their on-screen avatars, human players take their place in complex assemblages as just one type of actor among many. Ultimately, the cyborg plays an important role in highlighting the subversive potential of posthumanist SF,[34] challenging the heteropatriarchal and anthropocentric structures of modernity as "the dichotomies between mind and body, animal and human, organism and machine, public and private, nature and culture, men and women, primitive and civilized are all in question ideologically."[35] As posthuman subjects, players are trans-corporeal beings that emerge from complex player-game relationships, or, what should also be seen as meaningful player-game-*environment* interactions. For although the cyborg subjectivities enacted through *Abzû* and *HZD* are integral to their significance as posthumanist and feminist texts, the crucial role of the environment (whether physical or virtual), and its range of other-than-human actors in these assemblages, cannot be overlooked.

Animal and Machine-Animal Agency in *Abzû* and *Horizon: Zero Dawn*

In addition to the cyborg subjectivities that arise through *Abzû* and *HZD,* both games use certain rhetorical and gameplay elements to extend agency to other-than-human actors in the game world, namely animals and machine-animals. Both games work to decenter the human and subvert anthropocentric attitudes toward the environment that allow for continued human mastery over and exploitation of its nonhuman others. As Chang notes, the use of animals in environmentally focused video games can give rise to forms of multispecies thinking, wherein diffuse webs of agency created through player interactions with gaming hardware and software expand to incorporate these other-than-human beings as well.[36] Although, by virtue of their divergent narratives and gameplay features, both *Abzû* and *HZD* both make it evident that agency is not limited to the human, the extent to

---

[34]Serpil Oppermann, "Feminist Ecocriticism: A Posthumanist Direction in Ecocritical Trajectory," in *International Perspectives in Feminist Ecocriticism*, ed. Greta Gaard, Simon C. Estok, and Serpil Oppermann (New York: Routledge, 2013), 28.
[35]Haraway, *Simians, Cyborgs and Women*, 160.
[36]Chang, *Playing Nature*.

which each game is successful in creating these multispecies or posthumanist worlds differs significantly.

As they make their way through *Abzû*'s game world, players encounter beautiful coral reefs teeming with life, as well as devastated reefs to which they must restore life. The game's "meditation" mechanic allows players to leave the body of the diver avatar at certain instances and instead inhabit the consciousness of other aquatic creatures in the area, including solitary animals, such as sea turtles and manatees, as well as large schools of fish that swim together through the environment. While players can use the controller to jump between aquatic creatures, moving from one to the next, they are unable to control the animals themselves. Instead, players take a back seat in these moments, watching as lively schools of fish and other creatures swim across the screen, moving on their own accord. Similarly, *Abzû* also includes a "riding" mechanism, where players have the ability to have their diver grab onto certain large sea creatures, such as turtles, dolphins, or swordfish, in order to take a ride (see Figure 10.7). Once again, players have no control over the aquatic animals' movements, meaning they swim at their own pace and often in directions opposed to where players are attempting to go.

Through these riding and meditation functions, *Abzû* foregrounds both animal and technological agency in a manner that explicitly decenters the human. While the game itself controls what happens on-screen in these instances, this machine agency is connected to that of the real-world sea creatures on which the ones in *Abzû* are meticulously based, with the creators

FIGURE 10.7 *The android diver riding a sea turtle (Giant Squid Studios, Abzû, 2016, USA, © 505 Games).*

spending hundreds of hours conducting marine research in their making of the game.[37] This connection between the virtual and the actual is further solidified by the way the names of each species appear on the bottom of the screen whenever players use the mediation or ride functions. In a posthuman sense, nature here is technologized, while technology is naturalized.[38] Game studies scholar Saxton P. Brown posits that game environments are not always necessarily "beholden to the goal-directed behaviour of the user," and, as a result, "can lead to the user's more complex considerations of ecosystems and the nonhuman."[39] It follows then that, as *Abzû* players catch rides with sea turtles or embody schools of fish, a recognition of the agency of the animal within the game may also lead to a critical reflection on its existence outside the confines of the game world—including how its future survival may depend on human action.

Furthermore, Alaimo notes that oceans often seem like "alien" worlds to us, fostering a sense of otherness, a kind of "aqueous posthumanism," that may prevent them from becoming matters of pressing environmental concern.[40] She stresses the importance of recognizing the destructive impact humanity has had on its ecosystems, arguing for a "marine trans-corporeality" that "submerges us within global networks of consumption, waste, and pollution, capturing the strange agencies of the ordinary stuff of our lives."[41] Although the explosive mines uncovered throughout *Abzû*'s game world may not necessarily qualify as "ordinary stuff," they nonetheless demonstrate the material traces of unchecked human production and development. Thus while *Abzû* presents a clear challenge to anthropocentrism through core functions that decenter the human, attributing considerable agency to the other-than-human world, the game also makes a point of showing how human actions have devastating consequences for this world. To be trans-corporeal is to be vulnerable, for any harm we cause to the environment is also brought to ourselves.

Though biological animals play a minor role in *HZD*, occasionally running across the screen and providing meat and hides should players choose to hunt them, *machine-animals* constitute a significant dimension of the game in terms of both narrative and gameplay functions. These machine-animals are modeled on real animals, from docile creatures, such as deer, to much more hostile ones, such as panthers and birds of prey—again exemplary of the nature-technology entanglements within the posthuman convergence. While originally designed by Old World humans, these machine-animals

---

[37]GCD, "Creating the Art of ABZÛ," YouTube Video, 27:02, September 22, 2017, https://www .youtube.com/watch?v=l9NX06mvp2E.
[38]Braidotti, *Posthuman Feminism*.
[39]Saxton P. Brown, "The Garden in the Machine: Video Games and Environmental Consciousness," *Philological Quarterly* 93, no. 3 (2014): 384.
[40]Alaimo, *Exposed*.
[41]Ibid., 113.

are now created in large factories or "Cauldrons" as they are called in the game and are effectively machines created by other machines. As such, their production in the game world seems to occur largely outside of human influence, echoing Braidotti's sentiment that humans now "monitor" rather than control robots, as notions of self-organizing matter and autopoiesis now extend beyond living beings to include intelligent machines as well.[42]

Many of the machine-animals in the game were originally created by the AI GAIA as part of the terraforming process meant to restore the biosphere, with each "species" of robot undertaking a particular role in the revitalization of the Earth, such as purifying the air and water, recycling machine parts, and assisting with vegetation growth. However, following GAIA's destruction, they began to use their functions to fulfill their own needs and desires, separately from what they had originally been programmed to do. Even though technology is made by humans, it always exceeds human agency and intention, escaping the parameters of its original plans and goals.[43]

In *HZD*, not only are the machines self-replicating, but they also have their own dynamic ecology, as each machine plays a specific role within the techno-bios ecosystem. For instance, antelope-like machines known as "grazers" convert vegetation and other biomass into fuel to power the machines (see Figure 10.8), while bipedal machine-animals watch over

FIGURE 10.8 *The "grazers" (Guerrilla Games,* Horizon: Zero Dawn, *2017, USA, © Sony Interactive Entertainment).*

[42]Rosi Braidotti, *The Posthuman* (Cambridge: Polity Press, 2013).
[43]Hayles, *Unthought,* 84.

them to warn of any danger. Large, giraffe-like machines, appropriately
deemed "tallnecks," also make their way across the landscape to watch for
any potential threats, sending networked messages to all other machines
in the area. As in any biological ecosystem, the machines are inextricably
interconnected, relying on one another and the surrounding environment
for their continued survival. The fact that these machine-animals refuse to
stay within the intended boundaries set by their original human creators
again presents a challenge to anthropocentrism and is one of the primary
ways in which human agency is limited within the game world.

   The other-than-human agency of *HZD*'s machine-animals is also made
evident to a degree through some of the game's central mechanics, as players
must engage with these hybrid beings in particular ways. Namely, the hunting
of machine-animals plays a significant role in the game, as players must take
them down in order to scavenge for parts needed for crafting armor and
weapons and to progress through the story. However, unlike many other
AAA titles, where combat mechanics are fairly straightforward and enemies
can be defeated with a few well-timed hits, killing the machine-animals in
HZD is often a much more complex undertaking. When in the tutorial a
young Aloy and players are introduced to the mechanics of hunting, we are
taught that machines are to be respected, for they are immensely powerful.
This word of caution rings true throughout the game, as machine-animals
are often able to reduce Aloy's hit points to zero with two or three hits. As
such, players must learn certain methods for engaging with machines that
more closely resemble real-life hunting tactics. Rather than running directly
into combat using the "hack 'n' slash" button-mashing method associated
with many mainstream titles,[44] it is better to use the stealth option to track
and trap the creatures, paying careful attention to their movements so as not
to be caught by an oncoming attack.

   In some sense then, *HZD* features mechanics for relating to other-
than-human life forms similar to those in *Abzû*, wherein human agency is
undermined by virtual creatures who do not simply submit to the whims
of the player. In response to Jane Bennett's assertion that human bodies
are not independent actors but mere nodes in "a knotted world of vibrant
matter,"[45] Adenda Rivera-Dundas contends that video games are spaces of
shared materiality where world and player act on one another so that one
must acknowledge the agency of the other in order to move forward.[46] As

[44]Jesús Fernández-Caro, "Post-Apocalyptic Nonhuman Characters in *Horizon: Zero Dawn*:
Animal Machines, Posthumans, and AI-Based Deities," *Journal of Science Fiction* 3, no. 3
(2019): 43–56.
[45]Jane Bennett, *Vibrant Matter: A Political Ecology of Things* (Durham: Duke University Press,
2010), 13.
[46]Adena Rivera-Dundas, "Ecocritical Engagement in a Pixelated World," *Ecozone* 8, no. 2
(2017): 121–35.

such, games like *Abzû* and *HZD* that limit player interactions with and control of the environment emphasize the fact that the world exists in itself, beyond their scope or manipulation, forcing them "to critically inhabit a world in which human and nonhuman exist in an assemblage and not in Enlightenment-inspired power structures."[47]

However, while the sheer power of the machine-animals in *HZD* certainly makes them a force to be reckoned with, the agency afforded to them throughout the game is brought into question by another feature learned by players later on—an "override" mechanism that allows Aloy to effectively control certain machines (see Figure 10.9). In various side quests, players visit the Cauldrons where each type of machine is made, providing them with the knowledge and instruments they need to render these machines docile, and place them under their control. After overriding particular machine-animals, Aloy is then able to mount and ride them, thereby reestablishing traditional anthropocentric power structures based on human mastery. Thus, despite the way these machine-animals illustrate the simultaneous re-naturalization and de-naturalization of the posthuman convergence through the blurring of various normative boundaries, *HZD* is perhaps not as successful as games like *Abzû* in dismantling anthropocentric and patriarchal Western hierarchies largely based on the division between nature and culture. Unfortunately, *HZD*'s override mechanic reassumes

FIGURE 10.9 *Aloy riding a machine-animal that has been overridden (Guerrilla Games,* Horizon: Zero Dawn, *2017, USA, © Sony Interactive Entertainment).*

---

[47]Ibid., 126.

the human/nonhuman dichotomy, falling back on humanistic notions of dominance. Yet, it is important to note that this binary is never static, and mastery is never final or complete. Like *Abzû, HZD* also plays with a variety of connections between human and nonhuman actors, so that agency is constantly shifting throughout the diffuse webs of influence constituted by player-game-environment relationships.

Conclusions: Technology as Savior and Destroyer

I would like to close this chapter by returning to a central premise, foundational to both *Abzû* and *HZD*: the notion that technology is the simultaneous savior and destroyer of the natural world. Or, as Andrew McMurry puts it, "what technology has broken, more technology will fix."[48] Particularly recognizable in the increased production of "green" technologies in recent years, the hope that technological development will be our saving grace in the face of ecological crisis is perpetuated throughout the twenty-first century. On the one hand, the life-restoring android and the terraforming AI GAIA in *Abzû* and *HZD* seem to uphold this belief that more—or at least *better*—technologies are required in order to heal the planetary damage caused by humans. Yet, when these two games are understood through a posthuman feminist lens, the takeaway is not so much that addressing the planetary crisis rests on further technological production, but rather that if we want to address the damage in any genuine way, we cannot continue to see the categories of nature and technology (or human and nonhuman) as necessarily separate from or antithetical to one another.

Throughout *HZD*, the tension between technology as ecologically beneficial versus ecologically harmful is particularly evident, as players learn that the Old Ones were caught up in a seemingly endless cycle of needing to produce more "green" technology to counteract the environmentally detrimental effects of ongoing modern development and corporate greed. Faced with inevitable total ecological extinction, Dr. Elisabet Sobeck's ultimate solution was to create the AI GAIA (see Figure 10.10), who, while successful in her task of terraforming the Earth in order to restore vitality to the planet, has now lost control of her subordinate functions—including HADES, the failsafe mechanism threatening to wipe out all life on Earth once again. Not only named after the Greek goddess of the Earth, GAIA is also a reference to James Lovelock's Gaia Hypothesis, which proposes that the Earth is a self-regulated, integrated system—essentially a living organism

---

[48]McMurry, "Media Moralia," 498.

FIGURE 10.10 *The AI GAIA, personified as a holographic image of a woman made to resemble the Greek goddess (Guerrilla Games,* Horizon: Zero Dawn, *2017, USA, © Sony Interactive Entertainment).*

unto itself. Although Braidotti is critical of Lovelock's theory, as its notion of interconnected and holistic nature reestablishes problematic nature/culture binaries,[49] GAIA in *HZD* moves beyond such oppositions, demonstrating how nature and technology must now be understood as synonymous with one another. In the planet's precarious state, technology behaves in a similar manner to the natural world with which it is integrated, mimicking its processes of *both* creation *and* destruction.[50] The natural and technological are similarly interpenetrated in *Abzû*, particularly at the end of the game, as the android diver and great white shark work together to destroy the mines and factory ships responsible for environmental destruction and restore life to the ocean. In both *Abzû* and *HZD*, technology is understood to be an integral part of the ecosystem, rather than necessarily separate from it.

Contrary to some critics' beliefs that video games are merely temporary forms of escapism,[51] and therefore cannot be truly socially or politically meaningful,[52] from a feminist posthumanist perspective, the networks of agency and meaning that arise from video games do not stop within

[49]Braidotti, *The Posthuman*, 85.
[50]Lauren Woolbright, "Ecofeminism and Gaia Theory in Horizon Zero Dawn," *Trace Journal* 2, no. 1 (2018): n.p.
[51]Rachel Wagner, "The Importance of Playing in Earnest," in *Playing with Religion in Digital Games*, ed. Heidi A. Campbell and Gregory Price Grieve (Bloomington: Indiana University Press, 2014), 192–213.
[52]Jonathan Boulter, *Parables of the Posthuman: Digital Realities, Gaming, and the Player Experience* (Detroit: Wayne State University Press, 2015).

the boundaries of the games themselves. Rather, they extend outwards into the world to include a vast array of social, cultural, and ecological relationships and therefore have the potential to contribute meaningfully to an environmental ethic. Notably, *Abzû* and *HZD* both include emotive soundtracks and stunning visuals that inspire a sense of wonder and intimate connection within their digitally rendered environments. Indeed, the use of environmental realism in these games draws striking parallels between the game worlds and the real world on which they are modeled so that players are faced with a sense of how easily our planet could be lost if we are not careful. Describing video games as "mesocosms," Chang notes how they are like "mini-ecosystems" with unruly edges, emphasizing the porous boundaries between in-game and out-of-game realities.[53] She posits that environmentally realistic games create opportunities for establishing new relationships "outside those based on dominance and manipulation," where engaging with different kinds of individual and collective ecological agency can better our understanding of environmental issues.[54]

Importantly, as *Abzû* players ride the great white shark at the end of the game, this is the only time when they are allowed to take control of an animal's movements. Here, the game shifts the focus onto human agency, specifically our responsibility for addressing issues like ocean pollution. Similarly, taking on the role of Aloy in *HZD*, players must work with the AI GAIA to prevent another apocalyptic environmental disaster. The fact that GAIA is anthropomorphized, configured as holographic human woman, again highlights the necessity of human action in dealing with pressing issues such as climate change. Moreover, GAIA's feminine embodiment can be contrasted with the game's rendering of HADES, who is characterized only through a giant, threatening machine, and then later a robotic male voice: a disembodied existence associated with the supposed "neutrality" of heteropatriarchal Western systems.[55] Unlike HADES, GAIA's virtual materiality and capacity for empathy are foregrounded, emphasizing a posthuman feminist ethic that underlies *HZD*—a situated, "relational ethics of mutual dependence" that uses compassion and humility as a means of "bridging the differences between humans and non-humans."[56]

Much like GAIA who embodies the simultaneous re- and de-naturalization of the posthuman convergence, *Abzû* and *HZD* emphasize the importance of bringing a feminist ethics of care to our interactions with the other-than-human world, showing how video games are not only fundamentally participatory and interactive but also embodied and affective,

---

[53]Chang, *Playing Nature*.
[54]Ibid., 23.
[55]Alaimo, *Exposed*.
[56]Braidotti, *Posthuman Feminism*, 82–4.

wherein "everyday feelings transmitted across bodies and machines are interwoven."[57] As heterogeneous cognitive assemblages, *Abzû* and *HZD* reveal how players, games, and environments (virtual and otherwise) act with, through, and on one another in complex ways, bringing nature-culture tensions to the forefront as a means of questioning human superiority and dominance. Far from trivial escapism then, these games may have a lot to teach us about what it means to live in uncertain times, reminding us of the importance of reciprocity and respect as we work toward a better planetary future alongside naturalized and technologized others.

Like other posthuman feminist SF texts, games like *Abzû* and *HZD* show us that, as Haraway puts it, "[p]erhaps, ironically, we can learn from our fusions with animals and machines how not to be Man, the embodiment of Western logos."[58] In particular, the two games explored throughout this chapter can help us see that if we want to address the ecological crisis, we must start from the recognition that any notion of "pure nature" has always been a fantasy and that technology, like the humans that create it, is a part of nature, rather than somehow separate from or above it. By revealing that the boundaries between human and nonhuman, or self and other, are always contested and porous, *Abzû* and *HZD* remind us that although we are not the same, "'we' are all in *this* together."[59]

---

[57]Aubrey Anable, *Playing With Feelings: Video Games and Affect* (Minneapolis: University of Minnesota Press, 2018), xi.
[58]Haraway, *Simians, Cyborgs and Women*, 173.
[59]Braidotti, *Posthuman Feminism*, 104.

11

From Rogue Planets to Black Holes

Revaluing Death in *Melancholia* and *High Life*

Julia A. Empey

This chapter explores the nature of impending *post*humanity as a kind of posthumanism using Lars von Trier's 2011 film *Melancholia* and Claire Denis' 2018 film *High Life* as case studies. With reference to Timothy Morton's concept of "hyperobject," I read the planet Melancholia in von Trier's film and the black hole in *High Life* as hyperobjects, shifting human-centric notions of time, space, and objectivity and informing each film's audiovisual style. At the same time, I am interested in how this inevitable posthumanity can be read, as Nina Lykke argues, as a "vibrant death," and how the in/ability to come to terms with death becomes the motivation for life extension and death-denial characteristic of transhumanism. I read Morton and Lykke alongside Patricia MacCormack's rebuking (in *The Ahuman Manifesto*) of posthumanism's inability to grapple with death and human insignificance. I argue that *High Life*, a film about space exploration gone terribly wrong, and *Melancholia*, a domestic melodrama caught up in the annihilation of the planet Earth, both suggest an optimistic ending for humanity that reads the "distribution of the value of life differently to the anthropocentric understanding of the world."[1]

Where *High Life* has a more critical posthumanist lens in its critique of the exploitation of science, *Melancholia* arguably presents a more generative feminist politics. Ultimately, both films demonstrate a "negation-of-life-as-salvation"[2] in the most productive and generative sense: death as a beginning, as a co-becoming, as life-affirming. Instead of upholding human life—and, by extension, life on Earth—as sacred and needing to be saved, both films suggest that the end of the world can be seen instead as a generative moment. Unlike other dystopian science fiction films, such as Danny Boyle's *28 Days Later* (2002), Roland Emmerich's *The Day After Tomorrow* (2004), or John Hillcoat's *The Road* (2009), neither *Melancholia* nor *High Life* is interested in humanity's actual or metaphysical salvation through technology, or in denying the apocalypse with humanity's remnant population. I am not interested in litigating humanity's death denial and death denial's merits or its failings—but I am interested in how *Melancholia* and *High Life* approach death and posthumanity by revaluing death and actively seeking death. In *High Life*'s final scene, Monte (Robert Pattinson) does not want to enter the black hole and die but does so at his daughter Willow's (Jessie Ross) behest. Monte has already been denied his humanity—he has been criminalized and has been cast off so far from human society that he is, in many ways, already dead. By rejecting human-centrism and the day-to-day performance of happiness, *Melancholia*'s Justine (Kirsten Dunst), the protagonist, is able to radically accept Melancholia's looming presence and does not view her own death as a tragedy but as a matter of fact. I read Justine's melancholia as a politics of negation that is a decidedly feminist rejection of modernity. Like Monte, Willow and Justine embrace their "vibrant deaths," an understanding of death that is not final, not because of radical life extensions or belief in an afterlife, but because of a shift in perspective on dead matter as vibrant, present, and continuing.

Through close readings of *Melancholia*'s Prelude and the final collision, and *High Life*'s opening sequence and the final encounter with the black hole, I argue that the wayward planet's and black hole's looming presences inform not just the characters' narrative progression but also the films' audiovisual style. Within both films, the hyperobjects shift how the characters relate not just to time and space but also to their (lack of) presents and futures. I am not making any definitive claims about which approach to death and the "end of the world" is the most productive, however. What I am interested

[1] Patricia MacCormack, *The Ahuman Manifesto: Activism for the End of the Anthropocene* (London: Bloomsbury Academic, 2020), 6.
[2] Russell J. A. Kilbourn, "Redemption Revalued in *Tristan und Isolde*: Schopenhauer, Wagner, Nietzsche," *University of Toronto Quarterly* 67, no. 4 (1998): 785.

in is how *Melancholia* and *High Life* revalue death as something to be anticipated and engaged with and not avoided. The end of the world is nigh—in either an existential apocalyptic sense or, individually, in one's own death.

Posthumanity and Death Denial

After *Melancholia*'s highly stylized Prelude, Part One, "Justine," focuses on her wedding reception. Justine (Kristin Dunst) performs happiness by initially capitulating to societal expectations, such as marriage, but finds these gestures to be meaningless. The film's first part leads it to be read as a family melodrama disguised as an apocalyptic film. It is not until Part Two, "Claire," that the apocalyptic visions in the Prelude are realized and Melancholia's approach is inescapable. In contrast, Part Two focuses on Claire's (Charlotte Gainsbourg) fear of her impending death, her husband John's (Kiefer Sutherland) fidelity to science, and Justine's embracing of the Earth's inevitable destruction. Melancholia crashes into the Earth, the world ends, "The End." *High Life*'s nonlinear narrative, told in a series of flashbacks,[3] follows Monte, a convict, who has been sent along with other convicts into space, ostensibly to harness a black hole as a potential energy source. Within the ship, a Humanist regime is enforced: he and his crewmates are subjected to medical experiments and sexual abuse—including rape and forced impregnation. Despite being millions of miles away from Earth, a post-Enlightenment model of "being human" is still strictly enforced. After some years, he and his infant daughter Willow are the only survivors. The film culminates with Monte and Willow entering the black hole.

Because of its posthuman qualities—for example, the ability to deconstruct Humanist notions of time through formal techniques and to render aesthetically specific affects and experiences—cinema is a productive space in which to work through the anxieties of annihilation. *High Life* does not explicitly state that humanity has ceased to exist, but it does not matter: Monte and Willow are trapped and there is no escape except through death. Monte sends messages back to Earth and keeps a log of his activities. This ritual of reporting is absurd to him; in a voiceover narration, he remarks that the films broadcast from Earth might be a ruse "to make us believe a return was possible." We get an answer to this question when a professor (Victor Banerjee) on Earth remarks that the messages and reports from the spaceship "now take years to get back

---

[3]For further discussion of *High Life*'s use of flashbacks and posthuman memory, see Russell Kilbourn's chapter "'Originary Twoness': Flashbacks and the Materiality of Memory in *Annihilation*, *High Life*, and *Arrival*."

to us. We'll be bone dust while they're still hurtling through space." This scientist, credited as the "Indian Professor," views the space program as immoral: "Radical experiments are taking place in outer space. Death row inmates are selected to be used as guinea pigs." The professor views what is being done to the crewmates as inhumane—"is this really how Occidental authorities hope to deal with criminals?"—But the inhumane treatment is the point. Humanism in *High Life* is the oppressive system through which life is ordered and controlled. Humanism judges who is allowed to be human, who will have their humanity denied, and the consequences of being rendered out of the human-centric world order. The inhumanity and immorality of what is being done to the crew and what is being withheld from them is part of the Humanist project. The crewmembers are trapped, and, more importantly, the professor explains, "we cannot even communicate with them."

The end of the world, according to Robert Sinnerbrink, "even one explored through cinema, demands either an immanent or a transcendent ethical response to the prospect of such an 'end.'"[4] Sinnerbrink reads *Melancholia*'s response as immanent, "this-worldly," and turns to the affective sublime in order to consider *Melancholia*'s particular interpretation of the end of the world. As Mark Cauchi argues, *Melancholia* is an "instance of what Friedrich Nietzsche called an "untimely meditation" on our cinematic and cultural apocalypticism—that is, it is a meditation that acts "counter to our time and thereby act[s] on our time."[5] The film "moves depressingly, mercilessly, inexorably to its dispiriting and devastating end."[6] This "devastating end" is known from the beginning: the film's opening shot is of Melancholia crashing into Earth, with the latter breaking apart, unable to absorb any impact while all life on the planet is summarily snuffed out. From the beginning, *Melancholia* "refuses any humanistic consolation or metaphysical comfort";[7] there is no world to preserve and humanity will be annihilated. *Melancholia*'s bleak prediction of no future is the death knell of the anthropocene and its larger entanglements and anxieties.[8] As Justine remarks: "The earth is evil. We don't need to grieve for it."

---

[4]Robert Sinnerbrink, "Two Ways Through Life: Postsecular Visions in *Melancholia* and *The Tree of Life*," in *Immanent Frames: Postsecular Cinema Between Malick and von Trier*, ed. John Caruana and Mark Cauchi (Albany: State University of New York Press, 2018), edited by John Caruana and Mark Cauchi, 29–46, 30.

[5]Mark Cauchi, "The Death of God and the Genesis of Worldhood in von Trier's *Melancholia*," in *Immanent Frames: Postsecular Cinema Between Malick and von Trier*, ed. John Caruana and Mark Cauchi (Albany: State University of New York Press, 2018), 106.

[6]Ibid.

[7]Robert Sinnerbrink, "Anatomy of *Melancholia*," *Angelaki* 19, no. 4 (2014): 113.

[8]I align myself with MacCormack, who "deliberately" avoids capitalizing the term throughout the *Ahuman Manifesto*.

According to Patricia MacCormack, the anthropocene is "the opening of the world."[9] To MacCormack, posthumanism does not, in fact, destabilize and remove the human from the center of the world; instead, as a counterpoint, she offers her reading of the "ahuman." The ahuman forsakes "human privilege through acts of ethical affirmation that open the world to the other and to difference without forsaking what the posthuman gave away—truth in experience, reality, materiality and life itself."[10] MacCormack maintains that even posthumanism upholds the human as sacred, as something that needs to be preserved, and is yet another "perpetuation of humanist egoism."[11] Where transhumanism wants to augment the human body to its highest capacity or experience radical life extensions or immortality, according to MacCormack, posthumanism "picked up a vitalistic turn which attempts to reinvigorate a positive end to anthropocentrism."[12] However, that vitalistic turn does not, in MacCormack's eyes, go far enough. Posthumanisms, often framed as "critical," while aiming to dethrone the human from the top of the world's hierarchy, do not desire that the human should be rendered obsolete; nor do they recognize that "[w]e humans are simply parts of a thing known as earth."[13] Critical posthumanism's main goals might be deconstructing humanism as a concept and rethinking the Enlightenment's legacy, but so what? As asserted in this volume's introduction, "unintentionally or unconsciously, the posthuman—even the critical posthmuman—is also a Man" so too, even in critical posthumanist thinking, the human is not fundamentally revalued because there is no revaluing of human life as anything but essential.

While I do not think *Melancholia* or *High Life* fully embody MacCormack's aims, upholding as they do "anthropocentric signifying systems of representation and recognition,"[14] they serve as an interesting counterpoint to other types of science fiction film. I read both films as part of a legacy of science fiction cinema that anticipates and negotiates possible futures by critically examining our present moment. Each of these films is interested in renegotiating death. This affirmation of life through death resists the transhumanist fantasies of continued life via technology, and, in turn, rejects critical posthumanism's essentializing of (human) life. Yes, there are critical posthumanists who discuss death and suggest a radical rethinking of death; for example, Rosi Braidotti does so extensively in *The Posthuman*. She suggests a need to "re-think death, the ultimate subtraction, as another

---

[9]MacCormack, *Ahuman Manifesto*, 1.
[10]Ibid., 11.
[11]Ibid., 6.
[12]Ibid., 11.
[13]Ibid., 5.
[14]Ibid., 10.

phase in a generative process."[15] Human life, in Braidotti's view, must not be extended, but it also must not be negated. Braidotti argues death is an experience that is "behind" us: "Being mortal, we all are 'have beens': the spectacle of our death is written obliquely into the script of our temporality, not as a barrier, but as a condition of possibility."[16] Thus, death pertains to a past that is "forever present [and] not individual but impersonal; it is the precondition of our existence, of the future."[17] I do not fundamentally disagree with Braidotti's assessment, but I want to extend her claims: I am interested in how the negation of human life—a true posthumanity, where human life no longer exists—can be life-affirming and generative.

Posthumanism, whether as a philosophical turn or as the transformation out of human embodiment, continues to uphold human life as essential. In line with MacCormack, I suggest a rejection of an essentialized understanding of human life, of life as "sacred," of life as something that needs to be clung to and preserved at all costs. I want to suggest instead that we read and embrace posthumanism as *post*humanity. By posthumanity, I mean the end of the human as an ontological category and as a species. Rereading posthumanism as posthumanity can take a variety of approaches: anti-natalism, intentional depopulation efforts, and/or the acceptance that human life is not tenable on Earth. From this posthumanism, there may emerge a generative and affirmative approach to death, and, in turn, an annihilation of "death denial."

Here I draw from Ernest Becker's understanding of "death denial": humans know they are mortal, their time on this Earth is finite, and they therefore devise various strategies to avoid this awareness.[18] These strategies include religion, life after death or reincarnation, or even just a general belief in human survivability as a species, regardless of Earth's circumstances. There have been critiques of how death denial is defined and deployed. Tradii and Robert trace a genealogy of death denial and then question the concept's validity. They maintain that Western death denial is based neither on historical fact nor in current practices, arguing that, as a concept, it needs to be done away with, and death studies should move toward the study of "what the living have done with the dead, as opposed to what they should have done or did not do."[19] I would amend this to say that humans are not in complete denial of the fact that they die, and that it is short-sighted to make sweeping generalizations about an entire species. In a Western context, however, death denial is still useful as a concept and practice, as

[15]Rosi Braidotti, *The Posthuman* (Cambridge: Polity books), 121.
[16]Ibid., 132.
[17]Ibid.
[18]Ernest Becker, *The Denial of Death* (New York: Simon and Schuster, 1997), 7.
[19]Laura Tradii and Martin Robert, "Do We Deny Death? II. Critiques of the Death-Denial Thesis," *Mortality* 24, no. 4 (2019): 386.

the fear of death, or the myopic need to live as if death is not part of the human equation, is still prevalent. What makes death denial so insidious is the innumerable ways humans either attempt to theorize or materialize life beyond death. It is easy to say that death is inevitable, but doing so does not fundamentally revalue death. As MacCormack argues, "even the death of human exceptionalism is unthinkable."[20] Essentially, rethinking death is one element, but how does this revaluing of life become actionable? In *Melancholia* death is unavoidable: the planet will crash into the Earth. *High Life* offers a more interesting turn: Monte and Willow actively choose to embrace death, not just to rethink their relationship to death, but to affirmatively move toward death.

In her discussion of vibrant death, Lykke categorizes death denial into two main branches: the medical and the religious-cultural. As Lykke prepares for the death of her beloved and then mourns her loss, she notes how death denial shapes her relationship to her dead beloved. Lykke views both medical and religious-cultural approaches as predicated upon a "dualist split between mind and body, and shar[ing] a basic contempting [*sic*] and instrumentalizing approach to flesh and matter."[21] The dead body has the "power to affect other bodies in a Spinozan sense"; that is, it has the ability to affect and be affected by others. The dead beloved is vibrantly present not just in memory but also "materially present as vibrant traces, as a fleshy posthuman materiality."[22] Lykke's rewriting of death, however, is not the normative approach. Death denial has not gone away so much as it has evolved. Now, technological enhancement and medical intervention allow for individuals to live longer; nevertheless, how death is understood and the affects around death signal unease, a discomfort, a tension.

Death denial in *High Life* manifests in the in vitro-fertilization experiments overseen by Dr. Dibs (Juliette Binoche), a Medea-like figure who murdered her children and her husband and then failed to kill herself. As a character, Dibs both enforces Humanist ideology but is also dehumanized and rendered monstrous.[23] Dibs is myopically focused on these experiments to the point of obsession and violence. Time and again, the women crewmembers either fail to get pregnant, or they miscarry, or the fetus is stillborn. Humanity living on and being able to continue reproducing in space is a type of fantasy: even after life on Earth for humans is no longer viable, human

---

[20]MacCormack, *Ahuman Manifesto*, 6.

[21]Nina Lykke, *Vibrant Death: A Posthuman Phenomenology of Mourning* (New York: Bloomsbury Publishing, 2022), 8.

[22]Ibid., 9.

[23]See Chapter 13, "Coming to Terms with Our Own Ends: Failed Reproduction and the End of the Hu/man in Claire Denis' *High Life* and Pella Kågerman and Hugo Lija's *Aniara*" for a further discussion of Dibs' characterization and *High Life*'s reproductive politics.

reproduction in space is a "get out of annihilation free" card. It is through these experiments (and the monitoring of the crewmembers' bodies) that humanism is enforced. But death denial also operates in more subtle ways. The crew recycles their waste—both food-based and bodily—lest they run out of water to drink or food to eat. In the film's opening scenes, before the title card, Monte tells an infant Willow, "Don't drink your own piss, Willow. Don't eat your own shit. Even if it's recycled and even if it doesn't look like piss or shit any more. It's called a taboo." This instruction from father to daughter has been read as Monte trying to maintain a certain level of normalcy, but it does not matter. Monte does need to drink and eat his piss and shit, lest he die (Balsom para. 4). Taboo therefore becomes something that can and should be broken in order to deny death; even for Willow, taboo holds no meaning.

In *Melancholia* death denial is summarily rejected, and the characters that cannot come to grips with their impending deaths, in particular Claire and her husband, John, are given no consolation. Only Justine, who has summarily rejected the importance of human life, is able to understand and accept the imminent planetary collision. Danielle Verena Kollig argues that von Trier frames the apocalypse "either as an event contributed to through human interaction or as an enjoyable spectacle that, despite its definite and terminal effect on life nonetheless excludes the audience."[24] The audience is also denied the usual metaphysical comforts of apocalyptic science fiction film. Reading the apocalypse, and, in turn, death, through *High Life* and *Melancholia*, leads to questions of time, kinship, and human-centrism, questions displaced by the appearance in the films' respective diegetic worlds of *High Life*'s black hole and the planet Melancholia.

Hyperobjects

According to Timothy Morton, hyperobjects are "things that are massively distributed in time and space relative to humans" and can manifest innumerably: black holes, oil fields, Styrofoam cups, plastics, icebergs, and so on can all be hyperobjects. It is these hyperobjects that are the harbingers of "*the end of the world*, rendering both denialism and apocalyptic environmentalism obsolete."[25] Morton reads hyperobjects simultaneously

---

[24]Danielle Verena Kollig, "Filming the World's End. Images of the Apocalypse in Lars Von Trier's Epidemic and Melancholia/Rodar el fin del mundo: Imágenes del apocalypsis en Epidemia y Melancolía, de Lars Von Trier," *Amaltea. Revista de mitocritica* 5 (2013): 86.
[25]Timothy Morton, *Hyperobjects: Philosophy and Ecology after the End of the World* (Minneapolis: University of Minnesota Press, 2013), 2.

as discreet objects and as unfathomable concepts that operate beyond time. The hyperobject in *Melancholia* is obvious: the planet; likewise, in *High Life* the black hole is a looming specter that haunts the crew. But what is the *effect* of either of these hyperobjects in these specific contexts? As hyperobjects, what do they *mean*?

I am specifically interested in how the planet Melancholia's and the black hole's impact as hyperobjects are mediated through both films' audiovisual style. I want to argue, following MacCormack, that the "liberation of the world is not the romance of an inconceivable hyperobject made aesthetic [. . .] when it is taken out of the anthropocentric eye of aestheticization for self-gratification."[26] In other words, the hyperobject does not inherently turn away from anthropocentricism or destabilize the human; if anything, it affirms the human gaze as all knowing. As Stacy Alaimo argues, feminist methodologies are "conspicuously absent from this speculation about hyperobjects, which despite the footprints, leave the human thinker intact."[27] The hyperobject becomes a way of projecting humanism and does not in fact liberate the world; rather, it is the vastness and the unknowability of the Earth—and, by extension, the cosmos—that "reminds us that we have the dubious honour of being utterly inconsequential in a meaningful way."[28] If anything, Morton is unnecessarily fatalistic:

> The end of the world has already occurred. We can be uncannily precise about the date on which the world ended. Convenience is not readily associated with historiography, nor indeed with geological time. But in this case, it is uncannily clear. It was April 1784, when James Watt patented the steam engine, an act that commenced the depositing of carbon in Earth's crust—namely, the inception of humanity as a geophysical force on a planetary scale. Since for something to happen it often needs to happen twice, the world also ended in 1945, in Trinity, New Mexico, where the Manhattan Project tested the Gadget, the first of the atom bombs, and later that year when two nuclear bombs were dropped on Hiroshima and Nagasaki. These events mark the logarithmic increase in the actions of humans as a geophysical force. They are of "world-historical" importance for humans—and indeed for any lifeform within range of the fallout— demarcating a geological period, the largest-scale terrestrial era.[29]

Humans transformed what the world could be, for better and for worse. The anthropocene is indeed the opening up of the world in the mass extraction

[26]MacCormack, *Ahuman Manifesto*, 177.
[27]Stacy Alaimo, "Material Feminism in the Anthropocene," in *A Feminist Companion to the Posthumanities*, ed. Cecilia Åsberg and Rosi Braidotti (Cham: Springer, 2018), 52.
[28]MacCormack, *Ahuman Manifesto*, 177.
[29]Morton, *Hyperobjects*, 7.

of resources (as if human agriculture was not a significant moment, or when our first ancestor killed another being for sustenance), but to call it the end of the world is to give humans a more dubious honor than we deserve. There is no single moment where the world has ended because the world has not ended, and to argue that it has is to once again order the world in Humanist terms. The world will live on—with or without us—but one day, this world will not exist anymore, not because of human activity, however, but because the Sun will expand and the Earth will be engulfed by it. *Melancholia* depicts this inevitability in its Prelude and Justine embraces this end, her vibrant death.

MacCormack maintains that the "apocalypse will not come with an explosive bang or a diluvian wave but with apathy and internalized despair."[30] This slow apocalypse is not immediately present in *Melancholia*: in the film's Prelude the planet crashes into Earth—or rather, the Earth crashes into Melancholia, is shattered and subsumed—and fade to black. The "end of the world" is cataclysmic and final. Robert Sinnerbrink points to *Melancholia*'s "radical gesture of world-sacrifice" and that von Trier's "aestheticization of world-destruction" has "the paradoxical ethical meaning [. . .] of preparing for a post-humanist beginning."[31] By comparison, *High Life*'s ending is similarly final: Willow and Monte enter the black hole—fade to white. Like Sinnerbrink, I am interested in how there are different worlds that are sacrificed in the films. There is no Earth being sacrificed in *High Life*, but the world that Monte and Willow have cocreated together is sacrificed for a new beginning through their deaths via the hyperobject. Moreover, Monte has been living through a slow apocalypse that began when his dog was murdered—his world ended that day. *Melancholia* has the slow apocalypse of which MacCormack speaks, but it starts with Justine's melancholia causing her life to implode. Communal and familial bonds are tested and (mostly) shattered, well before the Earth itself is obliterated.

High Life approaches the end of humanity as that slow apocalypse. The film is ambiguous on whether humanity has truly ended and whether the crew is its last remnant; it does not matter, because the crew cannot return to Earth. The only thing that can be done is to move slowly toward the black hole. The film's nonlinear narrative displaces Monte and, in turn, the viewer. According to the ship's calendar, Monte has been in space for 7,650 days, but according to Earth time he has been gone for 210 years. Time has expanded for him; he is beyond human time while he is in space. This expansion of time makes Monte's punishment and exile to space even more cruel and full of retribution: everyone and everything he has ever known is most likely gone—including the family of the child he killed.

---

[30]MacCormack, *Ahuman Manifesto*, 177.
[31]Sinnerbrink, "Anatomy of *Melancholia*," 112.

Melancholia's Prelude and *High Life*'s opening sequence

Melancholia's Prelude turns "cinematic images into moving *tableaux vivants* evoking a variety of aesthetic moods."[32] Painterly in quality, the slow-motion digital compositions, set to the "Prelude" from Wagner's *Tristan and Isolde* (a piece that recurs throughout the film) convey the film's aesthetic vision and von Trier's imagining of the apocalypse. These digital compositions are formally unlike von Trier's usual style, which consists of subjective handheld camera movement, unmotivated cuts, and discontinuous editing—all characteristic of the "Dogme 95 Manifesto," with its "Vows of Chastity"; initially an inside joke among filmmaker-friends that became widely influential.[33] The Prelude makes references to Pre-Raphaelite art and Andrei Tarkovsky's filmography (particularly *Solaris*), hovering "ambiguously between romantic sublimity, historical homage, theological allusion, and cinematic self-reflection."[34] That the Prelude's visual style contrasts so starkly with the rest of the film signals the film's topics and themes. The Prelude becomes the "sticking-point for the film, a moment that we return to incessantly, because it can never be surpassed."[35] The Prelude is referred to repeatedly throughout the film, moreover.

Melancholia's opening shot, a close-up of Justine's face, is uncanny: she barely moves, she is disheveled, and her face expresses little to no affect. Her face is "a portrait of melancholia, of time arrested and congealed, with just the barest flicker of movement visible on her face, eyes, and hair."[36] Mikkel Krause Frantzen reads the Prelude as "a temporal disjunction; formally, the time is utterly out of joint."[37] The human figures move slowly, uncannily, while the background remains almost completely still. In a long shot, Claire clings to her son Leo (Cameron Spurr) and pulls him across the eighteenth hole of their family's golf course, her face stricken with agony. In another shot, Justine, Claire, and Leo in their wedding finery are posed across the palatial estate's lawn, while Melancholia, the moon, and the sun loom overhead. Frantzen reads these images as "Two temporalities . . . constantly contrasted, from the human to the planetary level, where planet Earth and

---

[32]Ibid.
[33]Gabriel Giralt, "Dogme 95 and the Reality of Fiction," *Kinema: A Journal for Film and Audiovisual Media* (Fall 2003): 1–2. https://openjournals.uwaterloo.ca/index.php/kinema/issue/view/285.
[34]Sinnerbrink, "Anatomy of *Melancholia*," 112.
[35]Steven Shaviro, "MELANCHOLIA, or, The Romantic Anti-Sublime," *SEQUENCE* 1, no. 1 (2012): 13.
[36]Sinnerbrink, "Anatomy of *Melancholia*," 112.
[37]Mikkel Krause Frantzen, *Going Nowhere, Slow: The Aesthetics and Politics of Depression* (Alresford: John Hunt Publishing, 2019), 161.

the planet Melancholia also belong to two discrete regimes of time."[38] This expansion of time through slow-motion reflects how hyperobjects "do not occur 'in' time and space, but rather emit spacetime" (90). In essence, because hyperobjects exist outside of human time, in that they have either been around for significantly longer or will exist for significantly long after, they operate within their own time. It is not just Melancholia that disrupts Justine's relationship to time and space, but her own experience of melancholia and how her mental health shapes her perspective of the world around her. Justine's melancholia is itself a hyperobject.

According to Yorick Le Saux, *High Life*'s director of photography, the "mood" they wanted to capture was that of Andrei Tarkovsky's *Stalker* and, in his eyes, like Tarkovsky's film, *High Life* is "ultimately a story of what happens inside human beings' bodies and minds."[39] *High Life*'s opening sequence follows Monte *after*; after his rape, after the crew is all dead, after Willow's birth, where he is utterly alone save for his infant daughter. The opening shot tracks across the ship's garden. Close-ups of various gourds, leaves, and grasses, all speckled with water, and then of a shoe. Shots of the spaceship's interior, shrouded in darkness, and devoid of life, until Willow starts to cry so loudly it almost drowns out the score. The camera tracks into a room where Willow is playing in a makeshift playpen. The voyeuristic camera captures moments that possibly should not be seen. The two films are voyeuristic but stylistically contrasting. The camera work in each film sheds light on how each director conveys their characters' affects and subjectivities: von Trier's camera movement is almost self-consciously voyeuristic as it quickly sweeps across crowds and the landscape and is almost claustrophobic in the tightness of the close-ups on Justine and her family's faces. In contrast, Denis' camera caresses in its gentle tracking and movements, often pulling back at high angles, holding the characters at a distance or tight on their faces and the messiness of the body: its blood, its piss, its humanness.

Monte is outside the ship; the vastness of black space surrounds him. Despite his attempts to comfort her, Willow's cries increase until she is screaming. Monte drops a wrench and it drifts into the infinite black of space. He returns to the ship. In a high-angle long shot, Monte appears to be dwarfed within the room, and questions occur to the viewer: Why are there so many spacesuits? Where are the other people? Why are this man and his baby left alone? This sequence culminates with Monte deciding to "jettison everything that is unnecessary. I'm fully aware of the consequences." "Everything that is unnecessary" is the crewmember's dead bodies, held in

---

[38]Ibid.
[39]Yannick Le Saux, "Eye Piece: DP Yorick Le Saux Mixed Digital With 35MM and Heavy Prep With On-Set Improvisation To Shoot *High Life*," MovieMaker.com, February 20, 2021, https://www.moviemaker.com/eye-piece-high-life-dp-yorick-le-saux/.

cryostasis. Before he jettisons them, he puts them in their spacesuits, almost like a mourning ritual, because, once their bodies are disposed of, Monte and Willow will be alone. The final remnants of other people are summarily ejected into space. The task is laborious, Monte grunts and groans as he carries the bodies, the camera tracks his struggle, and then it is over, the bodies are gone. It should be noted that it will not be possible for these bodies to decay: there is no life in space, no bacteria, and it is cold. These crewmembers will forever be entombed in their suits, free-falling through endless space. The bodies float down and across the screen and then the film's title appears: *HIGH LIFE*.

Threaded through these opening moments are memories of Monte's life on Earth as a child, running through the woods with his beloved dog and his friend-turned-murderess. Child-Monte drops a bloody rock into a well; a close-up of his bloodied hand in sharp relief against the dark interior, light reflecting on the water. According to Nicholas Devlin, *High Life*'s "flashbacks represent co-existing worlds: earth and the space station, the past and the present, pre-sexual experimentation and postsexual experimentation, before prison and after prison."[40] Stylistically, *High Life*'s flashbacks are shot on 16mm film, whereas the rest of the film is shot digitally. These flashback sequences, from Monte's, Boyse's (Mia Goth), and other's perspectives, including the Indian Professor, give insight into who these characters are and why they are never to return, but also signal the characters' relationship to time, memory, and the (lack of a) future. Frantzen's reading of *Melancholia*'s Prelude, that time is out of joint and that there are multiple temporalities at play, also applies to *High Life*. Moreover, like *Melancholia*'s Prelude, *High Life*'s opening sequence gestures toward the broader themes, ideas, and visuals that are explored within the film. Both openings are referents that are returned to time and time again, stylistically and thematically.

Melancholia's Prelude and *High Life*'s nonlinear narrative structure demonstrate that time is out of joint and beyond human in both films. According to Morton, the hyperobject's unfathomability, due to it being beyond or outside of human time, is what makes relations with these objects untenable. The black hole is the justification for Monte and the crew's exile, but it cannot be engaged with, for to do so, one is most likely to die. Melancholia, in turn, is world-shattering and world-ending, not merely in the annihilation of Earth, but in Justine's dismantling of her own life at her wedding reception. Melancholia becomes the objectification of Justine's melancholia, and *High Life*'s black hole is a specter that haunts the crew. These hyperobjects, by changing perceptions of time, in turn, highlight the characters' relationship to the future—or lack thereof.

---

[40]Nicholas Devlin, "Sci-Fi and Truth: Saturated Subjects in the Films of Claire Denis and Jordan Peele," in *From Cogito to Covid* (London: Palgrave Macmillan, 2022), 76.

Depression and No Future

Mikkel Krause Frantzen defines depression as a "chronopathology, characterized by the loss of (the ability to imagine) the future. Not the loss of a precise future but precisely the loss of future itself." Reading alongside Mark Fisher's work on capitalist realism and hauntology, Frantzen argues that "depression can be viewed as the pathological mirror of contemporary capitalism."[41] In his reading of *Melancholia*, Frantzen views the film's ending as happy, providing "an impetus" for what Frantzen calls "an eschatological hope."[42] Frantzen reads depression as an experience of a lost future, one that cannot be experienced and has been rendered absent. In *Melancholia*, Justine experiences "a frozen future" that manifests not only as a pathologized psychological state but which "is also asserted bodily, as a kind of slowness, inertness or pure immobility. The surrounding movements fixate her as immovable."[43] Justine is rendered out of time and, therefore, out of social life. Her lack of desire to "be happy" at her wedding, her inability to shake her melancholia, is also her rejection of these constructs. Likewise, Monte and Willow are also rendered out of time. Mark Fisher argues that twenty-first-century culture is marked by "anachronism and inertia"[44] and that "this stasis has been buried, interred behind a superficial frenzy of 'newness,' of perpetual movement. The 'jumbling up of time,' the montaging of earlier eras, has ceased to be worthy of comment; it is now so prevalent that is no longer even noticed."[45] As the spaceship hurtles through space toward the black hole at 99 percent the speed of light, Monte and Willow are suspended in time. Yes, Willow grows to her adolescence, but it is not a "future." Fisher's use of "future" here is drawn from Franco Berardi's text *After the Future*:

> I am not referring to the direction of time. I am thinking, rather, of the psychological perception, which emerged in the cultural situation of progressive modernity, the cultural expectations that were fabricated during the long period of modern civilization, reaching a peak after the Second World War. These expectations were shaped in the conceptual frameworks of an ever progressing development, albeit through different methodologies: the Hegel-Marxist mythology of Aufhebung and founding of the new totality of Communism; the bourgeois mythology of a linear development of welfare and democracy; the technocratic mythology of the all-encompassing power of scientific knowledge; and so on.[46]

---

[41]Frantzen, *Going Nowhere, Slow*, 11.
[42]Ibid., 157.
[43]Ibid., 163.
[44]Mark Fisher, *Ghosts of My Life: Writings on Depression, Hauntology and Lost Futures* (Alresford: John Hunt Publishing, 2014), 6.
[45]Ibid.
[46]Franco Berardi, *After the Future* (Chico: AK Press, 2011), 18–19.

The future can never be experienced; it is frozen and, in turn, the present cannot be experienced either. Fisher argues that the slow cancellation of the future, to put it as simply as possible, is due to a consistent nostalgia feedback loop, and that culture "has lost the ability to grasp and articulate the present. Or it could be that, in one very important sense, there is no present to grasp and articulate any more."[47] In essence, to have no future, one also does not have much of a present, and moreover, what is experienced is cyclical and unending.

Despite Monte's attempts, Willow does not experience a future. She will not know or experience progressive modernity, experience the ramifications of neoliberalism, or life beyond the dyad of her and her father—she has no future. Time has expanded so much for her and Monte in space that they have lived beyond humanity and there is seemingly no end to their circumstances. It is tempting to read Willow as experiencing a posthumanist future, one beyond the scope and limits of human-centric modernity, but what it means to be human is still mediated to her through the images that are relayed from Earth. I find these images—from the drama-turned-pseudo-documentary *In the Land of the Head Hunters* (1914) and specifically of an Indigenous man performing a religious ceremony[48]—as a way of interpreting Willow's subjectivity as these images are shown over and over again. She is shown either watching the screen or in the foreground, the images playing behind her. These images also highlight Willow's own relationship to time. The image of the Indigenous man and his ceremony are repeated over and over again. The Indigenous man in the film is that consistent nostalgia feedback loop, suspended out of time and rendered into an image without referent. Willow is, in a sense, like the man on the film: unable to age, grow, or experience life—she is suspended in time, denied history, denied a future, and in turn, because she has no future she has no present. Thus, the future is something that she does not experience, and in turn, neither does Monte.

Likewise, I read Justine's melancholia as a type of refusal: a refusal of modernity and its trappings that promise a future it cannot deliver. She refuses marriage, employment, and to capitulate to human-centrism and exceptionalism and to the medicalization of her melancholic perspective.

[47]Fisher, *Ghosts of My Life*, 9.
[48]*In the Land of the Head Hunters*, is a silent film directed by Edward S. Curtis. Depicting "a dramatization of the life of the Kwakiutl peoples of British Columbia," the film "revolves around the chief's son, who must contend with an evil sorcerer in order to win the hand of a beautiful maiden." The film was not meant to be read as a documentary but nevertheless was viewed as one upon its release. What sets the film apart from its contemporaries is that it depicts Indigenous life precolonization and was shot entirely on location and with heavy consultation from the Kwakiutl people. See Brad Evans and Aaron Glass' essay "In The Land of the Head Hunters," in *Return to the Land of the Headhunters: Edward S. Curtis, The Kwakwaka'wakw and the Making of Modern Cinema*.

Justine's family views her depression as irrational, an irritation. Justine's melancholia is cast as something that should not be admired or taken seriously: it is selfish; it is excessive; it is, in John's words, "unbelievable"— and yet, in the film's second part, "Claire," Justine is the person who can understand and accept her impending death.

Vibrant Death

For Justine, Melancholia the hyperobject becomes life affirming, it awakens her and makes sense of her depression. I read Justine's approach to death as generative and even life affirming. Vibrant death as a concept takes inspiration from Jane Bennett's "conceptualization of "vibrant matter"[49] and its reference to seventeenth-century monist philosopher Benedict Spinoza's concept of *conatus*,"[50] which is "the striving of all matter to persevere."[51] "Vibrant death" infuses death with the ever-present life force of *zoe*. Lykke frames this revalued death as a symbiotic relationship between *thanatos* and *eros*: these forces are "ontologized as totally intertwined."[52] Vibrant death takes death from a calamity and something that can be avoided either through biomedical intervention (or, possibly, digitization of consciousness, or by technologically augmenting the human body), or through belief in an afterlife. Instead, death, and its associated affects, such as grief and mourning, is reimagined and revalued as generative and life affirming. As MacCormack argues, "death is an imaginative, pro-ethical activist technique to end the human and open the world rather than the human's lamentable end as the end of the world."[53] Death, moreover, is "anthropomorphically absenting, but for the earth and its nonhuman occupants, [it is] richly liberating."[54] Vibrant death is an interesting way of thinking through the apocalypse, because, instead of viewing "the end of the world" as final, the vibrant matter that makes up all life remains. While *Melancholia* literally depicts the end of the world, this posthumanity should not need to be avoided, but may be embraced. *High Life*'s final scene also sees an embracing of death by Monte and Willow. Lykke rejects the pathologization of her mourning as "excess" and suggests a cripping of mourning: an "exploration and resignification of the pathologized subject position of the excessive mourner."[55] I see a

[49]Jane Bennett, *Vibrant Matter: A Political Ecology of Things* (Durham: Duke University Press, 2010).
[50]Lykke, *Vibrant Death*, 8.
[51]Ibid., 7.
[52]Ibid.
[53]MacCormack, *Ahuman Manifesto*, 97.
[54]Ibid.
[55]Lykke, *Vibrant Death*, 42.

similarity between Lykke's lived experience of mourning her dead beloved and Justine's melancholia, which is also read by her family as excessive and selfish. Both experience an entanglement with both life and death that is difficult to comprehend because it rejects Humanist understandings of life and death.

Justine's entanglement with Melancholia is demonstrated through the film's mise-en-scène, particularly when Justine herself becomes "vibrant matter."[56] Returning to the film's Prelude, I argue that Justine experiences a "co-becoming" with Melancholia.[57] In the tenth shot of the Prelude, Justine is in medium close-up at the center of the frame and, as she lifts her hands and gazes at them, sparks and lines of electricity stream from her fingertips.[58] I read this shot as Justine experiencing a generative moment, of Melancholia affirming her subjectivity, and, further, her rejection of human-centrism. If we read the Prelude as signaling the film's aesthetic and psychological mood and, as Steven Shaviro argues, as a departure point that the viewer is returned to repeatedly over the course of the film, then this moment can be seen as Justine expanding beyond the confines that have been placed upon her (Figure 11.1).

FIGURE 11.1 *Justine (Kristen Dunst) experiences a "co-becoming" with Melancholia (Lars von Trier (dir.),* Melancholia, *2011).*

---

[56]Bennett, *Vibrant Matter*, 3.
[57]Lykke, *Vibrant Death*, 8.
[58]Sinnerbrink notes that the moths surrounding Justine in the seventh shot could be read as a biblical reference "to a passage in Isaiah, referring to moths and mortality in the face of God's infinite power" (Sinnerbrink, "Anatomy of *Melancholia*," 115). The moths could also be read as an allusion to the Exodus plagues (God sends lice, flies, and locusts as the third, fourth, and eighth plagues, respectively). Ecological collapse as a sign of God's wrath features in the Old Testament prophets. It is possible that the birds falling from the sky in the opening shot are also a reference to apocalyptic visions in the Old Testament; see, for example, Book of Hosea 4:3.

The hyperobject Melancholia bears a type of witness to Justine's melancholia. Justine recognizes that there is "something rotten in the humanist myth of progress, our rationalist faith in redemption from catastrophe through science and technology."[59] Justine's relationship with Melancholia is not limited to the moments in the Prelude. While her family is trying to cope with and even rationalize themselves out of the prospect of imminent death, Justine is calm, even taking pleasure in Melancholia's approach. At one point, Claire sees Justine "moon-bathing" in Melancholia's light; in a long shot, Justine is aglow and naked, gazing up at the planet. In a series of shot-reverse shots between Justine and Melancholia, it is as if the two bodies are indeed looking at one another, Melancholia the hyperobject affirming Justine's feelings of her own insignificance and the emptiness of everyday life. In a sense, Melancholia becomes Justine's beloved, with whom she cannot wait to be united in a final, mutual, annihilation.

In contrast, for much of *High Life*, the black hole does not bring Monte comfort, and becomes something that needs to be avoided at all costs. After being forcibly impregnated and then giving birth to Willow, Boyse murders Nansen (Agata Buzek) and takes her place in a shuttle that is meant to loop around the black hole, unbeknownst to the remaining crew. The sequence cuts between Boyse in the shuttle and Monte as he watches her on the ship's radar. As Boyse moves closer to the black hole, she begins to stretch and compress in the black hole's gravitational field. To depict Boyse's spaghettification, the remaining light is stretched out into thin bands, her face barely illuminated, the nondiegetic score chaotic, until Boyse is summarily crushed. Boyse's death is violent—she would rather be rent apart than continue to live within the Humanist framework. I read Boyse's death as her moment of refusal. She refuses to be experimented on, she refuses to pretend that she wants Willow (thereby rejecting patriarchally enforced maternalism), and refuses to capitulate to life any longer. She would rather violently co-become with the black hole, the hyperobject, than be human.

After Boyse's death, the remaining crewmembers die in quick succession. Mink (Claire Tran) attacks Dibs in retaliation for the experiments and Nansen's death, only for Monte to murder her; Dibs ejects herself into space, after confessing to Monte that she raped him and Willow is his child; and Tcherny (André Benjamin) is subsumed into the garden. Arguably, before Willow and Monte enter the black hole, Tcherny also experiences a type of co-becoming with the garden, which he tends throughout the film: "this little garden is teaching me to enjoy the present." The garden reminds him of Earth; it is life-sustaining and caring for it is life-affirming. After Boyse's violent death, Tcherny cannot maintain the ruse of life on the ship. In a medium shot, he removes his shoes, lies down in the garden, and fades

---

[59]Sinnerbrink, "Anatomy of *Melancholia*," 104.

FIGURE 11.2 *Tcherny (Andre Benjamin) is subsumed within the garden (Claire Denis (dir.),* High Life, *2018).*

into the Earth. Through a fade and superimposition, his body is visible, then only the Earth, and then a mound of soil, as he becomes one with the garden's matter. Tcherny's death is unlike the others because his is the first "life-affirming" death in the film (Figure 11.2).

Lykke notes that "the mourning 'I' does not have a place in Western philosophy."[60] It must be said, though, that "the affective state of utter devastation" as well as the desire to become one with the dead beloved has become a staple within Western art and culture, notably in Wagnerian Romanticism. Specifically, this desire "has been figuratively embodied by the romantic couple, where the one left behind by the other's death performs a 'love-death'" or Liebestod.[61] The most obvious allusion to the Liebestod in *Melancholia* is the extensive use of the "Prelude" from Wagner's *Tristan and Isolde.* The "Prelude" operates on two levels: as part of the nondiegetic film score, but also as a thematic through-line for the film. With regard to the latter, as previously stated, Melancholia can be read as Justine's beloved for whom she yearns. For Justine, the negation of her life is her salvation, salvation from a life she does not want to live, salvation through "unity" with Melancholia. Frantzen asks whether what comes alongside, or maybe after, capitalist realism is depressive realism, an idea where "depressed persons are not depressed because they have a distorted or delusional view of reality, but because they have a more accurate perception of reality than

---

[60]Lykke, *Vibrant Death*, 11.
[61]Ibid.

people who are not depressed."[62] While I resist the idea of pathologizing Justine's melancholia, I am not romanticizing it either. Within the film's diegetic world, there are serious consequences for Justine: her marriage ends, she loses her job, and she is in conflict with her family—she is not well. She is not well because the world around her is not well. The consequences Justine faces manifest because she rejects the unwell world and embraces a new beginning in her death and reunification with Melancholia. I read Justine's longing for Melancholia as her turning away from humanism and its trappings. It is in the unfathomable and unknowable hyperobject that Justine's antihumanist subjectivity as a melancholic woman is finally embraced. This desire for a relationship with Melancholia is manifested through the film's repeated use of *Tristan and Isolde*'s "Prelude," first played in the film's "Prelude" and then throughout as Justine experiences her extreme moments of melancholia. This nondiegetic music becomes a sign of Justine's melancholia and Melancholia's leitmotif. Interestingly, the music is only used in direct association with Justine until Claire tries to flee with Leo to the village. When Claire realizes that she cannot run away from Melancholia the music is heard again. Curiously, von Trier never moves beyond the opera's "Prelude." While the music is cut and fragmented (the musical counterpart to how the images and visual motifs within the film's Prelude are reutilized and reconceptualized throughout the film), it never fundamentally changes. The music never builds to the "love-death" movement within the piece. It is as if von Trier will not allow for a release of the tension, of the reunion in death until the final moment of the film.

Conclusion: The End, Embracing *Post*humanism

High Life moves unrelentingly toward its ending, giving almost no relief. Willow is now an adolescent and more areas of the ship need to be shut off to save energy. When another ship like theirs comes across their radar, Monte still clings to the idea of being rescued: "There might be other people onboard," to which Willow replies, "So?" "They might be able to help us." Willow replies, "We don't need help." As it is, only dogs are found aboard, whatever human crew was there are dead and the dogs too have turned to eating each other and subsisting on their own waste. The dogs are shot with a handheld camera in reduced light, barely illuminated. Monte briefly holds a puppy but does not return with it, to Willow's rebuking: "It'll die in there, it's cruelty," to which Monte responds, "What do you know about cruelty?"

---

[62]Frantzen, *Going Nowhere, Slow*, 11.

The sequence with the dogs reminds us that, until Willow, Monte's most significant relationship is with his dog. One of the few moments in which Monte has a strong emotional reaction (that does not lead to a violent encounter) is when he tears up in the garden as he disinfects himself after encountering the dogs. Monte's subjectivity is intertwined with his dog. As they tend the garden, Monte asks if "Tcherny" is his real name. It is not: a Russian instructor called him that, "I think it means black." The conversation is in a series of shot-reverse shots; the camera is tight on Monte's face. When asked about his relationship with his parents, Monte replies. "Nah. I was raised by my dog." According to Devlin, Monte's dog's murder is "the condition around which all other events circle,"[63] and his inability to reconcile with his dog's death or give Willow that type of relationship with another being causes him grief. That Monte killed because his dog was murdered causes him shame; he has even wiped his prison records so Willow will not know his great sin. Monte broke the ultimate taboo: he valued nonhuman life above human life when he killed his friend in retaliation for her murdering his dog.

It is after the dogs that Monte agrees to take Willow into the black hole. Willow's longing for the black hole is similar to Justine's longing for Melancholia. She can "feel it"; she has been, to use Lykke's words, ontologized and intertwined within the spaceship and the broader cosmos itself. Even during her conception, images of the Orion constellation play across the screen as Dibs coos over Boyse's stomach, willing conception. As they suit up for their final journey, Willow asks Monte if she looks like her mother; he tells her no. Monte is framed in medium shot, Willow's back to the screen; she asks him: "my nose? My mouth?" Monte tells her no; the camera zooms in to a close-up on his face as he looks at his daughter: "You're special. So different. You're like no one else. And I love that." What makes Willow special is that she, unlike Monte, is able to imagine and accept a different type of life, one that is affirmed through death.

With Melancholia's impact imminent, Claire tries to console herself and make a plan. She wants "to do this the right way," "this" being her death. Claire, to comfort herself, falls back into her previous stances of performance, of denial. Sitting on the patio, drinking wine, Claire remarks, "That would make me happy." In a series of shot-reverse shots, with the camera tight on both of their faces, Claire tearful and Justine contemptuous, Justine summarily rebukes her: "I think it's a piece of shit." It is tempting to read Justine as selfish or irrational, and her apparent callousness toward Claire as reprehensible. But Justine does not fear her death; what she feared was living an empty life with no relief. She does not see her life as essential, and therefore is unafraid to lose it.

---

[63]Devlin, "Sci-Fi and Truth," 78.

It is simplistic to read Justine's remarks that "the earth is evil" and that there is no other life in outer space, as nihilistic or as expressing a death wish. I read this statement as Justine affirming that the Humanist world around her is evil and must be forsaken. Unlike her family, who scolds her for her depression, and makes no attempt to listen to her, Justine demonstrates care. Justine cares deeply for her nephew Leo; his emotional comfort is paramount to her. After rejecting Claire's plan for the end, she keeps her promise to her nephew to help him build a "magic cave" out of wooden sticks. After all has been stripped away, in her final moments, Justine chooses to be present with her nephew. Whereas so much of her life up to this moment has been full of passivity, as her death looms, she makes an active choice. The "Prelude" begins to play again; the magic cave sits on the golf course. In a medium shot, Justine wraps her arms around Claire, a visual echo of how Claire often held Justine up during her periods of melancholia. The three of them sit in the magic cave; the camera pans down and across their bodies. Melancholia's imminent approach is reflected in the lighting: their faces are washed out; the world is almost completely devoid of color, muted tones of gray, white, and blue. The camera cuts to a close-up on Claire, then Leo, and then a pan up to Justine. The three hold hands and wait for impact. In the final, stunning shot, Melancholia approaches, unfathomably large. Leo and Justine remain still, Claire convulses, even tries to cover her head for a moment, as if that might save her, but they are engulfed in flames. The noise of Melancholia's impact continues and then fades—the end (Figure 11.3).

As Monte and Willow leave the ship in the shuttle, there are final glimpses of the ship's interior, including a final shot of the garden, now overgrown, lush, and seemingly expanding out of its initial parameters. This shot of the garden suggests there is still life remaining on the ship, for

FIGURE 11.3 *Justine (Kristen Dunst), Claire (Charlotte Gainsborough), and Leo (Cameron Spurr) embrace Melancholia (Claire Denis (dir.),* High Life, *2018).*

FIGURE 11.4 *He (Robert Pattinson) says, "Shall we?" (Claire Denis (dir.),* High
Life, *2018).*

now. Monte and Willow approach the black hole; they too hold hands as
they approach their end, their faces illuminated by the black hole's golden
light. They make their final approach, and then a cut. Monte is shot in
profile, mirroring the earlier profile shot at the film's beginning. He is still
illuminated by the black hole, his profile outlined in yellow light, only he
is not in his suit, and nor is Willow. It is in this final moment that the most
crucial question is asked by Monte: "Shall we?," to which Willow replies:
"Yes" (Figure 11.4).

   These two endings, in my reading, signal a posthuman beginning. As
MacCormack maintains, choosing the "death of humankind remains
possibly the most unthinkable thing for the anthropocene,"[64] and these
films embrace the unthinkable. There is the ultimate revaluing of human
life and death, and by extension, the annihilation of death denial. At the
end, the characters actively choose to engage and become one with the
hyperobject. *Melancholia* presents the end of humanity as cataclysmic and
beyond human control, but *High Life* demonstrates that posthumanity can
be an active choice. Even still, Justine refuses to be rendered consolable. I
read Justine's turn toward Melancholia as an affirmation of her subjectivity
as a depressed woman who is tired of the patriarchal and capitalistic world
within which she has been forced to live. Even though Melancholia brings
her death, at the same time it destroys the empty performances of human-
centrism. Interestingly, after the screen fades to white and then to black, the
"Prelude" begins to play again, as if to suggest despite the end of the human,
the end of the "anthropocentric eye of aestheticization," traces of that
vibrant matter remain. In *High Life*, in turn, Willow's entanglement with

---

[64]MacCormack, *Ahuman Manifesto*, 145.

the black hole makes it possible for her to deny her "no future," through her death and co-becoming with the black hole, and with her father. In his death, Monte is released from the human-centric world that criminalized and condemned him because he valued nonhuman life above all else. Instead of being suspended within time with no end, they embrace their end, and in turn, humanity's end. *Melancholia* frames death as something to be embraced, and *High Life* frames death, by extension, posthumanity, as an active choice—"Yes." Within posthumanity, death is transformed into "an articulation of the vitality and vibrancy characterizing all matter."[65] *Melancholia* and *High Life* present a framing of posthumanity that is not nihilistic, but life affirming, vital, and transforming.

---

[65]Lykke, *Vibrant Death*, 7.

12

"Originary Twoness"

Flashbacks and the Materiality of Memory in *Annihilation*, *High Life*, and *Arrival*

Russell J. A. Kilbourn

This chapter analyzes the representation and significance of memory in a posthumanist context through three examples of contemporary "art house" SF films: Denis Villeneuve's *Arrival* (2016) and Claire Denis' *High Life* and Alex Garland's *Annihilation* (both 2018). For the purpose of the argument, I focus here on materiality, to be defined later, as the main axis of memory in what I call the posthumanist SF memory film. Each of these films offers an important critique of the epistemological and aesthetic legacy of the Enlightenment Humanist subject and its received structures of identity, especially memory. Where *Annihilation* advances a sophisticated transhumanist thesis, and *High Life* presents an oblique, open-ended critique of long-standing Humanist assumptions, *Arrival* offers the most radical revaluation of memory on both thematic and formal levels, countering the productively ambiguous endings of the other two films with a nontranscendent resolution that can only come from a view of memory and history alike as intertwined and immanent, recursive, yet open-ended.

Critical posthumanism presents a deliberate challenge to the Enlightenment Humanist narrative that has dominated Western thought for the last three centuries, embodied subsequently by the modern liberal and now neoliberal Humanist subject. The necessary deconstruction of this subject, and the political, ideological, cultural, and economic structures that sustain it, was initiated by feminist theory, in particular new materialism, which remains among the most significant of the various posthumanist approaches.[1] For Stacy Alaimo, new materialism allows for the thinking of "the subject as a material being, not as a transcendent, utterly rational subject but as a being subject to the agencies of the compromised, entangled world, plac[ing] us within a posthumanist and environmentalist domain."[2] Feminist new materialism styles itself as an antidote to the so-called "retreat from materiality" represented by social constructivist approaches.[3] The anti-representationalism of much posthumanist materialist theory, however, in its hubristic confidence in the transparent communicability of knowledge, puts it at odds with a formal analysis of much contemporary popular media, in particular narrative cinema. For instance, the opening paragraph of Karen Barad's 2003 essay, "Posthumanist Performativity: Toward an Understanding of How Matter Comes to Matter":

> Language has been granted too much power. The linguistic turn, the semiotic turn, the interpretative turn, the cultural turn: it seems that at every turn lately every "thing"—even materiality—is turned into a matter of language or some other form of cultural representation. The ubiquitous puns on "matter" do not, alas, mark a rethinking of the key concepts (materiality and signification) and the relationship between them. Rather, it seems to be symptomatic of the extent to which matters of "fact" (so to speak) have been replaced with matters of signification (no scare quotes here). Language matters. Discourse matters. Culture matters. There is an important sense in which the only thing that does not seem to matter anymore is matter.[4]

Despite Barad's probable objections, the materiality that precedes discourse, the "matter" of which she punningly writes—like God, the subject, affect, or Woman (no scare quotes here)—is itself only apprehensible by means of, well, discourse (in the most inclusive tense) and the ongoing possibility of representation. As Alaimo puts it, "the discursive realm is

---

[1]See Rosi Braidotti, *Posthuman Feminism* (Cambridge: Cambridge: Polity Press, 2022) for a recent assessment of feminism's relation to critical posthumanism.

[2]Cecilia Åsberg and Rosi Braidotti, eds., *A Feminist Companion to the Posthumanities* (Springer International, 2018), 4.

[3]See, for example, Stacey Alaimo and Susan Hekman, "Introduction: Emerging Models of Materiality in Feminist Theory," in *Material Feminisms*, ed. Alaimo and Susan Hekman (Indiana University Press, 2008), 10.

[4]Karen Barad, "Posthumanist Performativity: Toward an Understanding of How Matter Comes to Matter," *Signs: Journal of Women in Culture and Society* 28, no. 3 (2003): 801.

nearly always constituted so as to foreclose attention to lived, material bodies and evolving corporeal practices."[5] To state the obvious, however, there are no "lived, material bodies" in the "discursive realm" mapped out in the books and films we all consume daily. In response to Barad's famous claim, then, I propose the amendment that "language," broadly construed, can never be granted enough power. Or rather: it is always dangerous to underestimate the power possessed by language, in its very nature as a human construct. Barad's efforts to go beyond later twentieth-century developments, such as Foucault's concept of a historical episteme as the nexus of discourse, knowledge, and power, are laudable, but it is a mistake to overlook poststructuralism's fundamental insights into the operation of knowledge regimes via specific discourses upon the bodies of some to the benefit of others. It is not possible to either understand or negotiate the effects of "biopower" on embodied identities in the twenty-first century without taking account of "material-discursive relations" in the Foucauldian sense.[6] The discursive basis of materiality (not to speak, for the moment, of the material basis of discourse) is well illustrated in Barad's term "mattering," which is not a genuine neologism but a play or pun on matter, as in materiality, and what "matters," as in what is significant or meaningful. To quote the 2019 *Posthuman Glossary* entry: "Mattering is a kind of posthumanist performativity that emphasizes matter's capacity to matter, to achieve significance in its being *as* doing. Matter here is not ground or essence, but agentive, 'produced and productive, generated and generative.'"[7] For Barad "[t]he concept of mattering thereby expands the dynamics of performativity to include nonhuman bodies and practices as well as human ones."[8] But does any of this matter when it comes to analyzing films and books? Reductively, yet productively, speaking, the issue is with Barad's insistence on the Latinate prepositional prefix "intra-" (*within*), as in her theory of "intra-agential realism." Grounded in a parsing of phenomenal reality's subatomic substratum (my term), Barad postulates that relations always already precede every *relata*—in other words, there is never an initial agential subject or acted-upon object; there is, rather, the relation: relations precede *relata*, all down the line. Barad's ideas appeal

---

[5]Alaimo and Hekman, "Introduction," 10.
[6]See also Donna Haraway re the inseparability of the "material-discursive" (Alaimo and Hekman, "Introduction," 11).
[7]Karen Barad, *Meeting the Universe Halfway: Quantum Physics and the Entanglement of Matter and Meaning* (Durham and London: Duke University Press, 2007), 137; Rosi Braidotti and Maria Hlavajova, eds., *Posthuman Glossary* (Bloomsbury, 2019), 245. In extending "Butler's concepts of gender performativity and materialization into the concepts of posthumanist performativity and mattering," Barad intends the latter term (mattering) as congruent with *becoming* (vs. *being*), a gerund indicating a state of permanent dynamism, a "doing rather than an attribute" (246).
[8]Braidotti and Hlavajova, eds., *Posthuman Glossary*, 246.

to a contemporary generation by instantiating a principle of radical equity whereby no one and no thing is ever first; everything, all phenomena, is/are always already *preceded by a relation* as "the ontological primitive."[9] For Barad, to coin a phrase, there is (or should be) no "originary oneness" but only ever (in the words of Austrian-Jewish theologian Martin Buber) an "originary twoness."[10]

The idea of "originary twoness" manifests in *Annihilation*, first in the doppelgänger theme, wherein each protagonist confronts their Shimmer-produced double, with disastrous results. The film ends, however, after a kind of posthumanist underworld journey, with a very different kind of couple, leaving behind the dead-end of the doppelgänger to reaffirm the "primal" heteronormative pair. *High Life*, by contrast, rejects this model early on, in the ship's doctor's artificial insemination experiments—not to speak of her association with the mythical Medea, famous for killing her husband and children. In the end, in a shift to a very different intertext, the two protagonists resemble a new Adam and Eve, despite their relationship as father and daughter. Only *Arrival* avoids the primacy of the couple, shifting among two, one, and three: the (heteronormative) family triad of mother, father, and child, in an ironically tragic roundelay of agency crossed with fate.

This tension between "intra-"/within and "inter-"/between is crucial for any analysis that seeks to exploit Barad's rich ideas in actual cultural-aesthetic analysis. The productive relations that determine the film-text itself (screenplay, direction, camerawork, editing, postproduction, distribution, projection or streaming, viewing, whether in a theatre or at home, etc.)—these relations can only be described as taking place "between," as *inter*-relations, insofar as their respective "*relata*" *precede* each productive encounter in this complex process. Barad's ideas may be useful for a cinematic analysis, but not at this level of production and spectatorship. Where Barad's notion of intra-agential realism applies—as an ontology and ethics rather than an aesthetics, ironically—is within the *content* of the film-text, on the level of story, character, theme, and so forth; in short, as metaphor. This is the level at which this chapter engages with Barad's ideas, where the primary focus is on the use of specific aspects of narrative film "language," especially the

---

[9]Barad, "Posthumanist Performativity," 815, n. 20; "[N]othing stands separately constituted and positioned inside a spacetime frame of reference, and no divine position for our viewing pleasure exists in a location outside the world" (Karen Barad, "Invertebrate Visions: Diffractions of the Brittlestar," in *The Multispecies Salon*, ed. Eben Kirksey (Durham: Duke University Press Books, 2014), 229).

[10]Martin Buber, *I and Thou*, trans. Walter Kaufmann (New York: Touchstone, 1970), 32. Buber died in 1965. Re Buber and "originary twoness" see R. J. A. Kilbourn, "Affect/Face/Close-up: Beyond the Affection-Image in Postsecular Cinema," in *From Deleuze and Guattari to Posthumanism: Philosophies of Immanence*, ed. Christine Daigle and Terrance McDonald (Bloomsbury, 2022), 147–69.

flashback, to convey story information but also in the service of exploring the nature and value of memory in a critical posthumanist context. Finally, on a purely descriptive level, for film analysis the preposition "between" is difficult to abandon as it allows one to address the irreducible presence of (a minimum of two) discrete "actors" in the text; individual entities who may come to merge, agentially and "intra-actively," but only within the fictional world of the film.

The Materiality of Memory: The Flashback in SF Cinema

Garland's adaptation of Jeff VanderMeer's 2014 novel, *Annihilation*—which also intertextualizes Samuel Beckett's 1955 novel *Molloy*—tells the story of a biologist who volunteers for an expedition into an alien-contaminated zone known as the "Shimmer," where her conceptions of self and her own embodiment are irrevocably transformed. In Denis' *High Life*, by contrast, the tropes of a feminist critique of a masculinist-humanist system are superseded by an inquiry in which questions of gender, sexuality, race, reproduction, and power come face-to-face with the prospect of species extinction. An adaptation of American writer Ted Chiang's "Story of Your Life" (2002),[11] *Arrival* retains a number of the main story elements, its most productive challenge to the adaptive process emerging in the translation of Chiang's unusual mixture of verb tenses to convey the future anterior nature of the protagonist's relationship to her daughter's life and death (e.g., "I remember a conversation we'll have when you're in your junior year of high school"). Of the three films, only *Arrival* self-reflexively thematizes memory, in the protagonist's attaining to retrocognition.

"Memory" here encompasses the manner in which each film is structured around subjective flashbacks and an understanding of materiality as a way of talking about the relations between and among different media. In this reading—in a direct rebuttal of new materialist approaches—the first-order materiality of the medium (of the process of mediation/representation) is always interacting with the second-order on-screen level of represented matter/materiality. Memory therefore operates simultaneously on at least two, interdependent, levels: audiovisual form versus thematic and narrative content. Matter, in its relation to the human, links these various modalities of memory.

More prosaically, "memory" in cinema is often reduced to the near-ubiquity of the flashback, a classic cinematic narrative technique for

---

[11]Ted Chiang, *Stories of Your Life and Others* (New York: Vintage Books, 2002).

representing or mediating a relationship to the past in the midst of the film's present-tense flow.[12] In this reading, the flashback is often (but not always) tied to a particular character or at least to a subjective perspective internal to the diegesis; therefore, the past to which the film "flashes back" is an individual or personal one and not an objective view of "history" per se. Second, and relatedly, the classical flashback is always ultimately in the service of the narrative present; the past, as such, is returned to or brought back in order to illuminate or clarify some aspect of the main story, or the characters' lives, and does not "exist" in or for itself. These truisms about the flashback hold across the various commercial genres, as this aspect of a basic grammar of classical narrative film style remains largely unchanged in the face of categorical, thematic, or tonal difference.

The frequency and ubiquity of the flashback in Classical Hollywood filmmaking, for instance, recapitulates in modern form the Homeric in medias res. As audiovisual phenomenon the cinematic flashback can be cognitively disruptive, compelling a greater self-awareness in the viewer's experience of interpreting the film. This became more obvious with the emergence of the postwar international "art" cinema, which saw a great deal of formal experimentation, in part because its practitioners were unconstrained by the budgetary pressures of a studio system such as that of mid-century Hollywood. Postwar "auteurs" (so-called) were more or less free to reinvent the language of narrative film, an impulse that was quickly embraced as a new stylistic orthodoxy, whose effects continue to be felt well into the twenty-first century.

More than one study of the postwar art film, or modernist art cinema, makes the point that, in this modality, the fairly clear and consistent understanding of the classical flashback as narrative device is disrupted, yielding a variegated approach to the representation of the past, the relationship of present and past temporalities, the function and significance of the flashback as narrative device, and what this means for the ongoing attention to individual character and identity. With respect to genre, it is significant that a popular form like science fiction proved amenable to its own "art cinema" treatment, from Kubrick's *2001: A Space Odyssey* (1968), to—in a kind of Cold War cinematic space race—Tarkovsky's *Solaris* (1972). Films such as these demonstrated the natural fit between a genre like SF, with its occasional recourse to literal time travel (for instance), and the cinematic manipulation of time (and space) through editing and other techniques. What better venue than SF for the overt and self-reflexive cinematic exploration of

---

[12]Re the cinematic flashback see Maureen Turim, *Flashbacks in Film: Memory and History* (New York: Routledge, 1989), 4–5. See also Russell J. A. Kilbourn, *Cinema, Memory, Modernity: The Representation of Memory from the Art Film to Transnational Cinema* (New York and London: Routledge, 2010).

the complexities of time and memory in the constitution of the protagonist's interior life? This trend has continued and increased in significance in the intervening decades, issuing in such films as *Arrival*, *Annihilation*, and *High Life*. In the following section, I will briefly analyze and compare the use and significance of the flashback in each.

The Flashback: *Annihilation*

Annihilation's protracted precredit sequence opens with Lena's (Natalie Portman) interrogation scene at the "Area X" military base. This present-tense scene establishes not only the film's diegetic frame but also the epistemological theme of ignorance or unknowing: across the film Lena refrain is, "I don't know." In a flashback to outer space, some three years before, a meteorite speeds toward Earth, smashing straight into the base of the "Southern Reach" lighthouse. The vibrantly colored computer-generated meteor is echoed in the grayscale microscope slide of cancer cells dividing, in a jump ahead to an intermediate temporality, soon before Lena's husband Kane's (Oscar Isaac) return. The next scene's establishing shots of Lena's house, in particular the staircase, will become important mnemonic chronotopes for the viewer's engagement with the Shimmer in subsequent scenes. A long shot of Lena in her living room precedes a straight cut to a brief "memory" (a flashback-within-a-flashback) of happier times, Crosby Stills and Nash's "Helplessly Hoping" playing in the background, first extra-diegetically, then diegetically, with Kane's appearance at the foot of the stairs. After disappearing in the Shimmer one year before, he returns to Lena, like the humanoid entities generated by the sentient planet in Tarkovsky's *Solaris* (1972), simulacral emanations of the human characters' memories. Lena interrogates Kane, in an echo of the opening scene, Kane's repeated response likewise, "I don't know." An abrupt cut to an ambulance interior as Lena rushes Kane to the hospital, unmarked secret service vehicles in hot pursuit. This concludes what amounts to the film's Prelude, as, in the next scene, after a title card ("Area X"), Lena wakes up in a hospital-like room, having been sedated by the men who took Kane from the ambulance. The film then unfolds in temporal counterpoint, shifting back and forth, among three different time frames, from the interrogation scene in the present to Lena's sojourn at Area X and her journey with the rest of the team into the Shimmer, punctuated by flashbacks-within-flashbacks of herself and Kane, in the film's ironically juxtaposed backstory. There is a significant interruption right after the team enters the Shimmer, however: framed in a medium shot, they enter the wall of prismatic light and the scene cuts to another title card ("The Shimmer"). The next scene opens with a close-up on Lena's naked back as she has sex with her colleague, Dan (David Gyasi), a flashback disguised as a dream. Lena wakes up in her tent in the Shimmer;

FIGURE 12.1 *Kane's (Oscar Isaac) reappearance (Alex Garland (dir.)*, Annihilation, *2018).*

FIGURE 12.2 *Staircase in an abandoned house (Alex Garland (dir.)*, Annihilation, *2018).*

she is anxious and confused, then learns that neither she nor any of her teammates remembers the previous few days (Figures 12.1 and 12.2).

Josie (Tessa Thompson), the team's physicist, informs them that their "comms equipment," like their sense of time, is blocked by the Shimmer, a diagnosis updated in a subsequent scene when she realizes that the radio signals and other wavelengths are actually being refracted, along with everything else, including their DNA. It becomes apparent that Lena's flashbacks (within the principal structuring flashback to the Shimmer) are motivated by events within the diegesis: after the team discovers the soldier's splayed corpse in the pool at the abandoned military base, her memory of the day of Kane's departure recurs, again as if in a dream. Lena then examines the sample from the man's body, in a microscopic image that echoes the earlier frames of cancer cells. The team (minus Sheppard [Tuva Novotny], who has been killed by a mutant bear) reaches an abandoned house deliberately constructed as an uncanny double of Lena's own house, recognizable from the flashback scenes. In a Tarkovskian echo, the carefully manipulated mise-en-scène posits the Shimmer as a giant refracted reproduction of Lena's affective inner life. The film progresses in this manner, images from present, past, and deeper past, blending, doubling, reflecting, and refracting, until it is no longer clear which is the "original," whether ontologically or chronologically, since the Shimmer guarantees that everything in the film is affected by its influence—although it must be noted that this temporal refraction (metaphorical, if not literal) occurs only on the level of diegetic form, and not within the story-world. Lena's quest, despite the film's flashback structure, is ultimately circular: to the lighthouse and back. When Josie and Anya (Gina Rodriguez), after Sheppard's death, express their desire to return rather than go forward, Lena convinces them that going forward is the best way to go back, in an allusion, on the horizontal, to the classical katabasis of Virgil's *Aeneid* (bk. 6), by way of Dante's *Inferno*, but ultimately the pre-Socratic philosopher Heraclitus: the way up is the way down. This paradoxical going-forward-to go-back movement is paralleled in both *High Life* and *Arrival* but with very different ramifications in each case.

An excellent example of this technique occurs in the midst of the abandoned house scene: Lena, a biologist, discovers that her own blood cells are mutating like those of the Shimmer's other victims. In a side-on medium shot she slumps on the table in despair; a cut to the opening flashback to Kane's uncanny return shows him, in a graphic match, at the table in their kitchen, slumped forward in pain, his organs failing. Another cut to the flashback to her adulterous affair, seen before, but this time it continues. The juxtaposition here is deliberate: as others have noted, the editing generates an association for the viewer between Lena's "infection" by the Shimmer and the guilt she feels for having cheated on Kane. Then, in an abrupt ellipsis, a POV shot of Anya (as a paramedic, the only nonscientist) hitting Lena with her gunstock cuts straight to another brief flashback to Kane's original departure. Lena had neglected to reveal to the others her connection to the one person who had returned from the Shimmer, who they had all watched disemboweling his comrade in the video left in the abandoned military base. When Lena comes to, Anya confronts her with the locket containing a tiny photo of Kane. Their team gradually unravels, one by one, like all the others, leaving only Lena.

The film's final scene returns to the opening interrogation; Lena explains to Lomax (Benedict Wong) that the Shimmer was never really destroying anything, it was merely changing everything, radically, "making something new." In a medium shot, as she reaches for a glass of water, a tattoo is visible on her forearm: a snake eating its own tail, the "Worm

Ouroboros" from Norse mythology—the same tattoo visible on the arm of the splayed man in the military base swimming pool, and which she did not have before the Shimmer. The snake that swallows its own tail represents a process without end or terminus, but it can also stand for the ceaseless state of becoming of all things, ever-changing in form but never disappearing altogether.

The Flashback: *High Life*

Like *Annihilation*, *High Life* begins with a lengthy precredit sequence, its plot also structured around a deceptively straightforward journey but with an even more ambiguous ending. The film's going-forward-to-go-back theme operates more on the conceptual level, in what appears to be a relentlessly linear journey forward, toward the future, and the journey's end. This linearity is broken up on the formal level, however, by the complexity of the flashback structure and conceptually by the film's incorporation of certain unorthodox ideas about time travel and black holes, all conditioned, but not determined, by the subjective affect of Monte's (Robert Pattinson) memories. *High Life* opens with a protracted pan across the spaceship's lush onboard garden, then close-ups of dew-speckled vegetables worthy of a nature documentary, culminating in a shot of a single half-buried boot: a trace of human presence presaging its absence. *High Life* opens in a more expansive present than *Annihilation*'s framing interrogation scene, covering the period from Monte's daughter Willow's infancy to the onset of puberty. This is clear from the sound bridge that links the opening scene with the next: infant Willow's crying, as her father repairs some minor damage on the ship's hull. The long opening sequence establishes his relationship with his infant daughter, as the only surviving members of the original crew. Monte talks aloud as he feeds, washes, and prepares Willow for bed: "If my old man could see me now," presaging the first flashback to his past on Earth as a boy, when he killed a girl who had killed his beloved dog. The flashback sequences are shot in naturalistically colored 16mm, while the present-tense action is filmed in cold blue-and-gold digital. The opening sequence continues, jumping back and forth between present Monte in the ship and his childhood self, back on Earth, with his dog and the little girl. Like *Annihilation*'s flashbacks to Lena's life with Kane, these images are clearly anchored to Monte's character. Denis gives us enough fragments to piece together the primal scene of Monte's original sin: the crime that sets in motion his current voyage, which appears to have no scheduled terminus. As we learn in a subsequent flashback, the crew was never meant to return to Earth.

In the continuation of this long opening sequence, Monte jettisons the bodies of his dead shipmates, in order to conserve energy. The experience

leaves him shaken, as he recalls Boyse (Mia Goth), the young woman
to whom he was attracted. The flashbacks to earlier times on the ship,
however, are visually distinct from those to his childhood on Earth, shot
digitally with the same blue-gold tonality. There is also an intimacy to the
shipboard scenes that is absent from the childhood flashbacks, which are
characterized by long and medium shots. The onboard sequences in all time
frames involve more close-ups and camera mobility. At this point as well,
over twenty minutes in, Monte's sporadic voice-over begins. He complains
about the random video images that still arrive, despite traveling enormous
distances: "These fucking images from Earth. I can't believe they still make
it here. After all this time. Just like viruses chasing after us. Parasites. Those
random images. Maybe they were programmed to keep us on a leash. Make
us believe a return was possible." Finally, Monte sleeps as Willow sleeps,
with another flashback to Earth, as if it were a dream, as if return were only
possible in this form. A series of brief close-ups, alternating with Monte in
the present, confirms the subjective basis of these flashback images: the red-
haired girl, the dead dog, the boy's feet in the creek by its body, his hand
picking up a rock. The empty forest lane, the girl lying dead on a blanket
of dead leaves. The subjectivity is suddenly disrupted: a straight cut to a
high-angle shot of a train traveling across a wintry European landscape.
The camera moves down into a near close-up with the train, then a cut to a
compartment interior, two people talking across the table. A young woman
(Juliette Picollot) interviews a South Asian professor (Victor Banerjee),
representing the viewpoint of the nonoccidental "other," critiquing the West
without implicating himself. As he reveals, the ship's crew members are
"[d]eath-row inmates selected to be used as guinea-pigs" on a one-way trip.
"Their messages and reports now take years to get back to us. We'll be bone
dust, while they're still hurtling through space."[13] By the end of the film,
the ship will have been traveling for some eighteen years, which, because
of relativity, is equal to 210 years on Earth. This means that at the film's
climax, Willow (Jessie Ross) is thirteen years old. Some five years of their
mission went by before Monte was left alone with his infant daughter, and
everyone they left behind on Earth is long dead, despite the fact that those
on board the ship have lived only eighteen-and-a-half years. Poignantly, this
sequence cuts straight back to Monte on the ship, helping Willow take her
first steps. A brief shot of Dr. Dibs (Juliette Binoche) intrudes, ghost-like,
then flashes of a defiant Boyse, first on the ship, then earlier, back on Earth,
in a different 16mm flashback to her life as a teenage delinquent, hitching
a ride on a freight train. In another voice-over, Monte explains the origins
of the space program: viewed as disposable, these prisoners are given the

---

[13]Cf. Christopher Nolan's *Interstellar* (2014), which deals with comparable paradoxes of the
space-time continuum, black holes, deep space travel, fatherhood, and parent-child relations.

option of "serving science."[14] It becomes clear why Boyse is always angry. Cutaways to Dibs' empty gynecological chair and incubator underline the most important manner in which these prisoners "serve science": the men provide semen and the women are subjected to artificial insemination, in the hope of producing a healthy baby in space, potentially guaranteeing the survival of the human species. The story's middle act lingers in the recent shipboard past, just prior to Willow's birth.

The crew had been conditioned to see the voyage's purpose in terms of a different narrative, however. Monte (in voice-over) explains:

> We were at the half-way point. Four more years to our destination. We had to begin the deceleration maneuver so the ship could approach a black hole, one of the closest in our galaxy. A small one. This is the main goal of our mission. Our class-1 suicide ride. To check if we could capture a black hole's rotating energy. And we, heroes, would provide humanity with almost boundless resources.[15]

The only "return," as noted, however, is on the conceptual level. "At 99% the speed of light," Monte continues, "the entire sky converged before our eyes. This sensation, moving backwards even though we're moving forwards, getting further from what's getting nearer. Sometimes I just can't stand it." There is a sense, in the film's thematic (it not structural) recursivity, however, that the fact that Willow has "no future" may not really matter (Mackey and Sendur, ch. 13). As *Annihilation*'s Ouroboros symbol suggests, the future is the past and vice versa.[16] In *High Life*, the black hole becomes the radically negative focal point of their paradoxical journey.

From Flashback to Flash-forward: *Arrival*

Arrival opens on a black screen, giving way to a slow downward pan from inside Louise Banks' (Amy Adams) house, after dusk, a bottle of wine and

---

[14]In Hans' terms, they have been "recycled" (Simran Hans, "*High Life* First Look," Sight and Sound, December 28, 2018).

[15]Monte calls this "their Penrose process." Theorized by Sir Roger Penrose, the "Penrose process" is a mechanism "whereby energy can be extracted from a rotating black hole. The process takes advantage of the ergosphere—a region of spacetime around the black hole dragged by its rotation *faster than the speed of light*, meaning that from the POV of an outside observer any matter inside is forced to move in the direction of the rotation of the black hole" (Wikipedia; emphasis in original).

[16]Films with veritable chiasmic structures, ending in more or less the same point at which they began, so as to (in principle) begin all over again, ad infinitum, are extremely rare in the history of narrative cinema. For a rare example, see David's Lynch's *Lost Highway* (1997); see Kilbourn, *Cinema, Memory, Modernity*.

two glasses on the table before the picture window. "I used to think this was the beginning of your story," Louise explains enigmatically in voice-over. Unlike its more classical application in *Annihilation* and *High Life*, *Arrival* offers a truly innovative use of the flashback as both functional trope and thematic focus. Unlike the other films, in which a linear journey-narrative is complicated by a contrapuntal flashback structure—going backward to move ahead—*Arrival*'s recursive structure begins as it ends, with a montage of brief scenes of Louise and her daughter, the palindromically named Hannah, at various ages, including her birth. "Come back to me," Louise says to the newborn, followed soon after by a deathbed scene, as Hannah, now an adolescent, lies dying of a rare disease. In voice-over, Louise introduces the idea that time, or rather life, does not necessarily move in a straight line with a clear beginning, middle, and end. As she remarks, "[m]emory is a strange thing. It doesn't work like I thought it did. We are so bound by time. By its order."

Like Lena in *Annihilation*, Louise is a university professor. The story proper begins as her class in linguistics is disrupted by news of alien spacecraft arriving at twelve separate locations across the globe: "the day they arrived." An expert translator, Louise is conscripted by the military for a top secret assignment to help establish contact. En route to the landing site, she encounters new co-worker Ian (Jeremy Renner), a theoretical physicist. They begin to meet with the aliens, within the spaceship, at prescribed intervals; Louise quickly discovers that they have a writing system ("Heptapod B") that humans can learn. The more she is able to communicate with the aliens, the better she can understand them, and, ultimately, herself, through her profoundly altered relationship to time.

The room in which the scientists meet with the aliens is nick-named "the Nave," invoking Christian ecclesiastical architecture, but also sharing its etymology with "ship." This nave is divided by a transparent window or screen on either side of which the two species confront one another. *Arrival*'s 2.39:1 aspect ratio is well-suited to the wide two-way screen through which Louise and Ian communicate with the Heptapods, and upon which they view them. Both prepositions ("through" and "upon") are justified, in that the screen-within-the-screen visually echoes, mis-en-abime-like, the one-way screen on which we view *Arrival*. In Chiang's story the aliens communicate with humans not through two-way screens but via devices nicked-named "looking glasses,"[17] with attendant echoes of Alice. The film exploits its status as audiovisual text in order to show what appear to be Louise's memories of her child. Her gradual mastering of Heptapod B triggers disturbing visions of herself with a little girl who might be her daughter. At first these appear to be flashbacks, related to the film's opening sequence; later, we realize that

---

[17]Ted Chiang, *Stories of Your Life and Others* (New York: Vintage Books, 2002), 95.

she doesn't know who the girl is, and that these images are a retrocognitive flash-forward to the future-yet-to-be. Eventually, the Heptapods deliver the message "offer weapon," arousing the human authorities' suspicions. Soon there is panic over the meaning of this directive, construed as some kind of threat or as an attempt to sow discord between nations. On the verge of global war, Louise realizes that her uncanny fragmentary visions and the international crisis are intimately linked, and that by learning Heptapod B she has gained the ability to see the future. At the last minute she averts disaster by calling General Shang, the Chinese leader, on his personal phone. She gives him a message that he in turn whispers to her in one of her future visions, at which point present and future meet: present Louise dialogues with her future self in order to ensure that the present plays out in such a way as to ensure the future that will bring this all into being, and so on.[18] Not only can Louise see the future; counterintuitively, the future has an impact upon the present. As implied even more overtly with the inclusion in Chiang's story of Fermat's principle of least time (which explains optical phenomena such as refraction, stating that "the route that [a] light ray takes is always the fastest one possible"[19]), it is not simply a matter of free will versus a predetermined outcome; it is not either/or but both/and. In *Arrival*, present and future are in a dynamic mutual feedback relationship, intra-actively transforming memory into a productive force for change within life but predicated on the awareness that death and loss are not only inevitable but necessary for life.[20]

The Heptapods' written language is their gift to Louise, at once opening the door to a future that will be, *and* allowing her to see that she is free to choose her future.[21] In a sense, each option mirrors the other, because, with the gift of the Heptapod language, the future is the past and vice versa. Again, as Ian explains in a voice-over montage, the Heptapods' semasiographic written language has no relation to their spoken language: "Unlike speech, a logogram is free of time. Like their ship, or their bodies, their written language has no forward or backward direction. Linguists call this non-linear orthography. Which raises the question: is this how they think?" Villeneuve wisely refrains from illustrating this process, instead eternalizing their "thoughts" as fully formed utterances addressed to Louise. In the film, "Heptapod B" comprises hundreds of symbols, all based on the perfect circle, inflected in various ways with what appear to be the equivalent of diacritic

[18]Louise (Amy Adams), like Lena (Natalie Portman) and Monte (Robert Pattinson), is a kind of feminist spin on the "white saviour" stereotype of commercial and art cinema alike, through whose selfless actions the world is saved.
[19]Chiang, *Stories of Your Life and Others*, 117.
[20]See William Brown and David Fleming, "Through a (First) Contact Lens Darkly: *Arrival*, Unreal Time and Chthulucinema," *Film-Philosophy* 22, no. 3 (2018): 340–63.
[21]Cf. Chiang, *Stories of Your Life and Others*, 203.

marks. These visual signifiers are produced by the Heptapod "speakers" as a form of writing radically alien from that to which most Indo-European speakers are accustomed. During a communicative exchange, each symbol appears, evanescent, smoke-like, lingers momentarily in the air, a circular shape signifying something, then slowly disappears, returning to nothing— each utterance foreshadowing the disc-shaped ships on which the aliens depart by literally disappearing into thin air. In this "nonhuman" language the film offers a clear example of the crucial role played by any human language in its materiality as mediating force, as literal medium of communication, facilitating any communicative act. As the scenes between Louise and the Heptapods make clear, any communicative act requires a minimum of two interlocutors and a medium of communication, a language. To look at it the other way around, any language requires a medium to function, to be a language. This inescapable fact is eloquently and ironically borne out in the scene of Louise's final encounter with the aliens.

Memory, Materiality, Language

Shot on both digital and 16mm, with a much smaller special effects budget than the all-digital *Annihilation*, *High Life* is also structured contrapuntally around judiciously spaced flashbacks, gradually revealing how the protagonist arrived at the situation in which we find them at the film's outset: Lena (in *Annihilation*) under interrogation after her improbable escape from the Shimmer, her fellow teammates dead or vanished; Monte (in *High Life*) alone with Willow on board a space ship whose perpetual outbound journey ironically allegorizes humankind's best hope for long-term survival, the crewmembers all convicted felons who have opted for this special mission from which none will ever return. The two films thus share the same basic one-way journey or quest structure, although in *Annihilation* one team member, Lena, does return (facilitating the film's determining retrospective structure). In each film the secondary characters are killed off, one by one, underlining the protagonist's potential radical aloneness. That said, each protagonist is also matched, by the end, with another person, whether spouse or child, together with whom they constitute a kind of neo-primal couple: the last humans who are also—in potential posthumanist terms—the first.

In *Annihilation*'s climax, Dr. Ventress' (Jennifer Jason Leigh) final lines, spoken in the meteorite-carved tunnel beneath the lighthouse, come directly from Samuel Beckett's 1955 novel *Molloy*,[22] in which the titular character

---

[22]The first in a trilogy, including also *Malone Dies* and *The Unnamable*.

is tracked down by another, named Moran. By the end, Moran and
Molloy's identities appear to merge, a possible influence on *Annihilation*'s
doppelgänger theme. The specific passage occurs in the book's second half,
immediately after Moran has announced to his son that they will depart that
evening in search of Molloy, the protagonist of the book's first half:

> I did as when I could not sleep. I wandered in my mind, slowly, noting every
> detail of the labyrinth, its paths as familiar as those of my garden and yet
> ever new, as empty as the heart could wish or alive with strange encounters.
> And I heard the distant cymbals, There is still time, still time. But there was
> not, for I ceased, all vanished and I tried once more to turn my thoughts to
> the Molloy affair. Unfathomable mind, now beacon, now sea.[23]

The final enigmatic phrase posits the mind as a paradoxical structure:
at once the objective, the source of illumination, and the encompassing
"unfathomable" matrix, within which the quest and its goal unfold, turn
and turn-about—an image with its literary corollary in St. Augustine's
Confessions.[24] In this reading, Lena's journey into the Shimmer becomes
a psycho-katabasis, a secular allegory of the mind's interior journey from
incomprehension to understanding. Beckett's *Molloy* is the account of two
different "quests," two different bodily trajectories, which may converge,
undecidably, into a single body. *Molloy* exemplifies a peculiarly Beckettian
disposition at the level of the narrative subject in its ambiguous bifurcation
into narrator and protagonist—a continuum of subjectivity, without clear
division. Beckett's main theme is precisely the crisis or catastrophe of identity,
and the representation of subjectivity—the modernist preoccupation with
"self-expression." His conclusion, though, is radically proto-posthumanist:
while a certain kind of "expression" may be possible, the "self" is not. In
Annihilation's climactic scene, *Molloy*'s reference to a "beacon" is literalized
in the lighthouse setting—at once the team's goal and (metaphorical) source
of illumination, of secret knowledge or "truth."[25] The film uses only the final
phrase from the *Molloy* passage, however, in a succinct articulation of what
will ensue should the Shimmer be left unchecked:

> Ventress [eyes inexplicably covered by skin]: "It's the last phase.
>   Vanished into havoc. Unfathomable mind, now beacon, now sea."
> Lena: "Dr. Ventress?"
> Ventress: "Lena? We spoke, what was it we said? That I needed to know
>   what was inside the lighthouse. That moment's passed. It's inside me
>   now."

---

[23]Samuel Beckett, *Three Novels: Molloy, Malone Dies, The Unnamable* (New York: Grove
Press, 2009), 106
[24]See, for example, *Confessions* 10.8 215–16.
[25]The setting is so hyperbolically archetypal as to obviate analysis.

Lena: "What's inside you?"

Ventress: [whispered] "It's not like us, [normal volume] it's unlike us." [Pause]

Ventress: "I don't know what it wants, or if it wants, but it will grow until it encompasses everything. Our bodies and our minds will be fragmented into their smallest parts, until not one part remains. . . . Annihilation."

Ventress frames the fear of the loss or dissolution of individual self— Schopenhauerian disindividuation—ambiguously. She gives herself over to a process that she defines as "annihilation" in the neutral technical sense of radical negation (to the point of nonexistence) as potentially positive force for change; perpetual transformation for its own sake, like Darwin's "natural selection," only without species-being as (nonhuman) "rationale" or "motivation."[26] This may illuminate certain implications of the film's title: what Robert Pepperell identifies as the tendency for all highly cognitively evolved species to generate the conditions for their own "erasure," auto-negation as the ultimate goal of adaptation and evolution.[27] As Ventress asks: "Isn't self-destruction programmed into us? Coded into each cell?"

This theme also emerges in *High Life*, but with a decidedly different affective spin. Monte's shipmate Tcherny (André Benjamin), quotes his wife, back home: "I'd rather sink into the earth after I've lost you than to sit around and grieve once you've gone off into your destiny." In the next scene, Tcherny appears to literally sink into the Earth of the ship's onboard garden, vanishing before our eyes in a simple in-camera effect, turning, it seems, into a mound of fresh Earth, leaving only a boot. In *Annihilation*, by comparison, Josie (the physicist) ends up transmogrifying in such a way as to blend in with the Shimmer's mutated anthropomorphic vegetation. As she explains to Lena a few moments before her disappearance (involving no special effects at all): "Ventress wants to face it; you want to fight it. I don't think I want either of those things." Neither opposing nor trying to understand it, she willingly acquiesces to its inexorable, refractive, force. Like Tcherny, Josie's agential "action" is also an act of radical passivity, a giving in, the

---

[26]See Jan Čapek re "Annihilation" as defined in physics: "the combination of a particle and its antiparticle (such as an electron and a positron) that results in the subsequent total conversion of the particles into energy" ("Strange Days in the Anthropocene: The Inhuman in 'The Colour out of Space' and *Annihilation*," *Supernatural Studies* 6, no. 1 (2019): 17). In folk tradition a subject and its double cannot occupy the same space at the same time; that is, to meet one's doppelgänger is to meet one's death. For Freud, the model of the "uncanny" (*unheimlich*) is the double. See Paul Coates, "Protecting the Exotic: Atom Egoyan and Fantasy," *Canadian Journal of Film Studies* 6, no. 2 (Fall 1997): 24.

[27]Robert Peperell, "Neuroscience and Posthuman Memory," in *Memory in the Twentieth-Century: New Perspectives from the Arts, Humanities, and Sciences*, ed. Sebastian Groes (New York: Palgrave Macmillan, 2016), 331.

fruit of the realization that to be assimilated to the Shimmer need not be like Ventress' experience of a violent loss of self, but a willful and even joyful merging with a posthuman polymorphous whole: the snake devouring its own tail, forever. Tcherny's action, by contrast, is a resignation, a giving in to a desire for disindividuated materiality (and therefore the cessation of desire), a literal becoming-posthuman by becoming post-humous/post-humus. Each is an act of radical humility: a literal making oneself low, a bringing oneself down to Earth. The difference in affective charge—Josie's positivity versus Tcherny's melancholia—speaks to differences in gender and narrative alike. In the language of feminist new materialism, while Josie's transformation might be readable as yielding a kind of second-order co-constitutive "transcorporeality,"[28] Tcherny's disappearance is just that: the human vanishes and only the earthy matter remains.[29] It must also be noted, moreover, that in each film the character who makes this unique decision is a person of color. And, where *Annihilation* in Josie's transformation presents the possibility for the transcendence of racially demarcated identity, through the veritable transcendence of the physical boundaries of the "human," *High Life* presents a darker outlook, whereby, of the ship's crew only Monte and Willow transcend their carceral subjectivity.

"Com-post-humanism"

Matter, soil, fecundity, growth, and decay: the metaphorics of natural cycles and recycling resonate across these texts, for better or worse, evident in the central role played by the onboard garden in *High Life*, not to speak of the wildly overgrown quality of the Shimmer in *Annihilation*. In both films, what Haraway once termed "com-post-humanism" signifies in both positive and more neutral posthumanist senses.[30] In both films, differently, at least one character returns to the soil or otherwise adapts in such a way as to unite or reunite with the "natural" world that is modifying itself in

---

[28]Alaimo's term (see, for example, "Material Feminism in the Anthropocene," in *A Feminist Companion to the Posthumanities*, ed. Cecilia Åsberg and Rosi Braidotti (Springer International, 2018), 49).

[29]See, for example, Timothy Morton: "What if hyperobjects finally force us to realize the truth of the word *humiliation* itself, which means being brought low, being brought down to earth?" (*Hyperobjects: Philosophy and Ecology After the End of the World* [University of Minnesota Press, 2013], 17). Cf. also Richard Kearney, who points out that *humus* is also the root of humour (*Anatheism* [Columbia University Press, 2011], 42). See also Haraway, "Anthropocene, Capitalocene, Plantationocene, Chthulucene: Making Kin," *Environmental Humanities* 6 (2015), who points out that "human" is etymologically related to "humus," i.e., compost (59–65), leading Francesca Ferrando to almost coin the term "com-post-humanism" (*Philosophical Posthumanism* [Bloomsbury, 2019], 108; 212 n. 7).

[30]Haraway, "Anthropocene, Capitalocene, Plantationocene, Chthulucene," 59–65.

response to those modifications that originate (ironically) with human intervention.[31]

Before Tcherny's disappearance leaves Monte and Willow alone on the ship, the other eight crew members all die far more unpleasant deaths, as a result of radiation, black hole "spaghettification," or by the weapon of choice: the garden shovel. Like Josie in *Annihilation*, Tcherny (whose name is a corruption of the Russian for "black," as in Chernobyl) is the only one whose death involves no violence whatsoever and is not even a death properly speaking: where he vanishes into the garden's soil, Josie (in *Annihilation*) presumably transforms into an anthropomorphic plant. In *High Life*, the ship's onboard garden links Tcherny's to Monte and Willow's fate in the film's ambiguous final scene. In Erika Balsom's words,

> A garden exists aboard the ship to produce food and, presumably, oxygen; it is a token of a lost nature. In images that bookend the film, it is overgrown, glistening with a dewy voluptuousness that is more-than-real. *High Life* knows that there can be no return to Eden, that the state of nature is marked by violence. But it asks us to consider the passion—and the terror—of crossing the event horizon to cast off the laws that bind us and live another day. Would this black hole be paradise or hell?.[32]

But it is not a matter of an either-or choice. As Tcherny remarks to Monte: "This little garden is teaching me to enjoy the present. Nothin' else really matters, man." The film's conclusion leaves us poised in between, neither in one place nor another, a state of radical undecidability.

The ambiguous negativity of Tcherny's "destiny"—sinking into the Earth—contrasts with the ambiguous positivity of Monte and Willow's ultimate fate, tied, it seems, to their status as the ultimate human couple. In an early scene, Monte explains the concept of taboo to his infant daughter: "Don't drink your own piss, Willow. Don't eat your own shit. Even if it's recycled and even if it doesn't look like shit." Monte's taboo train of thought—"Break the laws of nature, and you'll pay for it"—leads him to recall the origins of his life in one kind of prison or another, when as a boy he killed the girl with a rock because she killed his beloved dog. Thou shalt not kill: taboo. In a productive ambiguity the sequence elides the two

[31]See Mat Zoller Seitz, "High Life" (rev.) Roger Ebert .com (April 5, 2019). Accessed June 15, 2020. https://www.rogerebert.com/reviews/high-life-2019.
[32]Erika Balsom, "*High Life* Review: Claire Denis Probes the Outer Reaches of Human Taboos," *Sight and Sound*, June 2019.

senses of "natural law" being broken. In Balsom's words, once the other crewmembers are gone, Monte and Willow are left

> alone to live in an uninterrupted dyad. When a temporal ellipsis brings the narrative forwards some fifteen [sic] years and Willow appears as a young woman, the possibility of continuing life comes face-to-face with incest, the most fundamental prohibition of all. Denis courts this taboo, neither definitively breaking it nor exactly abiding by it. She exercises no moral judgement, instead offering a spectacular conclusion open to multiple interpretations.[33]

Thou shalt not kill and thou shalt not commit incest: the two prohibitions overlap, just as in *Annihilation* Lena's crime of adultery is consistently juxtaposed with her dawning awareness of being "infected" by the Shimmer. For Lena it always comes back to the motif of the dividing cell: two from one, whether healthy, cancerous, or refracted. The Shimmer does not destroy; it merely changes—everything. It becomes clear in *High Life* that Monte's caring for Willow is motivated not only by paternal love but by the species-based need to not be alone: originary twoness. At the end, as at the beginning, they are the only humans left—although, ironically, as Sendur and Mackey observe elsewhere in this volume, "the result is an affective and often uncomfortable viewing experience for those who are used to perceiving the world on the basis of humanist principles" (ch. X; p. 13) (Figure 12.3).

FIGURE 12.3 *Willow (Jessie Ross) saying "yes" (Claire Denis (dir.),* High Life, *2018).*

---

[33]Balsom, "*High Life* Review."

Conclusion

In a late sequence in *Arrival* Louise, linguist-translator, is rapt up, "translated," to the Heptapod spaceship, brought into the space on the *other* side of the screen through which all previous encounters had been mediated, the side occupied by the Heptapods; she goes through the screen, like Alice through the looking glass. Louise's "unmediated" encounter with the Heptapod is the opposite of Tcherny's voluntary sinking into the Earth, and, as the culmination of a long process of giving herself over to the alien language, and worldview, the strange complement, perhaps, to Josie's passive transmogrification. Louise does not resist the encounter with the other, and she goes well beyond merely understanding them; she comes to see and experience reality as they do, which means being able to "see" the future. "Costello," the Heptapod, refers again to the "weapon" mentioned earlier; in answer to her questions about their purpose in visiting Earth, "he" responds, drawing his answer in the medium in which they both stand, suspended: "Louise has weapon . . . Use weapon." And, finally, before departing forever: "Weapon opens time." The smoky circular figures hang in the space between them just long enough for her to read, then dissolve into nothing. The "weapon," as Louise eventually realizes, is really a gift: the capacity to see the future through her comprehension of a written language with no forward or backward linear directionality (Figure 12.4).

Arrival ends where it began: a black screen gives way to a slow downward pan from inside Louise's house, after dusk—identical to the film's opening, absent the two half-filled glasses of wine. The last chapter opens with Louise speaking, over top of footage alternating between the aftermath of the alien's departure and her future (?) domestic happiness: "So, Hannah. This is how your story begins. The day they departed." A male figure is visible, out of focus, in the background, Louise in close-up in the foreground. "Despite knowing the journey and where it leads, I embrace it. And I welcome every

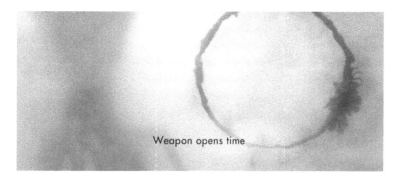

FIGURE 12.4 *"Weapon opens Time" (Denis Villeneuve (dir.), Arrival, 2016).*

moment of it." She knows already (always?) that her husband will leave her when he learns that she already knows that their daughter will die a teenager. Villeneuve intercuts these images with flashbacks to the earlier scene, as Ian in the "present" plays with Hannah, Ian in the "past" confessing that what surprised him the most was not meeting "them" but meeting *her*, Louise. Like the attachment to language itself, this is a romantically Humanist twist in a film otherwise highly attuned to the potentialities of human-alien encounter. As they embrace in both temporalities, we are reminded that this is the perspective of a woman who can see her "whole life from start to finish."

High Life ends with Monte and Willow in an escape craft, on the brink of entering the back hole, which will either annihilate or transform them— their fate remains suspended. The film's final line, Willow's emphatic "yes" to Monte's "Shall we?" offers the end-of-time affirmation missing from *Annihilation*, which concludes with its transhumanist protagonists rightly doubting their human "authenticity." But where *High Life* stops short, as it were, on the threshold, *Arrival* goes all the way, and back again, offering the most positive, albeit Humanist, vision of all: even in the face of the certain knowledge of her not-yet-existent daughter's death, we already know what her answer will be when Ian asks, "Do you want to make a baby?"

13

Coming to Terms with Our Own Ends

Failed Reproduction and the End of the Hu/man in Claire Denis' *High Life* and Pella Kågerman and Hugo Lija's *Aniara*

Allison Mackey and Elif Sendur

Nature was the same, as when she was the kind mother of the human race; now, childless and forlorn, her fertility was a mockery. . . . Why are there fruits, or flowers, or streams, man is not here to enjoy them?

MARY SHELLEY, *THE LAST MAN* (VOL III, CH. 2)

Actors, as well as actants, come in many and wonderful forms. And best of all, "reproduction"—or less inaccurately, the generation of novel forms—need not be imagined in the stodgy bipolar terms of hominids.

DONNA HARAWAY, "THE PROMISES OF MONSTERS"

In this chapter, we examine how the "end" of humanity is figured through a reconceptualization of human reproduction in recent science fiction films fundamentally invested in contemplating the future of the human species, Claire Denis' *High Life* (2018*)* and Pella Kågerman and Hugo Lilja's *Aniara* (2018). While both of these films reflect what Eva Horn has identified as "one of mankind's most ancient fantasies,"[1] we argue that they each imagine the end of the world in very different registers. Claire Denis' affective technique, including her nonlinear and alienating editing, sensual camera, and claustrophobic interiors, cinematically creates what Karen Barad calls "intra-actions," where the primacy of the human is constantly undermined.[2] This decentering of the human sparks a suspension of anthropocentric concepts, as sex, reproduction, and parenthood are put into question in ways that move beyond a Cartesian logic. By contrast, *Aniara*, with its continuity editing and narrative structure, still takes human experience as central, rehearsing the science-fictional trope of a lifeboat spaceship only to undo it in favor of extinction and total destruction. Hence, in these films we see two forms of posthumanist cinema: *High Life* provides a posthumanist experience through refusing to succumb to Humanist logic and anthropocentric technique, while *Aniara* plays with generic conventions only to disturb them by leaving no space for humans to survive their apocalypse. Reading these films through one another, another narrative emerges: a polyphonic "alter-tale," as Serenella Iovino and Serpil Oppermann put it, "that includes the vital materiality of life, experiences of nonhuman entities, and our bodily intra-actions with all forms of material agency as effective actors."[3] Comparing these films alongside critical posthumanist, feminist-materialist, and material-ecocritical thinkers, we analyze how they figure reproduction without generation as a rethinking of relations of body and production, while at the same time commenting on posthuman futures.

We would like to begin by acknowledging the circumstances under which we write this chapter, as academics from different hemispheres thinking together about the possibilities of survival amid a global pandemic when we are losing members of our and other species daily.[4] Even if the "apocalypse" is decidedly slower than science fiction usually envisions (the long-awaited

---

[1]Eva Horn, *The Future as Catastrophe: Imagining Disaster in the Modern Age*, trans. Valentine Pakis (New York: Columbia University Press, 2018), 21.

[2]Karen Barad, "Posthumanist Performativity: Toward an Understanding of How Matter Comes to Matter," *Signs* 28, no. 3 (2003): 826, https://doi.org/10.1086/345321.

[3]Serenella Iovino and Serpil Oppermann, "Material Ecocriticism: Materiality, Agency, and Models of Narrativity," *Ecozon European Journal of Literature Culture and Environment* 3, no. 1 (2012): 88, https://doi.org/10.37536/ECOZONA.2012.3.1.452.

[4]We met during the NeMLA 2020 event in Boston during our panel "Multispecies Becoming: Coming to Terms with Our Own End" at the very beginning of March 2020. This was one of the last conferences to take place in person and, when we were there, Boston was starting its first wave of Covid-19. Less than one week after this event, the global pandemic was declared,

invasion of alien species or sudden meteor strike has been replaced by fear of a tiny crowned virus hunting us one by one, as well as the slow violence of environmental degradation, species' extinction, and a gradually warming world), the catastrophic nature of our situation renders the timing of this piece particularly pertinent: our precarity as a species has been laid bare now more than ever as we endure what Rosi Braidotti sums up as "the disastrous planetary consequences of our species and the violent rule of sovereign Anthropos."[5] It is precisely at this moment that questions pertaining to the damages caused by the reigning mode of production to racialized, gendered, sexualized, and all other onto-political forms of "otherness" have become crucial. The anthropocentric, Eurocentric, and Humanist legacies that we have inherited insist on asking the same old questions based on an abstracted notion of the "human," overwriting the emergence of other kinds of questions that might lead to novel answers. We contend that *High Life* and *Aniara* can help us to address some of these questions from the plane of reproduction, the body, and multispecies becoming(s).

High Life takes place in a box-like spaceship where ten convicts have embarked on a journey toward a black hole to experimentally extract energy for a world that may no longer be there. Rather than waiting to die in prison after being given life sentences, they are offered a chance at redemption: "We were scum, trash, refuse, that didn't fit into the system, until someone had the bright idea of recycling us to serve science," Monte's voice-over tells us, though the specifics of just how they can save humanity by going into space remains unexplained. Unlike other science fiction narratives that focus on the search for alternative forms of energy (for instance, Christopher Nolan's 2014 *Interstellar*), this film does not give us scientific details about how such energy would be extracted, or even how urgently it is needed. Instead, Denis' film concentrates on Monte and his daughter, Willow, a miraculously conceived child born onboard the spaceship as a result of the obsessive reproductive experiments that a mesmeric Dr. Dibs (Juliette Binoche) conducts on the ship's inmates. The film moves back and forth between timelines, sometimes including abrupt flashbacks illuminating the past earthly lives of some characters, and at other times using dynamic cuts to show the everyday lives of the inmates. These shifting temporalities have disorienting effects that prevent spectators from anchoring themselves in a coherent and linear narrative. There are two key timelines in the film: the first is centered on Monte and his daughter as the last survivors of this dark journey, coming to terms with an unknown future. The second key temporal timeline is grounded on the process of artificially inseminating female

---

everything was shut down, and sickness and death began to take their place in our everyday landscapes.
[5]Rosi Braidotti, *Posthuman Knowledge* (Cambridge, UK: Polity Press, 2019), 10.

inmates and is composed of a series of increasingly violent events (rape, murder, and suicidal deaths) leading up to the birth of Willow, revealing life on the ship in all its bodily sensuality. There can be no return to Earth for Monte and Willow, and, for all we know, they might be the last specimens of an all-but-extinct species.

Aniara ponders similar ideas about human life, death, and human extinction: yet, unlike Denis' film, *Aniara* uses classical editing techniques to ground viewers in a linear narrative, in which we watch Emelie Garber's nameless character—referred to only as Mimarobe—who is responsible for the ship's mimetic-memory machine, called MIMA, which placates passengers with memories of idealized Nature while they travel between the devastated Earth and their new home on Mars. Unlike Denis' little box of a spaceship, *Aniara* is reminiscent of a cruise ship complex, with shopping malls, playgrounds, gaming arcades, restaurants, and spas, making the journey effortless for those who can afford this escape to humanity's "Plan B." In the first week of a supposedly three-week journey, a collision with a seemingly incidental piece of space junk sets *Aniara* off course and without fuel to turn back, leading to a series of inauspicious events eventually ensuring the passengers' prolonged death in deep space. *Aniara*'s narrative arc follows the stages of this slow death through the eyes of Mimarobe, marking the passing of time (hours, days, weeks, and years) to show the gradual disintegration of every social system, and indicating the failed project of a flawed species that continues to attempt to reproduce the *status quo* amid this catastrophic crisis.

Aniara and *High Life* both engage with the figure of the "endangered human."[6] In her seminal 1964 essay, "The Imagination of Disaster," Susan Sontag suggested that, through watching science fiction films, "one can participate in the fantasy of living through one's own death and [. . .] the destruction of humanity itself."[7] The crucial difference in the twenty-first century is that the "trauma" produced by mid-twentieth-century awareness of the possibility of human extinction through nuclear annihilation has mutated into a distinctly Anthropocene-era awareness of our precarious position somewhere between "the fourth industrial revolution" and the "sixth extinction."[8] As visual narratives about humans floating aimlessly in the vast expanse of outer space, each film also echoes the shift from Kenneth Boulding's "cowboy economy" to the "spaceman economy," from a conception of space as the new frontier (the "once-open, once-free horizon

[6]Ibid., 86.
[7]Susan Sontag, "Imagination of Disaster," *Commentary Magazine*, October 1965, 49, https://www.commentarymagazine.com/articles/susan-sontag/the-imagination-of-disaster/.
[8]Braidotti, *Posthuman Knowledge*, 3.

of expansive possibility, which previously drove American history"[9]) to an awareness of limit and scarcity. To be sure, "from a perspective inside one of these spaceships [. . .] life is a state of fragile and even hellish enclosure, at constant risk of either deadly shortages or deadly exposure to the void outside."[10]

Neither *High Life* nor *Aniara* fit neatly within the tradition of catastrophic sci-fi scenarios that showcase a linear framing of the apocalypse, especially given that a singular remarkable event bringing about the end of the world is never pinpointed.[11] Whereas, for Eva Horn, catastrophic fictions "enable the analysis of a society's fragility while outsourcing it to a distant future, to the imagination, or to science fiction,"[12] in these films it is precisely because there is no sudden event that destroys the Earth, precipitating a mechanism whereby some survive and others die, that they also do away with something else that Sontag identifies in her essay: that is, a sense of coming to terms with—or resolving—one's own end.[13] Significantly, the only living things that remain at the end of both of these films are the plants that accompanied the humans on their journey into space and are decidedly *non*human forms of life.

In what remains of this chapter we concentrate on how, in (re)presenting imminent species' extinction, each film exhibits anxieties about futurity by focusing on the failure of human sexual and social reproduction. These failed visions of reproduction and relations of care are associated with a specifically female body, on the one hand, and are mediated by dependence on distinct forms of *techné* brought onto the spaceships as a way to reproduce human life in a new milieu, on the other. In *High Life*, human dependence on technology is figured by the inmates' use of the masturbation machine, known as the "fuckbox" and by way of the monitors that broadcast "random images from earth," which keep the humans on board the ship invested in a certain vision of humanity by projecting that same

---

[9]Gerry Canavan, "Introduction: If This Goes On," in *Green Planets: Ecology and Science Fiction*, ed. Gerry Canavan and Kim Stanley Robinson (Wesleyan University Press, 2014), 6.
[10]Ibid., 7. The destructive consequences of globalized capitalism (human expansion, consumption, and resource extraction) are hinted at in both films. In *Aniara*, passengers are figured as settlers migrating to their new life as colonizers on Mars, while *High Life* is framed by grainy footage from *In the Land of the Headhunters*, a 1914 white settler "'ethnographic' film."Hannah Paveck, "No Other Voice: Claire Denis's 'High Life' Another Gaze," May 27, 2019, https://www.anothergaze.com/no-voice-claire-deniss-high-life-feminism/.
[11]Eva Horn provides a historical account of end-of-the-world narratives, from the classic monotheistic model of apocalypse as "revelation," to "secular" sci-fi where the figure of the "last man" looks back to the revealing event, and—with the benefit of hindsight—discerns the mistakes that led to the catastrophe. This temporal logic invokes the possibility of a different human-made future, instead of an apocalypse to come, thus providing cathartic relief for viewers.
[12]Horn, *The Future as Catastrophe*, 97.
[13]Sontag, "Imagination of Disaster."

flawed vision of humanity into space and thus into the future. In *Aniara* we have MIMA, a form of artificial intelligence designed to mirror human beings' pleasing memories of the planet that they were in fact responsible for destroying, in a therapeutic, and even palliative, fashion. In both films, the birth and uncertain survival of a baby becomes a central motif: however, unlike "the closing image of a human fetus hurtling through space in Stanley Kubrick's *2001: A Space Odyssey*," which, according to Haraway, "completed the voyage of discovery begun by the weapon wielding apes at the film's gripping opening" by becoming a projection of the "self-made, reborn man, in the process of being raptured out of history,"[14] the babies in these films have no future. What does it mean to focus on the reproduction of the species in a milieu where there is no futurity? We suggest that, to differing degrees and in very different registers, each film is also telling another story, one that encourages viewers to look beyond the human in order to see the relational ontologies and multispecies connections that in fact sustain human life, a vision that challenges anthropocentric humanity's "eco-phobic" and "pathological inability to see connections."[15]

Failing Reproduction

One of *High Life*'s main timelines explores the reproductive experiments carried out by Dr. Dibs, who is obsessed with creating viable fetuses in space. In exchange for a dose of a sedative that helps them cope with their hopeless existence onboard the ship, male inmates (with the exception of Monte, who insists on strict celibacy) regularly visit Dr. Dibs' office to have their sperm harvested. Due to high radiation levels, the doomed reproductive experiments usually result in the death of the pregnant women or their babies soon after birth. Dr. Dibs' is established as a maternal figure within the spaceship "family": she is responsible for caring for the inmates and for producing children, something to which she claims she is "totally devoted." In a deliberate reference to the mythical figure of Medea, however, Dibs is on the ship in the first place because she has been convicted of killing her own children.[16] She is thus a monster posited at the threshold that separates the proper and improper mother, destabilizing boundaries that are taken for

---

[14]Donna Haraway, "The Promises of Monsters: A Regenerative Politics for Inappropriate/d Others," in *The Monster Theory Reader*, ed. Jeffrey Andrew Weinstock (Minneapolis, London: University of Minnesota Press, 2020), 316.
[15]Simon Estok, "Theorizing in a Space of Ambivalent Openness: Ecocriticism and Ecophobia," *ISLE* 16, no. 2 (2009): 9.
[16]Dan Schindel, "'Claire Denis on Black Holes, Olafur Eliasson, and the Making of High Life' Interview with Claire Denis," *Hyperallergic*, April 16, 2019, http://hyperallergic.com/495099/claire-denis-on-black-holes-olafur-eliasson-and-the-making-of-high-life/.

granted.[17] As a mother who has murdered her children but is obsessed with childbirth, crying inconsolably when the babies die, Dr. Dibs is not simply an abject mother: she is a figure that restructures normative conceptions of motherhood. She refuses to be the ideal caring, selfless mother, yet she still performs acts of care for others. Through her sexual, desiring (and desired) body she is a figure that questions the very notions of creative power and the function of reproduction.

Dibs' body is far removed from what Shildrick calls the "clean and proper" body; in a scene that we will elaborate on shortly, Denis' camera focuses on a close-up of the scar on her abdomen, which resembles a grotesque self-inflicted cesarean. Given that the boundary between the outside and the inside of the body ensures its unity and intactness, the skin becomes a container; Sara Ahmed posits that scars threaten this unity, negating the "integrity of the body; [the scar's] form is a rem(a)inder of the failure of such integrity as the measure of well-being."[18] The lack of wholeness signified in Dibs' scar is carefully examined by Denis' camera through a panning close-up that renders her body leaky and thus anxiety-producing for viewers.[19] Yet Denis does not only show the leaky, porous, and improper body of Dibs as a monstrous mother; almost *every* body in the film is shot to reveal their scars, wounds, and imperfections, playing with this ontological anxiety in a way that brings it into question. Therefore, these bodies, with their scars and leaks, already threaten a conception of intact, unitary self, a prerequisite for the Cartesian mind. Instead, we have monstrous bodies that leak milk and semen, and blood and pus, constantly reminding us of the untenability of a unitary self.

---

[17]For monster theorists, the monster is a figure that threatens borders and stable meanings, perceptions, and the illusion of normalcy by revealing their constitutive instabilities. For example, Cohen theorizes the monster as dwelling at the gates of difference, Shildrick reads the monster as dissolving the boundaries of that which is "proper," and Canguilhem marks the monster as determinant of the norm. Dibs, therefore, with her witchlike appearance, her murderous actions and her desiring body, becomes a monstrous figure threatening the stable limits of motherhood. Jeffrey Jerome Cohen, *Monster Theory: Reading Culture* (University of Minnesota Press, 1996), 17; Margrit Shildrick, *Embodying the Monster: Encounters with the Vulnerable Self* (SAGE, 2001), 16; Georges Canguilhem and Therese Jaeger, "Monstrosity and the Monstrous," *Diogenes* 10, no. 40 (1962): 38, https://doi.org/10.1177/039219216201004002.
[18]Sara Ahmed, "Animated Borders: Skin, Colour and Tanning," in *Vital Signs: Feminist Reconfigurations of the Bio/Logical Body*, ed. Margrit Shildrick and Janet Price (Edinburgh: Edinburgh University Press, 1998), 47.
[19]This leakiness is one of the very features of women's bodies that has posited them as inferior, unreliable, and irrational in Western thought, since "[a]s the devalued processes of reproduction make clear, the body has a propensity to leak, to overflow the proper distinctions between self and other, to contaminate and engulf," which has, "in the conventional masculinist imagination," rendered women themselves, as "objects of fear and repulsion," "capable of generating deep ontological anxiety." Janet Price and Margarit Shildrick, *Feminist Theory and the Body: A Reader* (New York and London: Routledge, 1999), 3.

Two scenes, namely, Dr. Dibs' rape of Monte and the scene where Boyse's
breast milk leaks from her engorged breasts after giving birth to Willow, can
serve to enlighten how Denis engages with reproductive discourse in the film.
During her rape of a heavily sedated Monte, Dibs simultaneously embodies
both masculine and feminine forms of the monstrous incubus/succubus,
what Braidotti calls "one of the earliest theories of artificial insemination."[20]
After this nonconsensual act, the camera shows a close-up of Monte's sperm
leaking from her vagina when she collects his "gift" in her cupped hands,
filling a syringe and depositing it into Boyse. Dr. Dibs gently blows onto and
rubs the young woman's belly, speaking directly to the as-yet-to-be conceived
fetus and willing the baby into being. Denis immediately cuts to a shot of
the Orion Nebula, again resonating with the "star child" shot at the end of
2001 and equating the magnificence of the solar system with the miracle
of conception, marking this rape as an act of creation by a woman who,
with this action, is finally able to complete her magnum opus. The mother
figure here, as a consummate creator deliberately associated with the figure
of the "witch," is physically, spatially, and discursively detached from any
conventional understanding of care, womanhood, or its sacredness.

In the next scene, a devastated Boyse examines her breasts, horrified
by the dense, grainy breast milk leaking onto her naked body. Her breasts
produce milk but the baby is not there, suggesting that the biological mother
is neither available nor inevitable in Denis' vision. Through Denis' celebrated
command of the sensual camera,[21] she opens motherhood to questions of
radical alterity, since the only acts of care in the film are performed by a child-
murdering, forcefully desiring doctor, and a celibate man. This muddying of
roles and identities, together with the separation of desire and reproduction,
takes human desire and sexual relations out of the equation, seeking to
divorce the final product—babies—from their kinship networks.

Echoing Boyse's captive pregnancy and her forced detachment from
the film's "perfect" baby creation, the figure of motherhood in Aniara is
ambivalent at best. The protagonist's girlfriend Isagel becomes pregnant
accidentally, the result of a ritualistic orgy worshipping a defunct MIMA, and
ultimately fails to perform the kind of happy and hopeful motherhood that

[20]Rosi Braidotti, "Signs of Wonder and Traces of Doubt: On Teratology and Embodied
Differences," in Feminist Theory and the Body: A Reader, ed. Janet Price and Margarit Shildrick
(New York and London: Routledge, 1999), 291.
[21]Denis is a master of bodily and affective cinema in her use of camera and mise-en-scène.
Critics like Beugnet, Hole, and others underline the director's unique approach to the body:
for example, while Beugnet illustrates Denis' use of fragmented bodies not as sexually
objectification à la Hollywood but as a "progressive invocation of bodies," Hole reads the way
she uses the surface of bodies as hiding an interiority while opening up an ethical relation to the
Other. Martine Beugnet, Claire Denis (Manchester University Press, 2004), 193; Kristin Lené
Hole, Towards a Feminist Cinematic Ethics: Claire Denis, Emmanuel Levinas and Jean-Luc
Nancy (Edinburgh University Press, 2016), 5.

is expected from her. Instead, she undoes the nuclear family by killing herself and her offspring. Five years after the initial incident, the ship is shown in disarray: as in *High Life* (as well as in both of these films' precursor, *Solaris*) dirt, disorder, and waste have taken over the shiny shopping mall corridors in direct proportion to the desperation and hopelessness of the people on board. In this abysmal atmosphere, the camera shows Isagel playing with her six- or seven-month-old baby in the swimming pool. The baby floats in the water with Isagel's support. A close-up shows her stoic but expressionless face looking at the baby, as she gently lets his head sink under the water and does not pull him back up. Suddenly, a colleague enters the scene calling her to the bridge: they have apparently discovered a possible rescue pod that is fourteenth months away. Isagel pulls the baby out of the water, in an indication that there may still be hope. However, this scene of failed rescue proves that there is no help coming from outside, and Isagel eventually kills the child and herself. Here, the figure of the baby as symbol of futurity and temporality par excellence, what Lee Edelman identifies "as the emblem of futurity's unquestioned value,"[22] remains intact, since with their deaths *Aniara* erases any hope of futurity for the ship's passengers. In this way, the film plays into the trope of the salvation of the nuclear family (albeit a queer one) surviving the end of the world, a trope that Horn identifies as one of the basic gestures of the catastrophic end of the world narrative,[23] by folding it on itself, and showing reproduction without generation.

(Post)humanist Camera: Life Beyond Human Extinction

While both films posit human reproduction as a central trope in their meditations on the experience of extinction, we argue that *High Life* operates on a particularly posthumanist level when it comes to form. Understood in Rosi Braidotti's terms as a convergence of two critical stances, posthumanism is a critique of humanism and of anthropocentrism, without reducing them to the same thing.[24] Her conceptualization is in line with many scholars who

---

[22]Lee Edelman, *No Future: Queer Theory and the Death Drive* (Duke University Press, 2004), 4.

[23]Horn, *The Future as Catastrophe*, 99.

[24]Braidotti undoes the distinction, based on Aristotle's *Politics*, between *zoe* and *bion*, refusing to distinguish between animal and human forms of life. Both words can be translated as "life," yet there are various interpretations of the difference between them. For example, Giorgio Agamben grounds his concept of "bare life" on a distinction between *zoe* as animal life and *bion* as political life. Braidotti, *Posthuman Knowledge*, 8; Giorgio Agamben, *Homo Sacer: Sovereign Power and Bare Life*, trans. Daniel Heller-Roazen (Stanford: Stanford University Press, 1998).

view posthumanist discourse as a new plane from which to radically rethink Western premises about subject-object relations, logocentric discourses, and material ontologies, where an able-bodied, male, cisgender, white human is taken as the neutral center of experience of the "we" of humanity. Instead, the posthuman is premised ultimately on multiplicity, where a nonuniversal "we" is assumed.[25] Similarly, Donna Haraway proposes the concept of *sympoēsis* as a new way to form different ontological relations with others and ourselves, where a coproduction of selves is performed without the mastery of a human subject.[26] In this relation, we can think of Karen Barad's questioning of "the givenness of the differential categories of 'human' and 'nonhuman,' examining the practices through which these differential boundaries are stabilized and destabilized."[27]

The underlying concern in these and other accounts of posthumanism is the capacity to shift the epistemological plane of questions that have been asked (and answered) so far in Western thought: this would involve a shift from the perspective of an Anthropos that presumes the hegemony of the human—as a self-enclosed subject, subsuming everything else under his embodied logocentric being—to a much more fluid, immanent plane of relationality, where this perspective is undone and held accountable to a logic of multiplicity. By undoing the undifferentiated human as the subject of the relation where the undifferentiated nonhuman (animal and other) life forms, as object, must be subsumed, it becomes possible to not only subvert anthropocentric discourse but also open spaces for political and ethical questions about the relations between and among animals and other nonhuman forms of life, where the human is merely one *relata* among many. A similar dismantling of the human as apex is being done in a multitude of areas of contemporary theory, yet a simple decapitation of the apex-hu/man is not enough. As Barad notes,

[T]he point of challenging traditional epistemologies is not merely to welcome females, slaves, children, animals and other dispossessed Others (exiled from the land of knowers by Aristotle thousands of years ago) into the fold of knowers, but to better account for the ontology of knowing.[28]

---

[25]Braidotti, *Posthuman Knowledge*, 9.
[26]As opposed to Anthropos, Donna Haraway proposes a turn toward the figure of the Medusa to "give faciality a profound makeover," and deliver a "blow to modern humanist (including technohumanist) figurations of the forward-looking, sky-gazing Anthropos." Donna Haraway, *Staying with the Trouble: Making Kin in the Chthulucene* (Durham: Duke University Press, 2016), 53–4.
[27]Barad, "Posthumanist Performativity," 803.
[28]Karen Barad, "Invertebrate Visions: Diffractions of the Brittlestar," in *The Multispecies Salon*, ed. Eben Kirksey (Durham: Duke University Press Books, 2014), 222.

In other words, there is a difference between knowing that this universal "we" has been imagining an undifferentiated mass in the exclusionary form of a white cishet man, and making radical changes in the way epistemologies, aesthetics, and ontologies operate without this simultaneously exclusive and universal "we."

High Life partly manages to operate on this novel level, in which the "we" is in constant becoming, and the result is an affective and often uncomfortable viewing experience for those who are used to perceiving the world on the basis of Humanist principles. A central scene in the film that illustrates the disintegration of borders between human and nonhuman, as well as between nonhuman actors (technology/animal), is when Dr. Dibs enters a special room designed to keep the prisoners' sexual desires in check by means of a special machine contained in a room that some characters refer to as "the fuckbox." The room is located downstairs in the mechanical belly of the ship, where containers full of liquids (presumably part of the ship's water/waste recycling system) are stored. We see a metal compartment with "black water" written underneath. Dr. Dibs walks past this compartment and enters the machine, sliding the cold, gray mechanical door closed behind her. She is immediately bathed in an erotic red hue, and what follows is a four-minute scene of disorienting, fluid, intense and disturbing masturbation, in which the goal does not appear to be pleasure; instead, the main stakes seem to involve testing the sensual limits of humanity. The masturbation machine—which is not shown in its entirety until the very end of the scene—is a mobile, metal stool with a dildo attached to it. After watching Dibs take off her clothes and let down her long, flowing mane of black hair, a close-up of her hands shows her gently sliding a condom onto the shiny metal dildo part of the machine. Against pitch-blackness, the scene only lights Dr. Dibs' naked upper back, slowly turning to her breasts and then to a close-up of the large scar across her lower abdomen. With wailing-siren background music composed especially for this scene by Stuart Staples from Tindersticks, a medium shot covering Dibs' back shows her gripping two suspenders that come down from the ceiling, while her body spins, turns, twists, and bends with rhythmic and arrhythmic movements. As the rhythm of her movement increases, Denis gives us accelerated cuts concentrating on different parts of her body. Against the empty black background, her skin folds in multiple directions, her body sweats, her muscles contract, and the metallic machine disappears as the camera concentrates on her body, now a body perhaps without a person. With vertiginous camerawork that revolves around Dibs' body, showing glimpses of flesh, scars, and pubic hair, the shot suddenly shifts to show us an X-ray vision of the metallic dildo engaged in its pendulum motion inside her body, suddenly reminding us that this is in fact a machine. Therein comes the ultimate transformation from this fleshy, machinic merger, when the machine that Dibs is riding becomes an animal: a close-up of her hand shows her caressing what looks like fur. The fur of

FIGURE 13.1 *Dibs (Juliette Binoche) becoming animal (Claire Denis (dir.),* High Life, *2018).*

the animal merges with Dibs' pubic hair and with the rhythmic movements of her body when we finally see her face and then the whole machine. Her contorted body moves on top of the gray, wolf-like animal with its thick tail going around her bottom and caressing her. With a close-up on her now-relaxed face, she leaves the scene. What remains is the machine, now being sprayed by black water and cleaned by the circular scrubbing motion of what looks like mechanical brooms, similar to the kind used in automatic carwashes. Finally, from outside the "fuckbox," we see the machine oozing a white, sticky substance, something akin to sexual secretions (Figure 13.1).

These frenzied four minutes following the movements of Dibs' body merging with a machine (and then with an animal) is perhaps one of the most disturbing scenes in the film, yet these shifts from human to machine to animal undo any kind of objectification. The boundaries between the agential subjects of this act of masturbation—machine, body, and animal—are blurred, and we can no longer make sense of this scene anthropocentrically. Dibs herself becomes something monstrous, where the limits of the skin, the subject/human "I," and the other are utterly entangled. This muddling of the borders in the merger with machine and animal disturbs the primacy of what Margrit Shildrick calls the "self's clean and proper body," thus threatening the unity of being.[29] This merger through masturbation, an act that is supposed to be done sui generis, instead opens to include other beings or agencies, making Dibs' body both a space of multiplicity and an assemblage

[29]Shildrick, *Embodying the Monster*, 59.

with others. In this sexual act, we can catch glimpses of Haraway's cyborg along with Gilles Deleuze's becoming-animal. What we are not able to see in the shift from metal to fur is a singular conception of a woman who is reaching pleasure. The result is a machine-woman-animal amalgamation that does not make sense within a humanistic framework.

But perhaps the most interesting instance of Denis' posthumanist camera is in the film's opening shot of a lush green setting, where the camera pans from left to right on what looks like a dreamy garden at night. The overview of mossy wet ground covered by green vegetables and plants of all sorts ends with an abrupt cut, first to a close-up of textured green leaves, a luminescent dark green color, and then quickly to a cut of a wet yellow zucchini hiding between two large leaves, whose venation performs an almost tangible gesture. The digital camera effects become perceptible here, as the venation and the color are almost too real. The next cut is another close-up of an acorn squash on the ground followed by something very unexpected: a black boot, lying flat on top of the lush green as if it has, like the squashes, grown in the garden. The nondiegetic eeriness of the soundtrack accompanies this opening scene, where the fact that we are seeing the inside of a spaceship is not immediately apparent. This could just as well be an enclosed garden in the backyard of someone's house. This succulent and leafy picture that expands to encompass the first minute and a half of the film is slowly left behind through a plastic curtain, like the kind found in greenhouses or in factory farms. At the same time, a baby begins to cry. Along with these cries, now part of the diegetic background, the camera shows us the dirty, abandoned pallor of a spaceship, reminiscent of Tarkovsky's *Solaris*, with its empty gray stairs and off-white padded corridors. This spatial promenade ends with a view of baby Willow, approximately one year old, sitting by herself in the midst of a makeshift playpen looking at two computer screens that show codes in blue and red hues. She repeatedly murmurs "da-da" as she watches her father, Monte, in his spacesuit, doing repairs on the spaceship's exterior, on one of the monitors.

It is significant that this film about life onboard a spaceship opens with a vision of a lush fertile garden, instead of a traditional establishing shot where the spectator is introduced to the characters or to the setting. In fact, this garden forms a contrast in the overall spatial distribution of the film's claustrophobic and pallid interiors. The film intentionally begins in a nonhuman space and without a human lead, yet in many accounts of the film this initial shot is overlooked for the sake of a more human-centered sense of beginning. For instance, in her reading of the film, Hanna Paveck claims that the film opens up "with an exchange of voices: the cry of a baby,"[30] while David Sims describes the first image of the film as "a baby, seemingly

[30]Paveck, "No Other Voice: Claire Denis's 'High Life' Another Gaze."

abandoned on a spaceship."[31] These readings overlook the fact that, instead of centering on the baby or on the idea of human communication, the film instead opens with a lush, fecund image of vegetable life. This garden was perhaps created by human efforts but has seemingly long been abandoned, as is signaled with abundant weeds, overgrown vines, and the empty boot appearing as merely another vegetable among many, thus losing its sense of properly belonging to someone.

When we compare this scene with *Aniara*'s opening, the difference between their posthuman and Humanist approaches becomes clear: the film opens with what seems to be newsreel footage of catastrophic weather events and the destruction of the Earth—tidal waves, raging wildfires, and buildings toppling—and then cuts into a long shot of a technologically advanced space elevator ascending from a smog-covered Earth to a huge, futuristic, light-filled spaceship. Inside this transportation device, which to our eyes looks much like the inside of a commercial aircraft, we catch our first glimpse of the main protagonist, Mimarobe. The camera shows planet Earth getting further and further away, as a mother tells her small child: "want to say bye-bye to Earth?" Watching this film in the twenty-first century, through these opening images we can immediately ascertain the reasons why humanity has been forced to abandon the Earth. We are also introduced to the human character who we will be following and thus identifying with for the rest of the film. In this way, the film's premise is explained to the spectator in a way that refers to our present: the experience of the changing climate as a kind of "catastrophe without an event."[32] As Claire Colebrook asserts, "we can only imagine the present as the world, as what must be saved at all costs," and these first visual images speak to this present, establishing the immediacy of saving humanity.[33]

While *Aniara* provides a human-centered perspective from the beginning of the film, in *High Life* we are provided with no such narrative framing: in fact, until we see Monte in his spacesuit clinging to the side of the ship, surrounded by the vastness of space, the spectator has no way of knowing that this film is even set on a spaceship. There is no immediate explanation that can help us to make sense of the film, thus engendering an affective sense of confusion. Indeed, beside *Aniara*'s ultra-sleek model and sophisticated lighting, Monte's spaceship looks like a dirty matchbox. The decidedly unhygienic and nonstreamlined space of this ship is littered with old plastic water containers, makeshift playthings for Willow, and clunky monitors

---

[31]David Sims, "The Artistic Chemistry of Robert Pattinson and Claire Denis," *The Atlantic*, April 10, 2019, https://www.theatlantic.com/entertainment/archive/2019/04/robert-pattinson -and-claire-denis-talk-high-life-artistic-collaboration/586768/.
[32]Horn, *The Future as Catastrophe*, 80.
[33]Claire Colebrook, *The Death of the PostHuman: Essays on Extinction, Volume One* (Open Humanities Press, 2014), 43.

that look like leftover 2010 desktop models. This leaky and run-down space resonates with an aesthetic of "dirty technology," which "works by implying that technology is not a sterile, inanimate instrument that the human has mastery over," instead emphasizing "dirt and dampness," and suggesting "an animate, sweating, breathing life-force."[34] As an aesthetic concept, dirty technology "disrupts" our "normative, humanistically-inherited and instrumental perspective of technology by forcing us to consider technology as life,"[35] further blurring human-machine-nonhuman life boundaries.

Taken out of any kind of linear narrative orientation, the first twenty minutes of *High Life* show a father caring for the bodily needs of his baby: feeding, changing, singing to her, potty-training her, and sewing the arm of her doll. Monte's model of care, abstracted from the nonlinear framing of the story and presented prominently at the beginning of the film, challenges assumptions about gendered reproductive roles but is also, significantly, a model that opens out to include caring for that which is *non*human. While *Aniara* only makes vague references to the production of the algae on board the ship that sustains the passengers' lives, in this scene Monte is shown laboriously harvesting, cooking, and feeding the products of the garden to his infant daughter: he is also shown taking the vegetable scraps back to the garden to be composted back into the Earth. The film's nods to "trans-corporeal"[36] processes, such as decomposing—natural processes of which the human forms an integral part—present a challenge to prevailing anthropocentric notions of the human as a self-contained subject, somehow separated from and above the natural world.[37]

Even though there is the suggestion that, untethered to the "taboos" of human culture, the figure of Willow represents a potential (post)human futurity, Denis avoids reproducing the trope of reproductive futurism by refusing to let the baby have a future. Diverging from a Humanist and patriarchal path (gestured toward through hints of incest), instead Monte and Willow embrace ambivalence and obliteration by saying "yes" to a black hole; as they move away from the ship, the very same "random images from earth" continue to flash across the monitors inside. In contrast to the

---

[34]Norah Campbell and Mike Saren, "The Primitive, Technology and Horror: A Posthuman Biology," *Ephemera* 10, no. 2 (2010): 167.

[35]Ibid., 167.

[36]Stacy Alaimo, "Material Feminisms," in *Trans-Corporeal Feminisms and the Ethical Space of Nature*," ed. Stacy Alaimo and Susan Heckman (Bloomington and Indianapolis: Indiana University Press, 2008), 237–64.

[37]Similarly, Heather Sullivan proposes "dirt theory" as "an antidote to nostalgic views rendering nature a far-away and "clean" site precisely in order to suggest that there is no ultimate boundary between us and nature," and to challenge the assumption "that we can exist separate from our dirty planetary enmeshment." Heather Sullivan, "Dirt Theory and Material Ecocriticism," *Interdisciplinary Studies in Literature and the Environment* 19, no. 3 (2012): 515–31.

passengers of *Aniara*, who seem to need a screen of images to shield them from the dark void of space, Denis seems to be welcoming an alternative vision of futurity that would be premised on epistemological uncertainty and vulnerability. The same shot of the vegetable garden that sustains the prisoners onboard the ship closes the film: immediately before Willow and Monte leave the spaceship for good, Denis shows us this garden again, fertile, fecund, and greener than ever, as if to remind us that long after Monte and Willow (possibly the last humans in the universe) have gone, plant life remains with or without us. Framing the film in posthumanist terms, Denis' camera is telling us a story about the continuation of life—just not for "us."

Unlike Claire Denis' sensual close-ups, featuring skin, sweat, blood, and other bodily fluids, shots that simultaneously alienate and concretize the bodily experiences of the inmates, *Aniara*'s invisible camera and editing style follows the main protagonist, Mimarobe, in a linear fashion, narrating the harrowing story of the ship's passengers and crew. *Aniara* offers its own Humanist-framed critique of anthropocentrism through the figure of MIMA, the AI onboard the ship that is gendered as female, and whose function as a prosthetic memory device is to keep people placated while they are being transported to Mars. In a narrative that offers the viewer a gradual and intensifying sense of dread, the destruction of MIMA marks a shift in the communal environment from survivors of an unfortunate accident to a cruel community of punishers.

MIMA is introduced to us as a device that the first expeditioners to Mars used to remind them of their earthily experiences and thus keep them emotionally grounded and connected to home. A shiny, textured, pulsating rectangular unit that hangs from the ceiling, MIMA can read the memories of the people that sit or lie underneath, providing them with vivid visions of their peaceful and serene experiences of Earth. However, it is clear that MIMA is as much a dream machine as a memory machine; she is programmed only to show passengers idyllic scenes of an abstract and pure Nature, cleansed of any trace of human intervention. While the privileged passengers at first seem to only be interested in shopping and other vapid forms of entertainment, they develop an almost pathological addiction to the machine once they begin to experience the despair and sadness caused by knowledge of their impending doom. As a result, MIMA begins to show people "awful things" instead of the idealized vision of nature that she was designed to mirror. Once more and more people begin using MIMA, she becomes overwhelmed by the memories of pain, environmental destruction, and violence that she is supposed to filter out. Accusing humankind of intolerable cruelty, she refuses to serve their mimetic needs any longer: "My conscience aches for the stones. I've heard them cry their stonely [*sic*] cries [. . .] been troubled by their pains. In the name of *Things*, I want peace," she says, before exploding and leaving the Mimarobe as the default culprit to be punished for her loss.

MIMA's last words, as she "reduces herself" to human speech at the moment of her own destruction, remind us that human cruelty and carelessness are not only felt by humans but actually experienced in things themselves: her words thus hint at the possibility of another kind of relationship between people and the world, a relationship that might be understood through Karen Barad's sense of "intra-action," where things are not ordained in a subject-object relationship (where one subsumes the other) but, instead, are open to action among things through relationality and ontological equality. Barad asserts: "no-thing stands separately constituted and positioned inside a spacetime frame of reference, and no divine position for our viewing pleasure exists in a location outside the world."[38] In this repositioning, things (including "us") gain ontological reality as long as they are related to each other in a radical equality where an outside, superior position, such as that once occupied by Anthropos, is no longer tenable. MIMA reminds us that "nature is made, but not entirely by humans; it is a co-construction among humans and non-humans."[39] In a sense, MIMA, along with other things, is given the status of a living being, since her self-destruction is figured by some of the occupants of the ship as a suicide. MIMA's decision to self-destruct can be understood in terms of her mimetic function; as a machine designed to offer prosthetic memories of Earth, MIMA is driven to emulate the actions of the Earth itself, liberating herself from the human begins that are destroying her.[40] Since the nature that humanity has instrumentalized to the point of destruction does not have a voice, MIMA gives it one. Furthermore, recalling what Sontag identified as one of the functions of disaster cinema, MIMA enacts a simulacrum of humanity's own self-destructive urges by mirroring their own species' demise: "how horror blasts out, how grim it always is, one's destruction," MIMA says. Reflecting what Braidotti calls a "Gaia-oriented downsizing of human arrogance,"[41] this mirroring of humanity's anthropogenic annihilation is MIMA's last act before self-destructing, plunging the occupants of the ship into deep despair.

In spite of its Humanist-framed critique of anthropocentrism, *Aniara* also invites viewers to consider the possible continuation of life beyond human extinction in a curiously visual way. Just before the credits roll, viewers are provided with text that informs us that the year is now 5,981,407 and the ship (now completely devoid of human life) is orbiting the "Lyra constellation." The film ends rather abruptly with the spectacular image

[38]Barad, "Invertebrate Visions: Diffractions of the Brittlestar," 229.
[39]Haraway, "The Promises of Monsters: A Regenerative Politics for Inappropriate/d Others," 298.
[40]Perhaps this also explains why MIMA is female: her reproachful words, "I will be done with my displays. There is protection from nearly everything . . . but there is no protection from humankind," reflect the trope of a similarly anthropomorphized vengeful and indifferent Mother Earth, ridding herself of her parasitic children.
[41]Braidotti, *Posthuman Knowledge*, 39.

of this vibrant, blue-green (and decidedly Earth-like) planet, inviting us to wonder where this abundance of life might have come from. Given that, in a scene just a few minutes before, we see the algae farm overflowing the bounds of its' plastic containment, dripping onto the floor, the viewer is invited to consider that this might be what has happened to the plant life that humanity has taken for granted, once humans are out of the equation. Similar to *High Life*, then, the message seems to be that while it might be too late for humans, life *has* indeed gone on.

Conclusion

Providing a space in which to watch humanity dwindle and gradually disappear, both of these films engage with Anthropocene-era anxieties surrounding ecological species' guilt, reflecting the idea that to "heal or to cure at the scale of the planet is possible only through absolute annihilation and erasure of everything that makes the human possible."[42] In both cases, it is clear that there is no returning to the wasted Earth and that these doomed individuals might be all that is left of the human species. There are no happy endings or possible rescues. However, as Haraway reminds us: "It's not a 'happy ending' we need, but a non-ending. That's why none of the narratives of masculinist, patriarchal apocalypses will do. The System is not closed; the sacred image of the same is not coming. The world is not full."[43]

Braidotti wonders "who is this 'we' whose humanity is at stake?"[44] and both of these films invite us to keep this question at the forefront of our minds. Just *whose* ends are "we" coming to terms with as we watch these films? The spaceship represents what Peter Sloterdijk calls an "ontology of closed space."[45] With the ark, as with all forms of archive, there is an implication of selectivity, and the doomed humanity in both films is conspicuously white and/or European, reflecting a "distinct bias towards the anxieties of dominant cultures, ethnic groups and classes."[46] Sitting with the discomforting experience of leaving old models behind might be a way to encourage the emergence of other ways of thinking: "[f]ar from marking the rejection, extinction or the impoverishment of the human, the posthuman

---

[42]Ibid., 82.
[43]Haraway, "The Promises of Monsters: A Regenerative Politics for Inappropriate/d Others," 506.
[44]Braidotti, *Posthuman Knowledge*, 86.
[45]Peter Sloterdijk cited in Sabine Höler, "'The Real Problem of a Spaceship Is Its People': Spaceship Earth as Ecological Science Fiction," in *Green Planets: Ecology and Science Fiction*, ed. Gerry Canavan and Kim Stanley Robinson (Middletown: Wesleyan University Press, 2014), 104.
[46]Braidotti, *Posthuman Knowledge*, 82.

condition is a way of reconstituting the human," as a way to re-"negotiate who 'we' are."[47]

The "mark of posthumanism," suggests Sheryl Vint, rests in an "openness to change and newness, to becoming other and giving up on old categories when they no longer serve rather than defending them against inevitable change."[48] Ultimately, while in its empathetic narrative framing *Aniara* largely remains stuck within Humanist frameworks—in a sense offering a comment about its own inability to get beyond anthropocentric limits by narratively (re)enacting humanity's inability to imagine life beyond human time—*High Life* offers an affective experience of human ends. The latter's alienating, sensual, camera work, with its fixation on reproductive bodily fluids (ejaculation, gestation, lactation), points toward a decay of old models and corrupted processes, undoing object-subject relations and disturbing our capacity for individuation. Denis' film makes way for a posthuman futurity by choosing to make a leap into the black hole, in a radical decentering of the (hu)man. The result is a cinematic experience where the spectator is encouraged—if not forced—to give up the fantasy of "living through one's own death and . . . the destruction of humanity itself," as Sontag suggests,[49] and instead to sit with a sense of uneasiness. We are left with a cinematic experience where viewers are invited to approach the end of humanity critically and perhaps even a little uncomfortably.

---

[47]Ibid., 39.
[48]Sheryl Vint, "Conclusion: Toward an Ethical Posthumanism," in *Bodies of Tomorrow: Technology, Subjectivity, Science Fiction* (Toronto: University of Toronto Press, 2007), 175.
[49]Sontag, "Imagination of Disaster," 49.

BIBLIOGRAPHY

After Yang. Directed by Kogonada. A24, 2021. DVD.

Agamben, Giorgio. *Homo Sacer: Sovereign Power and Bare Life.* Translated by Daniel Heller-Roazen. Stanford: Stanford University Press, 1998.

Ahmed, Sara. "Animated Borders: Skin, Colour and Tanning." In *Vital Signs: Feminist Reconfigurations of the Bio/Logical Body*, edited by Margrit Shildrick and Janet Price, 45–65. Edinburgh: Edinburgh University Press, 1998.

A.I. Rising. Directed by Lazar Bodroža. Lions Gate Entertainment, 2018. DVD.

Air Doll. Directed by Hirokazu Koreeda. Engine Film, 2009. DVD.

Alaimo, Stacy. *Undomesticated Ground: Recasting Nature as Feminist Space.* Ithaca: Cornell University Press, 2000.

Alaimo, Stacy. "Trans-Corporeal Feminisms and the Ethical Space of Nature." In *Material Feminisms*, edited by Stacy Alaimo and Susan Hekman, 237–64. Bloomington: Indiana University Press, 2008.

Alaimo, Stacy. *Bodily Natures: Science, Environment, and the Material Self.* Indianapolis: Indiana University Press, 2010.

Alaimo, Stacy. *Exposed: Environmental Politics and Pleasures in Posthuman Times.* Minneapolis: University of Minnesota Press, 2016.

Alaimo, Stacy. "Material Feminism in the Anthropocene." In *A Feminist Companion to the Posthumanities*, edited by Cecilia Åsberg and Rosi Braidotti, 45–54. Cham, Switzerland: Springer, 2018.

Alaimo, Stacy, and Susan Hekman. "Introduction: Emerging Models of Materiality in Feminist Theory." In *Material Feminisms*, edited by Stacy Alaimo and Susan Hekman, 1–19. Bloomington: Indiana University Press, 2008.

Anable, Aubrey. *Playing With Feelings: Video Games and Affect.* Minneapolis: University of Minnesota Press, 2018.

Aniara. Directed by Pella Kågerman and Hugo Lija. Film Capital Stokcholm, 2018. DVD.

Annihilation. Directed by Alex Garland. Paramount Pictures, 2018. https://www.amazon.com/Annihilation-Natalie-Portman/dp/B079YYHM9Z.

Applegate, M. "Imagining the End of Late Capitalism in Shane Carruth's *Primer* and *Upstream Color.*" *Theory & Event* 19, issue 2 (2016). John Hopkins University Press, muse.jhu.edu/article/614363.

Arduini, Tina. "Cyborg Gamers: Exploring the Effects of Digital Gaming on Multimodal Composition." *Computers and Composition* 48, no. 1 (2018): 89–102.

Åsberg, Cecilia, and Rosi Braidotti, eds. "Feminist Posthumanities: An Introduction." In *A Feminist Companion to the Posthumanities*, edited by Cecilia Åsberg and Rosi Braidotti, 1–22. Cham, Switzerland: Springer, 2018a.

Åsberg, Cecilia, and Rosi Braidotti, eds. *A Feminist Companion to the Posthumanities*. Cham, Switzerland: Springer, 2018b.

Aster, Ari, and Jack Reynor. "Jack Reynor Wanted to Change Our Expectations of Horror Movies. So He Went Fully Nude." *Esquire*, Hearst Digital Media, July 3, 2019. www.esquire.com/entertainment/movies/a28262830/jack-reynor-ari-aster -midsommar-interview-nudity/.

Astle, Randy. "'Our Culture is in Our Language': Lisa Jackson on her VR Film *Biidaaban: First Light* and Indigenous Futurism." *Filmmaker*, July 23, 2018. https://filmmakermagazine.com/105184-our-culture-is-in-our-language-lisa -jackson-on-her-vr-film-biidaaban-first-light-and-indigenous-futurism/# .YpGAIBNBxAc

Atanarjuat: The Fast Runner. Directed by Zacharias Kunuk and Norman Cohn. Isuma-Igloolik, 2002. DVD.

Attebery, S. "Ecologies of Sound: Queer Intimacy, Trans-corporeality, and Reproduction in *Upstream Color*." In *Gender and Environment in Science Fiction*, edited by Brigitte Barclay and Christy Tidwell, 131–49. Lanham, Boulder, New York, and London: Lexington Books, 2019.

Backe, Hans-Joachim. "Within the Mainstream: An Ecocritical Framework for Digital Gam History." *Ecozone* 8, no. 2 (2017): 1–17.

Bakhtin, Mikhail. *Rabelais and His World*. Translated by Helene Iswolsky. Bloomington: Indiana University Press, 1984.

Balsom, Erika. "*High Life* Review: Claire Denis Probes the Outer Reaches of Human Taboos." *Sight and Sound*, June 2019.

Balsamo, Anne Marie. *Technologies of the Gendered Body: Reading Cyborg Women*. Durham: Duke University Press, 1996.

Barad, Karen. "Posthumanist Performativity: Toward an Understanding of How Matter Comes to Matter." *Signs: Journal of Women in Culture and Society* 28, no. 3 (2003): 801–31. https://pdfs.semanticscholar.org/3846/2c1ed106c55 ac6f4a2729ef639d9b4e83537.pdf?_ga=2.15125055.822278286.1594999801 -1514558440.1594999801

Barad, Karen. *Meeting the Universe Halfway: Quantum Physics and the Entanglement of Matter and Meaning*. Durham and London: Duke University Press, 2007.

Barad, Karen. "Invertebrate Visions: Diffractions of the Brittlestar." In *The Multispecies Salon*, edited by Eben Kirksey, 221–41. Durham: Duke University Press Books, 2014.

Bennett, Jane. *Vibrant Matter: A Political Ecology of Things*. Durham: Duke University Press, 2010.

Bennett, Tara. "*Annihilation* Director Alex Garland is OK If You Don't Understand His Movie." *Syfywire*, February 26, 2018. Available online: https://www.syfy .com/syfywire/annihilation-director-alex-garland-is-okay-if-you-dont-get-his -movie (accessed May 22, 2021).

Berardi, Franco "Bifo." *After the Future*. Chico: AK Press, 2011.

Berger, John. *Ways of Seeing*. London: Penguin, 2008.

Berlant, Lauren. "Intimacy: A Special Issue." *Critical Inquiry* 24, no. 2 (1998): 281–8. https://www.jstor.org/stable/1344169.

Berlant, Lauren. "A Properly Political Concept of Love: Three Approaches in Ten Pages." *Cultural Anthropology* 26, no. 4 (2011): 683–91. https://www.jstor.org/ stable/41336309.

Beugnet, Martine. *Claire Denis*. Manchester: Manchester University Press, 2004.

"Biidaaban: First Light." National Film Board of Canada, 2018. https://www.nfb .ca/interactive/biidaaban_first_light/.

BioWare. *Mass Effect*. Electronic Arts. Playstation 3, 2007.

BioWare. *Mass Effect 2*. Electronic Arts. Playstation 3, 2010.

BioWare. *Mass Effect 3*. Electronic Arts. Playstation 3, 2012.

Bishop, James. "Analysis: On FemShep's Popularity in *Mass Effect*." *Gamasutra*, September 8, 2010. https://www.gamasutra.com/view/news/120927/Analysis _On_FemSheps_Popularity_In_Mass_Effect.php.

Bittarello, Maria Beatrice. "Another Time, Another Space: Virtual Worlds, Myths and Imagination." *Journal of Virtual World Research* 1, no. 1 (2008): 1–18.

Blackstock, Cindy, and Pamela Palmater. "Canada's Government Needs to Face Up to its Role in Indigenous Children's Deaths." *The Guardian*, July 8, 2021. https://www.theguardian.com/commentisfree/2021/jul/08/canada-indigenous -children-deaths-residential-schools.

"Blade Runner - Awards." IMDb. https://www.imdb.com/title/tt0083658/awards/ (Accessed August 30, 2021).

Blade Runner 2049. Directed by Denis Villeneuve. Warner Bros. Entertainment, 2017. DVD.

Bordwell, David with Kristin Thompson. *Christopher Nolan: A Labyrinth of Linkages*, 2nd ed. Madison: Irvington Way Institute Press, 2019.

Bould, Mark. *Science Fiction*. Abingdon, Oxon: Routledge, 2012.

Boulter, Jonathan. *Parables of the Posthuman: Digital Realities, Gaming, and the Player Experience*. Detroit: Wayne State University Press, 2015.

Boyan, Andy, Matthew Grizzard, and Nicholas Bowman. "A Massively Moral Game? *Mass Effect* as a Case Study to Understand the Influence Of Players' Moral Intuitions on Adherence to Hero or Antihero Play Styles." *Journal of Gaming & Virtual Worlds* 7, no. 1 (2015): 41–57.

Braidotti, Rosi. *Nomadic Subjects: Embodiment and Sexual Difference in Contemporary Feminist Theory*. New York: Columbia University Press, 1994.

Braidotti, Rosi. "'Signs of Wonder and Traces of Doubt: On Teratology and Embodied Differences.'" In *Feminist Theory and the Body: A Reader*, edited by Janet Price and Margarit Shildrick, 290–301. New York and London: Routledge, 1999.

Braidotti, Rosi. "A Critical Cartography of Feminist Post-postmodernism." *Australian Feminist Studies* 20, no. 47 (2005): 169–80. Routledge. https://doi .org/10.1080/08164640500090319.

Braidotti, Rosi. "Posthuman, All Too Human: Towards a New Process Ontology." *Theory, Culture & Society* 23, no. 7–8 (2006): 197–208. https://doi.org/10.1177 /0263276406069232.

Braidotti, Rosi. "Feminist Epistemology after Postmodernism: Critiquing Science, Technology, and Globalisation." *Interdisciplinary Science Reviews* 32, no. 1 (2007): 65–74.

Braidotti, Rosi. *The Posthuman*. Cambridge and Malden: Polity, 2013.

Braidotti, Rosi. "Metamorphic Others and Nomadic Subjects." *Artmap*, 2014. Oliver Laric: November 22, 2014–January 17, 2015. https://artmap.com/ tanyaleighton/exhibition/oliver-laric-2014.

Braidotti, Rosi. "The Critical Posthumanities; or, Is Medianatures to Naturecultures as *Zoe* is to *Bios*?" *Cultural Politics* 12, issue 3 (2016): 380–90. Duke University Press. DOI:10.1215/17432197-3648930.

Braidotti, Rosi. "Posthuman Critical Theory." In *Critical Posthumanism and Planetary Futures*, edited by Debashish Banerji and Makarand R. Paranjape, 13–32. India: Springer, 2016. https://doi.org/10.1007/978-81-322-3637-5.

Braidotti, Rosi. "Posthuman Feminist Theory." In *The Oxford Handbook of Feminist Theory*, edited by Lisa Disch and Mary Hawkesworth, 673–98. Oxford: Oxford University Press, 2016.

Braidotti, Rosi. "Four Theses on Posthuman Feminism." In *Anthropocene Feminism*, edited by Richard Grusin, 21–48. Minneapolis: University of Minnesota Press, 2017.

Braidotti, Rosi. "A Theoretical Framework for the Critical Posthumanities." *Theory, Culture & Society* 6, issue 6 (2018): 31–61. SAGE Publications, May 4. https://doi.org/10.1177/0263276418771486.

Braidotti, Rosi. *Posthuman Feminism*. Cambridge: Cambridge: Polity Press, 2022.

Briggs, John. *Fractals: The Patterns of Chaos: A New Aesthetic of Art, Science, and Nature*. New York: Touchstone, 1992.

Bristow, Joseph. *Sexuality*. London: Routledge, 2011.

Brown, P. Saxton. "The Garden in the Machine: Video Games and Environmental Consciousness." *Philological Quarterly* 93, no. 3 (2014): 383–407.

Bukatman, Scott. *Matters of Gravity: Special Effects and Supermen in the 20th Century*. Durham: Duke University Press, 2003.

Campbell, Norah, and Mike Saren. "The Primitive, Technology and Horror: A Posthuman Biology." *Ephemera* 10, no. 2 (2010): 152–76.

Canavan, Gerry. "Introduction: If This Goes On." In *Green Planets: Ecology and Science Fiction*, edited by Gerry Canavan and Kim Stanley Robinson, 1–24. Middletown, CT: Wesleyan University Press, 2014.

Canguilhem, Georges, and Therese Jaeger. "Monstrosity and the Monstrous." *Diogenes* 10, no. 40 (1962): 27–42. https://doi.org/10.1177/039219216201004002.

Carbone, Marco Benoit, and Paolo Ruffino. "Apocalypse Postponed: Discourses on Video Games from Noxious Objects to Redemptive Devices." *GAME* 1, no. 1 (2018): 27–37.

Carbonell, C. D., M. Hauskeller, and T. D. Phillbeck. *The Palgrave Handbook of Posthumanism in Film and Television*. London: Palgrave Macmillan, 2015.

Cauchi, Mark. "The Death of God and the Genesis of Worldhood in von Trier's *Melancholia*." In *Immanent Frames: Postsecular Cinema Between Malick and von Trier*, edited by John Caruana and Mark Cauchi, 105–28. Albany: State University of New York Press, 2018.

Chang, Alenda Y. *Playing Nature: Ecology in Video Games*. Minneapolis: University of Minnesota Press, 2019.

Chang, Justin. "Review: Natalie Portman Braves the Scary, Enveloping Sci-fi Perils of 'Annihilation.'" *Los Angeles Times*, February 21, 2018. Available online: https://www.latimes.com/entertainment/movies/la-et-mn-annihilation-review-20180221-story.html (accessed May 22, 2021).

Chiang, Ted. *Stories of Your Life and Others*. New York: Vintage Books, 2002.

Frampton, Daniel. *Filmosophy*. London: Wallflower Press, 2006.

Frantzen, Mikkel Krause. *Going Nowhere, Slow: The Aesthetics and Politics of Depression*. Alresford: John Hunt Publishing, 2019.

Freud, Sigmund *The Uncanny*. Translated by David Mclintock. London: Penguin Books, 2003.

Galloway, Alexander R. *Gaming: Essays on Algorithmic Culture*. Minneapolis: University of Minnesota Press, 2006.

Gan, Elaine, and Nils Bubandt. *M25–M50*. Minneapolis: University of Minnesota Press, 2017.

Garland, Alex, and Kevin Vlk. "Annihilation | Alex Garland | Talks at Google." *Talks at Google*, YouTube Video, 30:27, February 22, 2018. https://www .youtube.com/watch?v=w5i7idoijco.

GCD. "Creating the Art of ABZÛ." YouTube Video, 27:02. September 22, 2017. https://www.youtube.com/watch?v=l9NX06mvp2E.

Geraci, Robert M. *Virtually Sacred: Myth and Meaning in World of Warcraft and Second Life*. Oxford: Oxford University Press, 2014.

Geraghty, Lincoln. "Love's Fantastic Voyage: Crossing between Science Fiction and Romantic Comedy in Innerspace." *Extrapolation* (Pre-2012) 47, no. 1 (2006): 123–33. https://doi.org/10.3828/extr.2006.47.1.12.

Giant Squid Studios. *Abzû*. 505 Games. Nintendo Switch, 2016.

Giralt, Gabriel. "Dogme 95 and the Reality of Fiction." *Kinema: A Journal for Film and Audiovisual Media* (Fall 2003), 1–6. https://openjournals.uwaterloo.ca/ index.php/kinema/issue/view/285.

Gomel, Elena. "Posthuman Voices: Alien Infestation and the Poetics of Subjectivity." *Science-Fiction Studies* 39, no. 2 (2012): 177–94. https://doi.org/10.5621/ sciefictstud.39.2.0.0177.

González, Jennifer. "Envisioning Cyborg Bodies: Notes from Current Research." In *Cybersexualities: A Reader in Feminist Theory, Cyborgs and Cyberspace*, edited by Jenny Wolmark, 264–79. Edinburgh: Edinburgh University Press, 1999.

Gorber, Jason. "*Night Raiders*: Danis Goulet on Crafting a Distinct Dystopian Vision." Toronto Film Critics Association, February 28, 2022. https://torontofilmcritics.com/ features/night-raiders-danis-goulet-on-crafting-a-distinct-dystopian-vision/.

Graham, Elaine L. *Representations of the Post/Human: Monsters, Aliens and Others in Popular Culture*. New Brunswick: Rutgers University Press, 2002.

"Green-Skinned Space Babe." TVtropes. https://tvtropes.org/pmwiki/pmwiki.php/ Main/GreenSkinnedSpaceBabe.

Groes, Sebastian, ed. *Memory in the Twentieth-Century: New Perspectives from the Arts, Humanities, and Sciences*. New York: Palgrave Macmillan, 2016.

Grosz, E. *Jacques Lacan: A Feminist Introduction*. Oxfordshire: Routledge, 1990.

Grosz, E. *Volatile Bodies: Toward a Corporeal Feminism*. Oxfordshire: Routledge, 1994.

Guardians of the Galaxy. Directed by James Gunn. Marvel Studios, 2014. DVD.

Guerilla Games. *Horizon: Zero Dawn*. Sony Interactive Entertainment. PlayStation 4. 2017.

Hamblin, Sarah, and Hugh C. O'Connell. "Legacies of Blade Runner." *Science Fiction Film and Television* 13, no. 1 (2020): 1–14.

Hanich, Julian. *Cinematic Emotion in Horror Films and Thrillers: The Aesthetic Paradox of Pleasurable Fear*. New York: Routledge, 2010.

Haraway, Donna. "Situated Knowledges: The Science Question in Feminism and the Privilege of Partial Perspective." *Feminist Studies* 14, no. 3 (1988): 575–99. https://doi.org/10.2307/3178066.

Haraway, Donna. *Simians, Cyborgs and Women: The Reinvention of Nature*. New York: Routledge, 1991.

Haraway, Donna. "Promises of Monsters: A Regenerative Politics for Inappropriate/d Others." In *Cultural Studies*, edited by Lawrence Grossberg, Cary Nelson, and Paula A. Treichler, 295–337. New York: Routledge, 1992.

Haraway, Donna. *The Companion Species Manifesto: Dogs, People, and Significant Otherness*, vol. 1. Chicago: Prickly Paradigm Press, 2003.

Haraway, Donna. *The Haraway Reader*. New York and London: Routledge, 2004.

Haraway, Donna. "A Cyborg Manifesto: Science, Technology, and Socialist-Feminism in the Late Twentieth Century." In *The International Handbook of Virtual Learning Environments*, 117–58. Dordrecht: Springer, 2006.

Haraway, Donna. *Staying with the Trouble: Making Kin in the Chthulucene*. Durham: Duke University Press, 2016.

Haraway, Donna. "A Cyborg Manifesto: Science, Technology, and Socialist-Feminism in the Late Twentieth Century." In *Manifestly Haraway*, 3–90. Minneapolis: University of Minnesota Press, 2017.

Haraway, Donna. "Symbiogenesis, Sympoiesis, and Art Science Activisms for Staying with the Trouble." In *Arts of Living on a Damaged Planet*, edited by Anna Tsing and Heather Swanson. Minneapolis: University of Minnesota Press, 2017, 25–50.

Haraway, Donna. "The Promises of Monsters: A Regenerative Politics for Inappropriate/d Others." In *The Monster Theory Reader*, edited by Jeffrey Andrew Weinstock, 459–521. Minneapolis and London: University of Minnesota Press, 2020.

Harvey, Alison, and Stephanie Fisher. "'Everyone Can Make Games!': The Post-Feminist Context of Women in Digital Game Production." *Feminist Media Studies* 15, no. 4 (2014): 576–92. https://doi.org/10.1080/14680777.2014 .958867.

Hauskeller, Michael, Thomas D. Philbeck, and Curtis D. Carbonell. "Posthumanism in Film and Television." In *The Palgrave Handbook of Posthumanism in Film and Television*, 1–7. London: Springer, 2016.

Hayles, N. Katherine. *How We Became Posthuman: Virtual Bodies in Cybernetics, Literature, and Informatics*. Chicago: University of Chicago Press, 1999.

Hayles, N. Katherine. "Traumas of Code." In *Critical Digital Studies: A Reader*, edited by Arthur and Marilouise Kroker, 25–44. Toronto: University of Toronto Press, 2008.

Hayles, N. Katherine. *Unthought: The Power of the Cognitive Nonconscious*. Chicago: Chicago University Press, 2017.

Hearne, Joanna. *Smoke Signals Native Cinema Rising*. Lincoln: University of Nebraska Press, 2012.

Heaven, Dan. "'The Future Starts with an Image': Wanuri Kahiu's *Pumzi* (2009)." *Alluvium*, June 4, 2021. https://www.alluvium-journal.org/2021/06/04/the -future-starts-with-an-image-wanuri-kahius-pumzi-2009/.

Henderson, P. "The Sun Never Set on the Human Empire: Haunts of Humanism in the *Planet of the Apes* Films." In *The Palgrave Handbook of Posthumanism in Film and Television*, edited by Curtis D. Carbonell, Michael Hauskeller, and Thomas D. Philbeck, 321–9. Palgrave Macmillan, 2015.

Her. Directed by Spike Jonze. Warner Bros. Entertainment, 2014. DVD.

Herbrechter, S. "Critical Posthumanism." *Critical Posthumanism: Genealogy of the Posthuman*, 2017. https://criticalposthumanism.net/critical-posthumanism/#:~ :text=Critical%20posthumanism%20is%20a%20theoretical,%2C%20ghosts %2C%20angels%20etc.

Herbrechter, S. "Critical Posthumanism." In *Posthuman Glossary*, edited by Rosi Braidotti and Maria Hlavajova, 94–6. London: Bloomsbury Academic, 2018.

High Life. Directed by Denis, Claire. Alcatraz Films, 2018. DVD.

Hiller, Brenna. "Loving FemShep: BioWare's First Lady Finally Steps Forward." *VG24/7*, 2011. https://www.vg247.com/2011/07/19/loving-femshep-biowares -first-lady-finally-steps-forward/.

Hole, Kristin Lené. *Towards a Feminist Cinematic Ethics: Claire Denis, Emmanuel Levinas and Jean-Luc Nancy*. Edinburgh: Edinburgh University Press, 2016.

Höler, Sabine. "'The Real Problem of a Spaceship Is Its People': Spaceship Earth as Ecological Science Fiction." In *Green Planets: Ecology and Science Fiction*, edited by Gerry Canavan and Kim Stanley Robinson, 99–114. Middletown: Wesleyan University Press, 2014.

Horn, Eva. *The Future as Catastrophe: Imagining Disaster in the Modern Age*. Translated by Valentine Pakis. New York: Columbia University Press, 2018.

Iovino, Serenella. "Posthumanism in Literature and Ecocriticism." *Relations Beyond Anthropocentrism* 4, no. 1 (2016): 11–20.

Iovino, Serenella, and Serpil Oppermann. "Material Ecocriticism: Materiality, Agency, and Models of Narrativity." *Ecozon European Journal of Literature Culture and Environment* 3, no. 1 (2012). https://doi.org/10.37536/ECOZONA .2012.3.1.452.

Irigaray, Luce. *I Love to You: Sketch for a Felicity within History*. Translated by Alison Martin. New York and London: Routledge, 1996.

Irigaray, Luce. *To be Two*. Translated by Monique M. Rhodes and Marco F. Cocito-Monoc. New York: Routledge, 2001.

Irigaray, Luce. *The Way of Love*. Translated by Heidi Bostic and Stephen Pluhacek. London: Continuum, 2002.

Irigaray, Luce. *In the Beginning, She Was*. Translated by Stephen Pluhacek. London: Bloomsbury, 2013.

Ivanchikova, Alla. "Machinic Intimacies and Mechanical Brides: Collectivity between Prosthesis and Surrogacy in Jonathan Mostow's *Surrogates* and Spike Jonze's *Her*." *Camera Obscura: Feminism, Culture, and Media Studies* 31 (2016): 65–91.

Jackson, Lisa, dir. *Biidaaban: First Light*. National Film Board of Canada. 8 min, 2018. http://lisajackson.ca/Biidaaban-First-Light-VR.

Jagoe, Eva-Lynn. "Depersonalized Intimacy: The Cases of Sherry Turkle and Spike Jonze." *ESC: English Studies in Canada* 42, no. 1 (2016): 155–73. DOI: 10.1353/esc.2016.0004.

Jameson, Fredric. "Progress versus Utopia; Or, Can We Imagine the Future?" *Science Fiction Studies* 9, no. 2 (1982): 147–58.

Jeffers McDonald, Tamar. *Romantic Comedy: Boy Meets Girl Meets Genre*. London and New York: Wallflower Press, 2007.

John, Tracey. "The Thoughts Behind Miranda's Behind In Mass Effect 2." *Kotaku*, 2010. https://www.kotaku.com.au/2010/04/the-thoughts-behind-mirandas -behind-in-mass-effect-2/.

Jollimore, Troy. "'This Endless Space between the Words': The Limits of Love in Spike Jonze's Her." *Midwest Studies in Philosophy* 39, no. 1 (2015): 120–43.

"Jurassic Park." IMDb. http://www.imdb.com/title/tt0107290/awards/ (Accessed August 30, 2021).

Jurassic World: Fallen Kingdom. Directed by J. A. Bayona. Universal Pictures, 2018. DVD.

Juul, Jesper. *Half-Real: Video Games Between Real Rules and Fictional Worlds.* Cambridge, MA: MIT Press, 2005.

Kahiu, Wanuri. "Afrofuturism in Popular Culture." TedxNairobi, 2012. https:// www.youtube.com/watch?v=PvxOLVaV2YY.

Kara, Selma. "Anthropocenema: Cinema in the Age of Mass Extinction." In *Post-Cinema: Theorizing 21st Century Film*, edited by Shane Denson and Julia Leyda, 750–84. Falmer: REFRAME Books, 2016.

Kareem, Soha. "Mashing Our Buttons: On Romance and Sex in Video Games." In *The Secret Loves of Geek Girls*, edited by Hope Nicholson, Expanded ed., 119–23. Milwaukee: Dark Horse Books, 2016.

Keller, Sarah. "The Exquisite Apocalypse." In *Anxious Cinephilia: Pleasure and Peril at the Movies*, 181–224. Columbia University Press, 2020.

Khurana, A. K. *Theory and Practice of Optics and Refraction*, 2nd ed. Noida: Elsevier, 2008.

Kickasola, J. G. "Leading with the Ear: *Upstream Color* and the Cinema of Respiration." *Film Quarterly* 66, issue 4 (2013): 60–74. Berkeley. DOI: 10.1525/fq.2013.66.4.60.

King, Geoff. *Film Comedy*. London and New York: Wallflower Press, 2002.

King, Tiffany Lethabo. *The Black Shoals: Offshore Formations of Black and Native Studies*. Durham: Duke University Press, 2019.

Knight, Chris. "Danis Goulet's Film a First for New Zealand-Canada Indigenous Co-operation." *National Post*. June 26, 2020. https://nationalpost.com/entertainment/ movies/danis-goulets-film-a-first-for-new-zealand-canada-indigenous-co-operation.

Kohn, Eric. "'Annihilation' Review: Natalie Portman Stars in a Stunning Sci-Fi Thriller from the Director of 'Ex Machina.'" *Indiewire*, February 21, 2018. Available online: https://www.indiewire.com/2018/02/annihilation-review -natalie-portman-alex-garland-1201930892/ (accessed May 22, 2021).

Kollig, Danielle Verena. "Filming the World's End. Images of the Apocalypse in Lars Von Trier's *Epidemic* and Melancholia/Rodar el fin del mundo: Imágenes del apocalypsis en *Epidemia y Melancolía*, de Lars Von Trier." *Amaltea. Revista de mitocritica* 5 (2013): 85–102.

Kornhaber, Donna. "From Posthuman to Postcinema: Crises of Subjecthood and Representation in *Her*." *Cinema Journal* 56, no. 4 (2017): 3–25. DOI: 10.1353/ cj.2017.0038.

Kristeva, Julia. *Powers of Horror: An Essay on Abjection*. Translated by Leon S. Roudiez. New York: Columbia University Press, 1982.

Kuhn, A. *Alien Zone II*. London and New York: Verso, 1999.

Kurzweil, Ray. *The Singularity Is Near: When Humans Transcend Biology*. New York: Viking, 2005.

Lacan, Jacques. *Seminar XX (On Feminine Sexuality, The Limits of Love and Knowledge: Encore)*. Translated by Bruce Fink. New York: Norton, 1999.

Lan, Kuo Wei. "Technofetishism of Posthuman Bodies: Representations of Cyborgs, Ghosts, and Monsters in Contemporary Japanese Science Fiction Film and Animation." PhD diss., University of Sussex, 2012. http://sro.sussex.ac.uk/id/eprint/40524/.

Lange, Amanda. "'You're Just Gonna Be Nice': How Players Engage with Moral Choice Systems." *Journal of Games Criticism* 1, no. 1 (2014): 1–16.

Lars and the Real Girl. Directed by Craig Gillespie. MGM, 2007. DVD.

Lavigne, Carlen. "'She's a Soldier, not a Model': Feminism, FemShep and the *Mass Effect 3* vote." *Journal of Gaming & Virtual Worlds* 7, no. 3 (2015): 317–29. https://doi-org.ezproxy.lib.ryerson.ca/10.1386/jgvw.7.3.317_1.

Le Saux, Yannick. "Eye Piece: DP Yorick Le Saux Mixed Digital With 35MM and Heavy Prep With On-Set Improvisation To Shoot *High Life*." MovieMaker.com, February 20, 2021. https://www.moviemaker.com/eye-piece-high-life-dp-yorick-le-saux/. (Accessed May 16, 2022).

Lee, Benjamin. "*Annihilation* Review—Natalie Portman Thriller Leaves a Haunting Impression." *The Guardian*, February 21, 2018. Available online: https://www.theguardian.com/film/2018/feb/22/annihilation-review-natalie-portman-thriller-leaves-a-haunting-impression (accessed May 22, 2021).

Levinas, Emmanuel. *Totality and Infinity*. Translated by Alphonso Lingis. Pennsylvania: Duquesne University Press, 1969.

Lidchi, Henrietta, and Suzanne Newman Fricke. "Future History: Indigenous Futurisms in North American Visual Arts." *World Art* 9, no. 2 (2019): 99–102. DOI: 10.1080/21500894.2019.1627675.

Lima, Leandro Augusto Borges. "Configurative Dynamics of Gender in Bioware's Marketing for the Mass Effect Franchise." *Kinephanos* 7, no. 1 (2017): 165–97. https://www.kinephanos.ca/2017/configurative-dynamics-of-gender-in-biowares-marketing-for-the-mass-effect-franchise/.

"Lisa Jackson's *Biidaaban: First Light*." CBC Arts (2018). https://www.cbc.ca/player/play/1323281475810.

Longfellow, Brenda. "Indigenous Futurism and the Immersive Worlding of *Inherent Rights/Vision Rights*, 2167 and *Biidaaban: First Light*." August 30, 2019. https://methodsandresearch.files.wordpress.com/2019/08/indigenous-futurism-and-immersive-worlding-1.pdf.

Lousley, Cheryl. "Ecocriticism and the Politics of Representation." In *The Oxford Handbook of Ecocriticism*, edited by Greg Garrard, 155–71. Oxford: Oxford University Press, 2014.

Lykke, Nina. *Vibrant Death: A Posthuman Phenomenology of Mourning*. New York: Bloomsbury Publishing, 2022.

MacCormack, Patricia. *The Ahuman Manifesto: Activism for the End of the Anthropocene*. New York: Bloomsbury Publishing, 2020.

Mandelbrot, Benoit B. *The Fractal Geometry of Nature*. New York: W. H. Freeman and Company, 1977.

Marche, Stephen. "Canada's Impossible Acknowledgement." *The New Yorker*, September 7, 2017. https://www.newyorker.com/culture/culture-desk/canadas-impossible-acknowledgment.

Marks, Laura U. "Thinking Multisensory Cinema." *Paragraph* 31, no. 2 (July 2008): 123–37. http://www.jstor.org/stable/43151879.

Marshall, Dave, ed. *The Art of the Mass Effect Universe*. Milwaukie: Dark Horse Comics, 2012.

Marshall, L. "*Upstream Color*: Nature, Love, Survival." *Queen's Quarterly* 120, issue 3 (2013), Queen's Quarterly. https://link.gale.com/apps/doc/A347408434/LitRC?u=queensulaw&sid=LitRC&xid=28df8f5a.

Mass Effect 2 Collectors' Edition Art Book. Roseville: Prima Games, 2010.

Massumi, Brian. "The Autonomy of Affect." Parables for the Virtual: Movement, Affect, Sensation, 23–34. Durham, N.C.: Duke University Press, 2002.

Maurice, Alice. "'Use your White Voice': Race, Sound, and Genre in *Sorry to Bother You*." *New Review of Film and Television Studies* 21, no. 1 (2022): 88–100.

Mayward, J. "Parabolic Transcendence in Time and Narrative: Shane Carruth's *Primer* (US 2004) and *Upstream Color* (US 2013) as Post-Secular Sci-Fi Parables." *Journal for Religion, Film and Media* 6, no. 1 (2020): 17–36. University of Graz. https://doi.org/10.25364/05.06:2020.1.2.

McGowan, Todd. "Looking for the Gaze: Lacanian Film Theory and Its Vicissitudes." *Cinema Journal* 42, no. 3 (2003): 27–47.

McMurry, Andrew. "Media Moralia: Reflections on Damaged Environments and Digital Life." In *The Oxford Handbook of Ecocriticism*, edited by Greg Garrard, 487–501. Oxford: Oxford University Press, 2014.

McRae, Andrew. "Life in State-Run Boys' Homes: 'These were Cells . . . All You Could Hear was the Screams.'" *Radio New Zealand*, May 3, 2021. https://www.rnz.co.nz/news/national/441709/life-in-state-run-boys-homes-these-were-cells-all-you-could-hear-was-the-screams.

Melancholia. Directed by Lars von Trier. Zentropa Entertainments, 2011. DVD.

Melzer, Patricia. *Alien Constructions: Science Fiction and Feminist Thought*. Austin: Texas University Press, 2006.

Mendlesohn, Farah. "Introduction: Reading Science Fiction." In *The Cambridge Companion to Science Fiction*, edited by Edward James and Farah Mendlesohn, 1–12. Cambridge: Cambridge University Press, 2003.

Merchant, Carolyn. *Ecological Revolutions: Nature, Gender, and Science in New England*. Chapel Hill: University of North Carolina Press, 1989.

Merriam-Webster. "Annihilation." n.d. Available online: https://www.merriam-webster.com/dictionary/annihilation#related-phrases (accessed July 20, 2022).

Meyer, Angela, Amelie Cserer, and Markus Schmidt. "Frankenstein 2.0.: Identifying and Characterising Synthetic Biology Engineers in Science Fiction Films." *Life Sciences, Society and Policy* 9, no. 1 (2013): 1–17.

Midsommar. Directed by Ari Aster. A24, 2019. https://www.showtime.com/movie/3474663?i_cid=int-default-1004&r=s&o_cid=19969182313_19947259571_19942911399_holdback.

Miles, Margaret. "Carnal Abominations: The Female Body as Grotesque." In *The Grotesque in Art and Literature: Theological Reflections*, edited by James Luther Adams and Wilson Yates, 83–112. Grand Rapids: Eerdmans, 1997.

Mirzoeff, Nicholas. "On Visuality." *Journal of Visual Culture* 5, no. 1 (2006): 53–79.

Mitchell, David T., and Sharon L. Snyder. *Narrative Prosthesis: Disability and the Dependencies of Discourse*. Ann Arbor: University of Michigan Press, 2000.

Molloy, Missy, Pansy Duncan, and Claire Henry. *Screening the Posthuman*. Oxford: Oxford University Press, 2023.

Morton, Timothy. *Hyperobjects: Philosophy and Ecology after the End of the World*. Minneapolis: University of Minnesota Press, 2013.

MPC Film & Episodic. MPC *Blade Runner 2049* VFX Breakdown, 2018. https://www.youtube.com/watch?v=x8ZnqCKZABY.

Mulvey, Laura. "Visual Pleasure and Narrative Cinema." *Screen* 16, no. 3 (1975): 6–18.

Munkittrick, Kyle. "Why Mass Effect is the Most Important Science Fiction Universe of Our Generation." *Pop Bioethics*, 2012. http://www.bioethics.net/2012/02/why-mass-effect-is-the-most-important-science-fiction-universe-of-our-generation/.

Muru-Lanning, Charlotte. "Chelsea Winstanley and Ainsley Gardiner on *Night Raiders* and Indigenous Storytelling." *The Spinoff*. March 23, 2022. https://thespinoff.co.nz/atea/23-03-2022/chelsea-winstanley-and-ainsley-gardiner-on-night-raiders-and-indigenous-storytelling.

Nayar, Pramod K. *Posthumanism*. Cambridge: Polity, 2014.

Ndalianis, Angela. *The Horror Sensorium. Media and the Senses*. Jefferson: McFarland, 2012.

Neale, Steve, and Frank Krutnik. *Popular Film and Television Comedy*. London and New York: Routledge, 1990.

Neimanis, Astrid, and Rachel Loewen Walker. "*Weathering*: Climate Change and the 'Thick Time' of Transcorporeality." *Hypatia* 29, no. 3 (2014): 558–75.

Nguyen, Josef. "Digital Games about the Materiality of Digital Games." *Ecozone* 8, no. 2 (2017): 18–38.

Night Raiders. Directed by Danis Goulet. Alcina Picture, 2021. DVD.

Ogoyo, Acee. "'The Elizabeth Warren of the sci-fi set': Author Faces Criticism for Repeated Use of Tribal Traditions." *Indianz.com*, June 24, 2020. https://www.indianz.com/News/2020/06/24/the-elizabeth-warren-of-the-scifi-set-au.asp.

Oppermann, Serpil. "Feminist Ecocriticism: A Posthumanist Direction in Ecocritical Trajectory." In *International Perspectives in Feminist Ecocriticism*, edited by Greta Gaard, Simon C. Estok, and Serpil Oppermann, 19–36. New York: Routledge, 2013.

Oppermann, Serpil. "From Material to Posthuman Ecocriticism: Hybridity, Stories, Natures." In *Handbook of Ecocriticism and Cultural Ecology*, edited by Hubert Zapf and De Gruyter, 273–94. Berlin: De Gruyter, 2016.

Parker-Flynn, Christina. "Joe and the 'Real' Girls: *Blade Runner 2049*." *Gender Forum*, no. 66 (2017): 69–74.

Parrinder, Patrick. *Learning from Other Worlds: Estrangement, Cognition, and the Politics of Science Fiction and Utopia*. Liverpool: Liverpool University Press, 2000.

Paveck, Hannah. "No Other Voice: Claire Denis's 'High Life.'" *Another Gaze*, May 27, 2019. https://www.anothergaze.com/no-voice-claire-deniss-high-life-feminism/.

Peperell, Robert. "Neuroscience and Posthuman Memory." In *Memory in the Twentieth-Century: New Perspectives from the Arts, Humanities, and Sciences*, edited by Sebastian Groes, 330–3. New York: Palgrave Macmillan, 2016.

Plantinga, Carl. *Moving Viewers. American Film and the Spectator's Experience*. Berkeley: University of California Press, 2009.

Plumwood, Val. *Feminism and the Mastery of Nature*. London and New York: Routledge, 1993.

Powell, Anna. *Deleuze, Altered States and Film*. Edinburgh: Edinburgh University Press, 2007.

Price, Janet, and Margarit Shildrick. *Feminist Theory and the Body: A Reader*. New York and London: Routledge, 1999.

Pumzi. Directed by Wanuri Kahiu. Focus Features, 2009. DVD.

Raheja, Michelle H. *Reservation Reelism: Refacing, Visual Sovereignty, and Representations of Native Americans in Film*. Lincoln: University of Nebraska Press, 2011.

Rains, Haley. "I Am Who I Say I Am: Reclaiming Native American Identity through Visual Sovereignty." *Imagining America*, September 28, 2021. https://imaginingamerica.org/i-am-who-i-say-i-am-reclaiming-native-american-identity-through-visual-sovereignty/.

Ramírez, J. Jesse. *Against Automation Mythologies: Business Science Fiction and the Ruse of the Robots*. New York: Routledge, 2020.

Rhee, Jennifer. *The Robotic Imaginary: The Human and the Price of Dehumanized Labor*. Minneapolis: University of Minnesota Press, 2018.

Riesman, Abraham. "How *Annihilation* Designed Its Unnatural Horrors." *Vulture*, February 23, 2018. Available online: https://www.vulture.com/2018/02/how-the-annihilation-bear-and-other-horrors-were-designed.html (accessed May 22, 2021).

Rivera-Dundas, Adena. "Ecocritical Engagement in a Pixelated World." *Ecozone* 8, no. 2 (2017): 121–35.

Roanhorse, Rebecca, Elizabeth LaPensee, Johnnie Jay, and Darcie Little Badger. "Decolonizing Science Fiction and Imagining Futures: An Indigenous Futurisms Round Table." *Strange Horizons*, January 30, 2017. http://strangehorizons.com/non-fiction/articles/decolonizing-science-fiction-and-imagining-futures-an-indigenous-futurisms-roundtable/.

Robinson, I. "The Critical Cinematic Cartography of *My Winnipeg*." *Canadian Journal of Film Studies* 23, no. 2 (2014): 96–143. Toronto: University of Toronto Press.

Russo, Mary. *The Female Grotesque. Risk, Excess and Modernity*. New York: Routledge, 1994.

Rutsky, R. L. "Mutation, History, and Fantasy in the Posthuman." *Subject Matters: A Journal of Communication and the Self* 3, no. 2 and 4, no. 1 (2007): 99–112.

Schindel, Dan. "Claire Denis on Black Holes, Olafur Eliasson, and the Making of *High Life*." *Hyperallergic*, April 16, 2019. http://hyperallergic.com/495099/claire-denis-on-black-holes-olafur-eliasson-and-the-making-of-high-life/.

Sharf, Zack. "'Annihilation' Draws Comparisons to Kubrick, Aronofsky, Cronenberg, Tarkovsky, and More in Rave Reviews." *Indiewire*, February 21, 2018. Available online: https://www.indiewire.com/2018/02/annihilation-critics-stanley-kubrick-aronofsky-cronenberg-1201931113/ (accessed May 22, 2021).

Shaviro, Steven. "MELANCHOLIA, or, The Romantic Anti-Sublime." *SEQUENCE*, 1.1 (2012).

Shechtman, Anna. "What's Missing from *Her*." *Slate*, January 3, 2014. https://slate.com/culture/2014/01/her-movie-by-spike-jonze-with-joaquin-phoenix-and-scarlett-johansson-lacks-a-real-woman.html.

Shildrick, Margrit. *Embodying the Monster: Encounters with the Vulnerable Self.* London: Sage, 2001.

Shildrick, Margrit. "Monstering the (M)Other." In *Embodying the Monster: Encounters with the Vulnerable Self*, 28–47. London: Sage, 2002.

Shildrick, Margrit. "Why Should Our Bodies End at the Skin?: Embodiment, Boundaries, and Somatechnics." *Hypatia* 30, no. 1 (2015): 13–29. Cambridge University Press.

Shildrick, Margrit, and J. Price. *Vital Signs: Feminist Reconfigurations of the Bio/logical Body.* Edinburgh: Edinburgh University Press, 1998.

Siemienoqicz, Rochelle. "*Coming Home in the Dark*—Director James Ashcroft Talks Tension on a Budget." *Screen Hub*, September 10, 2021. https://www.screenhub.com.au/news/features/james-ashcroft-on-making-nz-thriller-coming-home-in-the-dark-1472580/.

Sims, David. "The Artistic Chemistry of Robert Pattinson and Claire Denis." *The Atlantic*, April 10, 2019. https://www.theatlantic.com/entertainment/archive/2019/04/robert-pattinson-and-claire-denis-talk-high-life-artistic-collaboration/586768/.

Sinnerbrink, Robert. *New Philosophies of Film: Thinking Images.* New York: Continuum, 2011a.

Sinnerbrink, Robert. ("Re-enfranchising Film: Toward a Romantic Film-Philosophy." In H. Carel and G. Tuck, *New Takes on Film Philosophy*, edited by Havi Carel and Greg Tuck, 25–47. London: Palgrave Macmillan, 2011b.

Sinnerbrink, Robert. "Cinematic Belief." *Angelaki* 17, no. 4 (2012): 95–117. DOI:10.1080/0969725X.2012.747332.

Sinnerbrink, Robert. "Anatomy of *Melancholia*." *Angelaki* 19, no. 4 (2014): 111–26.

Sinnerbrink, Robert. "Two Ways through Life: Postsecular Visions in *Melancholia* and *The Tree of Life*." In *Immanent Frames: Postsecular Cinema Between Malick and von Trier*, edited by John Caruana and Mark Cauchi, 29–46. Albany: State University of New York Press, 2018.

Smelik, Anneke. "Film." In *The Cambridge Companion to Literature and the Posthuman*, edited by Bruce Clarke and Manuela Rossini, 109–20. Cambridge: Cambridge University Press, 2017. https://doi.org/10.1017/9781316091227.

Snowpiercer. Directed by Bong, Joon-ho. Anchor Bay Entertainment, 2013. https://vuw.etv.org.nz/tv/vod/view/130432.

Sobchack, Vivian. "The Virginity of Astronauts: Sex and the Science Fiction Film." In *Alien Zone: Cultural Theory and Contemporary Science Fiction Cinema*, edited by Annette Kuhn, 103–15. London: Verso, 1990.

Sobchack, Vivian. "Love Machines: Boy Toys, Toy Boys and the Oxymorons of *A.I.: Artificial Intelligence*." *Science Fiction Film and Television* 1, no. 1 (2008): 1–13. https://doi.org/10.3828/sfftv.1.1.2.

Sontag, S. "The Imagination of Disaster." *Commentary Magazine*, no. 65 (1965): 42–8. Commentary Inc, New York. https://americanfuturesiup.files.wordpress.com/2013/01/sontag-the-imagination-of-disaster.pdf.

Spiegel, Simon. "Things Made Strange: On the Concept of "Estrangement" in Science Fiction Theory." *Science Fiction Studies* 35, no. 3 (2008): 369–85. www.jstor.org/stable/25475174.

Squier, Susan Merrill. "The Uses of Literature for Feminist Science Studies." In *Liminal Lives: Imagining the Human at the Frontiers of Biomedicine*, 25–57. Durham: Duke University Press, 2004.

Stang, Sarah. "The Broodmother as Monstrous-Feminine: Abject Maternity in Video Games." *Nordlit* 42 (2019): 233–56.

Sullivan, Heather. "Dirt Theory and Material Ecocriticism." *Interdisciplinary Studies in Literature and the Environment* 19, no. 3 (2012): 515–31.

Sullivan, Heather. "The Ecology of Colors. Goethe's Materialist Optics and Ecological Posthumanism." In *Material Ecocriticism*, edited by Serenella Iovino and Serpil Oppermann, 80–94. Bloomington: Indiana University Press, 2014.

Suvin, Darko. *Metamorphoses of Science Fiction: On the Poetics and History of a Literary Genre*. New Haven: Yale University Press, 1979.

Tallerico, Brian. "Annihilation." *RogerEbert.com*, February 23, 2018. Available online: https://www.rogerebert.com/reviews/annihilation-2018 (accessed May 22, 2021).

Tasker, Elisabeth. "Did the Seeds of Life Come from Space?," *Scientific American*, November 10, 2016. Available online: https://blogs.scientificamerican.com/guest-blog/did-the-seeds-of-life-come-from-space/ (accessed May 22, 2021).

Taylor, Astra. "The Automation Charade." *Logic*, August 1, 2018. https://logicmag.io/failure/the-automation-charade/.

Telotte, J. P. *Replications: A Robotic History of the Science Fiction Film*. Chicago: University of Illinois Press, 1995.

Than, Ker "The Building Blocks of Life May Have Come From Outer Space." *Smithsonian Magazine*, February 2013. Available online: https://www.smithsonianmag.com/science-nature/the-building-blocks-of-life-may-have-come-from-outer-space-3884354/ (accessed May 22, 2021).

Turkle, Sherry. *Alone Together: Why We Expect More from Technology and Less from Each Other*. New York: Basic Books, 2011.

Ussher, Jane M. *Managing the Monstrous Feminine: Regulating the Reproductive Body*. Routledge, 2006.

Vint, Sheryl. "Conclusion: Toward an Ethical Posthumanism." In *Bodies of Tomorrow: Technology, Subjectivity, Science Fiction*, 171–90. University of Toronto Press, 2007.

Vint, Sheryl. "Introduction: Science Fiction and Biopolitics." *Science Fiction Film and Television* 4, no. 2 (2011): 161–72.

Vint, Sheryl. "Vitality and Reproduction in *Blade Runner: 2049*." *Science Fiction Film and Television* 13, no. 1 (2020): 15–35.

Wagner, Rachel. "The Importance of Playing in Earnest." In *Playing with Religion in Digital Games*, edited by Heidi A. Campbell and Gregory Price Grieve, 192–213. Bloomington: Indiana University Press, 2014.

Waldby, Catherine. *The Visible Human Project: Informatic Bodies and Posthuman Medicine*. London: Routledge, 2000.

Waldby, Catherine. "Introduction." In *The Oocyte Economy: The Changing Meaning of Human Eggs*, 1–22. Durham: Duke University Press, 2019.

Watts, Alan W. *The Wisdom of Insecurity*. New York: Pantheon Books, 1951.

Whissel, Kristen. "Vital Figures: The Life and Death of Digital Creatures." In *Spectacular Digital Effects: CGI and Contemporary Cinema*, 91–130. Durham: Duke University Press, 2014.

Wilde, Tyler. "Ranking the Best and Worst of the Mass Effect Games." *PC Gamer*, August 7, 2015. https://www.pcgamer.com/ranking-the-best-and-worst-of-the-mass-effect-games/.

Williams, Evan Calder. *Combined and Uneven Apocalypse*. N.p.: John Hunt
    Publishing, 2011.
Williams, Linda. "Film Bodies: Gender, Genre, and Excess." In *Film Genre Reader
    IV*, edited by Barry Keith Grant, 159–77. Austin: University of Texas Press,
    2012.
Willumsen, Ea Christina, and Milan Jacevic. "Avatar-Kinaesthetics as
    Characterisation Statements in Horizon: Zero Dawn." *Digital Games Research
    Association* 18 (2018): 1–4.
Wolfe, Cary. *What is Posthumanism*? Minneapolis: University of Minnesota Press,
    2010.
Woolbright, Lauren. "Ecofeminism and Gaia Theory in *Horizon Zero Dawn*."
    Trace Journal 2, no. 1 (2018): n.p.
Yao, Xine. "Midsommar: The Horrors of White Sympathy." *Avidly: A Channel of
    the Los Angeles Review of Books*, Los Angeles Review of Books, August 13,
    2019. avidly.lareviewofbooks.org/2019/08/13/midsommar-the-horrors-of-white
    -sympathy/.
Žižek, Slavoj. *The Parallax View*. New York: MIT Press, 2006.
Zoe. Directed by Drake Doremus. Amazon Studios, 2018. DVD.

CONTRIBUTORS

Sarah Best is a Ph.D. student in religious studies at Wilfrid Laurier University, in Waterloo, Ontario, Canada. She has an MA in English and Digital Humanities from Carleton University, in Ottawa, Ontario, Canada, as well as an MRes in Social Anthropology from the University of St. Andrews, Scotland. Her ongoing dissertation research is situated at the intersection of science and technology, environmentalism, and new religious movements, focusing specifically on science-based nature religions. She has previously written about video games and other media through a posthumanist lens and finds this theoretical framework helpful for understanding complex relationships between nature and technology.

Meraj Dhir is a Ph.D. candidate in the History of Art and Architecture Department at Harvard University in Cambridge, Massachusetts, where he is completing his Ph.D. thesis on film style and aesthetics in the films of Robert Bresson. His previous publications include book chapters in *Arnheim for Film and Media Studies* (2010), edited by Scott Higgins, an essay on contemporary editing norms in *Editing and Visual/Special Effects* (2016), edited by Charlie Keil, as well as an essay about the industry trade journal Cinemaeditor for *The Velvet Light Trap*. His research interests include the history of film style, aesthetics, and the relationship between art history and film studies.

Julia A. Empey received her Ph.D. in English and Film Studies at Wilfrid Laurier University. Dr. Empey is an SSHRC Postdoctoral Fellow in the Faculty of English at the University of Cambridge, UK, and currently the book review editor at *Interconnections: The Journal of Posthumanism*. Her research and publication interests focus on contemporary literature and film, feminist and posthumanist theory, and science fiction literature, film, and media. Her other interests include ecocriticism, cosmopolitan studies, and political theory.

Russell J. A. Kilbourn is Professor and Chair of English and Film Studies at Wilfrid Laurier University, in Waterloo, Ontario, Canada. Dr. Kilbourn publishes on memory, film, comparative studies, critical posthumanism, and postsecular cinema. His books include *The Cinema of Paolo Sorrentino: Commitment to Style* (2020), *W.G. Sebald's Postsecular Redemption: Catastrophe with Spectator* (2018), *The Memory Effect: The Remediation of Memory in Literature and Film* (coedited with Eleanor Ty, 2013), and *Cinema, Memory, Modernity: The Representation of Memory from the Art Film to Transnational Cinema* (2010). Dr. Kilbourn is one of the founders of the Posthumanism Research Network (based at Brock University, St. Catharines, Ontario and Wilfrid Laurier) and an associate editor at *Interconnections: The Journal of Posthumanism*, and a member of the editorial board of the *Journal of Italian Cinema and Media Studies*. His current project is on posthuman memory.

Allison Mackey (she/her/hers) is Professor of Anglophone Literatures in the Department of Modern Languages at the Universidad de la República, Uruguay, and Research Associate in the Department of English at the University of the Free State, South Africa. Her research interests span the areas of human rights and literature, postcolonial literary and cultural studies, and environmental humanities, focusing on ethics/aesthetics/affect from decolonial, feminist, and critical posthumanist perspectives.

Missy Molloy is Senior Lecturer in film at Victoria University of Wellington in Aotearoa New Zealand. She coedited *ReFocus: The Films of Susanne Bier* (2018) with Meryl Shriver-Rice and Mimi Nielsen, and her teaching and research focus on women's, queer, and activist cinemas. Her recent publications include "Is *The Power of the Dog* a New Zealand film? National Identity, Genre and Jane Campion" (coauthored with Alfio Leotta, *Senses of Cinema* 2022), "Aotearoa pioneering LGBTIQ, Indigenous and environmental production: The case of *Rūrangi* in New Zealand" (*Journal of Environmental Media* 2021), and "Indigenous feminism revitalizing the long take: *Waru* and *The Body Remembers When the World Broke Open* (*Jump Cut* 2021). Her book *Screening the Posthuman* (coauthored with Pansy Duncan and Claire Henry) is forthcoming.

Emily Sanders (she/her) is a Ph.D. Candidate in Screen Cultures and Curatorial Studies at Queen's University in Kingston, Ontario. Her research focuses primarily on Anglo-Canadian cinema in the 1980s and 1990s, psychoanalysis, gender studies, and film theory.

Jerika Sanderson is a Ph.D. candidate in the Department of English Language and Literature at the University of Waterloo, Canada. Her research investigates representations of biotechnology and biomedicine in twenty-first-century science fiction and science communication. In general, she is interested in the intersections of biotechnology, biomedicine, and environmental issues, and her research engages with critical posthumanism and critical medical humanities.

Elif Sendur is a comparativist by training. She is a film, writing, and literature scholar working at the Rutgers University New Brunswick Writing Program (in New Jersey) and the editor of H-Film. Invested in questions pertaining to those convergences of Marxist politics and queer bodies in cinema along with questions asked by critical theory (especially French film theory) and posthumanist discourses, and she finds SF a fertile space to think about many of these intersections. Her recent work includes a study of weird in Claire Denis' cinema and a Marxist tracing of labor in weird literature.

Sarah Stang is Assistant Professor of Game Studies in Brock University's Centre for Digital Humanities, St. Catharines, Ontario, Canada. She is also the Secretary for the International Communication Association's Game Studies Division, the former editor-in-chief of the game studies journal *Press Start*, and the former essay editor for *First Person Scholar*. She received her Ph.D. from the Communication & Culture program at York University, and her research primarily focuses on gender representation in both digital and analog games. Her published work has analyzed topics such as female monstrosity, androgyny, parenthood, interactivity, and feminist media studies and can be found in journals such as *Games and Culture*, *Game Studies*, *Critical Studies in Media Communication*, *Human Technology*, *Analog Game Studies*, and *Loading*, as well as several edited collections.

Evdokia Stefanopoulou is a post-doc researcher in the School of Film, Aristotle University of Thessaloniki, Greece She received her Ph.D. in 2019 from the same school with the highest grade (A with distinction). She received a scholarship for Ph.D. candidates from the Hellenic Foundation for Research and Innovation (HFRI) (2017–19). She has published and presented papers in international conferences about science fiction film and television, gender, and posthumanism, among others. Dr. Stefanopoulou's monograph *The Science Fiction Film in Contemporary Hollywood* will be published in 2023.

Olivia Stowell is a Ph.D. student in the Department of Communication & Media at the University of Michigan, in Ann Arbor, USA, where she studies the intersections of race, genre, and narrative and temporality in contemporary popular culture, particularly reality television. Her work explores how popular media enables, forecloses, or projects different racial futures and possibilities, drawing connections between the time we spend "escaping" reality through popular media and the power relations that organize that reality. Her scholarship has appeared or is forthcoming in

Television & New Media and *New Review of Film & Television*, and her public writing has appeared in *Post45 Contemporaries, Novel Dialogue, Avidly: A Channel of the L.A. Review of Books*, and elsewhere.

Sarah Stulz is an independent scholar based in St. Gallen, Switzerland. She studied film at Universidad del Cine, Buenos Aires, where she earned her MA degree with a thesis on Chris Marker's post-cinematic essays.

Zorianna Zurba completed her Ph.D. in Communication and Culture, a joint program between Toronto Metropolitan University and York University, both in Toronto, Ontario, Canada. She holds an MA in Popular Culture as well as a TESOL Certificate. Zorianna currently teaches at Toronto Metropolitan University's Creative School.

INDEX

Milton Keynes UK
Ingram Content Group UK Ltd.
UKHW020628140923
428655UK00003B/38

9 781501 398407